DERADICALIZING VIOLENT EXTREMISTS

Terrorism remains one of the major threats facing the world community. While literature on the subject is dominated by discussion of the factors leading individuals and groups to join violent extremist, terrorist groups, the question of what can lead them to disengage from such groups is an equally important one. This book is the first study to provide a detailed analysis of both counter-radicalization and deradicalization programmes in eight Muslim-majority states, representing hitherto one of the largest, detailed, and most systematic inventories of such programmes in the world.

Drawing on detailed case-studies from a number of countries, the book:

- traces the historical evolution of violent extremist groups and individuals in each country case study, including the period before independence;
- describes in detail states' responses to this phenomenon in each period;
- provides important empirical analyses for counter-and-deradicalization policies and programmes based on extensive fieldwork and interviews with state officials, former radicals, and members of civil society organizations in each country;
- provides a first systematic evaluation of the effectiveness and success of these programmes and policies;
- focuses simultaneously on factors that have led to deradicalization at an individual or organizational level, and on the macro environment, both external-global and internal, that encourages counter-radicalization and deradicalization of groups and individuals.

The detailed comparative analyses allow the reader to identify conditions, both internal and external, which are conducive to both success and failure of counter-radicalization and deradicalization programmes, and the authors identify best practice and provide policy implications for states facing threats from violent extremism, as well as for international institutions and organizations working in the field of counter-terrorism.

Hamed El-Said is Chair and Professor of International Political Economy at Manchester Metropolitan University Business School.

Jane Harrigan is Professor of Economics at the School of Oriental and African Studies, University of London.

DERADICALIZING VIOLENT EXTREMISTS

Counter-radicalization and deradicalization programmes and their impact in Muslim majority states

Hamed El-Said and Jane Harrigan

Routledge
Taylor & Francis Group
LONDON AND NEW YORK

First published 2013
by Routledge
2 Park Square, Milton Park, Abingdon, Oxon OX14 4RN

Simultaneously published in the USA and Canada
by Routledge
711 Third Avenue, New York, NY 10017

Routledge is an imprint of the Taylor & Francis Group, an informa business

British Library Cataloguing in Publication Data
A catalogue record for this book is available from the British Library

Library of Congress Cataloging in Publication Data
El-Said, Hamed.
Deradicalizing violent extremists : counter-radicalization and deradicalization programmes and their impact in Muslim majority states / Hamed El-Said & Jane Harrigan.
p. cm.
Includes bibliographical references and index.
ISBN 978-0-415-52519-0 (hardback) – ISBN 978-0-415-52520-6 (pbk.) – ISBN 978-0-203-10324-1 (e-book) 1. Terrorism–Islamic countries. 2. Terrorism–Prevention. 3. Radicalism–Religious aspects–Islam. I. Harrigan, Jane. II. Title.
HV6433.I74E4 2012
363.325'16091767–dc23
2012006467

ISBN: 978-0-415-52519-0 (hbk)
ISBN: 978-0-415-52520-6 (pbk)
ISBN: 978-0-203-10324-1 (ebk)

Typeset in Bembo
by Taylor and Francis Books Ltd

MIX
Paper from responsible sources
FSC® C004839
FSC www.fsc.org

Printed and bound in Great Britain by the MPG Books Group

CONTENTS

ACKNOWLEDGEMENTS

Unlike a journal article, a newspaper column or a conference paper, important as they might be, books are peculiar products in the sense that they require a long time to write. They also demand and rely on a far greater deal of assistance from others. This is especially the case when they involve more than one author, thus calling for a tremendous amount of coordination, imposition of strict deadlines and strong constraints. This book is no exception.

We are particularly indebted to the Norwegian Ministry of Foreign Affairs, whose generous financial assistance made it possible to start and complete this first volume on 'Deradicalizing Violent Extremists: Counter-Radicalization and Deradicalization Programmes and their Impact in Muslim-Majority States'. Without the generosity of the NMFA, this book together with two other major international conferences, which provided important feedback that allowed us to refine our analysis and update the material of the book, would not have taken place. The first conference was held in Amman in the Arab Thought Forum (March 2010) under the kind patronage of HRH Prince Hassan bin Talal of Jordan, while the second took place in New York in the prestigious International Peace Institute (IPI) (June 2011). Both conferences hosted key policy makers, state officials and experts in the subject, whose comments and views have been vital in shaping the contours of the book. To all these individuals, we are also grateful.

A large debt of gratitude is held in the capitals of the countries which are represented in this book, particularly in Algeria, Amman, Cairo, Dhaka, Kuala Lumpur, Rabat, Riyadh and Sana'a. It would have been literally impossible to write this book without the commitment, dedication and enthusiasm of officials in these countries. Not only were they extraordinarily cordial, sociable and tolerant of our sometimes repetitive and sensitive questions, but also open and honest in explaining to us what was/is going on in their world of radicalization and counter-radicalization, as well as the delicate and complex prison environment. They welcomed us and facilitated our fieldwork, and were willing to share their knowledge and expertise with us. They kindly and magnanimously gave us a great deal of their time and patience. Their generosity and liberality knew no bounds.

A special debt is owed to Richard Barrett, the Coordinator of the United Nations 1267 Al-Qaeda Taliban Monitoring Team. Richard's rich personal network of connections in Muslim-majority states facilitated fieldwork for this book in the eight countries represented in this volume.

Our appreciation also extends to both Elaine Mercer and Tom Buckley, who edited the manuscript after the fieldwork and analyses were completed and helped to put the material together in its current form.

We are extremely grateful to all of those mentioned above as well as to the imams, scholars, scientists and civil society organizations involved in countering radicalization and deradicalizing those who crossed the line by committing or intending to commit violent extremist acts. As this book goes to show, they are a significant and an integral part of any effective and successful counter-radicalization and deradicalization genre. Their input and opinions on what works, how, when and where have furnished this book with a vital foundation upon which more assertive conclusions have been built and developed. Like their state officials, civil society entities have also astonishingly, generously and proudly provided ample information on their efforts in this genre.

The list of acknowledgements is much longer than has been mentioned or could be listed here. But the victims of terrorism, most of whom happened to be Muslims, should not be forgotten. Their loss, pain and sadness provided the main impetus for this work. Their stories ridiculed the trivial issues we often complain about here in our comfortable lives in the West. They constantly reminded us of the importance of putting things in perspective.

This book, in other words, is the accumulative experience of all those mentioned above. We as authors simply collected their stories and put them together in this volume. Acknowledging their assistance, however, in providing the stories that eventually constituted this book, does not imply participation in the intellectual ownership of the book. Nor does it mean that they might agree with everything we wrote and which reflects our understanding of their stories. Those who contributed so vitally to the completion of this book had no role whatsoever in its writing. This responsibility is solely the authors of this book.

Hamed El-Said

1

INTRODUCTION

Definitions and conceptual framework

Hamed El-Said

Introduction

Almost ten years after the infamous 9/11 attacks on the World Trade Center and the Pentagon, the subject of terrorism continues to occupy a significant place in international relations. In recent years, there has been a 'renewed interest' in the subject of terrorism (Horgan and Braddock 2010: 267), which is fuelled by proliferation of political instability and consolidation of Al-Qaeda and like-minded terrorist groups in such 'failed' or 'failing' states like Afghanistan, Pakistan, Somalia, West Africa, Libya and Yemen (Sharp 2011). In recent years, an important shift in focus, however, has taken place. Rather than focusing on what leads an individual or group to join a terrorist organization, the literature has now turned its attention into the equally significant question of what leads an individual or group to leave or turn against terrorism and their former colleagues (Bjorgo and Horgan 2008). A recent report by the International Institute for Counter Terrorism (IICT) summed up the shift in focus of literature in the following words:

> Recently, we have been witnessing a new phenomenon – key figures in the Islamic world, who in the past took part in armed Jihad or at least ideologically supported it, are now working to counter the radicalization process and to minimize recruitment to terrorist organizations. This phenomenon is known as "retraction" … [which] reflects, particularly on the part of authorities within the Muslim world, to harness the Islamic sources being used for radical indoctrination and to instead employ them as tools for fighting Islamic extremism.
>
> *(IICT 2011: 2)*

At least two factors have triggered this change in focus. First is the emergence of a new way of thinking with regards to violent militancy or terrorism. This followed a re-evaluation of efforts and policies to counter the phenomenon, not only in Muslim-majority states but also Muslim-minority or Western countries. This new school of thought first officially emerged in Europe following the 2004 and 2005 Madrid and London terrorist attacks respectively, and was triggered by the realization that many of the attackers were 'home grown terrorists' (Coolsaet and Swielande 2008: 158–9). As David Miliband, the UK's former foreign secretary, stated in 2009:

> European officials, including British officers quietly stopped using the phrase "war on terror" in 2006 … [because] the use of "War on Terror" as a Western rallying cry since 9/11 has been mistaken and may have caused more harm than good.
>
> *(Miliband 2009)*

Mr Miliband also summarized the gist of the new approach, which came as a result of 'a fundamental evaluation of our efforts to *prevent* extremism and its offspring terrorist violence' (*my emphasis*). The new approach treats radicalization as a process caused by an 'environment conducive' to radicalization and extremism that leads to terrorism.[1] As Sageman (2008) noted, nobody is born a terrorist. The European approach, therefore, focuses on preventing violent extremism from occurring in the first place by focusing on the 'root causes' or 'environment conducive to violent extremism'.[2]

Second, re-evaluating 'efforts to prevent extremism and its offspring terrorist violence' has been preceded by the emergence of 'new innovative approaches', the aim of which is to win the hearts and minds of segments of the population most affected by, and prone to, terrorist violence (Horgan and Braddock 2010: 267). For lack of a better name, such approaches are often referred to as counter-radicalization and deradicalization programmes.

Counter-radicalization and/or deradicalization are very loosely defined in the literature. Generally speaking, they refer to programmes introduced to cause a change in views and behaviour of detained and non-detained militants to abandon 'permanently … violent activities' (Chapo Central 2010: 5). They also aim at preventing the emergence of a new generation of terrorists in the future (IPI 2010).

Counter-radicalization and deradicalization programmes (referred to thereafter as Counter-derad programmes), have become increasingly popular in Muslim-majority states. Spared by Algeria and Egypt in 1997, the novelty of their application has become the basis for other, sometimes more comprehensive and sustained programmes, in Saudi Arabia, Malaysia, Morocco, Bangladesh, Iraq, Indonesia, Tajikistan, Yemen, Pakistan and Jordan. They have not only inspired other Islamic radical movements in Western countries, such as Liberation Party Factions in the United Kingdom, which have renounced violence and resorted to more civil means of expressing their objectives. They have also inspired many Western and Muslim-minority states, like the Netherlands, UK, Canada, Singapore and Australia (Ashour 2009: 13; Boucek 2008).

Although Counter-derad programmes 'have been deemed more successful' than traditional military approaches in winning 'hearts and minds' and preventing fomentation of future generations of terrorists (IPI 2010: 1), little remains known about these programmes' composition, sequences, timing and conditions conducive to their success or failure. As Horgan (2008: 18) emphasized: 'we know little about the processes of disengagement from terrorism, and even less about the multiplicity of routes via which individual terrorists come to leave terrorism behind'. While assessing deradicalization programmes in some Muslim-majority and Muslim-minority states, Horgan and Braddock (2010: 267) also recently noted that 'despite their popularity, data surrounding even the most basic of facts about these programs remain limited'. Seifert concurs: 'Exactly how' these programmes are 'accomplished is not entirely clear'. Finally, Ashour (2009: 3) eloquently assented when he summarized the 'lacunae in the literature on Islamism', in the following words; despite the fact that deradicalization programmes:

> ... had removed tens of thousands of former militants from the ranks of al-Qua'ida's supporters and acted as disincentive for would-be militants, there is not one single detailed book on the causes of de-radicalisation processes.
>
> *(Ashour 2009: 3)*

More importantly, and in spite of continued great and renewed interest in explaining violent extremism and processes of disengagement from terrorism, 'it is difficult to distinguish the variables that influence senior members in Jihad organizations to "retract" their radical beliefs and to understand the relationship between such factors' (IICT 2011: 3).

To be sure, some 'value-adding' research has recently emerged on the subject. Authors such as Omar Ashour (2009) have shed important light on the factors that led to the successful deradicalization of violent extremist 'organizations' in both Egypt and Algeria. Ashour's work focused on the deradicalization of the Egyptian Islamic Group between 1997–2002, the al-Jihad Organization after 2007 and the Algerian militant Groups between 1997–2009. Michael Jacobson (2010) has also produced an important study into what he terms 'the flip side' – 'those who decide to leave terrorist and extremist organizations', or the 'drop-out phenomenon' among 'individuals' rather than groups and organizations. Both Ashour's organizational framework and Jacobson's individual approach, however, largely tend to ignore the general or macro environmental conditions that catalyse the initial radicalization and any subsequent deradicalization. Hence, the conditions and environments, both national and international, under which such programmes can be nurtured and implemented more effectively and successfully remain unknown and under-researched (Cline 2009: 4).

This book, therefore, fills an important gap in the literature by focusing on the conditions conducive to successful Counter-derad programmes. This is achieved by studying and analyzing the Counter-derad programmes in eight Muslim-majority states, known for implementing successful Counter-radicalization, deradicalization or both programmes simultaneously. These countries are: Algeria, Bangladesh, Egypt, Jordan, Malaysia, Morocco, Saudi Arabia and Yemen. Although the number of programmes studied is relatively small, the book remains today the most comprehensive study of Counter-derad programmes in Muslim-majority states. It is the first detailed study of conditions conducive to successful Counter-derad programmes at the macro level, including national and international levels.

The main questions, which the book seeks to answer, are the following: what are the national conditions conducive to successful Counter-derad programmes in Muslim-majority states? What is the relationship between developmental states and radicalization and effective Counter-derad programmes? What is the relationship between strong/weak states and radicalization and the ability to fashion effective Counter-derad policies? What is the link between radicalization, Counter-derad on the one hand and external and global factors on the other? Who are the main actors and stakeholders involved in Counter-derad policies and efforts? And what are the transferrable lessons that can be derived from studying the experience of Muslim-majority states to other Muslim-majority and non-Muslim-majority states alike facing the threat of terrorism?

To address these questions and shed light on conditions conducive to successful Counter-derad programmes, the book studies policies in eight Muslim-majority states known for implementing policies and processes in this important area of national security. In addition to reviewing and relying on written material, media and library literature on the subject, the book relies heavily on fieldwork and personal interviews carried out with state officials, academics and experts, members of civil society organizations, Islamists and former radicals who graduated from Counter-derad programmes in their respective countries.

But first and before embarking on analysis of counter-derad-programmes in Muslim-majority states, it is important to provide definitions for the terms and concepts used throughout the book, as well as sitting the conceptual framework against which the analyses of the book will be based, including an explanation for conditions conducive to successful Counter-derad programmes.

Definitions and conceptual framework

First, we use the terms violent extremism, violent militancy and terrorism interchangeably in this book. The reason for using the term terrorism here is due to our belief that terrorism, which includes the killing of innocent people, both Muslims and non-Muslims, for whatever reason is non-Islamic and violates the basic tenets of Islamic faith. As the Qu'ran instructed the Prophet (Muhammad) to tell people in Surat Al-Ahqaf (part 26: 9):

> I am not a new thing among the Messengers (of Allah, i.e. I am not the first Messenger) nor do I know what will be done with me or with you. I only follow that which is revealed to me, and I am but a plain Warner.

Killing an innocent soul in Islam is a major sin and is not justifiable except in the case of a mistake. This is made clear in Surat Al-Nisa (part 5: 91), which states that: 'It is not for a believer to kill a believer except (that it be) by mistake'. In other words, the Messengers were not ordered to fight people, including those who do not believe in their messages. This particular responsibility – punishment – was made the sole responsibility of, and preserved for, the creator himself. As the Qu'ran stated in Surat Al-Ghashiyah (part 30: 23–6): ' … who turns away and disbelieves. Then Allah will punish him with greatest punishment. Verily, to Us will be their return; Then verily, for Us will be their reckoning'. We therefore do not shy away from using the term terrorism in this book to describe the killing of innocent people for political, ideological or religious motivations.

We do not however treat self-defence, or defending one's country and people from foreign aggression as terrorism. Jihad is rooted in the Qu'ran precisely for self-defence and nobody can undermine the true interpretation of jiahd. Yet Islam clearly and unambiguously delineated the boundaries of jihad and provided a powerful ethical and moral framework for resorting to jihadi activism. Deviating from the true principles and ethics of jihad, as defined and outlined by the Qu'ran and the Sunna, in order to consciously kill or harm innocent people for political, ideological or religious motivations is what we refer to as terrorism or violent extremism in this book.

By extending the above analysis, we also do not believe that terrorism is 'Islamic' or confined to groups and individuals belonging only to the Islamic faith either. Indeed, Muslims are latecomers to terrorism, and groups and individuals belonging to all other faiths and cultures have long resorted to terror tactics throughout history even before some radical Islamists did so (Laqueur 2007). As John Brennan, Assistant to the American President for Homeland Security and Counterterrorism, stated:

> Violent extremism is neither unique nor inherent to any one faith. Violence is something that every faith rejects but every faith had to confront … there is nothing – absolutely nothing – holy or pure or legitimate or Islamic about murdering innocent men and children … As families with relatives and friends around the world, you know that it is actually Muslims who have suffered most at the bloody hands of violent extremism. It is your Muslim brothers and sisters … who have paid the highest price. As one study recently noted, in recent years, nearly all of al-Qaida's victims (98%) have been innocent from Muslim countries …
>
> *(Quoted in Neuman 2011: 31)*

This is why we use the terms violent extremism, violent militancy and terrorism interchangeably in this book. We do accept the argument, however, that 'Today Islamist's radicalisation is the most prominent form of radicalisation … even … if Islam is not the essence' (Coolsaet and De Swielande 2008: 158); hence, the reason for our specific focus in this book on Muslim-majority states.

Second, we define radicalization as a change in the views and behaviour of groups and individuals towards embracing more uncompromising political and ideological positions and ideas, with willingness to take unusual and concrete actions to see them implemented. This does not necessarily mean violent actions. In fact, 'being radical … is not illicit – and even when it goes against the law, it can be legitimate' (ibid. 156). Embracing acts of violence and criminology for political or ideological motives (e.g. terrorism), the subject of this book, is illicit.[3]

Third, counter-radicalization is a term used to refer to measures and policies implemented to prevent the emergence or fomentation of a new generation of terrorists or violent extremists in the society. Counter-radicalization refers to antedate measures that are taken before groups and individuals become violent extremists, or to reduce the level of radicalization in the society. Counter-radicalization focuses 'on the communities that are targeted by terrorists for recruitment. The aim is to protect, strengthen and empower these communities so that they become resilient to violent extremism' (Neumann 2011: 7). Counter-radicalization measures are usually delivered through multiple channels and entities, with an unlimited range of relevant activities, none of which are coercive (ibid.). They can include such policies and measures as reforming religious institutions, organizing conferences and workshops to counter radical ideology, fighting corruption, implementing economic reforms to address deep rooted socioeconomic grievances, making greater use of mosques and media, including TV, satellite channels and the internet to expose the danger of terrorism and undermine recruitment and violent extremist thoughts in society. They can also include more reliance on civil society organizations' networks and reach to fight violent ideas and thought, as well as political reform and liberalization, improving freedom of expressions and human rights records of the country (Coolsaet and De Swielande 2008; Ashour 2009: 13; Boucek 2008; Horgan and Braddock 2010; Bjorgo and Horgan 2008; Neumann 2011: 7).

Fourth, deradicalization refers to measures and strategies taken to deradicalize or bring back groups or individuals to a previous point before becoming radical or before embracing violent extremist ideology and/or activism. They are ex-ante strategies, used to convince and encourage groups and individuals who have already become violent extremists to permanently repent and abandon violence. Such measures are usually implemented inside prisons and most often target detainees who have been linked to terrorism charges. They can also be used as a PR campaign to convince other violent extremists at large to renounce violence and rejoin their families and societies. They include such measures as religious dialogues inside prisons, history lessons to correct 'misleading' or 'distorted' information, involving families and civil society in encouraging violent extremists to repent. They can also have social, material and other selective incentives and inducements, as well as improving treatment of prisoners and the general environment of the prison (ibid.).

Conceptual framework

The study of deradicalization has hitherto lacked any 'theoretical account of the causes of the deradicalization process within armed Islamist movements' (Ashour 2009: 3), or even 'a basic conceptual basis for planning, evaluating and guiding' the deradicalization processes (Horgan and Braddock 2010: 267). Not surprisingly, Counter-derad programmes have recently been the subject of contentious debate. The most heated and relevant debate here is over whether such programmes lead to, or are even aimed from the very beginning at 'disengagement' or 'deradicalization' in the first place. Disengagement targets behavioural aspects and seeks to convince groups and individuals to permanently disengage and abandon violence. Deradicalization, on the other hand, is cognitive and therefore is a more challenging task. It implies a fundamental change in understanding core values and beliefs (Bjorgo and Horgan 2008; Ashour 2009; Chapo Central 2010: 5).

The available empirical evidence suggests that it is possible to change someone's behaviour without deradicalizing them. A widely quoted example here is Nasser al-Bahri, better known as Abu Jandal, Bin Laden's former bodyguard. Despite attending a dialogue programme in Yemen and publicly abandoning violence, Abu Jandal remained loyal to Bin Laden and continues to believe in Jihad (Peraino 2009).

Horgan has generally been more pessimistic, arguing that deradicalization programmes have led to less deradicalization and to more disengagement. Such programmes, Horgan and Braddock recently stated (2010: 279) 'appear to attempt to secure sustainable disengagement from terrorism' (also see Bjorgo and Horgan 2008). This led Horgan and Braddock to describe deradicalization programmes as 'risk-reduction initiatives', rather than deradicalization initiatives.

Such a statement is overly general and tends to ignore the fact that the outcome depends on the strength, coherence, goals and objectives of deradicalization programmes themselves, as well as on the competence and credibility of scholars and scientists involved. As Dr Abdulrahman al-Hadlaq, a Saudi senior official and advisor to Prince Muhammad Bin Nayef (who is responsible for Saudi's counter-terrorism and deradicalization efforts) stated: 'We do not target behaviour only. We work to change the ideology of the terrorists to guarantee no return to violence' (Personal interview, Riyadh August 2009).

The more recent empirical evidence, derived from, for example, Ashour's work on militant groups in Egypt and Algeria (2009: 3), moreover, clearly shows that some of these groups underwent a process of both 'behavioural and ideological transformations towards non-violence'. This is evidenced not only by the removal of thousands of former militants from the ranks of al-Qaeda and like-minded organizations and currently very low recidivism rate among graduates, but also by publications of 'several books in which they ideologically and theologically delegitimized violence'. The leadership of Moroccan Salafi Jihadi movement also recently underwent a similar process of behavioural and ideological transformation towards violence and published a recantation book in which it admits mistakes, renounces violence and calls for peaceful, non-violent forms of participation to achieve change and reform.

What is evident, however, is that such recantations and deradicalization have been more durable when initiated internally and unilaterally by a militant group (Ashour 2009). Moreover, Counter-derad programmes in Muslim-majority states studied in this book have been enacted by and implemented in countries that have no democratic regimes in most cases, save Malaysia perhaps. They have not therefore attempted to change the behavioural and ideological position of former militants towards democracy. In fact, undemocratic Arab regimes

> for years told the West and [their citizens] ... alike that [their] reluctance to introduce democratic reforms, keep harsh emergency laws in place and allow [their] hated security agencies to detain and torture with impunity were necessary to stop religious groups from seizing power.
>
> *(AP News 2011)*

It is not surprising that many former militants 'still uphold ... anti-democratic views' (Ashour 2009: 6), although many did embrace democratic forms too as the analysis of this book will demonstrate.

Associated with the previous point is whether deradicalization or disengagement takes an individual or collective form, 'depending on whether the process is led by, or aimed at, individuals or entire groups' (Neumann 2011: 16). In many cases, charismatic, former leaders of violent extremist groups have initiated deradicalization/disengagement internally before the state started to support such a process. Egypt is a case in point. (See chapter on Egypt in this edition.) Such a process has also taken either an individual (as in the case of Yemen) or a collective nature (as is the case in Algeria). In other cases, the state itself initiated a process of individual deradicalization/disengagement, as the Saudi case in this edition demonstrates. Models of deradicalization/disengagement have thus varied from one country or region to another and it is difficult to speak of one form of the phenomenon of deradicalization/disengagement. The outcome depends on the specificity of the group/individuals and general environment in which they operate.

Also, 'Deradicalization is rarely translated or used in Arabic descriptions of these programs' (Chapo Central 2010: 6). Most Muslim-majority states use such terminologies as *al-Hiwar, lajnat al-munasaha*, *'aadat ta'hil* (rehabilitation), *'aadat inkherat* (reintegration), *Qanoun al-Rahmah* (Mercy Law) and *Qanoun al-Wefaq al-Watani* (Clemency and Civil Accord), 'Peace and National Reconciliation' (*al-Salaam wa al-Wefaq al-Watani*), to describe their Counter-derad programmes. This confirms the point made earlier in this section, that is, Counter-derad programmes in most Muslim-majority states might have different goals, objectives and expectations from those existing in Western countries.

Last but by no means least, there is no silver bullet and Counter-derad efforts are 'incremental' at best (Chapo Central 2010: 7). Clearly, what works in one country or region might not work in another country or region and also change requires 'turning points' (ibid.), triggers or 'drivers' (DFID: 1). For example, it took the mother Egyptian Muslim Brotherhood Movement (MB) more than two decades before its leadership was able to deradicalize and dismantle the military wing of the movement (*Nizam al-Khass*) in the early 1970s. Also, although the IG declared a unilateral ceasefire in 1997, it was not before '2007 that the IG's deradicalization process looked to have been consolidated'. The process which started in 2007 by Dr Fadl (or Sayyid Immam Sharif), the Amir of the JO movement 'has been partially successful, however, as three factions within al-Jihad still refuse to uphold it. These factions also refuse to leave the organization ... The process is thus still ongoing at the present time' (All quotations from Ashour 2009: 2).

This led Ashour (2009: chapter one) to talk about four 'turning points' or factors responsible for and leading to deradicalization of groups. These are: charismatic leadership at the organizational level; repression by state; repression accompanied by various selective incentives and inducements and social external and internal interactions. Michael Jacobson (2010) complemented Ashour's work by focusing on 'individual' deradicalization and disengagement. He found such personal and idiosyncratic reasons like disappointment with leadership and life of Jihad, corruption within organizations, envy and jealousy as significant factors leading individuals to leave terrorism behind and even turn against their former colleagues.

While Ashour and Jacobson made important contributions, their organizational and individual frameworks, respectively, say little about 'the environment in which people are predisposed to extremist ideology' and which is politically, economically, socially, 'geographically and demographically diverse' (Levitt, 2011: 2). Ashour and Jacobson's approaches not only ignore the internal, but also the external environment conducive to successful/failure of Counter-derad programmes. For example, an EU commissioned study talked about 'factors outside the control of government initiatives', including possible links between foreign policies of Western governments and radicalization/deradicalization at national levels. The study also spoke of links between socioeconomic 'grievances' and radicalization/deradicalization (all quotations from Chapo Central 2010: 5–7). Similarly, a British government commissioned study talked of such factors as 'historical conditions, existing intrastate conflicts, poverty, corruption, ineffective governance, experiences of justice and security sector, ideology and external influences' as major drivers of radicalization and deradicalization in a country (DFID and FCO 2009: 5). The same study also re-emphasized the importance of studying the links between 'external influences', including polices of Western countries in Iraq, Afghanistan and Palestine, for example, and radicalization and deradicalization at national levels. Both the British and European Union commissioned studies empathised with the role of 'civil society and government stakeholders' in the process of deradicalization, with the International Crisis Group (2003a, 2003b and 2005) emphasizing the role of good governance and strong political state in achieving political stability and hence economic development, both seen as a prerequisite for successful deradicalization. A more recent study (2011) by the EU (PURSUE) focused on the significant role of civil society in countering radical narrative, arguing that initiatives by:

> Local civil society partners … strengthen the resilience of … communities to extremist ideologies and organizations at the local and national levels … prevent the spread of extremist ideologies … civil society-led interventions are a more sustainable, locally acceptable, and human rights-oriented approach to reduce this threat to national stability and international security … messages [promoted by civil society organizations] are more effective because they originate from the local population rather than the … government or external actors.
>
> *(PURSUE 2011)*

Even the US government, which has continued to pursue its 'war on terror' and expand global engagement and strategic communication abroad, relied on 'community engagement and town hall meetings with immigrant communities at home' (Levitt 2011: 1).

Finally, Lubeck (1998) stressed the role of a strong developmental state in reducing national political and ideological conflicts and violent extremism.

Hence, and without undermining Ashour's organizational framework and Jacobson's individual approach, the above analysis can be translated into a simple hypothesis regarding the macro conditions conducive to successful Counter-derad programmes. At least five variables are necessary for successful Counter-derad processes. These are: charismatic leadership at state level; strong state developmental capacity; strong state political capacity; dynamic and active civil society and positive external and regional environments. Six hypotheses can be derived from this proposition, which guides the analysis throughout the book.

Hypothesis 1: Counter-derad programmes require political will and trust. This is achieved more easily when new, charismatic leadership that has weak links with powerful domestic groups opposed to reforms arrives. Hence, Counter-derad programmes associated with new, charismatic leadership at state level have more chance of success than those linked to the same old regimes whose policies were largely responsible for radicalizing large segments of the population.

Hypothesis 2: Developmental states, that is, states with the ability to achieve sustainable growth rate, create jobs, improve equity, reduce corruption and manage relations with their ethnic groups are not only less exposed to violent extremism, they are also more able to fashion effective Counter-derad programmes when faced with the phenomenon of terrorism.

Hypothesis 3: States with strong political capacity, that is, states capable of defending their borders and societies, maintain law and order, and set the rules of the game for all members of society, are more capable of fashioning effective Counter-derad programmes than weak states. This is especially the case when such programmes are accompanied by reforms to address some or all of the existing socioeconomic and political grievances.

Hypothesis 4: Civil society organizations (CSO) have resources to create and multiply social networks in ways that the state cannot. They thus have the ability to reach even the most recalcitrant corners of society. Therefore, states with dynamic and active CSOs are in a better position to enact effective Counter-derad programmes than those without dynamic CSOs. This is especially the case when CSOs are invited by the state to take part in the delivery of Counter-derad programmes.

Hypothesis 5: The timing of Counter-derad programmes is important. Counter-derad programmes that are associated or accompanied with positive international and regional environments have a better chance of succeeding than those associated with negative external environments.

Hypothesis 6: Counter-derad programmes have a better chance of succeeding and enduring when ceasefire, renunciation of violence and call for peace is initiated unconditionally from violent extremist groups and not the state.

It is difficult to determine which of the above factors is more important when weighing the significance of each factor in determining the outcome of Counter-derad programmes, or creating conditions and environments conducive to successful Counter-derad programmes. However, as the analyses in this book will demonstrate, the last five factors seem to be intertwined and carry equal weight, and their presence is therefore necessary for effective processes of Counter-derad. The reason being is that some successful reforms (i.e. Egypt) were not associated with the arrival of new regimes. Nor were all new regimes able to implement necessary reforms to counter radicalization at societal level or even to deradicalize those who have already crossed the line in society. Jordan's King Abdullah is a case in point.

Methodology and structure of the book

The aim of this book, as mentioned earlier, is to investigate and identify conditions conducive to successful Counter-derad at macro level, including national, regional and international levels. To do this, the book relies on comparative case studies of eight Muslim-majority states known, rightly or wrongly, for having implemented or being in the process of implementing successful Counter-derad policies. The approach used in this comparative study is qualitative; one relies on both secondary and primary sources (personal interviews, interviews made by media and press with relevant individuals, declarations and statements made public by violent extremists or repented individuals).[4]

One of the major advantages of the qualitative, comparative approach used in this book, which relied on 7–14 days fieldwork in each country studied and the observation of authors and personal interviews, is that it generates data and information on a recent subject that currently suffers from a dearth of information, has little understanding and is under researched. Unlike most other work on the subject of Counter-derad programmes, this book also combines Western and Arabic sources of literature, thus providing authors with a vantage point by understanding and bringing in a local perspective. This book provides a comprehensive analysis for the Counter-derad programmes in eight Muslim-majority states. This not only makes this study the first detailed study of Counter-derad programmes in Muslim-majority states, but also, hitherto, as far as we know, the largest and most comprehensive inventory of conditions conducive to successful Counter-derad policies available in a single study. It represents Phase I of an on-going project, which aspires to study most, if not all, successfully known Counter-derad programmes that exist among United Nations Member States. In fact, Phase II of the project has already started, also benefiting from the generous funding of the Norwegian Ministry of Foreign Affairs. Unlike Phase I, Phase II will evaluate Counter-derad policies in at least six other countries, both Muslim-majority and Muslim-minority States. These are Mauritania, Sudan, Turkey, Thailand, the Philippines and Singapore.

Chapter 2 of the book begins by studying the environment that led, after 1997, to the deradicalization, 'from the mountains' of Algeria's largest Islamic militant group, the Islamic Salvation Army (AIS). Chapter 3, which analyses the new Bangladeshi caretaker government's efforts in countering rising tides of violent extremism in the country after 2005, follows this. Chapter 4 evaluates conditions that led to the deradicalization, from inside prisons, of Egypt's two largest armed organizations in the 1980s and 1990s, namely, Islamic Group (IG) and al-Jihad Organization (JO). Chapter 5 follows by demonstrating how the lack of political commitment and failure to promote competent and independent ulama and scholars undermined Jordan's Counter-derad efforts. Malaysia's historical and contemporary environments, which led to the evolution of the country's policies to first counter Communist insurgency between the early 1970s and 1989 and then Islamic radicalism thereafter are analysed in Chapter 6. This is followed by Chapter 7 which discusses one of the most far-reaching counter-radicalization programmes found in our eight country case studies, namely Morocco. The most internationally touted and hitherto sustained state-led deradicalization programme in Saudi Arabia is studied in Chapter 8, while one of the earliest recorded official efforts to introduce a debate programme with former radicals, one which inspired other similar programmes in the region and outside, namely the Yemeni Committee for Dialogue, is studied in Chapter 9. The final chapter summarizes the main points in the book and concludes with a summary of the main lessons learnt from Counter-derad programmes of Muslim-majority states.

Notes

1 Although the US continues to rely more on a 'hard', military approach to counter terrorism, it has recently paid more attention to 'soft' Counter-derad programmes. As Secretary of Defense Robert Gates has recently stated: 'military might will not defeat terrorism – what is needed is a mix of hard and soft power. Secretary of State Clinton called that recently smart power' (Quoted in http://learning-curve.blogspot.com/2009/07/comments-on-obama-inaugural-address.html).

2 The new thinking first emerged in London in 2005 when the British government 'developed a counter-terrorism strategy and set up programmes and plans to … combat' the threat of terrorism in the UK. The new programme, which became known as CONTEST, contains four principle strands: 'Prevent, Pursue, Protect and Prepare' (HM Government 2006:1). Shortly thereafter, the European Union introduced their Counter-Terrorism Strategy also in 2005 which likewise focuses on four key pillars: Prevent, Protect, Pursue and Respond. For more details on the EU strategy, see http://ec.europa.eu/justice_home/fsi/terrorism/strategies/fsi_terrorism_strategies_counter_en.htm. Initially, 'the EU CTS also embraced the same pillars as the UK's, but for intellectual property rights' issue, they had to replace Prepare with Respond' (Personal interview with a senior European official, Riyadh January 2011). Europeans have also played an important role in influencing thinking inside the United Nations, leading to the adoption one year later in 2006, to the United Nation's Global Counter Terrorism Strategy with its focus on 'Addressing Radicalization and Extremism that lead to Terrorism' (for more details, see Coolsaet and De Swielande 2008; El-Said and Barrett 2011).

3 Peter Neumann (2011: 15) defines radicalization as a process, a period through which an individual or group 'gradually move from radical – yet non-violent activism to being a terrorist bent on violence is what social scientists refer to as radicalization. While we accept the argument that radicalization is a process, we do not equate terrorism with radicalization, a common mistake in the literature'.

4 This approach is common among scholars on the subject and has been used by Ashour (2009), Bjørgo and Horgan (2008) and Horgan and Braddock (2010) in their study of similar programmes.

Bibliography

Ashour, O. (2009) *The De-Radicalisation of Jihadists: Transforming Armed Islamic Movements*, London: Routledge.

AP News (2011) *Mubarak's Fall Sparks Religious Parties' Rise in Politics, Dawn.Com*, February 28. Available HTTP: http://www.dawn.com/2011/02/28/mubarak's-fall-sparks-religious-parties'-rise-in-politics.html/print/

Bjørgo, T. and Horgan, J. (eds) (2008) *Leaving Terrorism Behind: Individual and Collective Disengagement*, London: Routledge.

Boucek, C. 'Saudi Arabia's "soft" counterterrorism strategy: prevention, rehabilitation, and aftercare', Carnegie Papers, Middle East Program, No. 97, September 2008.

Chapo Central (2010) *Delegation of the European Union to the Republic of Yemen: Engaging the Yemeni Minister of Religious Endowment on a Future Dialogue Centre*, Nicosia, Cyprus, October 23. PURSUE Taking a Local Perspective.

Cline, L. (2009) 'Changing jihadist behaviour: the Saudi model', *Small Wars Journal*, 10 April.

Coolsaet, R. and De Swielande, T. (2008) 'Epilogue: Zeitgeist and (de-)radicalisation', in *Jihadi Terrorism and the Radicalisation Challenge in Europe,* R. Coolsaet (ed.) London: Ashgate, 156–81.

DFID and FCO (2009). *Drivers of Radicalisation Study – Yemen*, London: DFID and FCO.

El-Said, H. and Barrett, R. (2011) 'Radicalisation and extremism that lead to terrorism', in J. Harrigan and H. El-Said (eds), *Globalisation, Democratisation and Radicalisation in the Arab World*, London: Palgrave McMillan.

HM Government, 'Countering international terrorism: the United Kingdom's strategy', July 2006.

Horgan, J. (2008) 'Individual disengagement: A psychological analysis', in T. Bjørgo and J. Horgan (eds), *Leaving Terrorism Behind: Individual and Collective Disengagement*, London: Routledge.

Horgan, J. and Braddock, K. (2010) 'Rehabilitating the terrorists?: challenges in assessing the effectiveness of de-radicalization programs', *Terrorism and Political Violence,* 22: 267–91.

International Crisis Group (ICG) (2003a) *The Challenge of Political Reform: Jordanian Democratisation and Regional Instability*, Amman/Brussels, 8 October 2003: Jordan has weathered the Middle East's recent storms, but to maintain stability it must decide how much democracy it now needs and can afford.

—— (2003b) *Red Alert in Jordan: Recurrent Unrest in Maan*, Middle East Briefing, Amman/Brussels, 19 February.

——(2005) *Jordan's 9/11: Dealing with Jihadi Islamism*, Middle East Report No. 47, Amman/Brussels, 23 November.

International Institute for Counter-Terrorism (IICT), *Retracting – Using Ideological Means for the Purpose of De-Radicalisation*, ICT's Jihad Websites ~Monitoring Group, Insights, IDC Herzliya, January 2011.

International Peace Institute (IPI) (2010) *A New Approach? Deradicalization Programs and Counterterrorism*, New York, IPI.

Jacobson, M. (2010) *Learning from Dropouts*, in *ForeignPolicy.com*, 1 February.

Laqueur, W. (2007) *Terrorism: A Brief History, in Countering the Terrorism Mentality, in Nonviolent Paths to Social Change, U.S Department of State, Bureau of International Information Programs*, EJournal. Available HTTP: <http://www.america.gov/media/pdf/ejs/ijpe0507.pdf#popup.> (accessed 11 September 2009).

Levitt, M. (2011) 'It's the ideology, Stupid', *Journal of International Security Affairs*, The Washington Institute for Near East Policy, 1–2.

Lubeck, P. (1998) 'Islamist responses to globalization: cultural conflict in Egypt, Algeria and Malaysia' in B. Crawford and R. Lipschutz (eds) *The Causes of Cultural Conflict*, Berkeley: International and Area Studies, 293–319.

Miliband, D. (2009) War on Terror Wrong, in the *Guardian*, 15 January.

Neumann, P. *Preventing Violent Radicalisation in America, Bipartisan Policy Centre*, National Security Preparedness Group, June 2011.

Peraino, K. The Re-education of Abu Jandal, *Newsweek*, June 2009.

PURSUE (2011) *Proposed Programme of Activities for Delegation of the EU to Yemen 2011–12*, European Union, unpublished report.

Sageman, M. (2008) *Leaderless Jihad: Terror Network in the Twenty-First Century*, Philadelphia: University of Pennsylvania Press.

Seifert, K. (2010) 'Can jihadis be rehabilitated? Radical Islam', *Middle East Quarterly*, pp. 21–30.

Sharp, J. M. (2011) Yemen: Background and U.S. Relations, CRS Report for Congress, *Prepared for Members and Committees of Congress*, Congressional Research Service, 7-5700, RL34170, 8 June. Available HTTP: http://www.fas.org/sgp/crs/mideast/RL34170.pdf

2

CLEMENCY, CIVIL ACCORD AND RECONCILIATION

The evolution of Algeria's deradicalization process

Hamed El-Said

Introduction

Very few countries in the world have suffered over the past 15 years as much as Algeria did from the phenomenon of violent extremism. As the Algerian President, Abdelaziz Bouteflika stated during a public speech in 2005:

> Algeria paid the highest price for survival, I mean tens of thousands of victims and more than $20 billion worth of losses, stifling development ... in addition to deterioration of Algeria's international standing ... How many more sacrifices must be reached above the 100,000 already documented until now before peace and stability are restored?
>
> *(Bouteflika 2005: 5)*

The high level of violence which Algeria experienced between 1991–2000 and which continues intermittently up to the present day, 'was a source of surprise to many observers of contemporary Algeria' (Spencer 1996: 93). In fact, it is the lack of 'more revolutionary and radical' forces which was 'something of a surprise' in post-Independence Algeria (Richards and Waterbury 1996: 285). The high level of intense violence in Algeria, in the 1990s, was also surprising, because after independence 'Algeria followed a secular, modernising and socialist path' (Spencer 1996: 93). It is also surprising because after independence in 1962, Algeria enjoyed periods of stability that were lacking in many neighbouring countries. The kind of violence that Arab regimes were embroiled in with violent extremist movements, such as those in Iraq, Egypt and Syria were totally absent from Algeria before and during the first two decades of independence after 1962. The mainstream religious movements, such as *Islah*, were well co-opted by, and incorporated into, the ruling party – the National Liberation Front (FLN). At least until the 1980s, recourse to violence by Algeria's religious groups was, as the International Crisis Group (ICG 2004a: 2 and 2004b) noted, 'all but non-existent ... '

Algeria, however, suddenly found herself in the early 1990s facing what many Western observers and think-tanks describe as a 'civil war' (Silverstein 2000; ICG 2004a & b). The pace, scale and speed of violence which took place after the cancellation of the 1992 elections led to a vast, and in many ways, irresistible focus on Algeria's post-elections period. This has given a misleading impression of a country historically troubled by its faith-based movements, one which is de-linked from its pre-elections history or a country with no deep religious roots as if Algerians discovered religion only after 1992. The upshot has been the neglect of longstanding historical, socio-economic and political factors, which played a key role in radicalizing a large segment of Algerians since independence and led to the outbreak of violence in the late 1980s and thereafter. The root cause of the country's problems is thus wrongly portrayed as beginning with 'the urban riots of October 1988' culminating in the army generals' coup that resulted in the cancellation of the 1992 elections (Spencer 1996: 93). As Jebnoun (2007: 3 and 12) put it, Algeria's problems 'can only be understood by taking the internal political situation into consideration from an emic perspective' and only by 'add[ing] an important socio-historical element to our analysis'.

This chapter does that. It takes a historical-analytical framework in its attempt to examine Algeria's evolution of violent extremism in the 1990s and thereafter. Algeria provides an interesting case study to verify and examine three key arguments, which are relevant to the main finding of the book in general and which this chapter seeks to establish with regard to violent extremism. First, the developmental capacity of state plays a key role in reducing the risk of violent extremism. Second, although new and charismatic regimes are important they are not sufficient for successful deradicalization and national reconciliation processes. Finally, deradicalization is most effective when a ceasefire is unilaterally declared and demanded by violent extremist groups and individuals, rather than from the state.

The chapter proceeds as follows. The next section traces the developmental capacity of the Algerian state since independence. Then it looks at the evolution of faith-based movements in Algeria and then the deradicalization process, which started in the country in the early and mid-1990s, is analysed. The final part summarizes and concludes with some remarks.

The Algerian state's developmental capacity: the roots of failure

One determining factor of the level of communal and violent activism in a country is the developmental capacity of its state. That is, the ability of the state to achieve sustainable development and equitable growth, manage unemployment and relations with ethnic communities, and overcome and control stifled bureaucracy, corruption and other forms of rent-seeking. Particularly, authoritarian states with weak developmental capacities lose legitimacy and sooner or later become subject to violent pressure from various societal forces (Lubeck 1996). Algeria is no exception.[1]

The new Algerian state emerged out of a bloody eight-year liberation war with colonial France between 1954 and 1962 during which more than one million Algerians were killed. Like elsewhere in the region, political independence (gained by

Algeria in 1962) raised both enthusiasm and political and economic expectations of the newly liberated nation. Having been colonized and exploited for more than 130 years by an aligned European power (France) that sought to assimilate Algerians into a completely different culture, *mores* and way of life, Algeria's new political elite sought, with popular bear, to minimize, even to eliminate any possibility of external economic dependence. The state thus hoped to achieve self-sufficiency at home in the midst of ethnically, demographically and geographically fragmented society and communities.

Almost immediately after independence, Algeria's political elite, in the form of the National Liberation Front (FLN), the single party which mobilized all Algerians during the war of liberation and assumed power thereafter, laid hefty claims to a strong dose of socialism. Despite the vagueness of the term and the real commitment of leadership, Algerian socialism seemed to incorporate two key strategies: large, heavily centralized, state-led industrialization and an 'extensive welfare program' (Richards and Waterbury 1996: 32). Accordingly, the first act of the newly independent state was to nationalize all agricultural land and factories that were taken over (or abandoned) by the departing European settlers and colonial state. Algeria's first president, Ahmed Ben Bella and the radical elements in the FLN were able to initially promote worker self-management in industry and agriculture as the basis for the country's economic policy following advice from friendly countries like Yugoslavia in particular. But this approach lasted for less than three years until 1965 when a military coup led by Houari Boumediene removed Ben Bella from power. Boumediene 'was obsessed with … national development' and industrialization (Richards and Waterbury 1996: 286).

Under Boumediene's presidency (which lasted until 1978), the state, this time following advice from the former Soviet Union, was placed firmly under a strong socialist, central planning path, with large state enterprises assuming a key role in the economy. Import Substitution Industrialization (ISI),[2] a fashionable industrial strategy at the time, was not only resolutely implemented by Boumediene's cabinet, but was also implemented far more religiously than elsewhere in the Arab World. Algerians were promised justice, equity, prosperity, sovereignty, independence and an integrated society. These 'socialist slogans' were implanted and embodied in the revolution's two most fundamentalist documents (the Tripoli Program of 1962 and the Charter of Algiers of 1964) and were meant not only to promote the new state's economic policies, but also to bind together a fragmented social force (Ayubi 1999: 123).

An unwritten social contract quickly developed between the new state and its society, whereby the former provides, free of charge, education and health to all Algerians, as well as jobs, subsidized basic commodities, utilities and other social services in return for loyalty from the latter. The strategy of industrial deepening which Boumediene's Government pursued was similarly reliant on heavily subsidizing industrial inputs and intermediates, as well as strong protection via tariff and non-tariff barriers and distorted macroeconomic policies (such as an overvalued exchange rate and very low interest rates that aimed at making capital available to national enterprises). These policies not only unintentionally squeezed out the private sector, but also created an inefficient economy via provision of total monopolies in the trade, financial, banking and insurance systems. The Algerian state 'was convinced of the need to have the Algerian economy firmly under its control' with state-led-large-scale industrial public projects aimed at both state building and state's societal total control, as well as preserving national independence (Ayubi 1999: 123 and 372). By the late 1960s and early 1970s, Algeria looked to many observers as a strong 'Marxist–Leninist' state 'similar to Cuba's' (Richards and Waterbury 1996: 285).

To meet the shortages of human capital which the country found itself experiencing following independence and to fulfil the promise of education for all Algerians, the education system expanded most dramatically during this period. The number of higher education students increased to 150,000 in 1984, in addition to another 5,000 students in administrative and professional training. This does not include the large number of personnel that were rushed to France for training following independence. As a result, the early years of independence saw state functionaries growing by 30 per cent per annum. By the end of the 1980s, the Algerian state was completely transformed, consisting of 26 ministries and around 39 large public organizations.[3] The state also became the largest employer, employing more than 800,000 functionaries, that is, 4 per cent of the total population and nearly 20 per cent of the labour force, with their wages and salaries accounting for more than 52 per cent of total current expenses by the late 1980s and early 1990s (Ayubi 1999: 305). This excludes the armed forces, whose number rose from 62,000 in 1962 to 65,000 and 130,000 in 1965 and 1984 respectively, in addition to another 25,000 paramilitary in 1984 (Owen 1992: 207).

Education and building human capital aside, incoherencies and irrationalities of state policies became apparent in the early 1970s. These, however, were temporarily concealed by large rents derived from the tripling of oil and gas prices in the mid-1970s. Instead of carrying out necessary reforms, large external rents lured the Algerian state to take further industrial policies based on more public ownership and further control of capital, trade and competition, all of which were controlled by one single party (the FLN) that used to marshal support from fragmented and different social groupings (Owen 1992: 142). Ironically, Algerian inward-looking industrial deepening was taking place at a time when other more successful developing countries, particularly those in East Asia like Korea, Taiwan and Singapore were reorienting their societies and restructuring their economies towards exportation and the global market (Lubeck 1996). It was the success of such reorientation and restructuring, which was carefully guided, led and governed by strong developmental states that earned these countries the epithet of Newly Industrializing Countries (NICs) (Amsden 1989; Wade 1990).

By the late 1970s, it was becoming apparent to both the Algerian regime and its opponents and proponents alike, that this model of development is not only irrational, but also unsustainable. The lack of competition and the presence of monopolies created and sustained by strong protectionist policies, led to waste, inefficiencies, high costs of production and widespread corruption. State enterprises and public sector organizations became a strain and a massive financial burden on the state treasury, necessitating the need to resort to foreign borrowing by an oil and gas rich state to keep them afloat.

Widespread corruption and black markets ensued from heavy protectionism and monopolies afforded to public enterprises and began to undermine the legitimacy of the regime whose ability to continue to provide what it promised in terms of jobs and prosperity to all Algerians was eroding very quickly. Large fiscal deficit, caused mainly by the need to continuously fund and subsidize large and inefficient state enterprises, along with overvalued exchange rates led to high inflationary pressures that wore down Algerians' living standards. State enterprises were no longer able to absorb more workers, leading to high and increasing unemployment rates (Owen 1992; Ayubi 1999). Industrial deepening or an emphasis on industry, led to a large neglect of agriculture, a typical problem faced by Rentier States that derive most of their revenues from external rents and attempt to use them for rapid urbanization (Luciani 1990). In Algeria, the neglect of agriculture followed independence and long preceded the massive hike in oil prices in the mid-1970s. Overvalued exchange rates further undermined agriculture export, production and employment, leading to a deterioration in the terms of trade for the rural economy *vis-à-vis* industry and therefore to considerable rural–urban migration. The 'location of … industries in and around the major cities of Algiers, Constantine, and Oran further stimulated rural-to-urban migration, already massive because of rapid population growth and the neglect of agriculture. This exacerbated the severe problems of cities' (Richards and Waterbury 1996: 230). During 1970–80, Algerian exports grew at an average rate of -0.5 per cent while imports grew at an average of 12.1 per cent, more than 25 per cent of which were food imports. The labour force working in agriculture declined from 67 per cent in 1960 to 31 per cent in 1980, while industry was only able to absorb 27 per cent of the total labour force in 1980, down from 12 per cent in 1960. On average, inflation grew at an annual rate of 9.8 per cent during 1965–80, while the total earnings per employee grew by a paltry average of 0.1 per cent between 1970 and 1980 (World Bank 1989: 165 and 177). By the late 1970s, unemployment was already in double digits (more than 16 per cent in the mid-1980s) and rapidly increasing, notwithstanding a relatively high GDP growth rate of 7.5 per cent (at purchaser value) between 1965–80 (World Bank 1989: 167).

Despite its large oil revenues and rapid economic growth rates, Algeria could not escape the internal incoherencies and contradictions of its state-led, inward oriented development policy.

> The key weaknesses of the Boumediene strategy were excess capacity, over centralisation, unemployment, massive rural–urban migration, and serious neglect of agriculture. These problems elicited half-hearted reform measures that helped delegitimize the government as they imposed hardship but failed to deliver a restructured economy.
>
> *(Richards and Waterbury 1996: 229–30)*

In urban areas, where the regime provided incentives for the young to migrate, there developed a shortage of housing, jobs and decent incomes. Where jobs existed in public sector enterprises, the low productivity of industrial workers and the high costs of operations caused by overcapacity, lack of scale economies and management problems, including weak factory discipline became the norm (Richards and Waterbury 1996: 229–30; Ayubi 1999). The capital-intensive nature of Boumediene's development strategy not only drained the treasury and necessitated having to resort to foreign borrowing, but also meant that few jobs were created for the increasing cohort of youth entering the labour market.

Pressure was thus mounting for a change in economic strategy, and increasing international and national indebtedness, totalling $22.9 billion in the mid-1980s was a critical factor in driving it (World Bank 1989: 205). Following the sudden death of Boumediene and the presidential inauguration of Bendjedid in 1978, the latter announced in 1980, a ten-year economic programme was rigorously put in place in 1982. The new programme aimed at reversing the previous development strategy of heavy, state-led industrialization, to light, small-scale industry based on the private sector. It also included austerity measures that drastically cut government spending, imports and recurrent expenditures, including freezing jobs and the wages and salaries of public sector enterprises and civil servants.

A new investment law, aimed at encouraging and attracting both private local and foreign investment through various financial and non-financial incentives was enacted in 1982. Within the first three years, the new investment law succeeded in increasing the number of small and medium-sized private enterprises to 4,800 accounting for 30 per cent of the industrial workforce. The new economic programme also aimed at reforming the public sector by breaking it up into smaller, more flexible and specialized units. Breaking up the 35–39 largest state enterprises produced between 322–500 smaller state enterprises.[4] This reduced state concentration, produced a more flexible structure without resorting to privatization, or transferring ownership structure which have become an integral part of the so-called structural adjustment policies designed and promoted by the IMF and World Bank since the late 1970s (Ayubi 1999: 374. Also see Owen 1992: 144; Richards and Waterbury 1996: 229–32).

To all intents and purposes, the 'Bendjedid government tried without much success' to restructure and transform the economy (CIA World Factbook 2010: 1). The austerity measures incorporated in Bendjedid's programme were 'Ironically probably more severe than an IMF structural adjustment program (SAP), Chadli's austerity smashed already shrinking living standards of urban population, reduced the availability of essential commodities, and further spiked unemployment, especially of secondary and university graduates'[5] (Lubeck 1996: 308). Roger Owen (1992: 144), while analyzing the social impact of Bendjedid's economic policies, also noted that:

> As elsewhere in the world, economic liberalisation led to greater inequalities of income, increasing unemployment and more obvious corruption, while cuts in subsidies and in imports were a stimulus to inflation, currency depreciation and the growth of black-market. As elsewhere, too, the consequent popular discontent ... presented all kinds of opportunities to the different factions within them, being subject to rival interpretations and providing both reformers and anti-reformers with political capital to be used as the situation allowed.
>
> *(Owen 1992: 144)*

While Bendjedid's economic programme did break up large public sector enterprises, it could not stop subsidizing them and therefore it could not change the incentive structure necessary to motivate them to become more efficient, less wasteful and more productive. Budget constraints, in other words, remained soft and were not hardened enough to encourage public enterprises to operate on a more commercial and autonomous basis. The government, fearing its impact on urban population, refused to devalue the exchange rate, the centrepiece of any IMF SAP,[6] which was necessary to stimulate production exports and jobs. Interest rates remained very low and negative in real terms, thus encouraging firms to resort to capital-intensive rather than labour-intensive production methods. The link between the new private sector and state enterprise remained symbiotic rather than competitive, with the former continuing to rely on the latter for inputs, orders and sales. The new reforms failed to stimulate a sufficient degree of competition necessary to improve efficiency and productivity.

The labour market also remained rigid and lacked flexibility. Under these circumstances, private and public enterprises refused to take on more workers, although the public sector was already characterized by massive redundancies and underemployment. As a result of the overvaluation of the currency, the agriculture sector, which the new economic programme of Bendjedid's government targeted, failed to stimulate agricultural production and exportation leading to a rapid increase in the importation of foodstuffs. This came to represent more than two thirds of total imports in late 1980s (Owen 1992).

Bendjedid also believed that carrying out similar reforms to those promoted by the IMF and World Bank in other developing countries would lead to the repayment of foreign debt and would therefore avoid entering into SAP agreement with the IMF and World Bank, as Algeria's neighbours Tunisia, Morocco and Egypt had been forced to do. Hence, 'Algeria deliberately avoided entering into an agreement with the IMF. Its reform was "structural adjustment with a nationalistic face", designed in part to avoid the perceived humiliation of "losing sovereignty" to the IMF' (Richards and Waterbury 1996: 231). The national autonomous reforms however, neither allowed Algeria to repay her debts, nor stopped her from borrowing more: in 1986 Algeria returned to the international capital market for more borrowings. By then, Algeria had 'accumulated one of the largest per capita external debts in the world' ($23 billion) (Ayubi 1999: 307).

By 1988, economic growth declined rapidly to -2.7 per cent from 5.2 per cent in 1984. With a population growth rate exceeding 3 per cent annually, living standards continued to be smashed. The crisis was taking place at a time when a vast cohort of students was exploding into the labour market. In the mid-to-late 1980s, 75–80 per cent of secondary students sitting for the Baccalaureate exam failed, only to join the 40,000–50,000 students rejected elsewhere from the educational system (Ayubi 1999: 397). During 1985–90, the labour force grew at an annual average rate of 4 per cent. The growth in employment lagged seriously far behind. The result has been acute unemployment and underemployment, which official estimates put at 26 per cent (unemployment) in 1990. Almost 65 per cent of all the unemployed in 1990 were 15 to 24 years of age, raising the unemployment rate within this age bracket to 41 per cent

(CIA World Factbook 2010: 1). By the late 1980s and early 1990s, more than 22.6 per cent of all Algerians were living below the poverty line (World Bank 2003: 236).

In October 1988, tensions reached their zenith when urban riots erupted. Sources differ on what exactly happened and how and whether violence by rioters preceded repressive crackdown by the authorities or vice versa. What was clearer, though, is that living standards were the immediate cause of the riots and that the latter (riots) were bloody. While Lubeck (1996: 308) estimated the number of deaths associated with the riots at 200, Richards and Waterbury (1996: 287) suggest that the 1988 bloody riots resulted 'in thousands of deaths'.

Appreciating the severity of the situation and the need for deeper reforms, the Bendjedid government pushed for further reforms, but this time under the auspices of the very same institutions which the President's cabinet had proudly avoided for so long, namely, the IMF and World Bank. In 1989, Algeria signed its first SAP with the IMF and the World Bank, whose reforms included more of the same austerity measures, which the Bendjedid government had been implementing since the early 1980s, as well as everything else the Bendjedid government had been avoiding. This included the massive devaluation of the Algerian Dinar, increasing interest rates rapidly, slashing further government spending and privatization of state-owned enterprises. Within months of implementing these reforms, the number of Algerians living under the poverty line shot up to more than 22 per cent, with the living standards of most Algerians continuing to deteriorate rapidly (El-Said and Harrigan 2006).

In June 1992, the government unilaterally terminated the IMF programme, particularly following the assassination of President Boudiaf, blaming riots and increased violence on reforms. Less than a year later, Algeria had to re-open negotiations with the IMF as the country, for the first time in its history, was no longer able to service its debt. By that time, violence had engulfed the country and development, as President Bouteflika publicly stated, was halted for almost ten years. Algerians today have developed several terminologies to describe the 1990s decade, including the 'Red Decade', the 'Big Fetna' decade (Ahsriyat al Fitna al Kubra) or simply the 'Ten Black Years' (Bara 2007: 4). This might sound reminiscent of the Latin American 1980s 'lost decade', except that the Algerian 'Red Decade' dwarfs that of Latin America's in terms of the scale of violence. It was far 'bloodier and much more destructive … at times very intensive', encompassing atrocities, massacres, kidnappings, maiming and predator practices (Berkouk 2009a: 2 and 2009b).

To sum up the key points of this section, the Algerian state lacked the developmental capacity to deliver on its promises of providing jobs, improved living standards and basic social welfare services, the minimum citizens can expect of their legitimate state. Widespread corruption in almost all state institutions further undermined the legitimacy of the regime, as well as forcing it to resort to external institutions to run the economy, particularly the IMF and World Bank. In the minds of every Algerian, resorting to such institutions was tantamount to a public open admission of failure of all reforms initiated since independence. The abandonment of the IMF programme in 1992 and the re-opening of negotiations with it in 1993 reinforced the popular belief of a divided regime, one incapable of effecting badly needed reforms either autonomously or with others. As the next section demonstrates, this not only invited all sorts of opposition to the state, but also, when the opportunity arose later, to carry arms and launch a high-intensity war, the aim of which was to bring the state down altogether.

Evolution of faith-based organizations in Algeria

Algeria, historically, lacked a strong indigenous scholarly tradition, a fact which was reflected in the absence of any highly regarded national Islamic institutions, such as al-Azhar in Egypt or al-Zeitouna University in Tunisia. As a result, Algerian Islamism was, from the very beginning, influenced by external intellectuals and educational institutions. This tradition goes back to the early twentieth century when young Algerians, escaping compulsory service in the French army, fled to neighbouring Arab countries and attended religious education in such institutions as al-Zeitouna and al-Azhar. There, these self-exiled young Algerians were influenced by neo-reformist intellectuals like Mohammed Abduh and Jamal-Din Al-Afghani, as well as Sheikh Hassan al-Bana's radical teachings, which had perhaps the most significant influence on Algerian Islamism before and after independence. Upon their return to Algeria after the end of the First World War, they 'established the Association of the Algerian *Ulema* and planted the first seeds of Islamism in Algeria' (Berkouk 2009a: 3 and 2009b). They also used, and heavily relied upon, Islam to mobilize Algerians against French colonialists. The link between Islam and politics is not a new phenomenon in contemporary Algeria:

> The various resistance movements against the French gained justification not only in the name of Algeria but also of Islam. They were *Jihadists* against infidel invaders. They were defined as acts obligatory for all Muslims. The French further consolidated this conception of colonial relationships by distinguishing Algerians from the settlers first by religion (not by race, ethnic origin or nationality), and only secondly by geo-ethnicity. Algerians were called Muslims and the others called Europeans. This, and other polices of selective assimilation aimed at stripping the Algerians of their Islamic identity, have not only further engrained the feeling of Islamic identity, but have also strengthened the belief in the sole righteousness of the Islamic model. Islam was, thereafter, a source of identity and a motive for liberation. It was this identity that the Islamic Reformist Movement (The Association of Algerian Ulema) was trying to establish and it was this motive that was later used by the FLN (National Liberation Front) to rally people around the nationalist agenda.
>
> *(Berkouk 2009a: 3 and 2009b)*

The Association of Algerian Ulema (*jam'iyyat al-'ulama al-muslimin al-jaaza'iriyyin*) (AOMA) was a reformist movement (*Harakat Islah*) established in the very early 1930s by Sheikh Abdelhamid Ben Badis, a leading and influential Algerian Islamic scholar. It was an extension of the *Salafiyya* movement[7] of the late nineteenth and early twentieth centuries, from which the Muslim Brotherhood Movement sprang in Egypt in the 1920s. Initially, the AOMA was not revolutionary; rather it was an anti-assimilation movement. Ben Badis' original objective was to mobilize his countrymen against the French occupation in order to preserve the Muslim identity of the Algerian nation threatened by France's assimilation policies that sought to undermine the Arabic language and Islamic faith. As Ben Badis himself stated, the Algerian Muslim nation:

> ... has its history, defined by innumerable great events; it has its linguistic and religious unity, it has its own culture, its traditions, and its customs both good and bad, as do all the other nations. Therefore, this Algerian Muslim nation is not France, it is not possible that it be France; it does not want to become France, and even if it wished, it could not be France.
>
> *(Cited by Ruedy 1994: 76. Also cited by Jebnoun 2007: 12)*

Before the establishment of the FLN in 1954, therefore, the reformist AOMA movement played a key role in preserving and reinforcing the Islamic identity of the Algerian nation, expressed mainly in resistance to France's assimilation policies. The establishment of the FLN in 1954, its mobilization of most Algerians against French occupation and its declaration of war of independence following the establishment of its army, The National Liberation Army (ALN), emboldened the national trend, reinforced resistance movement and weakened the apolitical-reformist trend. The AOMA, along with other movements and oppositional groups, was cajoled to join the nationalist trend, with its members participating in the FLN's ALN. The AOMA not only rallied to the FLN's war of independence, but also endorsed it, hence providing a strong religious justification for the FLN's resistance army and its policies. From the inception of the FLN on November 1 1954, the AOMA, along with other groups and movements, was incorporated into, and represented in, the FLN's leadership, a trend that continued to prevail after independence (ICG 2004b: 1). In return, the first FLN's political programme, published on the day it was established, had an important Islamic input: 'the restoration of sovereign democratic and social Algerian state in the framework of Islamic principles' (Spencer 1996: 98).

This symbiotic relationship between the FLN and AOMA continued after independence. The FLN subsequently adopted and made key ideas of the AOMA its own, including the 'promotion of a reformed, scripturalist and puritanical Islam as well as Arabisation ... ' (ICG 2004: 1). The first constitution of the Republic, published in 1963, not only declared Islam to be the main religion of the state, but also stipulated that the President must be a Muslim, hardly surprising in a country where the population, including all ethnic groups, are Muslims. In other words, although nationalist-socialist in nature, the new Algerian state was born Islamic nationalist, unlike the Baathist secular regimes in Iraq and Syria, or Egypt's Arab secular socialism under Nasser. As the ICG (2004: 1) asserts, 'Algeria's nationalism was explicitly Muslim'. Not unlike all the other newly born Arab regimes at the time, the Algerian state was born authoritarian, undemocratic and based on the co-optation of various nationalist and oppositionist groups and individuals (Spencer 1996; Richards and Waterbury 1996; Owen 1992; Ayubi 1999).

In 1966, the Algerian state established The Algerian Islamic Supreme Council, which was given a monopoly over the interpretation of the *shari'a* (Islamic) law and delivery of the fatwa (religious ruling) (Nozaffari 1996: 246). The Supreme Islamic Council, which played a key role in the state's educational apparatuses and in informing the state's official campaigns, was manned by veteran members of the AOMA. The latter's influence was also reinforced by and reflected in the 1976 National Charter, adopted by a referendum, which banned gambling and introduced the Muslim weekend (ICG 2004: 2).

During the state and institution-building phase in the 1960s and 1970s, veteran members of the AOMA also staffed the new Ministry of Religious Affairs. The latter were entrusted with the key responsibilities of supervising the religious sphere, including the religious curriculum of the state, establishing new Islamic institutions to train religious officials, as well as supervising and organizing the pilgrimage to Mecca. The Council also employed *imams* and turned them into salaried civil servants thus benefiting from access to an important forum, namely, mosques to preserve and reinforce Algeria's Islamic identity (ICG 2004: 2).

It was in the 1980s however, that active Islamism grew most rapidly in Algeria. In a manner reminiscent of Sadat's dangerous policy of using Islamists as a counterweight to the pro-Nasserists in the 1970s, Bendjedid, in order to open up space for his economic reform programme, followed a similar policy. Large sections of the FLN, army and bureaucracy not only opposed Bendjedid's reforms, but also 'impeded the shift to the market at every opportunity' (Richards and Waterbury 1996: 232). Bendjedid, therefore, encouraged the growth of Islamists as a counterweight to the pro-Boumediene elements in state apparatus, including the FLN, army and bureaucracy (ICG 2004; Owen 1992; Ayubi 1999; Richards and Waterbury 1996).

Through their domination of the Ministry of Religious Affairs and The Algerian Islamic Supreme Council, veteran leaders of the AOMA and now other Islamists that infiltrated state institutions and radicalized by the politics of the region launched a massive campaign in the late 1970s and early 1980s, both private and public, to sponsor the building of new mosques. This came to be known in Algeria as the 'Free Mosques' Campaign (FMC). The FMC started under Boumediene who condoned it as a social and political counterweight to undermine leftist groups, particularly inside universities, that arose against his policies in the second half of the 1970s. The FMC, however, was accelerated under Bendjedid, who saw in it a counterweight to the pro-Boumediene elements which staunchly opposed his economic programme, either in the FLN, army or bureaucracy. The FMC successfully resulted in the building of thousands of new mosques in different parts of the country but, in the absence of a political participation process, it also encouraged the emergence of clandestine Islamic groups and activities, all of which remained outside state control. The *imams* of the new mosques began perilously criticizing the failure of government policy, widespread corruption in state institutions and the failure to solve unemployment problems, and rising poverty and inequities. Accelerated plans under Bendjedid to build Islamic universities in Algiers and Oran, along with other centres of Islamic learning, directly benefited Islamist groups by providing them with new forums to spread their message and job opportunities. Even before the introduction of political reforms in the late 1980s, Islamists:

> ... had stronger grounds than other parties, religious and secular. The key to success, in the late 1980s, was an access of new social groups to these centres of learning, which expanded the domain of higher education to include the humble, the peasants and the sons of peasants.
>
> *(Spencer 1996: 101. Also ICG 2004: 3)*

In the absence of any democratic process, most faith-based groups and organizations in post-independence Algeria focused on the *da'aw* (the calling for Islam) and charity provision as a means to access the hearts and minds of most Algerians and hence to transform society first from within and hence gradually bring about a bottom-up change in the country. As Professor Berkouk (2009a: 5 and 2009b), the Director of the Institute of Diplomacy and International Relations at the University of Algiers, explained, the first group of Islamists that emerged in the post-independence period:

> ... composed of Islamic welfare and religious groups, associations and individuals that reject the state's monopoly over the Islamic discourse and strive to recapture the initiative from the authorities by promoting charitable, cultural, educational and social initiatives. This is how all politically-oriented Islamic movements started in the sixties and the seventies. The associations, groups and individuals that belong to this category want to re-Islamize society through education, welfare and the spread of the moral code. In the case of Algeria, one can mention the association of *al-Qiyam* (values) in the sixties or *al-Irshad wal Islah* (an association belonging to the HMS party) and the former Islamic League (*al-Rabita al-Islamiya*) presided over by the late *Sheikh Sahnoun*, which served as an umbrella organisation for all the currents of the Islamic movements between 1988 and 1991.
>
> *(Berkouk 2009a: 5 and 2009b)*

As Bendjedid's economic and austerity programme of the 1980s included massive cuts in state spending, the state's ability to provide basic social services such as healthcare and education was weakened. As in other countries that implemented similar austerity measures in the 1980s and 1990s under the auspices of the IMF and World Bank, countries such as Jordan, Egypt and Morocco (Harrigan and El-Said 2009), severe cuts in state spending led to the withdrawal of the Algerian state from social welfare provision at a time of austerity and hardship. The consequence was the development of a welfare-gap, which was filled by various faith-based organizations that emerged in the 1970s and 1980s. In another context it has been shown how social welfare provision by faith-based organizations played an important role not only in undermining the legitimacy of the incumbent regime, but also in enhancing the legitimacy and popularity of the new providers. As Hamid and Kadlec wrote while analyzing the political impact of Jordan's Islamic Action Front's charity:

> With governments failing to provide an effective social safety net, Islamic groups have filled the vacuum, creating parallel institutions that provide jobs, education, and health care to constituents ... The Islamic Action Front ... By Fighting corruption and providing critical services ... are seen as the only viable alternative to ineffective state leadership.
>
> *(Hamid and Kadlec 2010: 2)*

Jebnoun (2007: 17) in his work on Algeria concurs: 'Furthermore, the failed educational system, sub-standard healthcare delivery system, and widespread poverty have significantly weakened political legitimacy'. This view is also shared by the International Crisis Group (2004a and 2004b), which asserted that the phenomenal and surprising expansion of the Islamist movement in the 1980s and early 1990s 'and its ability to acquire a mass base should be understood in terms of the alienation of many young Algerians from a state which seemed no longer to offer them prospects'.

Following the massive riots that broke out in October 1988 (known in Algeria as 'Black October'), Bendjedid decided to alter the country's economic strategy. He combined further economic reform with political liberalization (in early 1989). By that time, Islamists were already in a stronger position to benefit from the newly introduced democratization process than any other group in the country. The Islamists had benefited not only from their social welfare provision, but also from their access to mosques and the media to promote their *da'wa* and delegitimize a corrupt, politically bankrupt and developmentally failing regime. They also benefited from a new law that Bendjedid approved in 1988 and which allowed 'the free formation of association in Algeria without any prior approval by public authorities' (Richards and Waterbury 1996: 287).

The first act of the newly created Islamic movement, the Islamic Salvation Front (FIS), following their electoral win in the local and municipal elections in 1989, was not militant. It was to use the local municipalities, which they had won and now controlled to provide further welfare services to the poor and needy, particularly the urban poor that were most affected by the severe austerity measures which the Bendjedid government implemented in 1988–9 under the auspices of the IMF and World Bank and were accompanied by political reforms:

> The first activities of the movement headed by the FIS were born not of violence, but of a concentration of efforts to provide for the needs of those in overcrowded city quarters suffering most from the neglect of central government. The group's relatively young and vocal leaders offered, through the mosques, a variety of social services of the type withdrawn by the government for economic reasons or overstretched by the burgeoning population of cities like Algiers ... The provision of housing and other forms of social welfare by the FIS and its financial supporters in the disillusioned middle classes did more than fill gap where the government had abandoned urban population; it also restored a sense of dignity to younger generations and fuelled a propensity towards greater activism.
>
> *(Spencer 1996: 97 and 99)*

'Black October' therefore, and the economic and political reforms that ensued, should be seen as a popular response to the failure of the state's developmental model. A lack of alternative political venues for the Algerian youth to express their views and actions, as well as a rise in the popularity of faith-based organizations filling an important welfare function, all of which sparked a legitimacy crisis within the nationalist FLN party.

It is important to remember that not all Islamist groups that emerged in the 1980s and thereafter, were violent, called for violence, or believed in violence as the only means to bring about a change in the Algerian polity and society. 'It is worth noting' Professor Berkouk (2009a: 5) warns, 'that the Algerian Islamic Movement is neither homogenous nor monolithic. It is composed of a plethora of groups, associations and individuals with divergent convictions and ideational structures.' Even before democracy was introduced in 1989, various Islamic currents had already been distinguished in the Algerian society and continued subsequently to influence the evolution of Islamist expressions, the effectiveness of state's deradicalization and reconciliation policies, and the outcome of state-militants deliberations and discourse in general.[8] These various Islamic expressions can be divided into at least five main categories (ICG 2004; Spencer 1996; Berkouk 2009a).

The first category includes the veterans of the AOMA, which in turn can be divided into two sub-categories: the official and incorporated veteran leaders of the AOMA preserving the reformist tradition of Ben Badis under Abdelrahman Chibane who was minister of religious affairs from 1980–6 and, since 1998, President of the AOMA (re-established in 1991 as a legal association). It is from this sub-group, also known in Algeria as the intellectual current and which was influenced mainly by the thinking of the Egyptian and Syrian Muslim Brotherhood Movements, that the Algerian main Islamic parties HMS, An-Nahda and al-Islah sprang from (Berkouk 2009a: 4).

The second AOMA subgroup includes its dissident veterans which dominated the 'free mosques' and acted under the leadership of Sheikh Ahmad Sahnoun and Sheikh Abdellatif Soltani. This group operated outside official Islam and developed a radical discourse that attacked the moral decadence of the Algerian state and society, including widespread corruption among senior state officials and top state institutions. This current also acted as mentor to some of the more radical leaders of the FIS, such as Ali Ben Hadj (ICG 2004a and 2004b).

It is possible to categorize Ali Ben Hadj as belonging to the second current, which was influenced by the *Salafiyya* doctrine and which emerged following Bendjedid's lifting of restrictions on people's movements, particularly to Umrah and Hajj (pilgrimages) in the 1980s. This resulted in a large number of Algerians travelling to Saudi Arabia for both studentship and worship purposes. In Saudi Arabia, these Algerians were influenced by the intensity of religious discourse and life, and, when they returned to Algeria, they were saturated with *Salafiyya* doctrine, which they tried to spread throughout the country. Ali Belhadj, the radical and second most prominent FIS leader, was also associated with this current (Berkouk 2009a: 4).

Third, the Algerian current or the *Jaz'ara* (*Algerianists*), influenced by the Algerian Islamic thinker Malek Bennabi (1905–73) and distinguished by its modernist and intellectual view and outlook, as well as an acceptance of the Algerian national idea (ICG 2004: 2).

Fourth, the so-called Mustafa Bouyali's group that: 'belonged to none of the major currents of Islamist activism which had developed in the late 1970s and early 1980s' (ICG 2004: 2). Still, Bouyali became known for establishing the first violent movement in Algeria. For some, 'Mustafa Bouyali [is] perceived to be the first founder of the first Jihadist movement in Algeria' (Ashour 2009: 158). In the early 1980s, Bouyali gathered around him a small group of militants and formed the Algerian Islamic Armed Movement (MIA), which, during the early and mid-1980s, launched a series of attacks from Maquis of the hills surrounding Algiers against security posts to acquire weapons for their goal of an Islamic state (Spencer 1996: 97). Bouyali's religious credentials, however, were always questioned. What is known about him is that he certainly was a former Socialist and FLN member, who became disgruntled with the FLN policies and leadership. In 1987 Bouyali was caught and killed in an ambush by the security forces, but his 'dormant terrorist cells … were reactivated in 1992' and continue to be among the most radical and violent groups in Algeria today (Berkouk 2009a: 6).

The final category is known, in Algerian academic circles, as the 'methodical current' (Berkouk 2009a: 4 and 2009b: 4). This represents up to 1400 Algerians, most of whom served in Afghanistan in the 1980s with al-Qaeda and espouse a *takfiri* and Jihadi theology against both the Algerian state and society. They also espouse their own concept of an Islamic state based on *Khalifat* and thus oppose democratization and political liberalization as apostate and anti-Islamic. Developed in the late 1980s and early 1990s, this current and their followers represent today, along with the MIA, the nucleus of violent extremism and core of the most radical and violent groups in Algeria. Namely, the *Group Islamique or Arme* or Armed Islamic Group (GIA), *Group Salafiste pour la Pre'dication et la Combat* or the Salafi Group for Preaching and Combat (GSPC).[9]

To summarize the key point of this section, failed developmental states, particularly authoritarian and undemocratic, represent a recipe for violent activism and political instability. In some cases, they can become a fertile ground for high-intensity military conflicts. When economic and political grievances reach their zenith, as they did in Algeria in 1988, action-oriented activities such as demonstrations and riots can act as a catalyst for the involvement of groups and individuals with divergent ideological, economic, political and organizational backgrounds. While the 1988 Algerian riots had their roots in economic, political and social factors, the ensuing delegitimization of the regime, and particularly the FLN, attracted various groups and individuals of 'whatever nature' to join in the spoils (Richards and Waterbury 1996: 267). This process was to be repeated in 1992, following the Algerian army's cancellation of the 1992 elections. Not only did the level of violence in the post-1992 period dwarf, by far, any level of violence experienced in the previous periods since independence, its speed and intensity also created a temptation to focus on events post-1991–2.

Violence, deradicalization and reconciliation

Following the outbreak of riots in 1988, Bendjedid, as mentioned in the previous section, adopted a new approach and introduced more economic reforms that implied further and more severe austerity measures under the auspices of the IMF and

World Bank. This time, economic reform was combined with political reform. This included the introduction of free elections and a democratic process for the first time in the history of Algeria, a process which Roger Owen (1992: 137) referred to as 'the Algerian version of the Soviet perestroika'.

Within weeks of introducing the 'Algerian perestroika', more than 60 new political parties were created, many of which embraced Islamic values and principles.[10] This included the Islamic Salvation Front (FIS), created in July 1989. Out of all the 60 parties that existed during the 1990 local elections, none gained similar appeal to the FIS, leading to the latter's landslide victory in the 1990 local and municipal elections. In December 1991, its popular support was confirmed when the FIS achieved another landslide victory in the first round of national elections, which set it on a definite path to win the second round of national elections in 1992 and hence to control the parliament. To avoid such a scenario, the army generals deposed Bendjedid, announced emergency law, cancelled the elections, banned the FIS and followed that by arresting thousands of the FIS leaders, including Abbasi Madani and Ali Belhadj. This was the spark that gave birth to Algeria's 'Red Decade', or civil war that, according to other local sources (Berkouk 2009a: 7), 'caused over 200,000 deaths, 1.2 million internally displaced persons and more than 30 billion dollars in material damage. It was the most destructive terrorist dynamics in modern history that Algerians faced alone'.

Why the army generals intervened and cancelled the 1992 elections, their rationale and whether they were right or wrong, remains very controversial and has been contentiously, and extensively, debated elsewhere to warrant repetition (Richards and Waterbury 1996: 229–33 and 285-9; Owen 1992; Nozaffari 1996; Spencer 1996; Ayubi 1999; Jebnoun 2007; Hamid and Kadlec 2010). What is important here is the dynamics of peace, reconciliation and the deradicalization process that ensued. The focus in what follows, therefore, will be on the main factors that led to abandonment of arms by the large majority of militants in the late 1990s, a subject which hitherto has been neglected in the literature and received much less attention than it deserves. A brief description of the sequence and chronology of events as they unfolded since 1992 is necessary in order to effectively identify conditions conducive to a successful deradicalization process. To do this, we divide the period between 1992–2010 in Algeria into three main stages, or phases, in terms of the level of violence and the evolution of the deradicalization process.

First, the 1992–4 phase. This was marked by the consolidation of the militant groups reflected in the emergence of a cluster of factions, sometimes overlapping and interacting with one another, but which had one thing in common: most believed that only violence would help achieve their goals and hence they armed themselves for that purpose, although their motives were different. Some acts of violence carried out by these groups were perpetrated against the state and were determined either to restore the cancelled 1992 elections and democratic process or to bring the state down altogether and replace it with an Islamic state and create an Islamic society. This initially included the following: the MIA,[11] MEI,[12] GIA[13] and FIDA.[14] The Islamic Salvation Army *(Armée Islamique du Salut)* (AIS)[15] was founded in July 1994 and from the very beginning its aims and objectives were confined to the restoration of democracy and particularly the 1992 electoral results (ICG 2004: 10; Ashour 2009).

The second phase extends from 1995 to 1998. This phase represents the zenith of violence in Algeria, including explosions in public places; attacking state institutions, buildings and personnel; kidnapping of foreign and Algerian citizens;[16] massacres and atrocities, and even the degeneration of violence into predatory behaviour.[17] This phase also witnessed an increase in the state repression against and manipulation of radical groups, severe schisms between and among warring factions themselves, as well as further radicalization of some groups, particularly the GIA. The further radicalization of some members of the GIA led to the birth of a new, more radical splinter group in September 1998, the *Groupe salafiste pour la prédication el le combat* – GSPC, under the leadership of Hassan Hattab; a former GIA commander. Another radical group which split from the GIA and was created during this period was the LIDD (*Ligue Islamique pour le Da'wa et le Djihad* Islamic League for Preaching and Jihad), which was founded in 1996 by another former GIA commander, Ali Benhadjar. Unlike the GSPC, this group was dissolved in 2000. Finally, this phase was additionally characterized by the *beginning* of a successful deradicalization process by the AIS, the largest group to carry arms against the state. This process started in 1997 when the AIS's leadership declared a unilateral ceasefire but it was only completed successfully in the next final phase.

This final phase begins with the presidential victory of President Bouteflika in 1999 and lasts until 2010. This phase experienced not only the completion and successful deradicalization of the AIS in 1999–2000, but also of further radicalization of the GSPC, which in 2007, aligned itself with al-Qaeda and rebranded its name into al-Qaida in the Land of the Maghreb or al-Qa'ida in the Islamic countries of al-Maghreb (QICM). The group carried out its first operations, involving the simultaneous detonation of seven car bombs just before dawn on 13 February 2007 outside police and gendarmerie facilities in two provinces to the east of the capital (*The Economist* 2007). On 13 April 2010 the group carried out another operation when its members ambushed and killed at least seven Algerian security guards and a soldier working for a Turkish company responsible for a high-voltage electricity line near Bejaia, some 250 km (156 miles) east of Algiers. The attack was the deadliest since 22 October 2009 when rebels killed seven guards working for the Canadian company SNC Lavalin in Tizi Ouzou province, also part of the Kabylie area, where QICM has its stronghold (Reuters 2010). The GIA, GSPC and QICM remain today the only significant Islamist armed group still active in Algeria, along with HDS. Their total number ranges from a minimum of 500 to a maximum of 2000 (Interviews with Algerian officials December 2009). Other radical groups, such as FIDA and LIDD were dissolved in 1996 and 2000, respectively.

While investigating and analyzing the 'Causes of de-radicalization among Algerian [and Egyptian] armed Islamist groups' Ashour (2009: 111 and 120) concluded that 'four key variables' were vital in bringing about a successful deradicalization of armed Islamist groups in both Algeria[18] and Egypt.[19] These were: charismatic leadership at the movement level,[20] repression,[21] selective inducements[22] and interaction within and between radical groups and more moderate members of society.[23]

It is true that charismatic leadership at the movement level, the state's military strength, selective inducements and interaction are key and vital ingredients of a successful deradicalization process at the organization level. Such factors, however, ignore the general environment where such a process occurs, which is equally important for a successful deradicalization process. Some of the factors related to the general environment of the country where a deradicalization process is taking place includes the following: the role of a new, charismatic leadership at the national and country level, the role of civil society and the significance of a ceasefire and/or deradicalization process, stemming first and foremost from the militant groups themselves, as opposed to the state. The remainder of this section sheds some light on the significance of each of these factors in the Algerian context.

Deradicalization as stemming from militant groups

Before the AIS unilaterally declared a ceasefire in 1997, three unsuccessful deradicalization attempts took place during 1992–5. All three attempts were initiated by the Algerian state itself, rather than by the militant groups, and two of them were attempted before the AIS was formally created in 1994. In all of them, negotiations took place with the political, rather than the military wing of the FIS, although the political wing was not completely removed from the process.

The first attempt to find a peaceful resolution to the eruption of violence in Algeria took place in 1993, when General Liamine Zeroual, then Defence Minister, contacted the political leaders of the FIS, namely Abbasi Medani and Ali Belhadj in their al-Bilada military prison 'and asked them to call for a cessation of the violence perpetrated by armed Islamist organisations' (Ashour 2009: 113). Medani and Belhaj insisted first on restoring the FIS, the 1991 elections and the democratic process as a prerequisite for their intervention. These conditions were unacceptable to the generals of the army, including General Zeroual himself.

The second attempt took place in mid- to late-1994, at a time when the GIA and the militant groups in general were at their pinnacle in terms of strength, particularly following the unification of several armed groups under the GIA banner in May 1994, with rumours that they were preparing to storm Algiers. This led General Liamine Zeroual, who then headed the High Council of the State,[24] to deliver a public address calling for dialogue with the militants (Ashour 2009: 113–14). This was followed by a series of discussions with political parties, including indirect discussions with the leaders of the FIS in prison, by President Zeroual himself. The main conditions of the national dialogue 'stipulated that the FIS agree to renounce violence and accept the provision of the 1989 constitution, including a respect for political pluralism' (Spencer 1996: 95). In September 1994, Abbasi Madani and Ali Belhadji (the two FIS key leaders) were released after sending a letter to the president to the effect that the FIS was prepared to accept these conditions. Just as progress appeared underway, negotiations stalled mainly as a result of internal division among army generals, particularly between the so-called eradicators and conciliators, with 'moderate moves by one segment of the ruling elite (the so-called *conciliateurs*, grouped around Zeroual) are matched by harshly repressive countermoves by the *eradicateurs*, generally thought to be led by the chief of staff, General Lamari' (Richards and Waterbury 1996: 233. Also see Ashour 2009). In October 1994 negotiations were terminated and the initiative was given back to the 'military hardliners who had always opposed any form of accommodation with the FIS'[25] (Spencer 1996: 95).

The third and final attempt took place shortly after the second attempt, between November 1994 and January 1995, and was known as the Rome Accord (St. Edigio Platform). The Rome Accord incorporated all main (eight) political and opposition parties, representing 82 per cent of the vote cast in the last elections, including the FLN and FIS. It was the opposition parties that insisted on including the FIS in, and their presence at, the joint platform negotiations. While this reflected an awareness of the importance of the FIS for any peaceful and durable resolution in Algeria, it simultaneously meant sympathy for the FIS who had been denied the fruits of electoral victory in 1991 (Spencer 1996: 101). In January 1995, the negotiations led to what was described as 'a path breaking agreement' for the legalization of the FIS, commitment to democratic principles, pluralism and human rights, rejection of violence, fundamental liberties, including freedom of religion and thought, and universal suffrage. The Rome Accord seemed both a victory to, and a concession by, the FIS. A political victory since it called for the legal restoration of the FIS and democratic principles, a long lasting demand of the FIS from the very beginning and a concession because it moved the FIS away from what initially seemed a rigid anti-democratic and pro-Islamic state position. Political pluralism and fundamental liberties called for by the Rome Accord also reassured Berber-speaking ethnic groups, which always felt discriminated against by the state and thus their participation in militancy was rather obvious, if not strong. However, 'Neither the army nor its French backer embraced this accord as a basis for peace, so the Algerian government remained divided and war continued' (Lubeck 1996: 309). The breakdown of negotiations plunged Algeria into a vicious circle of violence, with the period between 1995–8 experiencing the worst decline into violence the country had ever seen.

Only when the AIS unilaterally and unconditionally declared a ceasefire in 1997 was the basis for a successful deradicalization and peaceful resolution for Algeria's political problems laid down. One sees a similar process taking place in Egypt, with both IG and JI, and in Libya with the Libyan Islamic Fighting Group (LIFG) recently unilaterally declaring ceasefire and abandoning violence too (Wallace 2010; Robertson and Cruickshank 2010). On the other hand, militant groups remain active in Yemen, Afghanistan, Pakistan and Somalia, to mention but a few, despite their respective state's call for a peaceful resolution for violent activism. Militants are unlikely to declare a ceasefire unilaterally if faced by a weak state that is incapable of calling the shots, defending its own borders and citizens, and delineating and enforcing the rules of the game in the country. As a former deradicalized Algerian Emir stated, 'we would not have come down from the mountains had we not started to lose the war' (Personal interview, Algiers December 2009).

This conclusion might wrongly be interpreted as a call for further state repression. On the contrary, we argue that state repression is, in most cases, responsible for radicalizing groups and individuals in a country and hence for the emergence of the kind of extremism that leads to violent activism. The 'link between lack of democracy' and human and basic political rights on the one hand and 'political violence' on the other, is now well recognized, acknowledged and established (Hamid and Kadlec 2010: 1; Krueger and Maleckova 2003). The point here is that unless the state is seen as strong enough to enforce its rules and regulations and is therefore respected by its own citizens, it will not be taken seriously by any group. Such a state will attract all sorts of individuals and groups to join militant opposition, including moderates, radicals, religious and secular alike.

While a unilateral and unconditional ceasefire from militant groups is a necessary condition for any successful deradicalization process, it is not sufficient. Although the AIS unilaterally declared an unconditional ceasefire in 1997, it was not before 1999 that the Algerian deradicalization process actually commenced and began to take hold. By then, a new and charismatic leadership had emerged in Algeria and become instrumental in securing and strengthening the deradicalization process.

The role of new and charismatic leadership

While the role of 'a united leadership or a charismatic leadership within the Islamist opposition' is by now well understood (Ashour 2009: 117), less so is the role of a country's leadership, which is equally 'always important' in any reform or deradicalization process (Richards and Waterbury 1996: 229).

As mentioned in the previous section, although the AIS unilaterally declared a ceasefire in 1997, it was not before 1999–2000 that the process of deradicalization got underway in Algeria. The main reason for this was the mistrust which built up over the years between the militant groups and most of the army generals, including the Algerian regime in the form of the retired General Liamine Zeroual.[26] As a former, deradicalized Emir stated:

> We had little confidence in the deradicalization process under the previous regime [General Liamine Zeroual]. Therefore, we had to wait until we were given concrete assurances this time that we and our families and relatives will be OK in case we lay down our arms. This only happened in 1999 and this is why we like this president [Bouteflika].
>
> *(Personal interview, Algiers December 2009)*

Retired General Liamine Zeroual could not absolve himself completely from the main interest group that supported him and in many ways brought him to power in the first place, the army. Despite being described as a moderate and a dialogist (Spencer 1996; Richards and Waterbury 1996), he could not ignore the interest of the *eradicateurs* in his army. As a result, General Liamine Zeroual's constantly changing policies and attitudes, partly to placate divergent army generals, failed to instil sufficient levels of confidence and trust in the deradicalization process. The militants could not, therefore, trust him with their lives and the lives of their relatives, families and sympathizers, all of whom became targets of the predatory behaviour that prevailed in Algeria in the second half of the 1990s. Worse, when some eradicators in the army initiated discussions with the AIS leaders in the second half of the 1990s and were becoming more in favour of a peaceful settlement with the militants, General Liamine Zeroual remained stuck in his past and therefore was incapable of moving the process forward. As Omar Ashour wrote:

> … the policies and political stands of the generals were changing, like most of the other variables, throughout the civil war. For example, Liamine Zeroual, often described as a patriot and a leading figure in the reconciliation camp and a dialogist for his part in initiating negotiations in 1993 was constantly opposing dialogue with the FIS, the AIS and other armed opposition groups from 1995 until his dismissal in September 1998. Arguably, one of the causes of his dismissal was his stand on the AIS unilateral ceasefire, which he refused to accept or even officially recognise.
>
> *(Ashour 2009: 112)*

This, in addition to his core military background and links, might also have made him seem complicit in the repressive, manipulative and brutal policies which the eradicators in his army allegedly followed and implemented against the militant groups and their families in the mid- and late-1990s (Jebnoun 2007; Silverstein 2000; Mellah and Rivoire 2005). It was these policies which further radicalized the GIA members in the late 1990s and which thereafter played a key role in undermining the emergence of a charismatic leader inside the GIA. The policies also prevented the interaction of the GIA's members with other, less radical groups; a factor that is now considered to be a prerequisite for any successful deradicalization process.

Finally, although General Zeroual was responsible for initiating the *Rahmah* (Mercy) Law in March 1995 as a goodwill gesture, this did little to enhance confidence in the deradicalization process or to ease the main concerns of the militants before 1997. In fact, the *Rahmah* Law offered very little acceptable incentives to the militants. The main beneficiaries of the law were only those 'individual[s] possessing weapons or explosions or other material means who gives them up voluntarily will … not be pursued judiciously' according to Article Number 3 of the Law (*National Gazette* 1995). The best militants could hope for from the *Rahmah* Law were small reductions in their sentences.[27] In fact, the *Rahmah* Law was accompanied by a new Anti-Terror Law,[28] which further empowered security forces,[29] introduced harsher measures against militants[30] and absolved security forces of any responsibility related to manipulation, atrocities or even disappearances of a large number of Algerians during violence.[31] In short, the state provided no real exit strategy and motive for the militants to abandon violence and lay down their arms.

The arrival of a new regime usually provides a country with a historically unique opportunity, which can be used by the new regime to introduce new and sometimes painful reforms, including a deradicalization programme. This is mainly because new regimes usually have weaker ties (if not severed) with current powerful interest groups opposed to reform and peaceful settlement with radicals. President Bouteflika's arrival in 1999, following his 1999 presidential elections, created such momentum. During his presidential campaign, President Bouteflika worked very hard to promote deradicalization with 'participation of all members of society' (Bara 2007). His 1999 election campaign's slogan was: 'I promise ... beyond Allah and beyond you not to save any effort and not to miss any opportunity for initiating whatever is required to extinguish the fire of *fitana* (division) as a first condition for national reconstruction' (Bouteflika 2005). Then he moved quickly to distance himself from the army, particularly the eradicator elements opposing most settlement with the militants. He thus publicly announced, in an attempt 'to present himself as the incontestable leader before Algerian generals' that, 'I refuse to be three-quarters of a president' (Jebnoun 2007: 16).

Following his election victory, Bouteflika initiated *Qanoun al-We'am al-Watani* (Civil Concorde Law – CCL), which extended incentives to a larger number of militants to join the deradicalization process. The key objective of the CCL was defined as:

> ... to find appropriate measures ... [and] suitable solutions to individuals who are both involving and involved in terrorist or destructive acts, and are expressing their desire to stop, with full conscious, their criminal activities and by giving the opportunity to achieve this ambition through civil reintegration in society.
>
> (National Gazette *1999)*

To this effect, the CCL included amnesties and pardons,[32] postponements of measures against certain individuals[33] and reductions in sentences.[34] These measures, in their totality, absolved thousands of military and auxiliary groups from crimes committed during the 'Red Decade'. The key condition for any individual or group to qualify for any of the above mentioned benefits is 'to notify the authorities about their decision to stop all terrorist activities and to come forward before the authorities voluntarily' (Article 1, *National Gazette* 1995: 3). Beneficiaries were also expected to fill a form, in which they should not only admit their responsibilities, but also describe the exact role they played in activities they committed or participated in.

To gain public support for his deradicalization programme, Bouteflika publically announced his deradicalization measures and insisted on a general referendum by the Algerian people: 'I suggested', Bouteflika declared:

> ... before *al-We'am al Watani* initiative which was ratified twice by the parliament, but I was not satisfied with that and went further for a popular referendum, which achieved a magnificent result, a result which was not achieved since the popular referendum that took place after Algeria's independence in 1962.
>
> *(Bouteflika 2005: 6)*

Although the 1999 CCL incorporated a much larger number of militants than the 1995 *Rahmah* Law did, it provided a genuine exit strategy for the militants and was associated with a drastic reduction in the level and extent of violence. It did not, however, eliminate violent threat altogether. For example, between 2000 and 2004, Algeria experienced 236 terror incidents, killing 1057 Algerians and wounding 582 (Figure 2.1).

The 1999 CCL, despite its quantitative and qualitative leap, left many questions unanswered. Some of these questions are pertinent to the reintegration and rehabilitation process of deradicalized groups and individualism such as: their political role, the fate of thousands of disappearances, the fate of those tried in absenteeism and are either inside or outside Algeria, compensations for all victims of 'national tragedy' including families of the deceased violent extremists, the role of the army in politics, as well as the FIS's political future and activism. In brief, the 1999 CCL did not go far enough to deal with the root causes of violent extremism in Algeria. President Bouteflika made this very clear in a public speech he delivered after winning the presidential elections in 2005 for a second term. In his speech, the President delineated the weaknesses of the 1995 CCL and why there was a need for a new, more encompassing and comprehensive initiative. In his speech, Bouteflika declared a number of new measures needed to achieve reconciliation, as well as explaining the rationale behind his new initiative (Charter for Peace and National Reconciliation – CPNR):

> Now security and safety have been restored as a result of the policy of *al-We'am al-Madani*. However, our national wound has not been healed yet because terrorism, whose evil has been reduced, has not been terminated completely, and we are determined to cut its throat with all possible means … Our wound also stems from what the national tragedy left in terms of effects and implications.

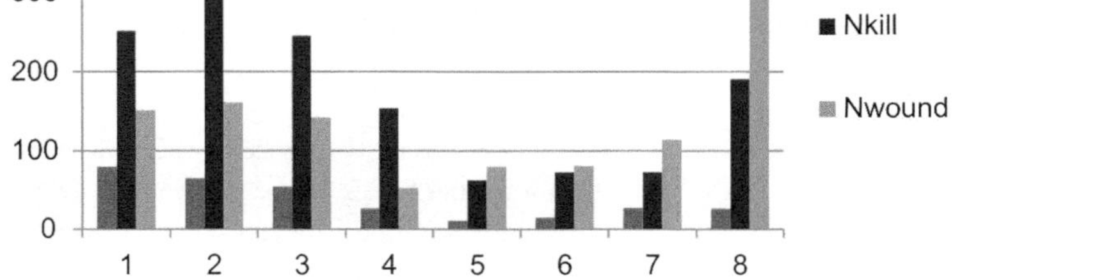

FIGURE 2.1 Total number of terrorist incidents, number killed and number injured in Algeria, 2000–07; 1 = 2000 and 8 = 2007.
Source: START National Consortium for the Study of Terrorism and Response to Terrorism, US Department of Homeland Security, University of Maryland, 2010.

> In addition to the increase in the number of families of our martyrs and victims of terror, there still a large number of other families who are stifled as a result of loss of their parents. And there are many other families who saw some of their members entering the hell pool of terror, live as a pray to poverty and deprivation. All of these families, without exception, are Algerian families who we share with the same home and the same ideology. Our orphans reach hundreds of thousands, some of whom lost their fathers while defending the country, while others died because they carried arms in the face of the same country. Many more other families found themselves alone without a breadwinner as a result of terror craze. But it is the Algerian nation that must embrace all of those orphans. It will take care of them and secure their future [and keep them and] ... their innocent hearts [away from] the roots of poisonous hatred and anger. These were the reasons that led me to ... initiate the national reconciliation process ... I feel that the national reconciliation is a persistent demand by the majority of our nation, without peace and reconciliation it will be impossible for any economic and social development path and for any effort made to modernise our country and to yield what we expect of in terms of results ... Let's bend the sheet without shredding it ... because there is no other mean to heal the wounds left by the national tragedy without national reconciliation.
>
> *(Bouteflika 2005)*

The CPNR, which was published on 29 December 2005, included three key measures. Firstly, measures that aim at 'Restoring Peace' and stability (Ministry of Justice 2006a: 5–7 and 2006b). These include dropping charges,[35] amnesties and pardons,[36] and reduction in sentences.[37] The only exception to these benefits are groups and individuals 'who committed collective atrocities, rapes or carried out explosives in public places, or participated in them or incited for them' (Article No. 10 of the CPNR. See Ministry of Justice 2006a: 7).

The second package in CPNR relates to measures that aim at supporting a national reconciliation and reintegration process. Examples of such measures include the right of the state to restore to every person who faced administrative dismissal as a result of the national tragedy, their previous job. If this is not possible, then they qualify for compensation (Article No. 25. Ministry of Justice 2006a: 10).[38] Another important measure in supporting reconciliation and reintegration includes taking care of the 'victims of the national tragedy' and 'deprived families who have been inflicted with the involvement of a family member in terrorist acts' (Article No. 27, Sections 2 and 3. Ministry of Justice 2006b: 15 and 19). The 'victims of the national tragedy' refers to missing persons who disappeared as a result of the national tragedy. Their number has been estimated between 6,000–10,000 (Ashour 2009). Families of the victims now qualify for compensation, although no information on their fate has been provided.

Compensation for the 'deprived families' is another important addition and invention of the CPNR. It refers to the families (particularly children, wives and parents), which have been 'inflicted' by the involvement of one of their members in terrorist acts, as a result of which he/she was either killed or imprisoned. The rationale here is not only to prevent holding innocent children responsible for acts they did not know about, let alone commit, but also to prevent turning them into angry individuals, seeking revenge for the loss/imprisonment of their family member. This is particularly true in the case of individuals who were the only or major breadwinner and their loss has deprived their children access to healthcare, education, a decent living standard and hence has undermined their social, economic and political mobility. In addition to financial compensation, health and education were also extended to the 'deprived families'.

Finally, the CPNR included 'preventive measures [to] prevent the national tragedy from being repeated'. This is to be done by 'prohibiting every person responsible for the excessive use of religion which led to the national tragedy from practicing any form of political activities whatsoever'. (All quotations from Article 26, Section 3, Ministry of Justice 2006a: 11.) In other words, the political rights of all former radical activists have been denied. They are neither allowed to participate in existing political parties or associations, nor allowed to establish new ones. The army and security forces, on the other hand, have been absolved of any responsibility in the atrocities and massacres that took place in the country during the 'national tragedy' decade. In fact, these groups were glorified for the role they played in defending the state and its institutions, and restoring peace and stability. 'Algeria was able to destroy the giant terrorism' President Bouteflika publically declared (2005: 1) 'because of the sacrifices of our security forces, at its head is the national popular army … with support from all nationalists.'

One further preventative measure that was introduced in 2006 is the anti-corruption law No. 01–06 (on 20 February 2006), which was enacted shortly after the 2005 CPNR and won overwhelming popular support through another referendum in September 2005 (Ministry of Justice 2006b). The aim of the law is to enhance credibility, and promote responsibility and transparency in the operations of both the public and private sectors. This is to be achieved by making employment in the public sector transparent, based on skill, fairness and qualification not personal connection, improve wage and salaries of public employees to reduce incentive for corrupt practices, prepare special training programmes to promote transparency and transfer the practice of good governance. Finally public officials have been urged to declare their property and wealth when taking up an employment in state.

Surprisingly, there has not been much mention of measures aimed at improving the human rights record in Algeria. The 1999 NCL made only one mention in this regard, reflected in Article 16, 'which guarantees the right of defence during the period when measured against persons involved in violent activities are under postponement period, as well as affording them the right to choose an attorney and appeal against the measure'. The 2005 CPNR made no mention to human rights of arrestees whatsoever.[39]

The role of civil society

Civil society is an important source of 'soft' power (Nye 2004). Participation in civil society organizations is considered an important ingredient of a healthy democracy, as it promotes bonds of solidarity and cooperation among members and therefore influences such variables as trust, tolerance and the creation of a participatory attitude, all of which are considered key variables for the functioning of a healthy democracy. All of this generates positive effects for democracy, participation, tolerance and co-existence with the other (Corral 2009: 1). Civil society organizations and associations therefore 'constitute important channels for actors promoting counter-measures' because they 'create networks and promote effective messages and initiatives in various constellations' (Ranstorp 2009: 5–6). With regard to violent extremism in particular, the state alone does not have all the necessary resources required for countering radicalization and extremism, and Non-Governmental Organizations (NGOs) through their extensive social networks and focus at the grass roots level, can complement the state's efforts and resources. Algeria is no exception.

Participation of all members of society was a key strategy consciously encouraged and supported by President Bouteflika from day one of assuming presidential responsibilities in 1999. During the 1990s, several civil society organizations sprang up in Algeria, facilitated by a 1988 law by Bendjedid himself, which allowed the free formation of an association without any prior approval from public authorities. One such important organization is the one created by Fatima-Zohra Flici on 26 December 1993 (National Organization of Victims of Terrorism – NOVT), following the assassination of her husband Dr Flici, described as the first Algerian intellectual to be assassinated by violent extremists.

NOVT has its own website (www.onvt-dz.com), which defines the objectives of the organization in terms of providing all sorts of psychological, medical, legal, administrative, housing and business creation support to members. Total membership of the organization today exceeds 80,000 and members themselves run the organization on a voluntary basis, relying on membership fees and donations from public and private organizations and individuals to fund their activities. All members come from families which lost one or more of their members to Algeria's civil war. Recently, the NOVT has compiled a list of 150,000 Algerian family victims and is seeking to incorporate all of them in its membership.

The NOVT's motto is 'Loyalty – Resistance – Sacrifice' (www.onvt-dz.com). In addition to representing and defending the interests of the families of the victims, which made large sacrifices for the sake of Algeria's future stability and development, the NOVT also seeks to counter radical and violent ideology. It is represented in all of Algeria's *willayat* (44 in total) and members hold weekly meetings to communicate information and to promote tolerance and a moderate interpretation of Islam. In addition to regular meetings, the NOVT organizes public campaigns, conferences, frequently prints newsletters and relies on other media outlets to reach its extensive and widespread membership, as well as society at large. In early 2008, the NOVT organized a high profile international conference 'on how to organize civil society's support for the global effort to end terrorism', to which they invited international experts and organizations, including the UN, as well as President Bouteflika himself, an effort that earned them further publicity and reinforced the role of civil society organizations in countering terrorism in Algeria (Fethi 2008).

More importantly, the NOVT has played an important role in promoting President Bouteflika's deradicalization and reconciliation programme. As Mrs Flici stated, the most important role played by the NOVT is:

> A mediator (*waseet*) role between families of the victims and state. We explained and interpreted the rules of the reconciliation program to the victims, what they meant exactly, their rights and responsibilities. We also functioned as a mediator between president and society. The president kept on saying the families of the victims told me this and that openly and publicly. We arranged for the president to meet some families of the victims for feedback too.
>
> *(Personal interview, Algiers December 2009)*

During the 1990s, victims of the families of the national tragedy refused to be equated with the families of the terrorists, let alone to accept compensation or state support for the families of violent extremists. This began to change with the coming to power of President Bouteflika in the late 1990s. The NOVT played an important role in convincing the families of the victims to accept Bouteflika's reconciliation programme:

> In 1995 we were opposed to any idea that equates between the victims and families of the victims on the one hand, and the terrorists or even the families of the terrorists, on the other. It was not until 1999's presidential elections which brought President Bouteflika who promised to end terrorism in the country. It was a new page in our history. First, and in a public speech, he said that we have no other alternative and reconciliation under the current circumstances is the best solution we can hope for. He followed a very clever approach. He kept on saying that there will be no progress without the approval and support of the victims and families of the victims. It was only after that we began to accept the idea of equity with the families of the terrorists.
>
> *(Personal interview with Mrs Flici, Algiers December 2009)*

Even President Bouteflika, in an opening message read to the participants of a 2008 international conference organized by the NOVT, recognized the role of civil society in the deradicalization and reconciliation process when he stated:

> It is now recognised that unified action by civil societies across the world is more necessary than ever before to contain and eliminate the terrorist threat … Terrorist victims have shown by voting, with courage and self-sacrifice, for the national reconciliation charter, to bar the way to blind extremism which turns to terrorist violence, supposedly in the name of Islam.
>
> *(Fethi 2008)*

Through their extensive social networks, dynamism, innovation and energy, civil society organizations, like NOVT, managed to convince the Algerian society to support and vote for Bouteflika's deradicalization, *We'am* and reconciliation programme. They thus played an important complementary and mediatory role and channel for actors, state and societal, promoting deradicalization and counter-measures. This role is today widely recognized and acknowledged inside Algeria:

> Civil society and political parties were also active in mobilising the population against this phenomenon. They were incremental in creating a modus operandi anchored in peace and national reconciliation. In fact, since 1999 both the Law on Civil Concord (1999) and the Law on Peace and National reconciliation (2005) were overwhelmingly endorsed by the population through referendum. Even bereaving members of the associations of victims of terrorism were actively involved in defending these principles and are still fighting for tolerance, peace and stability. The role of the community, therefore, was of a strategic importance in defeating terrorism ...
>
> *(Berkouk 2009b: 13)*

Conclusion

This chapter has examined the historical evolution of Algeria's Islamist movements, the country's violent extremism and its deradicalization and reconciliation processes since the early 1990s. In particular, it has focused on identifying the key factors affecting the Algerian deradicalization process as it has unfolded since the early 1990s.

At least three factors seem to have most influenced the Algerian radicalization environment and deradicalization efforts. The former include historically weak developmental capacity of the state followed by the weakened political capacity of the state in the late 1980s and early 1990s. The latter include the arrival of a new, charismatic leadership in 1999 and the role of civil society in countering radicalization and promoting deradicalization policies in the country.

Terrorism, although reduced, has not been eliminated from Algeria. A great deal remains to be done. Corruption for example, remains high, as well as the unemployment level, which today, is one of the highest in the Arab world. After 1993–4, Algeria abandoned a great deal of market-oriented reforms and reverted to its state-led developmental approach. The rise in oil and gas rents since the early twenty-first century has allowed the state to buy off its deradicalization and reconciliation programme, while denying political rights to its opponents. Improving the human rights record remains a challenge and the mistrust that has developed between the deradicalized militants and state's security forces, particularly the General Intelligence Department Officers, cannot be ignored. For the time being, most Algerians supported Bouteflika's deradicalization and reconciliation policies. Have they done so because they truly believe in their ability to deal with the root causes of violence in Algeria? Or is it because they were simply exhausted by the bloodshed, instability and atrocities? Will Algeria's past return to haunt it in the future? Only time will tell.

Notes

1 Other examples of failed developmental states include Iraq, Afghanistan, Pakistan, Somalia and Yemen.
2 ISI is the most tested industrial strategy in developing countries. It was designed by Latin American economists with the aim of reducing dependency on volatile external markets for primary products and on high-priced imports through economic diversification and local production of manufactured products. The key rationale is to move the economy from being traditionally dependent on exports of raw material and primary commodities to an industrial footing, where the new industries were expected to both produce goods previously imported (everything from textiles and shoes to refinery and sugar) and process raw material domestically (cottons, sugar, sugarcane, petroleum). See Richards and Waterbury 1996: 26.
3 According to Richards and Waterbury (1996: 230), Algeria by the early 1980s had more than '66 huge state-owned enterprises'.
4 Again according to Richards and Waterbury (1996: 230) 'some 66 huge state-owned enterprises were broken up into 474 smaller companies by 1985, with more following'.
5 IMF and World Bank promoted SAP in developing countries have generally been associated with negative social consequences. As Lubeck (1996: 294–5) noted, 'structural adjustment programmes (SAPs) – in developing states is invariably associated with economic dislocations. This means reductions in living standards and shocks to the governing coalition'. Also see Mosely, Harrigan and Toye 1991.
6 For full details on the elements of the IMF and World Bank Stabilization and SAPs, see Mosely, Harrigan and Toye 1991.
7 The Salafiyya Movement of the late nineteenth and early twentieth centuries was reformist and modernist in the sense that not only was it not anti-Western, but also called for the adoption and adaptation of Western modern sciences in order to overcome what it saw as decadence, atrophy and degeneration of Muslim society. Later in the 1920s it became anti-Western, particularly following the Belfour Declaration which promised the Jews a homeland in Palestine, the Sykes-Pickot Agreement which divided the Arab World between the British and French Empires and the Palestinian Revolution in the mid-1930s. See ICG (2004), Islamism in North Africa I, Middle East and North Africa Briefings, 20 April.
8 Berkouk (2009a: 4) divides them into three main currents: the intellectual current, the spiritual current and the methodical and most radical current. The ICG (2004) on the other hand, divides them into the following. First is the official and incorporated veteran leaders of the AOMA; the dissident AOMA veterans; the Algerian variants of Islamists influenced by the Egyptian Muslim Brotherhood and the Algerian current or the *Jaz'ara* (*Algerianists*). Finally, Spencer (1996) dwells most on the roots of the oldest current, the one which was established before independence and influenced by the Egyptian Muslim Brotherhood Movement and which included mostly AOMA members.
9 For detailed information of these groups, see Ashour 2009; ICG 2004: 10–11; Jebnoun 2007. Also see the next section.
10 Hence, it is misleading to argue that the FIS had no competition in 1989 and that was the only party available at the time of the 1991–2 elections, as, for example, the ICG (2004) argued. In fact, Islamist-oriented parties, such as Hamas (now HMS) and Al-Nahda were established in 1990. However, none gained the same appeal as the FIS. This is mainly because HMS and Al-Nahda were created by or with state support and therefore were seen by the masses as linked to the state. This is unlike the FIS, which was spontaneously created from the bottom or more from the Algerian grass roots.
11 *Mouvement Islamique Armé* (Armed Islamic Movement). This movement was led by Abdelkader Chebouti, which remobilized veterans of Mustafa Bouyali's earlier movement. It thus reawakened the earlier cell of the MIA which was created by Bouyali in the early 1980s. The MIA however, disintegrated after Chebouti's death in late 1993.

12 *Mouvement pour un État Islamique* (Movement for an Islamic State). The MEI was led by Saïd Makhloufi, a founder of the FIS who left the party in July 1991. Like the MIA, the MEI also disappeared after Makhloufi's death in 1997.
13 *Groupe Islamique Armé* (Armed Islamic Group). Although the group was founded in 1992 by Mansour Miliani and Mohammed Allal, it developed only after they had been superseded by other leaders, notably those drawn from Algerian veterans of the Afghan war. As we will see later in this section, this group remains among the most radical and violent groups in Algeria and in the second half of the 1990s and in 2007 underwent even further radicalization. They thus remain active in 2010.
14 *Front Islamique du Djihad Armé* (Islamic Front of the Armed Jihad). Former members of the Jaz'ara tendency founded the group. At one point, it rallied to the GIA but later resumed an independent existence before being eliminated in 1996.
15 Although officially formed in 1994, the first cells of the AIS were established in western Algeria in 1993 by elements of the MIA following the latter's disintegration. Leadership changed in 1994, with Ahmed Ben Aicha and Madani Mezraq, ex-FIS militants, assuming key leadership roles. Soon after its official establishment in 1994, the AIS became the largest group in terms of number of membership. Due to strong organizational and coordination links with the FIS, the AIS is usually described as a self-declared armed wing of the FIS. It was dissolved in 2000 following a unilateral ceasefire declared by the group in 2007 and a Clemency Law announced by President Bouteflika following his presidential electoral victory in 1999.
16 Kidnapping of foreigners increased in the post-2000 period. The most serious kidnapping operations took place between 22 February and 23 March 2003, when 32 tourists – 16 Germans, 10 Austrians, 4 Swiss, a Swede and a Dutchman – were abducted in the Illizi region of the Algerian Sahara. After secret undetailed negotiations, they were released in two stages: the first group in May 2003 and the second in August 2003. A female German hostage died in the desert and was buried there. But question marks were raised regarding who planned and was responsible for the operation, with some observers accusing the state of carrying out the operation in order 'to capture Washington's attention and ensure attendant arms sales' (Mellah and Rivoire 2005).
17 Again, question marks were raised over who exactly was involved in such predatory behaviour and the extent of the state's involvement in them. For more details, see Silverstein 2000; Ashour 2009.
18 In 1997–2000, the FIS not only managed to disarm more than 7,000 of its militants which made up the organization without causing any split, but was also able to influence several hundreds of other militants from smaller militant groups to join the deradicalization process (Ashour 2009).
19 In Egypt, al-Gama'a al_Islammiyya (Islamic Group of Egypt – GI) was the first to deradicalize itself in 1997–2000, followed by the al-Jihad Organization (JO) in 2007–present (Ashour 2009).
20 Ashour rightly argues that one of the reasons why the AIS was able to deradicalize its militant members in 1997–2000 was due to the presence of a unified and charismatic leadership in the form of Medani Mezraq that convinced both the political wing (FIS) and military wing (FIS militant members) without causing any split of the need for the abandonment of arms and reintegration into society. The GIA, on the other hand, did not have this type of leadership at any point in its history in 1992–2005. Most of the GIA leaders either lacked charisma or religious background or did not live long enough as most were assassinated either by the state's security forces or by internal feuding within the movement. Similarly, the presence of a charismatic and knowledgeable leadership in the form of Sayyid Imam al-Sharif (better known as Dr Fadel, a former ideologue of al-Qaeda who turned against the movement) also played a key role in convincing a large number of IG militant members to abandon their arms and adopt a more reformist approach.
21 Again, repression by the Egyptian and Algerian states was a common factor that convinced many militant groups and individuals to lay down their arms and abandon

violence. In the mid-1990s, for example, state's repression wiped out large parts of the Algerian GIA. As a former FIS Emir responded when asked about why the movement decided to lay down its arms and abandon violence in 1997: 'Because we were losing. We were very strong before 1995 but after 1995 the army turned things around and started to win and we started to lose' (Personal interview, Algiers December 2009).

22 Selective inducements are an important part of almost all deradicalization programmes, with the Saudi deradicalization programme, described by some observers as the most successful deradicalization programme in the world, pioneering the use of selective incentives (see Boucek 2008). Incentives can be material (financial support and allowances, regular income, financial support for marriage purposes, etc) or in kind (educational support, jobs and work related support, reduction of sentences, amnesties, etc).

23 Interaction refers to communication and dealings not only between the leadership and its militant groups, but also to interface with other non-religious, political opposition groups. This type of interaction was instrumental in rationalizing ideas of many Egyptian Islamist militants inside prisons. Although neglected in the literature, the Algerian government actively encouraged interaction between AIS members and Saudi prominent clerics by facilitating access to tape recordings of speeches by widely respected Saudi religious scholars to be sent to the radical groups in the mountains. 'These taped speeches played an important role in convincing us that violence is anti-Islam and in reinforcing the argument of the FIS leadership of the need to abandon violence' (Personal interview with a former AIS Emir, Algiers December 2009).

24 Following the cancellation of elections and declaration of emergency laws in 1992, the army generals revived Boumediene's secretive National Council of the Algerian Revolution (NCAR) in the form of The High Council of the State which ran the country in the absence of parliament and constitution in post-1992 and passed power, just like the NCAR did, to the army and intelligence department.

25 According to Spencer (1996: 95), Abbasi Madani and Ali Belhadj, following their release in 1994, required a full meeting of the FIS executive council to formulate a negotiating council. But because of residual doubt of participation or whether it will also include representatives of militant groups, contacts between the president and FIS stalled in October 1994, or rather were used as an excuse to end negotiations by the hardliners in the army. According to Ashour (2009: 113 and 114), what ended the talks this time was an interaction between Gouasmi (then GIA leader) and Ali Belhaj. A letter was found from Belhaj to Gouasmi after the latter was killed by security forces in late September 1994. Allegedly, Belhaj in the first part of the letter praises the struggle of armed Islamists in Algeria. In the second part, which was not published by the authorities, he called for conditional cessation of violence, theoretical argument to GIA leadership about legitimacy of dialogue and truce, and a warning to the GIA not to turn Algeria into another Afghanistan. Again, the hardliners published and used the first half of the letter to end negotiations.

26 Zeroual was the ninth President of Algeria from 31 January 1994 to 27 April 1999. He was born in Batna and joined the National Liberation Army in 1957 at the age of 16 to fight French rule of Algeria. After independence, he received training in Cairo, Moscow and Paris. In 1975, he took command of a military school in Batna and then in 1981 of the Cherchell Military Academy. He was then made Commander of the Tamanrasset military region in 1982, then the Moroccan border in 1984 and then Constantine in 1987. He became a general in 1988 and head of ground forces in 1989. After disagreeing with President Chadli Bendjedid about proposals for army reorganization, he quit in 1990 and briefly became ambassador to Romania. However, after Bendjedid was deposed by the military coup of January 1992, he became Minister of Defense in July 1993; in January 1994 he was promoted to head of the High Council of State. In November 1995, he was elected President, a post which he retained until the next elections. He was reputed to be politically dialoguist, supporting a partly negotiated solution to the Algerian Civil War. (From Wikipedia: the free encyclopedia, 2010. Available HTTP: http://en.wikipedia.org/wiki/Liamine_Zéroual.)

27 Article 4 of the *Rahmah* Law states that 'in case of individuals … committing crimes that caused the killing of another person or caused him permanent damage, then the worthy penalty will be: temporary imprisonment between 15–20 years, if the original penalty stated by the law was death penalty; temporary imprisonment between 10–15 years, if the original penalty was life imprisonment; in all other cases, the penalty will be reduced by half' (*National Gazette* 1995).

28 The Anti-Terror Law was issued in March 1995. Article number 87 of the law defined terrorism or destructive act as: ' … every act that targets the security of the state and national unity and safety of Algerian soil and the stability of the institutions and their normal operations through the following: spreading fear among the population and undermine security environment through physical or psychological attack against individuals or exposing their lives and freedoms or security to danger or their property; impeding traffic or freedom of travel in the roads or gathering and demonstrations in public places; attacking icons of the nations and the republic and digging and destroying graves; attacking public and private means of transportation and communications and occupying it without a legal permit; attacking the ocean or smuggling a material through the air or land … which might threaten the lives of humans, animals and environment; impeding the work of public authorities or freedom of religious practice and operations of institutions supportive of public sector; impeding the operation of public organisations or attacking their supporters or property or impeding the application of laws and regulations' (*National Gazette* 1995).

29 Article 6 of the law states that 'when the matter is related to issues to do with crimes defined as terrorist crimes, the investigator has the right to carry out any investigation or arrest during day or night and in any place over Algerian soil or order specialized judiciary police officers to do so'. Article 8 states that 'the period of arrest can be doubled when the matter is related to attacks against the security of the state, and be extended to 12 days in case of terrorist acts'. Article 29 states that 'if a witness did not turn up without a good excuse the criminal court has the right … to issue an order to bring him through force if necessary or postponing the case until a later date' (*National Gazette* 1995).

30 For example, Article 87/6 of the new law states that 'he will be punished by imprisonment from 5–10 years and AJ 100,000–500,000 every person who re-prints deliberately documents or prints or record documents that praise terrorist acts; 10–20 years and AL 500,000–100,0000 every Algerian who joins a terrorist or destructive group or organisation outside Algeria regardless of its shape or name even if its acts were not directed against Algeria; life imprisonment when the latter targets Algeria'. Article 87/7 states that 'punishable by imprisonment from 10–20 years and AL 500,000–100,0000 every person who illegally possesses or takes control or carries weapons or explosives or trades in them or imports them or exports them or manufactures them or fixes them or uses them without a license from the authorities; and he who knowingly sells white weapons or buys them or manufactures them for purposes against the law will be punished by 5–10 years imprisonment and AD of 100,000–500,000' (*National Gazette* 1995).

31 Article 2 of Law (No. 16) states that 'Articles 2, 3, 4 and 5 do not apply to officers of judiciary police that belong to the military security which have jurisdiction over all Algerian land'. Article 5 of Criminal Law (1995) defined 'The judiciary system [to] consist of the police and those in the national *darak*, *darak* men, military security which do not have a character of officers in judiciary police'.

32 Article 3 of the NCL states that pardons and amnesties (dropping charges) will be given to 'whoever joined a terrorist organization, inside or outside Algeria and did not commit or participate in any crime that can be characterized as a terrorist crime in the law such as the killing of a person or causing him a permanent disability, rape or used explosives in public or crowded places and informs the authorities about their decision to end all of their terrorist or destructive activities within 6 months of issuing this law and has come forward to the authorities voluntarily'. Article 4 of the NCL also extended amnesties to

'apply to those who possessed weapons or explosives or other material means and handed them in to the authorities voluntarily'. (For full details see the *National Gazette* 1999.)

33 Article 6 states that 'the postponement measure represents a temporary adjournment of measures [against certain individuals and groups] for a specific period of time the aim of which is to ensure the full correctness of persons subjected to adjournment measure'. Article 7 states that 'those who benefit from the temporary adjournment measures … are those individuals who in the past joined [terrorist or destructive] organisations … and who inform the relevant authorities within 6 months of the date of issuance of this law of their decision to end all terrorist or destructive activities and voluntarily coming forward to the authorities, either individually or in groups. Those who committed or participated in crimes that led to the murder of a person, or collective killing, attacks by using explosives against public or crowded areas or committed a rape crime are excluded from the provisions of this article'. Article 8 also extended the adjournment measures to 'those groups and individuals which were permitted to participate, under the supervision of the state, in fighting terrorism'. This is a clear confession of the role of the state in some of the atrocities that occurred during the 1990s, albeit indirectly. Article 8 also demanded that the beneficiates from the adjournment measures 'must take an honest oath to declare whatever weapons, explosives and other material means they have in their possession and hand them in to the authorities before them'. Minimum period of adjournment was set at 3 years and maximum at 10 years. The postponement period ends with the end of its period as determined by the law (3–10 years), after which individuals and groups, provided that their behaviour has been corrected, can be freed from these measures. Article 13 states that the maximum period of adjournment for 'persons permitted to serve the state in fighting terrorism and destructive acts, is a maximum of 5 years'. Article 18 states that 'In case of a person who is subject to postponement measure absolves himself from some of the responsibilities imposed on him, the postponement committee has the right to rescind the postponement decision'. Article 22 states that 'The postponement decision can be lifted prematurely based on a decision from the postponement committee if the person subject to the postponement measure is distinguished with an exceptional behaviour or manner in serving the country, or he provided sufficient evidences on his correctness'. However, this premature lifting can 'be conditional, but cannot exceed one year, after which the lifting becomes permanent and without conditions'. (For full details see the *National Gazette* 1999.)

34 Article 27 of NCL states that 'it is possible for persons who had previously joined terrorist or destructive organisations and informed the authorities within a period of 3 months of publishing this law about their decision to end all of their terrorist or destructive activities and did so voluntarily … to have their sentences reduced according to the following conditions: a 12-year maximum imprisonment if the original verdict was either death penalty or life sentence; reduction to 7 years from previous court verdict of 10–20 years; 3 year imprisonment when the maximum previous verdict was 10 years; the maximum penalty of all other cases also gets to be reduced'. Article 28 reduces the sentences to those who accepted temporary postponement (see previous endnote), even if they had belonged previously to terrorist or destructive organizations, according to the following conditions; a maximum of 8 years if the previous verdict was a death penalty or life imprisonment; a maxim of 5 years from a previous maximum verdict of 10 years and less than 20 years. Article 29 states that 'in all other cases, the persons which had previously joined terrorist or destructive organisations … and informed the authorities within 6 months of issuing this law about the decision to end all terrorist or destructive activities and did so voluntarily benefit from sentence reduction according to the following criteria: 15–20 years if the penalty is death; 10–15 years if the penalty is life sentence; the maximum sentence for all other cases is reduced by half'. The only exception to sentence reductions relate to groups and individuals who either committed a rape, collective or individual killings and used explosives in public or crowded places. (For full details see the *National Gazette* 1999.)

35 Beneficiaries from this section include five criteria: the persons who voluntarily gave themselves up to the relevant authorities between 13 January 2000 and 28 February 2006, that is, from the date of ending the operations of the CCL; the persons who decide voluntarily to give themselves up within 6 months of the date of issuance of the CPNR; persons who are inside or outside the country and who are pursued by the authorities for committing or participating in acts forbidden by the law and give themselves up voluntarily and end their involvement in these activities; persons tried in absentia and give themselves up voluntarily and end their involvement in these activities within 6 months of the date of issuance of this law; and persons who are imprisoned with no final trial/verdict against them. (These represent articles 6, 7, 8 and 9 respectively of CPNR. Ministry of Justice 2006a: 6–7 and 2006b: 4–6.)

36 Beneficiaries from this law include all persons who have been tried with a final court judgment issued against them for committing or participating in an act/s deemed illegal by the Algerian criminal and anti-terror law. (Article No. 16 of CPNR. Ministry of Justice 2006a: 9.)

37 Beneficiaries from this law include all of those which have been tried with a final court judgement against them but did not benefit from dropping charges against them or pardons. Also persons inside or outside Algeria which are pursued by state authorities for committing, or participating in, or enticing others to commit collective murders, rape or use of explosives in public places, but voluntarily give themselves up to the authorities within 6 months of the date of issuance of this law. (Article No. 18 and 19 of CPNR. Ministry of Justice 2006a: 9 and 2006b: 7–8.)

38 If they were still within the working age, then their previous jobs could generally be restored. If they had already passed the working age, then they qualified for compensation equivalent to the total amount of their salary lost since their dismissal, plus the normal pension that they would have received had they not lost their jobs. Although it was possible to restore the jobs of some individuals, the majority received compensations and for various reasons, it was not possible to restore their previous jobs. (Interviews with high-ranked state officials at the Ministry of Employment and National Solidarity, Algiers December 2009.)

39 Article 65 of Procedural Law No 22–06 of 20 December 2006 states that individuals should not be arrested without a trial for more than 48 hours. However, the same article adds that the authorities have the right to extend this period once after handing him over to the public prosecutor, who in turn has the right to extend this period twice with regard to cases related to state security, three times in cases related to organized crimes and five times in cases related to terrorism and destruction. Article 102 states that the accused has the right upon his arrest to contact an attorney freely but the investigating judge has the right to prevent him from doing so for a period of ten days (Ministry of Justice 2007: 26 and 43, respectively).

Bibliography

Amsden, A. (1989) *Asia's Next Giant: South Korea and Late Industrialisation*, Oxford: Oxford University Press.

Ashour, O. (2009) *The De-radicalisation of Jihadist: Transforming Armed Islamist Movements*, London: Routledge.

Ayubi, N. (1999) *Overstating the Arab State: Politics and Society in the Middle East*, London: I.B. Tauris.

Bara, R.M. 'The unselective truth and the un-punishable justice in the peace and national reconciliation', paper delivered in a seminar on the Place of Human Rights in Light of Reforms in Algeria, Nazel Al-Awarisi, Algiers, December 2007.

Berkouk, M. (2009a) 'Domestic Terrorism in Algeria', The Institute of Diplomacy and International Relations, Algerian Ministry of Foreign Affairs, Algiers.

—— (2009b) 'The Role of Civil Society in Combating Terrorism in Algeria', The Institute of Diplomacy and International Relations, Algerian Ministry of Foreign Affairs, Algiers.

Boucek, C. (2008) 'Saudi Arabia's "soft" counterterrorism strategy: Prevention, rehabilitation, and aftercare', Carnegie Papers, Carnegie Endowment for International Peace, No. 97.

Bouteflika,A. (2005) *Speech delivered on the occasion of the National Seminar for Regional Activities*, 14 August. Available HTTP: http://www.riassa.dz/arabe/discoursara/2005/08/html/D140805.htm

CIA World Factbook (2010) *Algeria: Labor and Employment, The Library of Congress Country Studies*. Available HTTP: http://www.photius.com/countries/algeria/economy/algeria_economy_labor_and_employment.html (accessed 29 March 2010).

Corral, M. (2009) 'Participation in Meetings of Political Parties, *orgAmericasBarometer Insights*', Latin American Public Opinion Project, *Insights* series, (pp. 1–5). Available at: www.AmericasBarometer.

The Economist, 'Bombs in Algeria', 15 February 2007.

El-Said, H. and Harrigan, J. (2006) 'Globalisation, International Finance and Political Islam in the Middle East and North Africa', *Middle East Journal* 60(3): 236–51.

Fethi, N. (2008) Algiers Conference Promotes Civil Society's Role in Fight Against Terrorism, Magharebia, Published in Magharebia on 28 March 2008. Available HTTP: *http://www.magharebia.com/cocoon/awi/xhtml1/en_GB/features/awi/reportage/2008/03/28/reportage-01*

Hamid, S. and Kadlec, A. 'Strategies for Engaging Political Islam', Freidrich Ebert Stiftun, Project on Middle East Democracy, January 2010.

Harrigan, J. and El-Said, H. (2009) *Aid and Power: the IMF and World Bank Policy Lending in the Middle East and North Africa*, London: Palgrave Macmillan.

International Crisis Group (2004a) 'Islamism, Violence and Reform in Algeria: Turning the Page', (Islamism in North Africa III), *Middle East Report* No. 29, 30 July. Available HTTP: http://www.crisisgroup.org/~/media/Files/Middle%20East%20North%20Africa/North%20Africa/Algeria/Islamism%20Violence%20and%20Reform%20in%20Algeria%20Turning%20the%20Page.pdf

—— (2004b) 'Islamism in North Africa II: Egypt's Opportunity', Middle East and North Africa Briefing No. 13, 20 April.

Jebnoun, N. (2007) Is the Maghreb the 'Next Afghanistan?' Mapping the Radicalization of the Algerian Salafi Jihadist Movement, Center for Contemporary Arab Studies, A. Edmund, Walsh School of Foreign Service Georgetown University.

Krueger, A. and Maleckova, J. (2003) 'Education, poverty and terrorism: Is there a causal connection'? *Journal of Economics Perspectives*, 17(4): 119–44.

Lubeck, P.M. (1996) 'Islamist responses to globalisation: cultural conflict in Egypt, Algeria and Malaysia', in *The Causes of Cultural Conflict*, B. Crawford and R.Lipschutz (eds). Berkeley: International and Area Studies, pp 293–319. Available HTTP: http://escholarship.org/uc/item/90v5s45r.

Luciani, G. (1990) *The Arab State*, London: Routledge.

Mellah, S. and Rivoire, J-B. (2005) *Who staged the tourist kidnappings?* El Para, the Maghreb's Bin Laden, Le Monde Diplomatique, February.

Ministry of Justice (2006a). *Texts Which Include the Execution of Charter for Peace and National Reconciliation*, Algiers, Ministry of Justice.

——(2006b). *The Practical Guide for the Implementation of Decree No. 01–06 Dated 27 February*, regarding the execution of Charter for Peace and National Reconciliation, Algiers, Ministry of Justice.

——(2007). *Procedural Panel Law*, Ministry of Justice, National Council for Education Work, Algiers.

Mosely, P., Harrigan, J. and Toye, J. (1991) *Aid and Power: The World Bank Policy-Based Lending*, London: Routledge, 2nd edn.

National Gazette (1995) The *Rahmah* Law, Law No. 11, 1 March and Laws No. 12–95, 25 February, Algeria, pp. 10–12.

——(1999) *Reestablishment of Civil Concorde Law*, Law No. 45, 13 July.

Nozaffari, M. (1996) 'Islamism in Algeria and Iran', in A. Salam Sidahmed and A. Ehteshami (eds), *Islamic Fundamentalism*, Oxford: Westview Press, pp. 229–47.

Nye, J. (2004) *Soft Power: The Means to Success in World Politics*, Cambridge: Cambridge Centre, MA.
Owen, R. (1992) *State, Power and Politics in the Making of the Middle East*, London: Routledge.
Ranstorp, M. (2009) *Preventing Violent Radicalisation and Terrorism: The Case of Indonesia, Stockholm, Centre for Asymmetric Threat Studies*, Swedish National Defence College.
Reuters (2010) *Rebels kill seven Algerian security guards*, 4 April. Available HTTP: http://af.reuters.com/article/topNews/idAFJOE63303G20100404.
Richards, A. and Waterbury, J. (1996) *A Political Economy of the Middle East*, London: Westview, 2nd edn.
Robertson, N. and Cruickshank, P. (2010) 'In a bid to thwart al Qaeda, Libya frees three leaders of jihadist group', CNN, 23 March. Available HTTP: http://edition.cnn.com/2010/WORLD/africa/03/23/libya.jihadist.group/.
Ruedy, J. (ed.) (1994) *Islamism and Secularism in North Africa*, New York: St. Martin's Press.
Silverstein, P.A. (2000) *Regimes of (Un)Truth: Conspiracy Theory and the Transnationalization of the Algerian Civil War, Middle East Report* 214 – Spring. Available HTTP: http://www.merip.org/mer/mer214/214_silverstein.html.
Spencer, C. (1996) 'The roots and future of Islamism in Algeria', in A.S.Sidahmed and A. Ehteshami (eds) *Islamic Fundamentalism*, Oxford: Westview Press, (pp. 93–108).
Wade, R. (1990) *Governing the Market*, Princeton: Princeton University Press.
Wallace, E. (2010) *Qadaffi son helps free anti-al Qaeda jihadists*, Geneva Lunch, 24 March. Available HTTP: http://genevalunch.com/blog/2010/03/24/libyas-notorious-abu-salim-prison-to-be-emptied/.
World Bank (1989) *World Development Report 1989: Financial Systems and Development*, Oxford: Oxford University Press.
—— (2003). *World Development Report 2003: Sustainable Development in a Dynamic World, Transforming Institutions, Growth, and Quality of Life*, Oxford: Oxford University Press.

3

THE RISE OF RELIGIOUS-BASED RADICALISM AND THE DERADICALIZATION PROGRAMME IN BANGLADESH

Jane Harrigan

Introduction

Islamic-based terrorist groups began to emerge in South Asia in the 1980s and now pose a serious threat to the region. This new religious militancy was shown by the fact that between 1998 and 2004, 22.6 per cent of world terrorist attacks took place in South Asia whilst 23.5 per cent took place in the Middle East and North Africa, making South Asia almost as terrorist prone as the more notorious Middle East.

Between 1999 and 2005 Bangladesh witnessed an upsurge in Islamic terrorism and the US Congressional Research Service identified confrontational politics, a poor system of governance, corruption and the rise of extremists as a threat to the moderate image of Bangladesh (Ahmed 2009: 189). In response, the country has adopted the four 'I' approach to counter-terrorism: 1) Incarceration; 2) Intelligence, including a recent thrust towards more civic-based community intelligence; 3) Intellectual intervention using religious discourse to counter radical interpretations of Islam and 4) Investment in all of the previous three approaches. The approach to dealing with an increased Islamic terrorist threat has predominantly been the first two of these Is, i.e. one of force with the focus on the pursuit of terrorists and incarceration, rather than on deradicalization and counter-radicalization programmes. The former approach has been demonstrated by the formation of the elite Rapid Action Battalion (RAB) to deal with the terrorist threat and increased criminalization more generally along with the passing of harsh new legislation which has enabled the execution of terrorist leaders. Indeed Bangladesh is the only country to have executed all top leaders of its major Islamic terrorist organization.

The country has a hybrid deradicalization cum counter-radicalization programme, which operates in three specific regions of the country. The programme, judging by its own criteria of success, seems to have been fairly effective. Despite its success, the limited spread of the programme and the lack of any prison-based rehabilitation programme of deradicalization mean that Bangladesh is well behind many other countries such as Singapore, Malaysia, Indonesia and Saudi Arabia when it comes to using deradicalization and counter-radicalization as a tool of counter-terrorism. In fact, Bangladesh's programme is very different from those witnessed elsewhere, focusing much more on prevention with a grass roots motivational approach, rather than developing a cure. Whilst many other countries have approached the criminal, Bangladesh has approached society with a focus on preventative measures well suited to the socio-cultural local environment. Using people of religious influence the programme is one of psychological warfare rather than rehabilitation.

The next section of this chapter provides a detailed overview of the social, cultural and political context in which Bangladesh's counter-radicalization and deradicalization programmes have been implemented. This is followed by an analysis of the terrorist threat in Bangladesh. The country's deradicalization and counter-radicalization programmes are then described and critically appraised.

The social, cultural and political context

Socio-cultural background

Bangladesh has a population of just over 140 million people squeezed into a land mass not much bigger than England and Wales, much of which is submerged during the monsoon season. This produces extreme pressures on the land and livelihoods, making the country one of the poorest in the world. With extreme poverty, very limited opportunities and increased exposure to Western aspirations, the majority of the population is vulnerable to radicalization. Society is also violent with increased criminalization in recent years and an estimated 800,000 illegal weapons and 1,000 illegal arms factories running mainly with foreign spare parts (Rahman 2002) and a police force of only 140,000. In this context, the question is why more people have not turned to extremism and violence. The answer seems to lie in the country's brand of Sufi Islam, secularism and tolerance. The tolerant nature of the country is shown by the fact that in the last 50 or 60 years there has been no communal riots. Many of the Bangladeshis who went to fight Jihad in Afghanistan in the 1980s returned to their country aiming to establish an Afghan-like Taliban state, but failed to realize that the fabric of their country was very different from Afghanistan, with religious force and fundamentalism generally unacceptable to most Bangladeshis. As such, few people have been infected with extremism, and most agree there is little future for religious-based terrorism in the country, not least because almost all imams in both rural and urban areas are vehemently opposed to it and make this known to their congregations. In addition, extensive poverty means that most people are too busy trying to make ends meet to be distracted by ideological pressures.

Another aspect of the socio-cultural context is the highly democratic and pluralistic cultural space with many festivals, both secular and religious, celebrated by all religions throughout the year in an atmosphere of tolerance with extensive media coverage. The country's cultural and traditional heritage binds people together in the celebration of festivals such as Bengali New Year and the Harvest Festival. Individualism is also a major component of the Bengali make up with people being too individualistic to be attracted to a monolithic and rigid Taliban-like state. Another binding factor is the lack of ethno diversity with a homogeneous race sharing the same living habits, food habits etc. leaving little room for extremist groups to exploit ethnic tension.

A feature of Bangladesh is the failure of the government to provide adequate basic services that has led to a vibrant NGO movement providing alternative services. This NGO movement has been effectively exploited by the government to help implement the country's deradicalization programme since communities are used to NGOs springing up to deal with a wide variety of issues. Civil society in Bangladesh is composed not only of NGOs but also of human rights activists, intellectuals, university teachers and the like, and this civil society has been actively involved in educating the masses about the existence of terrorism as well as putting pressure on the government to take action. Various national media are used by civil society for debates and consultations on the menace of terrorism. Although some of the Islamic NGOs have been accused of supporting terrorist activities, the majority of them have been actively engaged in working to educate and mobilize religious leaders and teachers to build up a resistance against the misinterpretation of Islam and the spread of terrorism. The extensive development-based work of NGOs is also expected to help check the growth of militancy in the longer run.

The media in Bangladesh is also strong and largely free from government control. In this respect, terrorist groups have failed to effectively exploit the media or to recognize the strength of the media in building a public opinion against terrorism and in exposing the existence of terrorist-based groups. After the major Islamic terrorist event of 2005, the entire media became united against the militants.

Religious background

Bangladesh is composed of four major religions – Islam, Christianity, Hinduism and Buddhism. The majority of the population is Muslim making the country the fourth largest Muslim country in the world. Although 88 per cent of the population are Muslim, the brand of Islam is predominantly the moderate, inclusive and tolerant Sufi and juristic Hanafi brand with little discrimination on the basis of religion. Sufis and saints from Asia converted Bangladesh to Islam resulting in a more humanistic Islam, which blended with local culture and religions such as Hinduism. Likewise Hinduism has been influenced by the Sufi tradition, and is less caste centred than in India. The majority of the population is religious minded but not fanatic and certainly the country is more secular and tolerant than India or Pakistan. Inclusivity is shown by the fact that all four major religions have their main festivals marked by national holidays and many common rituals are shared between religions. In addition, the bulk of the population identifies itself as much as being Bengali as Muslim and religious leaders have never advocated violence; even during the colonial period. The secular tradition is no doubt influenced by the fact that the Awami League fought the 1971 liberation war against Muslim Pakistan in the name of secularism so that Bangladesh could become a country for people of all religions.

The impact of the mosque and imams on society is extensive with over 500,000 mosques[1] in the country and the imam playing a key motivational role, which has been effectively exploited by the country's deradicalization programme. The majority of the population attends Friday prayer when mosques are full and the Friday sermon is an effective vehicle for the imams to spread their message. Sermons from imams in Bangladesh are noteworthy for their strong counter-radicalization messages. Imams and Islamic scholars are united against terrorism and communal disharmony and appear on television on a daily basis to teach a moderate interpretation on Islam. The profound influence of religious leaders was clearly shown by the role they played in encouraging the uptake of family planning over the past decade and a half.

The inclusive and secular nature of what is nevertheless a deeply religious society sets Bangladesh apart from countries such as India, Pakistan, Saudi Arabia or Afghanistan. To quote A.M.M. Shawkat Ali (2006: 34), ' … the vast majority of Muslims in Bangladesh are peace loving and not wedded to the ideal of religious fanaticism. There is a strong media, a vibrant civil society and a secular criminal justice system'.

The role of the madrassa education system

The increased role played by the madrassa education system is sometimes blamed for the emergence of religious radicalism in Bangladesh and some members of the Awami League government in power in 2010 have expressed the view that the religious education system is a problem and needs reform. Currently 22 per cent of children are madrassa educated, up from 17 per cent in 1998. This is largely a reflection of the poor state of the public education system. Since the 1990s, money has been flowing from the rich Middle Eastern states to fund madrassas in Bangladesh.

There are four types of madrassas in Bangladesh – Alia madrassas, Qawmi madrassas, Hafezia madrassas and Forkania madrassas, the former two being the most prominent with 25,201 Alia madrassas in 2004 and the number of Qawmi madrassas unaccounted for (Ahmed 2005). The Alia madrassas are controlled by the National Education Board and partially funded by the government and have a more liberal and broad-based curriculum with qualifications being accepted for higher education and many types of jobs. Qawmi on the other hand are largely independent of the government, with their own Board, and are privately sponsored and run, with a narrower religious-based curriculum resulting in a qualification that is not generally acceptable by employers. Some are run by veterans of the 1980s Afghan war and a very small minority are run by pseudo charities to promote an extremist agenda often prompting the government to take action against them.[2] It is these Qawmi madrassas that are generally perceived to be a problem. There have been two Commissions on madrassa reform and in 1986 a limited curriculum and syllabus reform programme was introduced bringing more secular subjects to the government controlled Alia madrassas.[3]

After the arrest and interrogation of many Jama'atul Mujahedeen Bangladesh (JMB) members following their bombing campaign of 2005, the security services produced a detailed profile of JMB membership and found that of the hard-core members only 5 per cent were madrassa educated. Despite there being a small number of JMB members with a madrassa-based education, the Qawmi madrassas do pose a potential threat.[4] Qawmi students usually come from poor economic backgrounds and graduates of these madrassas with their low quality, narrow education struggle to find mainstream jobs and many are left unemployed, or recycle themselves into the madrassa system as teachers or take other religious-based jobs. They have a poor sub-optimal education and a deep sense of religious duty. This leaves them vulnerable to the clutches of extremist groups and the obvious solution is a broad reaching, modernizing reform of the entire religious-based education system. It is, however, as much poverty and unemployment as it is a radical education that leaves these segments of society vulnerable, with recruitment into terrorist organizations often being motivated more by financial reward than ideological conviction.

Despite the perceived problem of the madrassa system there is certainly much less of a connection between madrassas and fundamentalism and extremism than in countries such as Pakistan and Indonesia. Indeed some have argued that the spread of extreme interpretations of Islam is much more pronounced amongst the well-off students in the private university system and elite private schools than it is in the madrassa system (Personal interview, Dhaka August 2009). One prominent Bangladeshi scholar has stated that:

> Madrassas have been made an easy scapegoat … the religious knowledge here in the madrassas is very fragmented. They don't teach the mystic, Sufi, civilization or tolerant part of Islam. They mainly deal with rules and regulations … But to equate that with militancy is something I have my reservations about. Militants could also emerge from secular groups. I don't think madrassas alone are responsible.[5]
>
> *(*New Age *21 August 2009a: 18–19)*

The role of migration

One of Bangladesh's biggest exports is its people. In the past two decades, many illiterate, semi-illiterate and semi-skilled workers have migrated on an unprecedented scale to the Middle East to work. The diaspora interacts with people back home through modern communication technology and also has a profound influence when they return. Consequently, millions have been influenced by a very different school of Islam, particularly the more conservative Wahhabism from the likes of Saudi Arabia, resulting in a confusion of their religious identity. The returnees to rural and semi-urban areas come back with relative affluence and become part of the local elite, influencing for example, local dress, with more returnees and their family wearing black burqahs and Saudi dress for Friday prayers, and affecting local traditions such as the old Sufi tradition of praising dead saints: 'Attack on religious shrines, jatras (folk theatre), fairs, cinema halls and non-Sunni Ahmaddiyas only indicate the confluence between the local perpetrators and Wahhabism' (Ahmed 2009: 30).

In addition, mosques and madrassas have received much of the remittances from migrants to the Gulf sometimes enabling the migrants to influence the content of what is taught in these mosques and madrassas. The government has failed to fully comprehend the influence of this more intolerant and conservative brand of Islam compared to the local Sufi and Hanafi brand.

Another older influence on radicalization has been that of the returnee Afghan war veterans who went to fight alongside the Taliban against the Russians in the 1980s as well as a smaller number who fought in Lebanon during the civil war. Over 3,000 went to fight and although only a small number returned, they came back with radical ideas and a significant number became involved in the madrassa education system. Significantly, although the CIA had encouraged them to fight and was responsible for popularizing the idea of jihad in the South Asia region, there was no form of rehabilitation programme once the fighters returned.

Political background

Bangladesh has a secular constitution and is committed to democracy. Nevertheless, most agree that the country currently suffers from a governance deficit. Two main political parties dominate politics. The Awami League led by Sheikh Hasina and the Bangladesh Nationalist Party (BNP) led by Begum Zia. Both parties are enmeshed in a web of crime and violence with many politicians having close links to criminals such as the Mastan[6] as well as having party-backed thugs in the universities and major industries such as textiles. To quote one observer: 'The political parties hardly have democracy inside them. They have invited the Mastans and brown shirts into their ranks and they are now the kingmakers ... The gap between militants and Mastans is not very much' (*New Age* August 21 2009a: 19).

The two political parties are often aligned to opposing business interests in different areas, resulting in arson attacks and other violence against property and businesses. Many of the politically linked criminal elements in society have moved beyond the control of the political parties although the latter still benefit financially from their activities. The links between crime and politics is shown by the fact that under the last BNP government, 82 per cent of MPs had criminal records while the figure for the current Awami League government is 46 per cent (Personal interview, Dhaka August 2009). The criminalization of politics has meant that the governance structure has become severely corrupted leading to a deep mistrust of political leaders and a confrontational style of politics. Street violence is also associated with the political process, the January 2007 elections being suspended by the Caretaker government[7] partly because of an eruption of extensive street violence and rioting in which over 100 people were killed. The opposition political party often exacerbates this situation by boycotting parliament and encouraging hartals (strikes) making the country unstable. Confrontational politics is intensified by the bitter rivalry between the two female leaders of the main parties. In short, politics in Bangladesh is often confrontational, violent, corrupt and un-transparent and religious-based terrorist groups have exploited this: 'If Islamic militancy has prospered in Bangladesh, it is as much due to the deficiencies and self-interested behaviours of mainstream political parties as to the strength of radical groups' (International Crisis Group 2006: 10).

Corruption and poor governance has also left a vacuum, enabling Islamic political parties to make an entrance at the national, political level and there has been a gradual Islamization of politics with religion used as a political tool. The post-1975 military regime delegalized the ban on religious parties and General Ershad who took over power in a coup tried to bolster his legitimacy with an appeal to religion, making Islam the state religion in 1988. During the 1996 election, the Awami League promoted itself as the champion of Islam and formed an alliance with the Islamic party Jamaat-e-Islami which it broke once it came to power. This was followed by an alliance between the BNP and Jamaat-e-Islami as well as one other smaller Islamic party and a secular party making it a four-party alliance which won the 2001 election with two Cabinet ministerial positions given to Jamaat-e-Islami members. Keen to win the support of pro-Islamic forces the Awami League signed a deal with Khelafaty-e-Majlis giving them the right to declare fatwa and to declare the Ahmadiyya sect as non-Muslims. As both the Awami League and the BNP attract a similar number of votes they need an alliance with a third party to gain power and the choice is usually the rightist Islamic parties. Despite the gradual Islamization of politics, and the deeply religious nature of the population, religion does not translate into votes, with Islamic-based political parties in the past two decades securing only around 7–10 per cent of the popular vote and needing to form alliances with the main political parties to gain any power. Even in coalition with one another, the Islamic parties could not win enough votes to form a government and their alliances with the Awami League and BNP usually force them to compromise their more extremist views when in power.

The Islamization of politics, especially under the 2001–06 BNP coalition government, is sometimes blamed for a political neglect of the Islamic terrorist threat until the wake-up call of the 2005 bombings. There have been numerous terrorist attacks on political leaders and civilians in the past. These include: the attack at the Bengali New Year's Day celebrations in Dhaka Park, the unsuccessful 2004 attack on the British High Commissioner in which two people were killed and the 21 August 2004 attack on the Awami League leaders in front of their headquarters in which 24 people, including the wife of the President, were killed and nearly 500 injured. In the context of confrontational politics, however, victims have tended to blame the attacks on the political opposition rather than see them as the work of religious extremists and this has resulted in a lack of serious police investigation.[8] By blaming each other, the two political parties failed to see the attacks as the work of a third, more sinister, force, and the attitude developed that if an attack was on an opponent it did not really matter:

> It has been a practice in Bangladesh to blame and prosecute opponents after the occurrence of violence in any part of the country without an impartial

investigation into the matter. Such a practice, however, diverts attention from conducting proper investigation and camouflages the actual perpetrators.

(Rahman 2009: 169–70)

In addition, many politicians from the mid-1990s onwards ignored JMB activities, especially in the northern belt of the country, as the group was perceived to be an effective social counter to the extreme left wing groups such as the Naxerlites who attacked private property and levied exorbitant taxes. Indeed much initial, local support for the JMB was the result of their protective role against the Naxerlites and other left-wing extremist groups and, the JMB was perceived by politicians and the public alike, more as a social than a religious group. More seriously, some have argued (the Awami League opposition during the 2001–06 BNP coalition government along with the foreign press and some members of the BNP government themselves who were subsequently expelled) that elements of the BNP coalition government actually patronized religious-based terrorist groups, particularly the JMB.[9] The Awami League while in opposition, along with the media, continued to warn of the growing Islamist threat but this was largely ignored by the BNP government who cited media hype in an attempt to discredit its government. If not compliant, the BNP was certainly complacent. The explanation often given is again that the BNP patronized the JMB in order to deal with the ultra left wing threat of the Naxerlites and other groups.

With the 2005–07 Caretaker government and the Awami League government which came to power in 2009 there has been a consensus amongst all parties that religious-based terrorism needs to be taken seriously and dealt with effectively, and a determination that Bangladesh will not become another Pakistan.[10] This new concern was partly prompted by the wake-up call of 2005 when Jama'atul Mujahedeen Bangladesh (JMB) orchestrated a wave of bombings in all but one of the country's 64 Districts and for the first time declared responsibility for the attacks which were incredibly well co-ordinated:[11] 'The spate of bombings on August 17 was perhaps the most elaborately planned operation, not only in Bangladesh, but also in the region, and perhaps ever seen anywhere else in the world' (Khan 2009: 150). 'The two incidents of bombings (on 24 August 2004 and the simultaneous country-wide bombings on 17 August 2005) exposed us to a heretofore unknown force, well organized and well trained to carry out destructive acts' (ibid.: 149).

In the same year two judges were killed in suicide bombings, the first time JMB had used such lethal tactics. The attacks indicated a strong network of synchronized activities amongst JMB activists. Under pressure from Western donors to take action (Rahman 2009: 182–3), the Caretaker government reacted swiftly. There were successful and quick apprehensions, and new legislation was passed that enabled the execution of six of the seven Shura Council leaders of the JMB for the murder of the two judges, as well as establishing the death penalty for patrons, financiers and trainers of terrorist activities with special tribunals set up to deal with such cases. An elite force, the Rapid Action Battalion (RAB), was also set up and part of RAB was deployed to deal with extremists. The new Caretaker government also reopened the case of the 2004 bombing of the Awami League rally and the Awami League government elected in 2009 has vowed to bring those responsible to justice.

The nature of the terrorist threat

Traditional non-religious terrorism

Terrorism in Bangladesh in the 1970s was primarily political with a large number of ultra left groups such as the Naxerlites as well as some nationalist and separatist groups amongst the tribal peoples especially in the Chittagong Hill Tracts region of the South East. The outlawed Naxerlite groups had bases, training camps, and arms supplies and were generally better organized and with more support than many of the religious-based terrorist groups that emerged in the 1990s. The ultra-left groups are also sometimes referred to as the Sharbahara[12] (the have-nots) with leadership in the hands of extreme left political parties who sought the destruction of capitalist society. The sources of funding for these underground groups were the forceful collection of tolls from the farmers, robbery and looting and it was in opposition to such groups that the government encouraged the activities of religious-based groups such as the JMB in the 1990s. Today the left wing political groups are of little political consequence but the Sharbahara groups still resort to arson, anarchy, subversive and extortion activities.

Terrorism in the Chittagong Hill Tracts from the late 1970s onwards took the form of a separatist movement by the tribal Chakma people with an armed insurrection against the government to press for more autonomy and in the extreme a separate homeland. India provided both funding and refuge for these groups. This movement was largely quelled with the signing of a peace accord in 1997 between the government of Bangladesh and the representatives of the tribal people. In addition to the organized terrorist groups, Bangladesh is also a route for small arms, narcotics and people-smuggling with its excessively long and unpatrolled borders and currently it is estimated that there are just over 1,000 politically and criminally motivated groups operating within Bangladesh. In addition, the Mastan groups effectively operate as micro level, local terrorists. Recently, international donors have expressed concern over the breakdown of law and order in the country.

Religious-based terrorism

The 1990s saw the rise of a new phenomenon in Bangladesh, religious-based terrorism. These ideologically motivated groups sought to use violence to bring about what they perceived as divinely commanded purposes, such as the introduction of Shariah law, often targeting broad categories of the population. Rumours of a rise in Islamic militancy started to appear in daily newspapers in Bangladesh as a result of the death threats issue by clerics on so-called murtads (apostates) who were seen to be violating Islamic ideals. These included prominent writers, NGO activists and academics.

Studies of the radicalization forces behind these groups in Bangladesh found that the drivers are often home grown to do with dissatisfaction with local politics rather than with strong links to international causes such as Palestine and international movements such as The Muslim Brotherhood, although there was some empathy with the Afghan and Iraqi problems.

One of the first groups to emerge in the early 1990s was Harakat-ul-Jihad-al-Islami (HuJI). In 1992 the Bangladesh chapter of HuJI demanded that the country become an Islamic state at a press conference in April and reportedly with the assistance of Osama Bin Laden's International Islamic Front intensified its subversive activities in 1996 when the Awami League came to power (*New Age* 21 August 2009b: 15). The organization became fully operational with the 1999 blast at the Udichi cultural programme in Jessore, which marked the beginning of a new age of religious-based terrorism in Bangladesh, killing 10 people and injuring about 100. Since then they have orchestrated regular attacks including attacks at the Bengali New Year celebrations (considered to be un-Islamic) in 2001, on the Awami League rally in 2004, on the British High Commissioner in 2004 and had a hand in the 2005 countrywide bombings. Currently it is reported that HuJI has some 2,000 hard core members (Khan 2009: 149).

The Jama'atul Mujahedeen of Bangladesh (JMB) emerged slightly later than HuJI, initially in the north west of the country, in order to help protect people from the taxes, levies and the general violence of the ultra-left Naxerlite groups. It is believed that the first major JMB terrorist incident was in 2002[13] followed by the bombing of a cinema hall in 2003. The group is dedicated to removing the country's secular government and imposing a Taliban-inspired Islamic theocracy in its place based on Shariah law. In addition, the group has denounced the American-led invasion of Iraq. They have targeted judges, lawyers, courthouses, cinema halls, NGO offices, intellectuals and cultural programmes.

Table 2.1 shows the extent of deaths and injuries due to religious-based terrorist incidents between 1999 and 2005. Most of the terror events took place during the four-party BNP coalition government of 2006–08. During this period, the attacks took on a new dimension, using grenades, suicide bombers and powerful gel explosives with extraordinarily large caches of arms and sophisticated weaponry apprehended. Despite the major crackdown on the JMB following the 2005 bombings, many are worried that it is in the process of successfully regrouping: 'Although fractured, the JMB has never been inactive and under the leadership of Maulana Saidur Rahman, the proscribed militant organization is believed to be strengthening itself' (*New Age* 21 August 2009b: 16).

TABLE 3.1 Deaths and injuries due to terrorist attacks in Bangladesh 1999–2005

	1999	*2000*	*2001*	*2002*	*2003*	*2004*	*2005*
Deaths	22	2	49	9	8	25	23
Injuries	130	22	225	156	8	170	120

Source: Rahman 2009: 168.

Groups have been trying to reorganize using the 'cut out' technique whereby splinter groups and cells are formed and each group is kept unaware of the others. Each group has a hard-core leadership which defines policy, an active cadre of shooters and bombers, active supporters who provide money, intelligence, legal and medical services, safe havens and forged documents as well as passive supporters and sympathizers.

Although JMB and HuJI are the two most effective and well known religious-based terrorist groups in Bangladesh there are a number of smaller ones such as Jagrata Muslim Janata Bangladesh (JMJB), Allahr Dal, Hijb-ut-Tuhid and Hijb-ul-Mujahedeen. In 2005 the *Daily Star* estimated that there were 30 Islamic militant organizations in Bangladesh (*Daily Star* 21 August 2005). In all, there are 12 outlawed groups in Bangladesh including five religious ones.

Although poverty was not found to be a major factor in radicalization in Bangladesh (Personal interview, Dhaka August 2009), most agree that social factors potentially help recruitment into these groups, including governance failure, poverty and the failure of government to mainstream the madrassa education system, particularly the Qawmi madrassas. Recent international factors, such as the war in Iraq and Afghanistan, US hegemony and globalization, and the feeling of international oppression and marginalization by many Muslims also helps. As already mentioned, during the decade from the 1990s to 2005 political parties also turned a blind eye to the growth of groups like JMB seeing them as a social movement to counter the leftist social movements. These religious groups, however, eventually turned against the government.

In summary, groups like JMB and HuJI have little grass roots support, a weak organizational infrastructure, and often recruit using the incentive of money rather than ideology. Their membership is minute compared to the total population of over 140,000 million, and they have not reached the scale of similar groups in Indonesia. These groups, however, have links into other types of criminality such as money laundering, arms and narcotics smuggling, and although they remain small, they are potentially deadly in their attacks. Despite the rise of religious-based terrorism, the daily lives of Bangladeshis are more affected by Mastans, thugs, criminals and political violence than by the activities of groups like JMB and HuJI.

The regional and international dimension to terrorism in Bangladesh

It is often argued that religious terrorism in Bangladesh does not have strong international links. Although ideologically different, neither HuJI nor JMB have strong international links although HuJI has more international and regional links than JMB with its founding father being a signatory to one of the early Al Qaeda documents. It is also likely that some HuJI members have received training in Pakistan and have footprints in attacks in India as well as raising money, explosives and arms from India.

In the crackdown following the 2005 wave of bombings, JMB and its leadership were largely dismantled but more recently, there are signs of regrouping with stronger international support. In March 2009, RAB unearthed an orphanage cum madrassa in Bhola used by JMB as a training camp. The madrassa was funded by a British Bangladeshi chemist under a UK-based charity organization, Green Crescent and contained a mini ordinance factory with huge amounts of firearms and explosives and remote control devices (*New Age* 21 August 2009b: 15). In the first half of 2009 RAB has arrested at least 48 members of JMB which is reportedly now obtaining arms and explosives from Pakistan, Myanmar, Thailand, India and China with fund management in Saudi Arabia and funding from Saudi, Kuwait, UAE, Bahrain, Libya and Pakistan. More recently, with the apprehension of Indian terrorists residing in Bangladesh and the discovery that many of the explosives and detonators for the 2005 attacks came from India there have been growing tensions between the two countries on terrorist-based issues, with India claiming that Bangladesh hosts terrorist camps for the North East Indian insurgents. Both Indian and Pakistani militants see Bangladesh as a safe haven although this does not necessarily mean they are trying to set up active groups in Bangladesh.

Regionally, Bangladesh is surrounded by terrorism with the insurgency movements in India's seven North East states, an insurgency in Myanmar, the Maoist insurgency in Nepal and religious-based terrorism further afield in Pakistan and Afghanistan. This host of regional influences, particularly given porous borders has no doubt affected Bangladesh and Bangladeshis often blame their own terrorist activities on attempts by India and others to destabilize the country. Even if there are only weak organic links with regional terrorist movements, some in Bangladesh nevertheless get ideological inspiration from them.

Although regionally influenced, Bangladeshi terrorism does not have a strong international flavour. Attacks are not carried out outside the country, and within Bangladesh the attacks are largely aimed at local rather than international targets, with the exception of the 2004-attempted assassination of the British High Commissioner, Anwar Chowdhury. As pointed out by Taj Hashmi:

> ... despite its poverty, backwardness and the preponderance of Islamic ethos in the mainstream of its politics and culture, Bangladesh is not just another Afghanistan, Iran, Saudi Arabia or even Pakistan. Despite having many striking similarities with the Islamic movements elsewhere, their Bangladeshi counterparts have striking dissimilarities with them as well.
>
> *(Hashmi 2004: 42)*

One of the features that distinguish the Bangladeshi groups is the fact that unlike say Al Qaeda, they do not strongly pick up on international issues such as Palestine, the Afghan and Iraq war, and the presence of US troops in Saudi Arabia. They are focused much more on domestic grievances. In addition, the religious-based terrorist groups have much less grass roots support than many of those based in other countries, with few people sympathizing with their domestic objectives.

this is consistent with sense of 'other' that I found.

Is religious militancy on the increase in Bangladesh?

The emergence of religious-based terrorism in the 1990s along with the increased Islamization of both politics and society as well as a more general decline in law and order has prompted some commentators to speculate that Bangladesh was about to degenerate into a new Afghanistan. The Western and Indian[14] media has become more concerned with Bangladesh since 2001. The debate about whether Bangladesh had become a haven for terrorists, including Al Qaeda, started with two publications in *Time* (Alex Perry 'Deadly Cargo' 21 October 2002) and *Far Eastern Economic Review* (Bertil Linter 'Bangladesh: A Cocoon of Terror' 4 April 2002). The Bangladesh government strenuously denied both reports. In November 2002, the Indian Deputy Prime Minister L.K. Advani raised concerns about the growing activities of Pakistan's Inter-Service Intelligence (ISI) and Al Qaeda in Bangladesh after the BNP coalition government came to power. In 2005, Eliza Griswold wrote an article in the *New York Times* about Bangladesh entitled, 'The Next Islamic Revolution?' The *Washington Post* published an article in August 2006 entitled 'A New Hub of Terrorism?: In Bangladesh, An Islamic Movement with Al Qaeda Ties is on the Rise'. *Intelligence Review* has also reported that Bangladesh is on the brink of becoming a failed state and a perfect target for Al Qaeda (Yasmin 2009: 98–9).

One of the factors that has prompted the above media speculation is the increased Islamization of society in Bangladesh. This has been evidenced by the adoption of more traditional and religious-based dress, such as the black burqah and an increased attendance at mosques especially by the young. This, it is important to stress, does not necessarily equate with an increased Islamic terrorist threat. Similar trends towards increased religiosity have been seen in the USA amongst evangelical Christians and the political right without prompting scares of Christian-based militancy and terrorism. Likewise, it is also possible for people to adopt extreme and fundamentalist religious views without this making them a terrorist. Much of the increased veil wearing is evidenced amongst university students and the upper middle classes and seems to be a knee jerk reaction against the geo-political response to 9/11 by the West as much as a manifestation of increased radicalization. In addition, much of the religious revivalism amongst the young is part of the self-actualization of youth and an intellectual, rather than a violent, social awareness movement to establish an Islamic way of life. Traditionally student politics and movements have always been very vibrant in Bangladesh, although Dhaka University does not permit any religious-based political groups to function. Certainly, socially and culturally people are now more aware of the global situation and many Muslims, including those in Bangladesh, have anti-USA and anti-globalization views but again this does not equate to militancy or terrorism.

Given the social and religious background outlined above, there seems little objective evidence that alarmist predictions will come true in Bangladesh. For example, the Bangladeshi response to the Danish cartoon was virtually non-existent compared to that in many other Muslim countries and the Global Peace Index in 2007 rated Bangladesh low in terms of radicalization, below Pakistan, India and even the USA. Increased outward manifestations of religious values do not seem to be symptomatic of increased militancy or terrorism. People from the whole strata of society, including most religious leaders, were united in their condemnation of the 2005 attacks, and popular hatred of the militants was also shared by their families, many of whom refused to bury those who were killed.

In terms of actual terrorist activities, these seem to have reached their peak in 2005. Since then the brutal crackdown and arrests, as well as the deterrent of the death penalty and a successful deradicalization programme, have all contributed to a decline in religious-based terrorist incidents.

The deradicalization and counter-radicalization programme

The objectives of the programme

The approach to counter-terrorism in Bangladesh has a three-pronged focus – law enactment, law enforcement and the battle of ideas. The deradicalization programme falls under the third prong. The battle of ideas contains the following elements:

- Delegitimization of terrorism.
- Deradicalization programme.
- Counter-radicalization programme.
- Media management.
- Comprehensive, consistent, sustained and prolonged think tank engagement.
- Model madrassa education.
- Literacy and academic platform.

Bangladesh has been running a hybrid deradicalization cum counter-radicalization programme since 2005. Deradicalization takes place on those who are already radicalized and indoctrinated, and aims to change their views and beliefs. Counter-radicalization aims to prevent the vulnerable from falling into the clutches of radicalized beliefs and views before they have done so. Bangladesh's programme is a hybrid in the sense that although it uses group profiling, its target group is a mixture of those who have already become radicalized and those who are just at the vulnerability stage. For the sake of simplicity, although it is a hybrid programme, we will henceforth refer to it as a deradicalization programme.

The objectives of the deradicalization programme have been listed as:

- To propagate the true spirit of Islam.
- To act as a platform to bring in both people having extreme views and also people with moderate outlook.
- To promote modern education like English, computer studies etc. along with Islamic education.
- To identify orthodox minded people and motivate them towards the actual spirit of Islam.
- To recruit potential agents to infiltrate the extremists' groups/institutions.
- Collection of information on Islamic issues, documentation of information and finally dissemination.

(Government briefing, Dhaka September 2009)

The deradicalization programme is essentially a motivational programme designed to expose the misconception of Islamic Jihad as a mission to kill and to change ideas peacefully. It uses religious leaders and other influential people to disseminate a peaceful and tolerant interpretation of Islam. The programme is run by a branch of the military that reports directly to the Prime Minister.

The deradicalization programme is a highly covert operation. Searches for information about the programme on the internet revealed not a single hit whilst most people in Bangladesh, apart from those directly concerned with the running of the programme, do not know of its existence. The military is particularly keen not to be publicly associated with any elements of the programme as the military and security services are generally perceived to be part of the state apparatus consisting of Western-educated moderates and it is felt that a perception of military and state involvement would alienate participants from the programme. In addition, the authorities are keen not to promote the image of Bangladesh as an extremist state requiring a state-sponsored deradicalization programme.

The establishment of the programme involved several phases of operation, including information collection, site selection, ground study and setting up NGOs and establishing NGO offices and staff to oversee the programme. The government chose to set up pseudo NGOs to run the programme. These NGOs were registered by the government and a local Islamic pro-Western community man was chosen to run each NGO. Three regions were chosen for the deradicalization programme – Cox's Bazaar, Bogra and Sylhet. These three areas were identified on the basis of historic incidents and events, including the recruitment levels of the major terrorist groups in each area. The programme initially started in Cox's Bazaar in the south east of the country in 2005 and was then extended to Bogra and Sylhet. Cox's Bazaar was chosen because of the tradition of insurgency in the region associated with Burmese refugees, a tradition of crime with transnational links and because of religious militant activity in the area. Sylhet was chosen because of the high level of out migration from this area and hence the potential for diaspora, returnee migrants and migrant remittances to affect the area as outlined earlier in this chapter. Bogra was chosen because of the perceived high level of JMB recruitment and general underground activities in the area. All three areas were also identified as having a high concentration of madrassas. The grass roots programme is essentially a village level rural and semi-urban programme rather than an urban programme, targeting village madrassas, mosques and imams.

Unlike many of the deradicalization programmes elsewhere, the Bangladeshi programme is not a prisoner-based rehabilitation programme but a broader based, society wide, motivational programme. Imams and religious leaders front the programme due to their high level of influence and authority in Bangladesh society. They have a long tradition of being able to influence people's views gradually without assaulting their religion as was seen in the successful family planning campaign. The religious leaders that are used are both from within the community as well as some more influential figures being brought in from outside. The programme targets students from madrassas as well as other individuals identified by the intelligence forces as prone to radicalization and militancy. More specifically, in the three areas the intelligence services carried out monitoring work of 4,200 people on their database, and targeted many of them for the programme. The programme offers workshops, seminars, conferences, roundtables and symposia. These are held at various venues, including some of the madrassas, mosques and community centres. They are funded by the government via the NGOs, with the latter being responsible for their operational running. These events are all very participatory, encouraging questions and answer sessions with the religious leaders and offering an open floor. Topics are not explicitly billed as deradicalization but rather include things like Islam and peace, Islam and modernity, Islam and pluralism, Islam and human rights, Islam and the role of Imams. Anti-terrorist themes and messages are inserted unannounced into the events. To quote one government official: 'This is deradicalisation unannounced – a covert form of psychological warfare' (Personal interview, Dhaka September 2009).

The government has deliberately adapted the themes of the events to the concerns of Bangladesh society. Sometimes the events are open to all and generally advertised, and sometimes they are put on for explicit target groups such as female madrassa students or imams. People are attracted with free lunches, teas or dinners and sometimes the incentive of a computer or cell phone demonstration or a movie. Timings are set so as not to clash with work or school time. In addition to the seminars, workshops etc., the government has also sponsored the publication of religious-based magazines to be distributed at madrassas and mosques free of cost. Again, the approach is very covert, with a wide range of general articles in the magazines with the subtle insertion of deradicalization and counter-radicalization messages. The use of NGOs as a front for all these operations, along with the local and village level approach, gives the programme a very decentralized character so that it is not seen as a government initiative.

Although only a small part of the programme, there is also a financial component that offers support to a limited number of individuals, often those graduating from Qawmi madrassas and unable to find work, including the 40 best madrassa graduates each year in each region. Small loans are offered to set up businesses such as tea stalls, rickshaw operation and the like as well as vocational training with small scholarships in such areas as mechanics, air condition maintenance and plumbing. These employment-generating programmes are again run by the three NGOs but funded by the government and are very popular since the NGOs do not levy interest or other charges on these micro loans, unlike many other similar NGO programmes.

Unlike many deradicalization programmes, the Bangladeshi programme does not impose any strict conditions on those who benefit from the programme such as renunciation of political activities or acceptance of informant status although some of those given loans and employment are encouraged to become informants with monetary rewards. The lack of conditionality is partly because of the covert nature of the programme, and a desire not to reveal its true intention as a mind-altering exercise.

Although Bangladesh does not operate a prisoner rehabilitation programme for imprisoned religious terrorists, the government has given some financial assistance to the families of a small number of those arrested, particularly to help with the education of their children. The aim is to prevent the spread of hatred and resentment into prisoners' families and to avoid their marginalization. The families of the six hanged JMB leaders were supported in this way. In addition, an attempt has been made to segregate religious terrorists in the prison system although the extreme overcrowding in the current prison system hampers the practical implementation of this.

Compared to the prison rehabilitation programmes that take a curative approach, the Bangladeshi programme focuses more on prevention rather than cure with a grass roots approach designed to catch the radicalized and those vulnerable to radicalization before they commit acts of violence. It is also designed to tap into the social, cultural and religious nature of Bangladeshi society as outlined earlier in this chapter, with a moderate, secular and tolerant society seen as susceptible to this type of motivational programme.

Criticisms of the programme

Some have argued that Bangladesh's hybrid programme is inappropriate and that a more focused and targeted programme is needed. The group profiling used to attract people to the workshops is criticized as poor because it assumes that just because one is, for example, the student of a madrassa one is radical or vulnerable. By differentiating such a person from the rest of society and targeting the programme on him or her, a sense of resentment may be fostered which drives the individual in a more radical direction. The covert nature of the programme, however, helps avoid such a trend. Workshops, seminars etc., are not explicitly billed as deradicalization events and other elements such as computer training are often mixed in to disguise the true intention of the event. Some still argue, however, that by being a hybrid the programme does not do either deradicalization or counter-radicalization well. An effective deradicalization programme, it is argued, needs to be highly targeted, including, specifically, the prison population, and needs to involve a whole raft of measures and individuals, including the family and the immediate periphery of the targets' social networks. The individual needs to identify himself as a radical before the process can become effective and multiple tools are needed to reintegrate him/her into society. An effective counter-radicalization programme on the other hand needs to be much broader and far reaching than the three regional programmes which just use seminars, focus groups and workshops, and instead needs to use a wide range of strategic communication networks, including television and the internet.

Some critics have argued that the Bangladesh programme could backfire in two ways. Firstly, if there is not an adequate level of acceptance for the programme and if individuals resent being targeted they may see this as an attempt by the state to infringe their identity. Secondly, there is the risk that people will attend the public events only in order to obtain a reward such as the financial incentives which are sometimes on offer or other incentives such as free food or free computer training and that they will not in any way be influenced by the messages on offer.

One weakness that affects the programme is the poor standard of religious scholarship in the country, since the programme relies on religious leaders and scholars to propagate its ideas. Although the programme is fronted by three pseudo NGOs it is effectively delivered by Imams and religious leaders rather than by civil society and many of these religious leaders are poorly educated and not particularly savvy.

The success of the programme

The success of the programme is hard to judge. The government has stated that its criteria of success are:

- The number of terrorist incidents.
- The level of local violence.
- Recruitment into religious-based extremist groups.

All three of these indicators have declined since the programme was launched. Certainly, since its peak in 2005 religious-based terrorism has declined in Bangladesh with only sporadic incidents between 2005–09. The government also claims that it has successfully reached its target groups, especially amongst the young, has mobilized public opinion against terrorism, has created a social awareness against extremism, has moderated extremist views and has reduced JMB recruitment and strongholds. There has also been an increased flow of human intelligence from local communities leading to more arrests and trails and fewer incidents. It is difficult, however, to ascribe causation. Some of the improvement might be due to the greater and more effective use of force in tracking down and apprehending the terrorists that came into place following the 2005 bombing campaign with the formation of RAB, the passing of new legislation and the introduction of the death penalty as a deterrent. This hard line approach by the government created a fear of joining radical, religious groups and has played a major part in the de-escalation of violence since 2005. The deradicalization programme, however, has undoubtedly had some positive effects in the three areas in which it operates. This is particularly the case in Cox's Bazaar and the government believes that the increased level of human intelligence provided by community members in the three areas may well be a positive spin off from the programme, although it may also be due to the monetary rewards offered for such intelligence to peers, friends and family.

Due to its nature, focusing on the individual rather than the terrorist group or imprisoned terrorists, the effects of such a motivational programme are not easy to observe and psychological warfare of this nature also takes time to become effective via gradual persuasive techniques. One indicator of success is the number of people who have been reached by the three programmes. By 2008 programmes in the three target areas had reached:

- 125 madrassas.
- 205 madrassa teachers.
- 500 senior madrassa students.
- 4,200 general madrassa students.
- 255 imams.
- 40,000 religious persons.

One notable aspect of the programme is that it has a very low budget with the government spending less than $100,000 per year in each of the three targeted areas. Critics of the programme, however, argue that the government has an excessively operational view of terrorism with a short to medium time horizon such that the lack of bombs and attacks are seen as the indicator of success. It is also argued, however, that whilst terrorist attacks may have gone down this does not necessarily equate to a decline in radicalization and potential longer term threats, and may lead to complacency regarding the longer term trends in society. It has also been argued that the role played by the military in helping the Caretaker government run the national agenda led to reduced attention being paid to general counter-terrorism operations enabling groups to reform behind the scenes ready for future attacks.

Other related programmes

In addition to the distinct deradicalization programmes run by the government in Cox's Bazaar, Bogra and Sylhet, a number of other ad hoc initiatives have been undertaken by the government and other bodies which contribute to deradicalization and counter-radicalization in Bangladesh.

The government has funded the production of a large number of sermon guides distributed via the Islamic Foundation[15] with sermons on such subjects as tolerance and non-violence. These are delivered at the sermon (Khutba) before the noon prayers on Friday. These sermons are used to tackle a broad range of social and religious issues and are attended by most people. The sermon guides include the guide 'No to Terrorism' which was circulated to all imams shortly after the 2005 bombings. In addition, a directive was sent to all imams by the Islamic Foundation to give Friday sermons against terrorism. It is generally agreed that the Friday sermon delivery by Imams throughout the country's 500,000+ mosques has been a highly effective means of diffusing extremism and violence amongst the Muslim community.

After the 2005 wave of bombings the Masjid Council[16] contributed to building public opinion against extremism and violence in Islam. The Council made strong statements along with the major religious leaders in the daily papers and on television, and produced a set of over 10,000 posters in both Bangla and Arabic containing statements and verses from the Koran that strongly condemned the link between Islam and violence. They also produced and distributed a book on a similar subject and ran a national conference with major leaders from all religions as well as government ministers. In addition, the leader of the Masjid Council as well as other leading Islamic scholars, appear regularly on television talk shows and use this forum to condemn violence. Some of the funding for these activities was provided on a covert basis by the DGFI as part of the Counter-Terrorism Bureau's broader mandate. The Masjid Council runs six imam training academies and USAID has funded an Imam training programme via these academies where part of the training is on how to remove the link between Islam and violence and extremism. Masjid Council vocational training for Qawmi madrassa graduates could also be seen as part of a broader approach to counter-radicalization.

The media in general played a major role in helping to build a broad national consensus against religious-based terrorism in the wake of the 2005 bombings: 'The role of the media assumes great significance in the fight against terrorism particularly in so far as it relates to the psychological and propaganda aspects of counter-terrorism' (Khan 2009: 144).

Television, for example, has aired a number of documentaries about religion and terrorism sponsored by the government. Other organisations such as the Bangladesh Institute of International and Strategic Studies (BIISS) have run large events such as 'The Roundtable Discussion on Countering Radicalization in South Asia: The Bangladesh Perspective' in May 2009 which received extensive media coverage. There have also been three multi-faith seminars in Dhaka to talk about terrorism and religion attended by religious leaders and funded by government, although not publicized as government activities.

The new government initiative

On 25 August 2009, the *Daily Star* announced a new counter-radicalization initiative by the Awami League government:

> Recognising the fact that anti-militant drive is not enough to uproot the evil of extremism from society, the government has launched a massive socio-political campaign, involving 14 different agencies, to educate people and closely monitor militant activities at the grass-roots level.
>
> (Daily Star *25 August 2009: 1)*

Spearheaded by the State Minister for Home Affairs, the campaign involves various initiatives to create awareness of the destructive nature of extremism. This will include holding campaigns, screening documentaries, training imams and organizing anti-militancy campaigns at madrassas and other venues. The Information Ministry has already prepared a documentary highlighting the negative impacts of militancy which will be screened at every village across the country. A major part of the initiative will be to continue the training and encouragement of imams to give sermons against militancy. Another aspect of the drive will be to involve the unemployed youth in various types of development work and vocational training via small loans.

In addition to the counter-radicalization aspects of the new programme, the programme will also take a new approach to monitoring and intelligence work at the local level. This will involve Ansar and the Village Defence Party (VDP). These two volunteer agencies are spread throughout the country into the remotest areas where RAB and the police do not have regular access. There is an Ansar/VDP team in each village consisting of 36 male and 36 female members who interact closely with villagers and are therefore quick to notice newcomers or suspicious activities at grass-roots level.[17]

The new campaign, although it involves many of the elements of the old approach, is a nationwide rather than a limited regional counter-radicalization programme and for the first time brings all agencies involved under one committee. Following a series of meetings since it took power in 2007, the Awami League government formed a high-powered committee on 20 April 2009. The committee, however, initially only met twice due to the resignation of the State Minister for Home Affairs. With a new minister having taken office in 2009, the committee has been reactivated and will meet once a month. Other members of the committee include the secretaries of the ministries of home, education, law, religious affairs, social welfare, local government and information as well as the Inspector General of Police, chiefs of the Directorate General of Forces Intelligence, Bangladesh Rifles, Ansar, VDP, National Security Intelligence and RAB and Director General of the Prime Minister's Office. Each of the ministries has been assigned a specific task. The Ministry of Religious Affairs, for example will be responsible for motivating imams against militancy via the Islamic Foundation. If the committee operates effectively, it should provide a more holistic approach to nation-wide counter-terrorism initiatives, as well as serving as the key reference and contact point for all those involved with such initiatives. This is a welcome improvement over the previous, somewhat ad hoc, arrangements. The new inter-agency perspective should provide a more strategic approach and reduce the inter-agency rivalry that has existed in the past. In addition, with its media coverage, the new approach is more open and transparent than the old, limited, military-led, deradicalization initiative.[18] It remains to be seen, however, how effective the new initiative will be or indeed whether it is just the new Awami League government wanting to be seen to be doing something new from the old regime.

Conclusion

Although Bangladesh is unlikely to become another Afghanistan, despite the predictions of some media pundits, and although the incidents of religious-based terrorism have declined significantly since 2005, the country still needs to take the threat of radicalization seriously. To this effect, it needs to tackle serious issues such as the prevalence of poverty and unemployment, the need to reform the madrassa system, the need for ongoing dialogue with moderate religious leaders and the need to improve governance. The country has a moderate, hybrid, deradicalization cum counter-radicalization programme that operates in three distinct geographical areas and the government has recently announced a new multi-agency approach to counter-terrorism more generally. The existing programme appears to have been successful, judged by the decline in terrorist incidents.

One area where future activities could be effectively extended is into a prisoner-based deradicalization programme. In 2009 Bangladesh had over 1,000 prisoners charged with religious-based terrorism, many of them arrested after the crackdown following the events of 2005 and given 10–15 year sentences. Before they are released back into society there is scope for a programme to help their reintegration via family support, rehabilitation in a controlled environment and demotivational programmes along with help finding employment on their release. Without such a programme this group represents a future threat to society.

The government has also expressed a desire to expand the current programme into more geographical areas, particularly in the north of the country. They would also like to do more work with imams and sermon guides, reform the madrassa education system, increase the number of motivational programmes especially for the poor and the young, expand their audio-visual library, increase the number of vocational training programmes and scholarships, and, more generally, increase public awareness against extremism and terrorism (personal interview, Dhaka September 2009). This is a clear acknowledgement that the threat cannot be dealt with by coercive powers alone but requires the participation of the whole society. The recently articulated new government strategy to involve society in a multi-agency, holistic approach is to be welcomed in this respect.

Notes

1 This means that on average there are nine mosques per square mile giving the country one of the highest concentration of mosques in the world (Ahmed 2009: 9).
2 For example in 2009, madrassas run by the Kuwaiti-based NGO, Revival of Islamic Heritage were investigated by the police, and the media often lists madrassas with finance coming from Middle East-based NGOs.
3 Subjects such as English, comparative religion, politics, sociology and computer studies were introduced and Bangla replaced Urdu as the medium of instruction.
4 Two Indian militants, Obaidullah and Mansur Ali, recently arrested in Bangladesh were teaching and had affiliations with madrassas in Jessore, Habiganj and Dhaka and five of the six Huji activists captured on 1 August 2009 by RAB were also teachers and principals at different madrassas (*New Age* 21 August 2009b: 12 and 15).
5 Some still disagree with Ahmed. For example, Kumar has stated that the Qawmi madrassas '... are a major factor behind the rise of Islamic extremism in Bangladesh. They spend a large share of their funds for arms training as part of preparations for Jihad' (Kumar 2005).
6 In the past the local Mastan was a Robin Hood type figure who helped secure services such as water connections for his locality. More recently they have become deeply involved in racketeering, extortion and serious crime such as money laundering, narcotics and arms trading. Many Mastan have themselves become politicians by virtue of donating money to the party and each Mastan has his armed cadre of thugs. It is estimated that there are around 1,050 Mastan groups operating in the country (Personal interview, Dhaka August 2009).
7 Under the constitution a non-elected Caretaker government takes power for three months at the end of each administration in order to run free and fair elections. In January 2007 extensive public disorder as well as the Awami League declaration that they would boycott the elections due to a rigged voter list prompted the Caretaker government, backed by the military, to postpone the elections and continue in power for two years whilst the military reformed the electoral list. Whilst in power the Caretaker government did a lot more than a Caretaker government is mandated to do, prompting some to declare it unconstitutional.
8 It is now generally accepted that the religious terrorist group HuJI was behind the 2004 attacks on the Awami League.
9 For example, on 19 February 1996, 41 HuJI members were arrested for running a training camp in Cox's Bazaar and sentenced to life imprisonment. However, under the coalition BNP government all 41 were released on bail by the High Court. An appeal by the accused reduced their jail term to 12 years but 36 had gone into hiding and were not rearrested. In response to donors' concerns that government was turning a blind eye to

terrorism, the BNP Finance Minister of Bangladesh termed the terrorist problem an international one which was difficult to contain by normal enforcement tools (*Daily Star*, 24 November 2004). In addition, the subsequently arrested JMB activists hinted at active collusion by the Jamaat-e-Islami coalition party in terrorist activities (*Daily Star* 25 August 2005). However, the BNP government did not entirely neglect the terrorist threat. In February 2003 it banned Shahadat Al Hiqma and in February 2005 banned both Jagrata Muslim Janata Bangladesh (JMJB) and Jama'atul Mujahedeen Bangladesh (JMB). It also started a crackdown on Islamic NGOs who were identified as having links with Islamic militant organizations, such as the Saudi-based NGO Al Haramaine Islamic Institute and the Kuwait-based Revival of Islamic Heritage Society.

10 The 2005–07 Caretaker government, although charged simply with getting the forthcoming elections up and running fairly, extended its activities beyond this. The military played a prominent role in the government such that some argue that this distracted them from their counter–terrorism activities. In addition the severe cyclone of 2007 was a distraction, although at the same time it hampered the terrorists' ability to function.

11 The 17 August 2005 attacks by the JMB involved the detonation of over 400 simultaneous explosions primarily targeted at government buildings and areas for public gatherings for official activities in regional capitals and Dhaka. The explosives were mostly non-fatal containing sawdust rather than lethal ball bearings but several people were killed and over 100 injured. Aimed at spreading mass panic the recently banned JMB littered the sites with leaflets espousing their grievances.

12 There was also a Sharbahara Party whose existence predates the formation of Bangladesh with much the same ideology as the Naxerlites who drew their inspiration from the Naxalbari movement in West Bengal. These groups had a dual identity, one involved in platform politics and the other in underground terrorist activities.

13 Following the arrests of JMB members after the 2005 JMB bombings interrogations led to an estimate of 6,739 active members, of which 216 were die-hard activists and a further 4,250 supporters. Of the active members 33 per cent were aged between 20–24 years and 20 per cent between 25–29 years and 24 per cent had received some kind of training. 16 per cent had only primary level education, 40 per cent secondary education to O Level and 16 per cent higher secondary education. Most recruits had joined up out of economic desperation rather than ideological conviction. The organization also had limited resources despite its well-orchestrated wave of bombing around the country in 2005. Money was obtained from local donations, Diaspora, migrant workers and Middle East-based NGOs. Nearly 1,400 people were prosecuted following these bombings and six of the seven leaders executed.

14 It is sometimes suggested that India has a vested interest in portraying Bangladesh as radical and ungovernable as this would tend to indicate a lack of viable statehood for its own seven North East states campaigning for independence. In the wake of the 2005 bombings the Indian intelligence agency RAW (Research and Analysis Wing) prepared a dossier for President Bush in order to show evidence that Bangladesh was about to become 'the next Afghanistan' and claiming links between Bangladesh extremists and Al Qaeda and Kashmiri-based groups such as Lashkar-e-Toiba and Jaishe-e-Mohammad (Walker 2006).

15 The Islamic Foundation is under the Ministry of Religious Affairs and controls all mosques.

16 The Masjid Council is a private committee cum council for mosques and all mosques in Bangladesh are expected to register as members.

17 Ansar/VDP members are mainly volunteers who receive little training and are mainly unarmed. They have uniforms and come under the control of the police and Ministry of Home Affairs, although they are not the same as an institutionalized police force. They reach into every village in Bangladesh. There are around six million members. They also run local banks, businesses and development projects to support the local community and are called into action in times of national emergency and disaster such as cyclones and floods.

18 It is as yet unclear whether the government initiatives in Cox's Bazaar, Bogra and Sylhet will continue under the new campaign.

Bibliography

Ahmed, I. (2005) *On the Brink of Precipice: Contemporary Terrorism and the Limits of the State*, Bangladesh Foundation for Development Research, Dhaka.

Ahmed, I. (ed.) (2009) *Terrorism in the 21st Century: Perspectives from Bangladesh*, The University Press Limited, Dhaka.

Daily Star, 24 November 2004, Dhaka.

Daily Star, 21 August 2005, Dhaka.

Daily Star, 25 August 2005, Dhaka.

Daily Star, 25 August 2009, *Govt. Takes on Terror Socially, Politically, Dhaka.*

Far Eastern Economic Review, 4 April 2002, *Bangladesh: A Cocoon of Terror.*

Hashmi, T.I. (2004) 'Islamic resurgence in Bangladesh: genesis, dynamics and implications', in S.P. Limaye, R.G. Wirsing, and Malik, M. (eds), *Religious Radicalism and Security in South Asia*, Asia Pacific Centre for Security Studies: Honolulu.

International Crisis Group (2006) 'Bangladesh Today', *Asia Report* no. 121.

Khan, S. A. (2009) 'Anti-terrorism and the role of the media', Chapter 6 in I. Ahmed (ed.), *Terrorism in the 21st Century: Perspectives from Bangladesh,* The University Press Limited: Dhaka.

Kumar, A. (2005) 'Islamic NGOs Funding Terror in Bangladesh', *South Asia Analysis Group*, paper no. 1531.

New Age, 21 August 2009a, *Madrassahs Have Been Made an Easy Scapegoat*, Dhaka.

New Age, 21 August 2009b, *Terrorism Without Borders*, Dhaka.

New York Times (2005), 'The Next Islamic Revolution?', January 23, 2005.

Rahman, A.B.M. (2009) 'Countering terrorism: response of stakeholders', Chapter 7 in I. Ahmed, (ed.), *Terrorism in the 21st Century: Perspectives from Bangladesh,* The University Press Limited: Dhaka.

Rahman, S.T. (2002) *Illegal Use and Trade of Small Arms and Light Weapons: An Assessment of Present Status of Bangladesh*, South Asian Partnership Bangladesh: Dhaka.

Shawkat Ali, A.M.M. (2006) *Faces of Terrorism in Bangladesh*, The University Press Limited: Dhaka.

Time, 21 October 2002, *Deadly Cargo.*

Walker, M. (2006) *India to Warn Bush of Bangladesh Terror.* Available HTTP: http://www.upi.com/international.

Washington Post (2006), 'A New Hub of Terrorism?: In Bangladesh. An Islamic Movement with Al Qaeda Ties is on the Rise.', August 2, 2006.

Yasmin, L. (2009) 'Bangladesh-India relations: neighbourliness beyond terrorism', Chapter 4 in I. Ahmed (ed.), *Terrorism in the 21st Century: Perspectives from Bangladesh,* The University Press Limited: Dhaka.

4

GROUP DERADICALIZATION IN EGYPT

The unfinished agenda

Jane Harrigan and Hamed El-Said

Introduction

Over the past fifteen years, Egypt has witnessed one of the most remarkable processes of deradicalization in the Muslim world. Between 1997–2007 the country's two largest violent Jihadist groups, *al-Gama'a al-Islamiyya* (the Islamic Group, henceforth referred to as IG) and the *al-Jihad* Organization (henceforth referred to as al-Jihad) renounced violence. Both were an instance of group, as opposed to individual, deradicalization whereby a Jihadist group collectively abandons violence. To quote Blaydes and Rubin in the case of the IG:

> No other religious terrorist group of this size to this date has offered a programme of religious re-interpretation on the scale of the experience in Egypt.
>
> *(Blaydes and Rubin 2008: 462)*

This is not the first time that Egypt experienced a process of deradicalization. In the early 1970s, the mainstream Islamic movement, the Muslim Brotherhood, underwent a similar process when it denounced violence and joined the political process. Omar Ashour (2009) has analysed the process of deradicalization in Egypt, both in the 1970s and during 1997–2007 and refers to three dimensions of the deradicalization process: behavioural, ideological and organizational. The behavioural dimension is the actual abandonment of violent activities; the ideological is the delegitimization of violence and the organizational relates to structural changes within an organization's leadership and structure including the dismantling of armed wings. In the case of the IG all three elements have been present. In the case of al-Jihad the organizational component is not yet complete, in that some of the leadership abroad as well as two factions of leadership in Egyptian prisons, have not accepted the deradicalization stance and it is unclear whether armed cells have been fully disbanded.

The success of the deradicalization process in Egypt is shown by the fact that neither of the two groups has been involved in any acts of violence since the end of 1997 and that both groups have strongly denounced the several acts of violence undertaken by smaller groups within Egypt since 1997. This is a remarkable achievement given the previous violent history of both groups who were responsible, jointly, for the assassination of President Sadat in 1981, as well as numerous other acts of violence. In the case of the IG, such acts included the assassination of a former speaker of parliament and the intellectual Farag Foda, the attempted assassination of Mubarak in Addis Ababa, in addition to at least four other attempts on his life. They also included attacks on tourists and Copts and the killing of police and security officers. The IG was even implicated in the 1993 World Trade Center bombing in New York. Both groups are also known former allies of al-Qaeda. In fact, during the 1990s the terrorist campaigns of both groups were responsible for over 1,000 deaths (Blaydes and Rubin 2008: 462).

Ashour (2009: 14) identifies four factors that can contribute towards a process of group deradicalization. He defines group deradicalization as:

> … a process of relative change within Islamist movements, one in which a radical group reverses its ideology and de-legitimises the use of violent methods to achieve political goals, whilst also moving towards an acceptance of gradual social, political and economic changes within a pluralistic context.
>
> *(Ashour 2009: 6)*

The four factors that can contribute to the above process are the correct combination of charismatic leadership at the organization level; state repression; interaction with other incarcerated individuals, both members and non-members of the same organization and selective inducements from the state and other actors.

The focus of this chapter is on the role of the state in the deradicalization process. In terms of the above taxonomy this involves looking at how the state may have facilitated various forms of interaction and the kinds of selective inducements it offered. Analysis is based on secondary sources as well as on a series of interviews with some key players in the process and Egyptian analysts and experts. The role of the Egyptian state in deradicalization is contentiously debated. Some refer to a state-sponsored 'deradicalization programme' or 'strategy' and place much of the credit for the deradicalization that took place on such a programme or strategy. Others deny that the state played a lead role and instead present the process as one emerging essentially from the leadership of the two radical groups in a unilateral fashion, with the state, after a delayed response, responding opportunistically to the initiative through the provision of various facilitation measures. The available empirical evidence, however, supports the latter argument (that deradicalization was spontaneous, emerging initially from within the two groups themselves). State facilitation, nevertheless, was undoubtedly necessary to move the process forward after it had started. Much can still be learnt from this.

Whether the state or the radical groups themselves initiated the deradicalization process, one thing is clear: the state, including the post-Mubarak Egyptian state could still do more to complete and consolidate the remarkable deradicalization process that has taken place so far. Deradicalization does not end at the prison gate and there is much that the state could still do to fully rehabilitate and reintegrate into society those repentant prisoners from the IG and al-Jihad. In addition, the lack of true democracy in Egypt and the failure to provide a space for groups and individuals to fully participate in the political process threatens to breed a new generation of radicals, as does the growing economic inequality in Egyptian society, the prevalence of corruption and a police and security apparatus that acts as if it is beyond the law. Without further reform, there is a danger that the pendulum might swing again. Just as the 1980s and early 1990s were a period of radicalization in Egypt, the first decade of the new millennium has been one of deradicalization. Yet without a concerted effort to consolidate this, an opportunity may be missed such that the 2010s become yet another decade of reradicalization.

The next section of this chapter offers a history of extremism and deradicalization in Egypt in the form of actions taken by the Muslim Brotherhood, IG and al-Jihad. This is followed by an assessment of the deradicalization undertaken by the latter two groups from the late 1990s onwards. The role of the Egyptian state in this process is assessed and we conclude by arguing that there is an unfinished agenda in Egypt in terms of the need for rehabilitation of reformed jihadists and the need for the promotion of a more inclusive socio-economic and political system.

A history of extremism and deradicalization

The deradicalization of the Muslim Brotherhood

Egypt is credited for creating the largest, most organized and most enduring Islamic movement in the Arab World, namely, the Muslim Brotherhood (MB). The MB was initially created by Sheikh Hassan al-Bana in 1928 as an apolitical movement, seeking to protect Muslims from what the movement perceived as aligned and corrupt Western influences of Muslim society brought about mainly by the British colonization of Egypt in 1880. To do this, Sheikh al-Bana sought to restore and modernize the traditional role of the mosque as a provider of education, healthcare, forum for debates and discussion, and a place for *da'wa* (proselytizing) and worship. Sheikh al-Bana, in other words, wanted to create a Muslim society whose main activities evolve around the mosque in an attempt to isolate Muslims from what he perceived as decadent and immoral Western influences brought about by European increased political and social penetration of the region (Al-Urdun Al-Jadid Research Centre 1996).

Although the MB was created in Egypt, Sheikh al-Bana and his colleagues sought to spread their message beyond Egypt. They advocated their 'views and policies outside Egypt thorough messengers and delegates, as well as via pamphlets and magazines published by the group and mailed to a number of prominent Arab and Islamic figures' (ibid. 15). It is not surprising therefore that the Egyptian MB has influenced events beyond its place of creation, affecting almost every Islamic movement in the Arab world. This led *The Economist* (2010) to describe the MB as a 'wellspring of modern Islamism'.[1]

Despite its apolitical upbringing, numerous factors led to the radicalization of several members of the MB after the Second World War. These included the increased Zionist threat in Palestine, the inability of the then frail Egyptian 'democratic' state to undermine the influence of the British in the country whose soldiers remained encamped around the Suez Canal since 1880, the shock of the defeat in the 1948 Arab–Israeli war and increased influence of socialists and 'communists' in the late 1940s and throughout the 1950s (*The Economist* 2010). In addition, 'King Farouk's and [later] Nasser's attempt to smash the organisation' had also led to further radicalization of some members (Harrigan and El-Said 2009a: 98. Also see Richards and Waterbury 1996).

Although the MB became more radical during 1948–68, it undertook a gradual process of deradicalization from 1968 onwards, when it denounced violence and dismantled its armed wing. Unlike the IG and al-Jihad, the MB today does not subscribe to Salafi-Jihadism, nor does it reject electoral democracy.

The first attempt to renounce violence by the MB took place in 1951 when its leader (The General Guide or *Murshid*) Hassan al-Hudaybi attempted to dismantle the armed wing known as the Special Apparatus (SA).[2] Lack of strong leadership however, meant that the attempt, which lasted from 1951–4, failed and led instead to factionalization. In addition, the MB had hundreds of thousands of members coalescing around different factions whilst the SA had thousands of members who were known to the SA leadership but not to the MB leadership, both of which made deradicalization difficult. It took almost two more decades and another failed attempt by weak leadership between 1964–5, before the MB fully denounced violence against the Egyptian regime and population, delegitimized violence through several publications, including al-Hudaybi's book *Preachers not Judges*, written in 1969 (al-Hudaybi 1985) which employed both ideological and theological arguments and dismantled all of its armed units, including the SA. This deradicalization process took place between 1969–73. Since then the MB, although still a proscribed organization, has been undergoing a process of further moderation, has participated in the political process by putting forward candidates standing as independents in both state and municipal elections and has vastly expanded its network of welfare services (Harrigan and El-Said 2009a). According to Ashour:

> These conditions indicate a successful, comprehensive de-radicalisation process that took place on the behavioural, ideological and organisational levels.
>
> *(Ashour 2009: 1)*

The success of the third MB attempt to deradicalize, in contrast to the previous two attempts, seems to be due to the fact that by the end of the 1960s al-Hudabyi had consolidated his position as a strong leader.[3] The success of this attempt was also due to the fact that on the third occasion the process was not just one of behavioural and organizational deradicalization, but was also supported by ideological deradicalization in the form of the *Preachers not Judges* book. This book provided a strong ideological and theological justification from the leadership for the abandonment of violence and provided a counter-argument to Takfir and Jihadist ideologies. It was also a critique of Sayyid Qutb's *Milestones*.[4]

Another factor in the success of the third attempt was the role played by the regime and it is this which is the main interest of this chapter. State repression during the 1950s and 1960s undermined the leadership and encouraged a return to radicalism. According to Ashour (2009: 64) this prevented some of the reformist leadership from interacting with other leaders, mid-ranking commanders and the grassroots, thus denying one of the four crucial ingredients in a deradicalization process namely, interaction. In addition the first two attempts were marked by a lack of any state-led inducements (apart from 1952–4 when Nasser's regime co-opted many of the MB and SA leaders and commanders by giving them government positions). Apart from the co-option attempt, Nasser's regime seemed uninterested in the process of deradicalization. By contrast, the third attempt which commenced amongst the leadership[5] in prison following the execution of Sayyid Qutb in 1966, was bolstered by selective inducements offered by Sadat's regime in the form of what Ashour (ibid.: 86) refers to as 'the Limited Accommodation Policy' initiated in 1971. The new regime, in response to the MB's renunciation of violence, was keen to promote the Islamist movement in general to counter the influence of the Nasserists and left wing groups in society. Hence in May 1971, several key MB leaders were unconditionally released from prison and the state security apparatus, namely the State Security Investigations (SSI) began talks with other MB prisoners including those from the SA and SO. According to Ashmawy (2005) the SSI showed a degree of flexibility, abandoning their initial demand that the MB provide political loyalty and support for the regime, which the MB felt they could not do and replacing it with the demand that they publicly renounce violence. The end result was an accommodation of the MB by the regime under which the MB ideologically renounced violence and dismantled its armed wing. In return, Sadat dropped the case against the armed wings of the MB and released all MB political prisoners. The released prisoners could return to their previous employment and with some restrictions, were allowed to perform peaceful *da'wah* (proselytizing) activities whilst the MB was given a public voice through the *al-Da'wah* Magazine, which commenced publication in 1976.

al-Gama'a al-Islamiyya

The origins of Jihadism can be traced back to Egypt in the 1960s and 1970s. Young Muslims became disillusioned with the MB and its inability to stand up to the repressive Egyptian regime. Many of them, especially those who were political prisoners, started reinterpreting the writings of Sayyid Qutb in a more radical and violent manner. This resulted in the development of *Takfirism* which rejected democracy and asserted that those who participated in the democratic process were infidels. With the Soviet–Afghan war this then developed into a more international Jihadist movement both in Egypt and abroad. Indeed, according to Ashour:

> ... to a large degree Takfirism and Jihadism are the products of repressive authoritarianism in Egypt and the consecutive failures of the Egyptian regimes to accommodate political opposition in a non-violent manner since 1953. These ideologies were exported at a later stage to the rest of the Arab world.
>
> *(Ashour 2009: 10)*

The IG emerged out of these more violent ideologies in the Egyptian universities in the mid-1970s.[6] The movement developed between 1974–89 and launched a major confrontation phase with the Egyptian regime between 1989–97 before deradicalizing. The IG was strongly critical of the MB's political pragmatism and its renunciation of violence against the regime. It advocated violence as one means of achieving socio-political change, along with proselytizing activities in mosques, universities and the streets. Following the IG's involvement in the assassination of President Sadat in 1981 many of the IG members were imprisoned in a regime crackdown that marked the first years of Mubarak's rule. During this period the IG developed into a predominantly Upper Egypt group and produced a large body of literature on the jurisprudence of violence by leaders such as Nageh Ibrahim and Kamal Habib which provided an ideological and theological justification for the use of violence and military tactics against the regime. In 1988 many of the IG members who were either not imprisoned or released from prison, travelled to Afghanistan to join the fight against the Soviets where they acquired military and guerrilla training and returned to Egypt in what marked the beginning of a concerted confrontation with the regime between 1989–97.[7] This confrontation was characterized by numerous assassinations and assassination attempts, bombings, attacks on tourists and Egyptian intellectuals, prison-based torture, curfews in Upper Egypt and the arrest of around 30,000 IG members and supposed sympathizers. By the end of the 1990s both the IG and the security apparatus were exhausted by the confrontation and this helped set the scene for the deradicalization phase which commenced in earnest in 1997.

al-Jihad

al-Jihad developed from a split with the IG that occurred between 1982–3 in the Turah prison, following disagreements over leadership, ideology and tactics (Ashour 2009: 46).[8] The new leaders of this smaller Jihadist group were Abbud al-Zumur and Ayman al-Zawhiri. The new group, who predominantly came from Lower Egypt, rejected the leader of the IG and advocated violence alone as the main route to achieving socio-political change. The main contrast between the IG and the new al-Jihad organization was that the former was largely Upper Egypt based and promoted change from below via proselytizing as well as via violence whilst the latter was mainly Lower Egypt based and was a secret society (a network of clandestine cells), which advocated change from above via covert military action rather than through public activism. Post-1984 al-Jihad became known as a distinct radical group with its own leadership and structure that had absorbed a number of cadres and leaders from other clandestine cells. It had branches in both Upper and Lower Egypt and multiple cells in Egypt's urban centres (Gunaratna and Bin Ali 2009: 282). In 1987 the leadership, including al-Zawhiri and Sayyid al-Sharif, moved to Afghanistan to escape the repression of the Mubarak regime and to train largely Egyptian recruits in military tactics. They were part of a small group of individuals who were established within al-Qaeda in 1988 and used recruits who often returned to Egypt to carry out terrorist activities.[9] Blaydes and Rubin (2008: 467) claim that during the insurgency of 1992–7, 90 per cent of attacks were carried out by the IG, but that al-Jihad had played a role in the insurgency and was involved in some important operations.

Following a brief sojourn in Sudan, which started in 1989, the leadership of Al-Jihad returned to Afghanistan in 1996. During the second phase in Afghanistan, al-Zawhiri started to develop close links with Osama Bin Laden and a split emerged in al-Jihad over whether it should adopt the Bin Laden tactics of concentrating on the external enemy such as the USA and Israel or continue to focus its struggle against the Egyptian regime. Al-Zawhiri opted for the former and continued to lead a faction of al-Jihad which merged with al-Qaeda, eventually becoming the second in command to Bin Laden and one of the most wanted terrorists in the world. According to Ashour (2009: 55–6) by the 2000s al-Jihad had split into four main factions. The largest group was that of the 2,000–3,000 militants in Egyptian prisons led by the old generation of leaders responsible for and imprisoned for the assassination of Sadat. The second faction was loyal to al-Zawhiri and joined al-Qaeda. The third group was led by those outside Egypt who opposed al-Zawhiri's internationalization of the group. The fourth and smallest faction consisted of al-Jihad leaders who disappeared after 9/11 and re-emerged in Egyptian prisons at a later date, most notably Sayyid Imam al-Sahrif who was eventually to lead the al-Jihad deradicalization process.

The deradicalization of the IG and al-Jihad

Although Egypt has a long history of deradicalization going back to the MB in the 1960s, the deradicalization of the IG and al-Jihad were qualitatively different from that of the MB, in that the former two organizations were much more violent Jihadist-based groups which rejected democracy and were based on a more puritanical and fundamentalist interpretation of Islam. Both groups wanted an Islamic state ruled according to Islamic law and called for an armed confrontation against the regime, which had failed to implement Islamic law and had signed a peace agreement with Israel. Hence the task of getting the IG and al-Jihad to renounce violence was potentially much more difficult than for the MB, particularly in the case of al-Jihad whose main course of action was militancy and violence and who operated clandestinely out of only loosely related cells; compared to the IG's more public social services and proselytizing work.

The initial response of the Mubarak regime to the insurgency of the 1990s was a harsh crackdown on Islamic militants and their sympathizers. In addition to rounding up the Islamists the regime also arrested family members, including women and introduced new anti-terror legislation which included the death penalty and limited detention without charge. Numerous terrorists were executed and torture was common in prison, as were extra-judicial arrests, military tribunals, arrests without warrants and prison stays without trials. In addition, the security apparatus were successful in dismantling the financial resources of the IG. Blaydes and Rubin (2008: 467) argue that initially these harsh measures produced the opposite of what was intended and spurred the Islamists onto further violence and garnered support for them.

The IG's deradicalization

In July 1997 the IG unilaterally declared a ceasefire. The announcement was made by Muhammad al-Amin Adbul during his court case number 235 when he read a statement signed by six of the IG's leaders declaring a permanent end to violence both at home and abroad.[10] The statement was unexpected by security and other officials, commentators and even some of the IG membership itself. As stated by Karam Zohdy, one of the group's leaders interviewed in prison by the journalist Makram Mohammed Ahmed:[11]

> He announced it inside the courtroom without seeking permission to do so or arranging it with anyone and without informing the police or any officials. Everyone came to a standstill with the (announcement of the) initiative due to their sheer amazement.
>
> *(Blaydes 2004b: 6)*

The ceasefire was contrary to the group's militant literature and the violence it had been carrying out during the 1980s and 1990s. Unfortunately, the leadership in favour of the ceasefire did not have full communication with, and control over, all armed groups in the IG and despite the public announcement of the ceasefire, elements of the group were responsible for the subsequent November 1997 Luxor massacre in which nearly 60 tourists were killed. This led to suspicion and doubts about the genuineness of the ceasefire both amongst the general public and the security forces. It was to take another five years before the IG's deradicalization process was consolidated.

Following the ceasefire declaration, leaders of the IG worked to complete and complement this behavioural deradicalization with ideological and organizational deradicalization. By March 1999 a consensus was reached amongst all IG leaders both at home and abroad to support what had become known in the media as the 'Initiative for Ceasing Violence' (ICV). To quote Karam Zohdy, the Luxor incident was a 'stab in the back' for the IG and the:

> … initiative was buried and not accepted at this time and it was said publicly (the *Gama'a* espoused) dialogue but secretly (they espoused) killing. The initiative continued to be moribund until 1999 when Doctor 'Amr Adbul Rahman[12] announced that he supported what the brothers in prison had announced on the issue of the initiative, then the brothers on the *Gama'a's shura* council abroad announced their support for the initiative. Thus the leadership of the *Gama'a* began to be represented by a single group backing the initiative and interaction began …
>
> *(Blaydes 2004b: 6)*

Following the consensus of 1999, the leadership in Egyptian prisons started work on a series of writings that were to become known as the *Muraja'at* (Revisions). This involved countering their previous ideology contained in earlier works such as *Mithaq Al-Amal Al-Islami* (The Charter of Islamic Action) which had been published in the early 1980s as well as countering other work which had been centred around *fiqh a-'unf* (Islamic jurisprudence justifying violence). Blaydes and Rubin refer to this aspect of the deradicalization process as ideological reorientation:

> We define ideological reorientation as a counterterrorism approach that seeks to change core ideological or religious beliefs of the terrorist group, thus bringing the beliefs of the group members in line with societal norms.
>
> *(Blaydes and Rubin 2008: 462)*

The events of 9/11, for which the IG felt partly responsible, spurred them on and made the Egyptian authorities take their initiative more seriously. By 2002 members of the IG's *Shura* (Council) had published a number of books which, contrary to their earlier works, produced an ideological and theological justification for a renunciation of violence and an end to their armed attempt to overthrow the Egyptian regime. Four books, authored by members of the *Shura* were issued in January 2002 as the *Tashih al-Mafahim* (Correcting Conceptions Series, Hafiz and Majid 2002). These provided both ideological and pragmatic reasons for abandoning violence and argued that it was wrong to kill civilians, tourists and security officers, denounced the practice of Takfir (excommunication of Muslims) and declared it wrong to wage Jihad against a Muslim ruler who does not apply *sharia* law.[13] The pragmatic stance argued that Islam had been harmed by Jihad with imprisonments, torture, a cutting off of financial resources and growing unpopularity of the IG amongst the Egyptian public, especially after the Luxor massacre which scared off tourists and harmed the income generation of many ordinary Egyptians. The fact that Islam had been harmed by Jihad was put forward as a reason why Jihad is Islamically forbidden in this case (Abdul Rahman *et al.* 2002: 66).[14] To quote Karam Zohdy in a prison interview with the journalist Makram Mohammed Ahmed:

> So, I do not rely in all of my arguments on legal justifications only, because I talk to unconvinced individuals not persuaded by this legal perspective. For that reason, I make them understand that even from a practical perspective they will not be able to revolt.
>
> *(Blaydes 2004a: 4)*

And 'Ali al-Sharif in the same interview:

> They did not reap anything from their fighting except threatening evil and this was an injustice to (the idea of) jihad. It is incumbent on people to understand that as long as the result of fighting is bad and the yield is evil, we cannot describe this fighting as legitimate. Rather, it is legally prohibited since Islam never brings evil.
>
> *(Blaydes 2004b: 9)*

This pragmatic approach and a reappraisal of the means to an end also appeared in much of the IG's revisionist literature:

> Jihad is neither the goal nor the intent. Jihad is the way to raise the banner of religion and god's word. And if Jihad can't achieve this, it is forbidden.
>
> *(Hafiz and Majid 2002: 45)*

The above books were followed by a number of others which provided an ideological and theological critique of al-Qaeda's ideology and strategy (Zohdy *et al.* 2002; Zohdy *et al.* 2003a) and a critique of the clash of civilizations, arguing instead for dialogue. In all, the IG leadership has produced around 25 volumes of work providing the basis of their ideological deradicalization.[15] Many of these works were first presented to scholars at al-Azhar[16] for approval. According to Ashour:

> The IG is the first, former Salafi-Jihadist movement which produced ideological literature that de-legitimised violence.
>
> *(Ashour 2009: 31)*

To quote one Egyptian diplomat:

> The way to deprive them of their ability to recruit is to attack the message. If you take Islam out of the message all that is left is criminality.
>
> (Guardian *2007)*

Ashour (2010) refers to this body of literature as ushering in a 'post-Jihadist era'. He argues that the new literature involves an inference shift:

> The theological arguments of Jihadism rest on the idea that literal orders from God supersede any rational calculations or material interest. This usually translates into an impetus to engage in armed confrontations against much stronger powers. In post-Jihadist literature, there is a shift to the idea that interests determine the interpretation of the text. If a confrontation, or any other behaviour, is likely to lead to negative consequences, it must be forbidden and should be avoided.
>
> *(ibid.: 1)*

The post-Jihadist era is defined as follows:

> On the ideological level, post-Jihadism involves de-legitimisation and discouragement of political violence in general as well as upholding theologically sanctioned pragmatism. On the behavioural level, it criticises Islamists who still engage in violence … , and on the organisational level, it aims to disband armed wings and secret units.
>
> *(ibid.: 2)*

One of the most important and difficult inference shifts that both the IG and al-Jihad had to make was on their previously uncompromising view that they should establish a *sharia* state. According to Gunaratna and Bin Ali:

> Their new argument was that "even if the ruler does not apply a law or laws from the Islamic *sharia,* he is not considered an infidel as long as he does not hold a position that his man-made rulings are better than the rulings of Allah". Thus, according to the new approach, there are extenuating circumstances for tolerating a ruler even if he refrains from applying *Sharia* law.
>
> *(Gunaratna and Bin Ali 2009: 284)*

In addition to its books, the IG has also issued several fatwas banning the use of violence and condemning the violence of other groups such as al-Qaeda. Some of its leaders also addressed the leadership of al-Qaeda including Osama Bin Laden and al-Zawhiri asking them to desist from violence (al-Anani 2009). Apologies have been issued for past terrorist attacks in Egypt that led to the killing of innocent civilians, tourists and government officials, even describing some of these deaths as martyrs.

Although renouncing violence the IG clearly stated that it wanted to remain as a political grouping seeking socio-political change and yet it continued to view democracy as Islamically illegitimate (Ashour 2009). The group's leader Karam Zohdy has argued, however, that the position on democracy may change in the future and that they may attempt to form a political party. In addition, some former IG members participated in the 2005 parliamentary elections.

The IG's leadership followed up their production of literature with a tour of prisons to convince the rank and file to abandon violence whilst also dismantling the armed wing of the organization. The latter process was relatively easy due to the fact that the armed wing only contained around 800–900 members, all of whom were known to, and controlled by, the leadership – this contrasts with the earlier difficulties experienced by the MB in dismantling the SO which had thousands of loosely controlled members.

Why was the 1997–2002 IG deradicalization process a success?

Ashour states that before the 1997 ceasefire there were at least 14 attempts to halt the violence between the IG and the State (Ashour 2009: 91). A pertinent question is why these earlier attempts failed whilst the 1997–2002 process was a success. Answering this question will help to identify the conditions that are necessary for the successful deradicalization of a Jihadist group and may well have some important policy implications for regimes that wish to encourage such a process by groups operating within their borders.

Earlier attempts to end the violence include possible efforts by Al-Azhar scholars to convince the IG leadership that violence is not sanctioned by Islam (on the disputed role of Al-Azhar see below); attempts by security officials to make the IG cease violence against tourists and ad hoc statements by individual IG leaders to renounce violence. One of the most publicised efforts was the so-called 'Committee of Mediation'.

The Committee was formed in 1993 and was led by two important Sheikhs, Muhammad al-Sha'rawy from Al-Azhar, a popular scholar who had a TV show and was a former Minister of Endowments and Mohammed Ghazali from Al-Azhar. Its membership was mainly drawn from moderate Muslims, including members of the MB, lawyers and intellectuals. Although the initiative seemed to emanate from the Sheikhs, it was supported by the then Minister of the Interior General Abdul Halim Abu Musa. The Committee of Mediation was met with a list of demands from the IG leadership, which included: releasing all detainees who were held without charge; improving prison conditions; ending the policy of renewing detention indefinitely; releasing female hostages who were taken to make their male family members surrender; ending torture and re-opening IG mosques.

The Committee of Mediation, along with other earlier attempts, ended in failure for several reasons. Firstly, the Al-Azhar scholars and the moderate Sheikhs did not have legitimacy amongst the members of the IG. They were seen as regime sympathizers and in some instances, agents of the state (Al-Azhar for example was seen to be closely allied with the Mubarak regime). Secondly, the IG leadership prior to 1999 were not united in their call for the cessation of violence. These reasons point to a number of important lessons. Firstly, genuine ideological delegitimization of violence cannot be imposed from, or initiated, outside the group, especially not by agents that are seen to be closely allied with the state or regime that the group is in conflict with. This does not mean that the state cannot help facilitate the process once it is underway or offer selective inducements to move the process forward, as shown below. Secondly, there must be strong leadership and a consensus amongst this leadership to end violence. Again, in terms of policy implications, there is much that the state can do to facilitate consensus by allowing the imprisoned leadership to interact. Indeed an important lesson is that rather than executing the leadership of a Jihadist group, as was done in Bangladesh, which can lead to group fragmentation and lack of strong leadership, imprisonment and proper interaction may well facilitate the process of deradicalization. An imprisoned historical leadership often gains legitimacy from the role it has played in the previous struggle against the regime, the hardship it has faced in prison and the fact that it has not been co-opted by the state. Indeed, Ashour concludes his study of deradicalization in both Egypt and Algeria with the statement that:

> The charismatic leadership of an armed Islamic organisation seems to be the decisive factor in the success or failure of any de-radicalisation process.
>
> *(Ashour 2009: 138)*

A third lesson is that behavioural deradicalization i.e. the verbal renunciation of violence by leaders may not be enough. Given that Jihadism is rooted in a strong literature giving a theological and ideological justification for using violence, this needs to be countered by an equally strong and persuasive literature that delegitimizes violence, which the earlier attempts at IG deradicalization lacked.

Another important lesson that can be learnt from the failure of the Committee of Mediation is that a consensus in society, the media and the regime in support of the deradicalization process needs to develop. Such a consensus was not present in 1993. The state-dominated media, as well as the left wing and secular media, strongly criticized the Committee of Mediation as well as the regime for negotiating with terrorists. The fact that the IG was allowed to issue the above list of demands reinforced this view. In addition, although the Minister of the Interior supported the initiative, it did not have the full backing of the regime and in response to the media outcry, Mubarak sacked this Minister. By contrast, although the 1997 ceasefire was initially treated with scepticism by many politicians, writers, intellectuals and the media, with very few people really believing that the IG would cease violence, the subsequent publication of revisionist literature, interviews with the leadership and state TV discussion programmes on the deradicalization process gradually helped build belief and support for the process amongst the wider public. This clearly shows that any deradicalization process is many sided and requires coalition and consensus building. Again, there is much that the state can do to help create such a consensus. This includes providing outlets to publicize a Jihadist group's new ideology and harnessing the media to support the effort – unlike 1993 (as discussed below). The lesson here is that deradicalization should not just be seen as a state policy or programme but a coalition effort involving civil society, the media, the state, the religious authorities and the radical group.

Timing is also critical. At the time of the 1993 Committee of Mediation, society and the regime clearly were not ready to accept a deradicalization process. By contrast, the 1997 Luxor attack and 9/11 were both events that shocked the public and the regime and made both more willing to consider seriously supporting and facilitating a deradicalization process. According to Muntasir al-Zayat, the lawyer who acted as a spokesperson for the IG ceasefire initiative, the language of both the IG and the government changed after the Luxor attack. The IG leadership strongly condemned the attack and the Minister of the Interior, Habib el-Adhy, told the government that they should trust the announcements of the IG (Personal interview, Cairo January 2010). Indeed the new Minister of the Interior represented a change after Luxor and was very good at advocating dialogue, and strongly believed that the regime should take full advantage of the IG initiative. According to the deputy IG leader Nageh Ibrahim:

> The event made us feel the extent of the importance of interfering forcefully and the necessity of resolving these problems.
>
> *(Blaydes 2004a: 23)*

The IG's strong denunciation of the 9/11 attack also helped shape public opinion. Likewise, according to Makram Mohammed Ahmed, by the late 1990s both the IG and the authorities were exhausted by the armed struggle and hence both were willing to negotiate (Personal interview, Cairo January 2010). To quote the IG leader Nageh Ibrahim:

> It is enough that I can say we have grown tired until we can stop the violence and the confrontation.
>
> *(Blaydes 2004b: 19)*

The IG also found a waning of public support after the brutalities of the Luxor attack (al-Hashimi and Goerzig 2007: 11).

In terms of timing, Makram Mohammed Ahmed argues that the state would have been wrong to have engaged in mediation in 1993 before the IG had ideologically deradicalized and changed their views since this would have been a compromise which would have legitimized the IG's still violent philosophy. In addition, unlike the 1980s and early 1990s when the IG issued demands in return for a possible ceasefire,[17] the 1997 ceasefire announced in court came with no strings attached. To quote Karam Zohdy and Nageh Ibrahim:

> ... we announced in it that we do not require conditions or make requirements but we want an end of military operations within the country and outside of it.
>
> *(Blaydes 2004b: 6)*

> This initiative does not seek reward and is not scared of anyone and not desiring anything and not afraid of anything ... Even in the basic statement of the initiative we did not ask for anything and we did not desire compensation ... we stopped issuing statements encouraging militant operations without qualification or condition and from a single side. Therefore, the statement of the initiative enjoyed the favour of a great deal of sincerity because we did not want one thing. We said that if we had achieved the stopping of bloodshed alone, it would have been enough. Thus it was not merely a bargain with the government.
>
> *(Blaydes 2004b: 21–2)*

Zohdy also acknowledges that attempts at deradicalization had been initiated in the early 1980s but that it took a series of critical events before this became serious:

> We were not late in attempting to reach a compromise (in fact these attempts) to reach a compromise have been going on since the 1980s. Thus, the initiative was not born on July 1997. Rather, the true initiative began in the beginning of the 1980s when we were trying to find a solution to this problem. Then things became serious and events escalated. We made a major effort and gathered the Islamic thinkers and searched widely in an attempt to find a correct Islamic legal solution for the situation we were in.
>
> *(Blaydes 2004b: 18)*

If we discount the earlier ad hoc and unsuccessful attempts, then it can be argued that the consolidated phase of the IG's deradicalization lasted only five years – 1997–2002, and was much quicker than that of the MB. Ashour (2009) attributes this to his four factors:

i) A strong leadership, with leaders abroad (mainly in Afghanistan) owing allegiance to the historical leadership in Egyptian prisons and a loyal following amongst the rank and file who considered obedience to their leaders as an almost religious duty;
ii) The effects of successful repression by the regime during the early 1990s that encouraged the leaders to pragmatically reappraise the effectiveness of violence;

iii) Interactions both with those external to the group, i.e. between the imprisoned IG leadership and imprisoned liberal intellectuals such as the human rights activist Saad Ibrahim, and within the group such as between the imprisoned leadership and the imprisoned rank and file;
iv) Selective inducements from the state such as better prison conditions.

Although state repression in the form of torture and harsh prison conditions cannot be recommended as a policy action to bring about deradicalization, the latter two variables, namely, interaction and inducements can be the focus of state policies and these will be discussed in more detail later in this chapter.

The role of consensus amongst the leadership and the obedience of the rank and file was stressed many times in Makram Mohammed Ahmed's prison interviews with IG leaders. According to one leader, Nageh Ibrahim:

> *Al-Gama'a al-Islamiyya* is distinct from other groups in that it is quasi-organised and that a very good deal of consultation takes place within it. We always consult with one another and with our rank and file who exchange opinions within us. We adopt an opinion based on *shura* and not in haste. The *Gama'a* is also distinguished by the high level of obedience found in it and the *Gama'a* trusts in its leadership as the leaders trust in the individual members and a mutual connectedness is found. If not for this connection then all of the base would not have accepted this new thought and the initiative would not gain the acceptance of everyone.
>
> *(Blaydes 2004a: 15)*

Another factor contributing to the success of the 1997–2002 deradicalization process according to one commentator on the process was the personal maturation of the leadership whilst in prison (Diaa Rashwan personal interview, Cairo January 2010). The leadership had formed the IG movement whilst they were still in their early twenties. Most came from modern universities and were studying subjects such as medicine and engineering not theology, and had little experience or knowledge of theological texts. Their radicalism came via contact with other radicals in the university environment not from an in-depth study of religious texts, and they had little time to think through their radical ideas. This changed, however, whilst they were in prison. They had time to read from various schools of Islam and to rethink their old ideas through a systematic Islamic logic. This is reflected in their revisionist body of literature, which contains many references to different strands of Islam and even liberal thought, unlike their earlier Jihadist works. One foreign diplomat in Cairo has drawn a lesson from this:

> The authorities eventually came to treat the prisoners as intellectuals not criminals and gave them the space to study.
>
> *(Personal interview, Cairo January 2010)*

The deradicalization of al-Jihad

The deradicalization of al-Jihad, Egypt's second largest Jihadist group, started in 2007 when it was announced that Dr Sayyid Imam al-Sharif (also known as Dr Fadl), the former leader of the group between 1987–93 and one of the group's leading ideologues was back in an Egyptian jail. Both al-Jihad and al-Sharif had close connections to al-Qaeda,[18] but in March 2007 the *al-Hayat* newspaper announced that al-Sharif and other leaders in prison were initiating a deradicalization process. By April, several of the al-Jihad leaders both in Egyptian prisons and abroad announced their support for the initiative and in November 2007 al-Sharif released a 111-page book entitled *Document for Guiding Jihad in Egypt and the World* (al-Sharif 2007). This book rejects his own highly influential Jihadist manifestoes from 1988. According to al-Anani the document was drafted in 2006 and discussed with imprisoned al-Jihad leaders, most of whom signed the document as well as being given to the Islamic Research Academy at al-Azhar for approval before it was published (al-Anani 2009: 3). This was followed a year later with the book *Unveiling al-Zawhiri's Deceptions* (al-Sharif 2008). As with the recent literature from the IG, this document provided an ideological and theological rationale for abandoning violence and Jihad and provided a strong critique of al-Qaeda's ideology and strategy. Again, mirroring the IG process, al-Sharif and other al-Jihad leaders toured Egyptian prisons between February and April 2007 to convince their followers to support the deradicalization process.

Although the al-Jihad process started in earnest in 2007 the group had been attempting deradicalization since 1997 when one of its leaders, Abbud al-Zumur, announced that he supported the IG's 1997 ceasefire initiative, whilst other leaders had sporadically announced that they wanted an end to violence. These earlier attempts failed largely due to the structure of al-Jihad, which contrasted to that of the IG. Although smaller, the former was less organized than IG and composed of multiple loosely related cells each with its own commander and taking different stances on deradicalization and offering allegiance to different factional leaders. Al-Jihad was also a secret society that focused only on covert action. Ashour also argues that the failure to provide theological/ideological literature by a leadership that lacked training in Islamic jurisprudence contributed to the earlier disappointing attempts to deradicalize by al-Jihad (Ashour 2009: 103). Success in 2007 might also be due to the demonstration effect from the IG process of deradicalization and according to one of the IG leaders, Karam Zohdy, IG leaders met with al-Jihad members in prison to discuss the deradicalization process (Blaydes 2004a: 20).

According to Ashour (2009), it was the re-emergence of the charismatic ideologue al-Sharif as leader of the deradicalization process that was a crucial element to its success in 2007. Unlike the IG, al-Jihad has not fully deradicalized at the organizational level, in that two factions based in Egyptian prisons[19] still oppose the process and one faction abroad, led by Zawhiri and in close alliance with al-Qaeda, also opposed and harshly criticized it, with al-Zawhiri writing *The Vindication* (al-Zawhiri, no date). These factions are refusing to dismantle armed wings. Despite the lack of full-scale deradicalization by al-Jihad, a number of smaller Jihadist groups have been influenced by the process in a domino like effect, attending the prison lectures given by al-Sharif and issuing statements to denounce violence. For example, the leader of the Takfir group Survivors from Hell issued a statement in support of al-Sharif's stance (Ashour 2009).

Despite the fact that al-Jihad has not fully deradicalized in an operational sense, al-Anani argues that:

> Sayyid Imam al-Sharif's reassessment was extremely important – more so than similar initiatives undertaken by al-Gama'a and by other groups in Egypt, Algeria, Saudi Arabia and Libya – for three interrelated reasons. First, al-Sharif's biography places him at the centre of Jihadi activity in the 1980s and 1990s … Second, al-Sharif was widely known as the most significant ideologue and legal philosopher of international Jihad, and his two major works had a substantial impact on young Jihadis in Afghanistan … Finally, al-Sharif is significant due to the evolution of his revisionist thought.
>
> *(al-Anani 2009: 3)*

As with the IG, al-Sharif's revision was a combination of a reinterpretation of Islamic texts and pragmatic rejection of violence to obtain political ends.[20]

The role of the Egyptian state in the deradicalization process

Analysis of documentation and commentary on the IG and al-Jihad's deradicalization process, as well as interviews with key players indicates a degree of ambiguity regarding the role played by the authorities in the process. Some argue, as al-Hashimi and Goerzig (2007) do in their paper *Change through debate – Egypt's counterterrorism strategy towards the Gama'a Islamiyya* and Blaydes and Rubin (2008) that the authorities adopted a 'two pronged' approach combining force with deradicalization, that the authorities had a clear and well developed strategy or a programme towards deradicalization. Likewise, Khatab (2009) argues that to contain radicalism the authorities adopted a strategy sponsored by the Egyptian state that dealt with the ideology, ideas and behaviour inside and outside detentions. The *Guardian* (27 July 2007) states that the Egyptian government's 'deradicalization programme' has successfully converted the IG which was once the largest Jihadist group in the Arab world and Gunaratna and Bin Ali (2009) make a similar argument. Others (personal interviews, Cairo January 2010) suggest that the leadership of the IG initiated the process unilaterally, and that the authorities simply reacted to this by offering facilitation of the process and provision of logistics, often in a delayed manner.

One area where there is particular controversy is whether or not the state sent religious leaders from both Al-Azhar and the MB to convince the leadership of the IG to review their stance on Jihad and violence, prior to and after the 1997 ceasefire announcement. According to Ahmad (2002: 6) al-Ahzar scholars have tried to influence the IG leaders on several occasions both inside and outside prisons. Likewise, Khatab (2009: 48) argues that the authorities created special entities of experts to teach and preach to the inmates, and to produce and foster counter-radicalization publications, movies, special TV series and programmes that dealt with radical ideas both inside and outside prison. Khatab also argues that the authorities left copies of anti-radicalization publications for inmates to read and made the works look old, as if well read, and periodically pretended to confiscate them. Blaydes and Rubin (2008: 469) argue that one commentator reported to them that the regime used MB members as intermediaries to persuade IG members to change their views. In return the government cut a deal with the MB that in exchange for convincing the IG of this new ideological stance, the MB would be permitted to operate politically and in civil society.

Other evidence, however, including information from key informant interviewees (Cairo January 2010) strongly deny that either al-Azhar scholars or MB members were initially sent into prisons and stress the unilateral nature of the declaration of ceasefire. IG leaders have pointed out that if the change of heart was due to persuasive actions initiated by the regime in prisons, then this would not explain why the leadership abroad also agreed to the deradicalization process. Stracke (2007) concurs; the deradicalization process within the IG and Al-Jihad, she argues, was a spontaneous, internally generated course of action, it 'was initiated by prisoners themselves' and was not the result of a thorough or well-planned deradicalization process planned and implemented by the state. In fact, Hosni Mubarak remained sceptical of any deradicalization and recantations until his very last day in office in early 2011. Mubarak once described early recantations by members of the MB, IG and Al-Jihad as feign repentances: 'They say they have renounced violence, but, in reality, they are responsible for all of this violence, and the time will come when they will be uncovered' (Quoted in Weaver 1995). Even after 1997, high ranked state officials remained 'initially sceptical of the prisoner's apparent repentance, which looked [for state officials] like a ploy for better treatment' (Wright 2008).

In fact, deradicalization would have started long before 1997 had the Egyptian state taken it seriously, believed in its sincerity and supported it. Not only were high-ranked state officials suspicious of the deradicalization process, but they also tried to sabotage it and prevent it from occurring before 1997. It was the attempt by Abdel Harith Madani[21] 'to broker a ceasefire between the two sides' (Islamists and state) that led to his arrest and torture to death on 26 April 1994 by Mubarak's security forces (Weaver 1995).

Even if one wants to assume that the Egyptian state did send religious leaders from both Al-Azhar and other institutions to convince the leadership of the IG and Al-Jihad to review their stance on violence prior to 1997, it is highly unlikely that that would have yielded any positive results. The al-Azhar had little credibility among Islamist militants. As the spiritual mentor of the IG, Sheikh Omar Abdel-Rahman, stated:

> You know, if al-Azhar had not neglected its duty, had it not become only a mouthpiece of the government, had it implemented Islamic Sharia law, you would not see any Islamic groups, like Gama'a, working as they are now. They wouldn't even exist, for it was only after al-Azhar forfeited its historical role that all these groups began popping up to fill the void. Every Islamic group working in Egypt now is trying to fill a vacuum created by al-Azhar.
>
> *(Quoted in Weaver 1995)*

It was not before a new Grand Mufti, Ali Gomaa, was appointed in 2003 that the Mufti himself began openly 'champion[ing] moderate Islam' through, among other things, 'his own television show and occasional columns in *Al-Ahram*' (Wright 2008). Al-Azhar's credibility was also undermined by its role to 'censor books that touch on religion', which confirmed its status as the regime's mouthpiece. And it was only 'recently [that Al-Azhar] launched the Azhari TV, a satellite channel promoting centrist, moderate Islam in a bid to stop the encroachment of Saudi-inspired fundamentalism' (All quotations from *The Economist* 2010).

However, although it seems that the state was not pro-active, it did play a facilitating role in the deradicalization process. For example, Egyptian security officers undertook a process of dialogue with both the IG and al-Jihad leaders prior to their successful deradicalization initiatives, but as argued above, the timing of these earlier efforts was not favourable to a successful outcome for various reasons. In addition, it is clear that the authorities gave the prisoners space to study theology, often for degrees, and ensured study material such as books and other religious texts were freely available. This included seminal Islamic texts and standard reference books on Islamic jurisprudence and interpretation. They also provided students with time and space for discussion amongst themselves. According to the IG leader Karam Zohdy, the group came to change their stance whilst in prison as a result of:

> … drawing on authoritative legal texts which we read during those years. You know that prison is a good place for reading and debate and ideological rethinking.
>
> *(Blaydes 2004a: 5)*

Also, regardless of whether we see the state's role as consisting of a well-defined pro-active strategy, or more one of opportunistic response to a process essentially initiated from within the Jihadist groups themselves, it is clear that the state had an important role to play in facilitating the process once it was underway. Indeed, of Ashour's four causal variables, two, namely selective inducements from the state and interaction with those both within and outside the group, show that the state has a potentially important role to play in any successful deradicalization process.

In Egypt, the Ministry of the Interior and state security allowed interaction within the group and this was crucial to the process. Not only were the IG and al-Jihad leaders allowed to interact in prison to discuss and form a consensus on the deradicalization process, but these leaders were also allowed to interact with mid-ranking commanders and the rank and file to convince them to support the process. People were moved between prisons to help spread the new IG ideology and those that did not support it were isolated. In the case of the IG, the imprisoned leaders were allowed to tour all the prisons holding intensive workshops, lectures and discussions for a period of ten months in 2002 and even before, whilst for al-Jihad the same process was permitted and encouraged between February and April 2007 (Wright 2008; Stracke 2007). According to an IG leader, all prisons were covered in the tour except the prison at Demnhour. Ashour has described this process as follows:

> Those tours and meetings aimed to illustrate the meaning of the ICV, to explain the new ideological perspectives, and then to address the questions, comments and critiques of the members. The historical leaders would first hold meetings with the second-in-line commanders to illustrate the general guidelines of the ICV and the new ideology. Then, there would be a "general assembly" where all the members would attend and meet with the historical leaders. The leaders would start with a discussion of the four new books, followed by an extended Q&A period. Afterwards, the leaders would meet with the members in their cells and in prison corridors to discuss the transformations directly in small groups.
>
> *(Ashour 2009: 98)*

Karam Zohdy also states that at the end of each prison tour the prisoners threw a party for the leaders and a document was produced expressing not only love for the leaders but 'satisfaction with the initiative'.

In the case of the IG, this was a massive task with the number of IG prisoners estimated to be between 15,000 and 30,000. The official prison tours of 2002 were the final stage in a much longer process that had lasted from 1997–2002 during which leaders had been debating with their followers in prisons across Egypt. Undoubtedly, however, the facilitation of the prison tour in 2002 by the authorities was a major factor in the success of the ceasefire and this has been acknowledged by the IG leadership itself (Zohdy *et al.* 2003b: 25), who pointed out that many of the mid-ranking commanders, and much of the grass roots following, had not initially supported the ICV. In convincing their followers to accept the ceasefire, the IG leaders stressed their own sacrifices in the previous struggle, including their long imprisonment and, in some cases, their impending death sentences. This gave them legitimacy in the eyes of their followers. To the general public they stressed, particularly in their interviews with Makram Mohammed Ahmed, that their revisionism was a genuine change of heart rather than a strategic calculation.

In February 2007, a similar styled three-month prison tour was arranged by the authorities for al-Sharif and other al-Jihad leaders to convince the imprisoned al-Jihad members to support al-Sharif's initiative. This was deliberately modelled on the successful IG prison tour and IG leaders such as Karam Zohdy and Dr Nageh Ibrahim accompanied al-Sharif on some of his tours to share their experience and encourage the process. Earlier meetings between the IG leadership and members of al-Jihad in prison may also have had a domino-like effect in helping to convince the al-Jihad group to adopt a similar deradicalization process. In addition to the prison tour, a conference was held in Fayyum prison during which al-Sharif's document was presented to hundreds of al-Jihad members and received their support.

Evidence also suggests that the authorities allowed imprisoned Jihadist leaders to interact with those from outside their own group. The imprisoned human rights activist Dr Saad Eddine Ibrahim (Ashour 2009) described how Jihadist prisoners were allowed to interact with him and other detained secular liberals and debated Islam, democracy and human rights. Ashour (ibid.: 97) argues that the influence of this can be seen in some of the modernist and post-modernist ideas contained within the IG's revisionist literature.

The IG had the task not just of convincing its members to abandon violence but to persuade the Egyptian public and the international community that they were indeed sincere in their revisionism. To facilitate this, the authorities allowed the IG to establish an official website where they placed much of their new literature as well as allowing some IG leaders to be interviewed on state television and satellite networks like *al-Jazeera* and *al-'Arabiya*. In addition, Makram Mohammed Ahmed, a well-respected journalist who had credibility for frank reporting, partly due to the earlier assassination attempt on his life by the group Salvation from Hell, was asked by the regime to report on the IG deradicalization process. This he did through a series of interviews with IG leaders in the Scorpion prison and through observing the meetings between four IG leaders and over 500 IG members in the Wadi al-Natroun prison. The interviews and observations were published in June 2002 in four issues of the magazine *al-Mussawar*.[22] Makram claims that his experience with the IG in prison convinced him that their deradicalization was genuine and his magazine articles generated strong feedback. In response to some feedback that questioned the genuineness of the conversion, he wrote a piece saying he was deeply convinced (Personal interview, Cairo January 2010). He also accompanied leaders on some of their prison tours to convince the rank and file. In his reporting he states that very often the rank and file themselves questioned the genuineness of their leaders' conversions and that each time the leadership was successfully able to persuade them that it was not a temporary tactical or strategic move, but a genuine and permanent conversion of beliefs. Al-Jihad was afforded similar assistance and al-Sharif's 'Revisions' books were serialized in the Egyptian paper *al-Misri al-Youm* and in London-based Arab dailies *al-Sharq al-Awsat* and *al-Hayat* as well as in Kuwaiti newspaper *al-Jarida*. The work was also placed on the official website of the MB (www.ikhwanonline.com) and Al-Jihad leaders were interviewed on Egyptian television.

The interviews published in *al-Mussawar* magazine were particularly helpful in convincing the public that the IG's change of heart was genuine. Quotes from the IG members and leaders such as the following were persuasive:

> Everybody was right to marvel at a person wearing a red outfit (those condemned to death row) and nevertheless to embrace new thinking, and there is a question of what a red outfit wearer gets out of adopting this thought despite the fact that he will not be released from prison to society.
>
> *(Blaydes 2004a: 14)*

Commenting on Karam Zohdy, Makram states that:

> I think that he was sincere when he said "we did not ask anyone for permission in this initiative and we do not lay down a single condition, and we do not demand anything from the state, and our goal and our intention was God's approval after a comprehensive review of the provisions of *sharia* and a

> complete study of the practical considerations of national welfare which emphasised the necessity of change of the thought of *Gama'a* and its programmes".
>
> *(Blaydes 2004b: 2)*

Although the authorities gave support to the IG's and al-Jihad's deradicalization process by facilitating interaction and providing selective inducements, the response seemed somewhat slow. According to Ashour:

> The Mubarak regime initially responded to the transformations with several negative signals including apathy, rejection, hesitation and suspicion.
>
> *(Ashour 2009: 31)*

According to one imprisoned IG leader:

> If the state had followed the style of discussion during the early period the problems and fighting that happened would not have happened as they did.
>
> *(Blaydes 2004a: 13)*

Karam Zohdy claims that after the Luxor incident the IG persevered with the initiative despite the initially disappointing state response:

> ... during the period in which the government was not prepared to accept the initiative we were trying to the extent that we could to communicate the initiative to all the brothers both domestically and abroad.
>
> *(Blaydes 2004a: 23)*

The delayed state response is perhaps not surprising given that pre-1997 efforts were accompanied by the IG's list of six demands and the initial ceasefire declared in 1997 was rapidly followed by the Luxor killings and due to the fact that, as argued above, in these early days the IG had not produced an ideological delegitimization of the use of violence. Nageh Ibrahim states that the Luxor incident led to state suspicion and set the initiative back by five years. After the initial suspicion, however, the state responded with a series of selective inducements. In 1998, the authorities ceased their violence and torture of imprisoned IG members and prison meals improved. By 1999–2000 prison visits, which had previously been banned, were reintroduced and visiting conditions gradually improved, including overnight stays and phone calls from relatives. Television and newspapers were provided, solitary confinement ceased, with two exceptions executions stopped and prisoners were moved to prisons closer to their homes. Brutal state actions against IG members in the community were also toned down and the image of the IG began to improve in media and political circles. The lawyer Muntasir al-Zayat was also allowed into the prisons to negotiate with the IG leadership. However, according to al-Zayat many of the improved conditions were simply normal prisoner rights as opposed to any special favours from the authorities. To quote Karam Zohdy from inside the notorious 'Scorpion' prison:

> The truth is that we cannot deny that circumstances have changed. The prison has become better in terms of its conditions and treatment has become exceedingly kind and generous despite the fact that this prison enjoyed a bad reputation. The development which occurred in it recently has changed conditions and improved circumstances of life inside completely.
>
> *(Blaydes 2004a: 29)*

Following 9/11 the authorities intensified their effort to promote the deradicalization process and to support the revisionist literature, much of which provided a critique of al-Qaeda. By 2002 the authorities had launched their full-scale effort to help the IG leaders disseminate new ideas both to their followers and the general public. Finally, in 2002 and 2003 the authorities started releasing IG prisoners, first in groups of hundreds and then thousands. Many of the historical leaders were released at the end of 2003. In April 2006, approximately 1,200 members of the IG and al-Jihad were released, including the deputy leader of the IG, Nageh Ibrahim. By April 2007, only several hundred IG members remained in prison and these were members who had been sentenced by military tribunals, state security or civilian courts and who had not yet completed their sentence (Ashour 2009: 102). Early release, however, was not an inducement offered by the state since all those released had already completed their sentences but were still being held. In the case of al-Jihad, similar state inducements were offered as well as an additional inducement of state support for court rulings that provided compensation for those detainees who had been tortured or held without charge. The IG leadership, however, are keen to point out that despite these selective inducements they did not cut a deal with the state and that the change of heart was due to genuine conviction rather than any inducements. According to the leader Nageh Ibrahim:

> We did not cut a deal. The initial announcement (was made) … regardless of whether the government gives something in exchange or not. We announced the initiative based on legitimate conviction with which we shall meet God.
>
> *(Blaydes 2004a: 17)*

According to one foreign diplomat in Cairo (Personal interview, Cairo January 2010) it is impossible to tell whether the improved prison conditions were a carrot in the sense of part of a deal, or whether they were simply a reward for a unilateral initiative.

A final area where the state has played a role in counter-radicalization, i.e. preventing people from becoming radicalized as opposed to deradicalizing those who have already adopted extreme views, was in ensuring that preaching in mosques and the curriculum in religious schools and universities remained moderate so that radical groups did not monopolize religious teaching. Those who preached in mosques were monitored and, more generally, the regime tried to mobilize civil society and refute claims that the regime was anti-Islamic. Al-Azhar scholars have been used by the regime to preach moderate Islam via the mass media, seminars and debates, and the al-Azhar education system promoted moderation from school level upwards.

In terms of the debate as to whether the Egyptian state had a clear deradicalization strategy or whether it simply responded to a unilateral initiative in an opportunistic manner, the view of one foreign diplomat in Cairo seems to offer a good conclusion:

> The truth is probably somewhere in between. The state had tried a number of methods, all of which had failed. People within the IG then started rethinking of their own accord. The state jumped on this to facilitate the process and use channels of influence. This included books, clerics, time to discuss amongst themselves and prison tours. They treated them as intellectuals not criminals and this is an important lesson. The government paid for publication of the books, although distribution was initially limited. Anything that was public knowledge about the process would have been facilitated by the government.
>
> *(Personal interview, Cairo January 2010)*

Despite the state role, the government has never given any formal official response[23] to the deradicalization initiatives of either the IG or al-Jihad and in general has done little to present the deradicalization process as a great success to the outside world. Makram Mohammed Ahmed, for example, says he has video recordings of his interviews with the imprisoned IG leadership, which provides a convincing testimony to their change of reviews and yet the authorities have so far refused to allow this to be broadcast (Personal interview, Cairo January 2010). Lack of publicity is perhaps because the state does not want to highlight its role such that, as with Bangladesh, legitimacy for the process is created by keeping the government's role covert.

An unfinished agenda

Rehabilitation and compensation

Deradicalization does not stop at the prison gates. Released prisoners who have renounced violence need to be rehabilitated into society and one notable feature of the Egyptian process is the failure to properly address this issue by the authorities. Many people interviewed in Cairo in January 2010 pointed to this weakness.

Thousands of former Jihadists have been released from Egyptian jails as a result of the deradicalization process. Their reintegration into society is very difficult, particularly in terms of finding jobs and marriage. Many suffer from very bad social conditions and some have even demanded that they be returned to jail where the conditions were better. Most of them are under the watch of security officers and in some instances, these officers help them find jobs and provide them with small stipends, but this is all very *ad hoc* and disorganized and does not consist of a comprehensive rehabilitation programme. Some commentators in Egypt, such as Diaa Rashwan (Personal interview, Cairo January 2010) have called for the formation of a fund by

Arab states to help rehabilitate former Jihadists in the region, but so far nothing has been forthcoming. General Ra'uf al-Minawy, the former spokesperson for the Ministry of the Interior, has also called for a fund to be created to assist former detainees with employment, financial assistance and psychological and medical treatment (Ashour 2009: 106). Placing the onus on the Egyptian state alone would give rise to resource problems. It is estimated that as many as 30,000 former Jihadists have been released in a country which is already suffering from high unemployment rates and government officials are worried about domestic criticism if they provide released prisoners with guaranteed jobs in the face of the general unemployment problem in the country. This is in marked contrast to countries like Saudi Arabia where the number of released prisoners is far smaller and where state resources are available to fund a comprehensive rehabilitation programme. Likewise, Western countries with deradicalization programmes that result in releases from prison have well developed social welfare programmes for society as a whole and parole systems that these people could benefit from.

The Egyptian experience is one of the few cases of deradicalization in the Muslim world in which ideological reorientation is not combined with some sort of approach aimed at improving the person's practical living conditions. This, however, may be one source of at least short-term success in that reformed Jihadists have not simply been motivated by a system of rewards and incentives such that they feign a change of views which is not genuine. Certainly, compared to Saudi Arabia and Yemen where there has been a degree of recidivism in programmes with high rewards, the Egyptian case has been much more successful in terms of lack of recidivism. In the longer term however, the failure to provide proper rehabilitation could well backfire.

It has been argued (Personal interview, Cairo January 2010) that the state deliberately ensures that the released prisoners do not find a job in order to keep them dependant on their security officer. In some instances, family members also face difficulties getting jobs in the public sector, such as in the police force or army. In addition to a compensation fund, the state could play a more proactive role in encouraging society to positively receive the released prisoners and encourage the private sector to provide them with employment. As one foreign diplomat in Cairo commentated, releasing prisoners without a comprehensive rehabilitation programme 'is like releasing 30,000 political bombs'. Certainly, the lack of a well-developed programme can increase the risk of recidivism. In addition, pull factors provided by state interventions can be an important incentive for individuals to abandon violence. Education, job training, economic support to individuals and their families, and new social networks are possible incentives to activists who may be tired of their underground life as a Jihadist.

One of the questions often asked at the group meetings between leadership and members in the prisons was whether there would be any compensation from the Egyptian regime for imprisonment without trial and/or torture. Many complaints have been filed in court for compensation. The judicial process is, however, slow with thousands of cases pending and many argue that the state is actually putting obstacles in the way of the court process (Personal interview, Cairo January 2010). Those cases that have been decided in court usually only award approximately $500 for each year held under administrative detention (the average period held under such detention is around ten years). The Ministry of the Interior, however, has still not made the majority of these pay-outs and the regime has used red tape and bureaucracy to stall on the payments. There have been far fewer cases lodged in the courts for compensation for torture and very few payouts.

Lack of socio-political reform

One foreign diplomat in Cairo (Personal interview, Cairo January 2010) has commented that the danger of radicalization or reradicalization in Egypt stems not so much from ideological and theological conviction, as from disillusionment with social and political conditions. These include an autocratic and undemocratic political structure that leaves very little room for independent political action, high levels of state corruption, growing economic and social inequality, and contacts with a police and security apparatus that acts as if it is above the law. If deradicalization is to permanently succeed in Egypt such that there is no recidivism and no new recruits to Jihadist movements these factors need urgent attention. As Ashour has argued, there is a history in the region of 'repressive autocrats breeding violent theocrats' (Ashour 2009: 89) and in the case of Egypt the Takfir and Jihadist movements grew in prisons out of opposition to repression by the state.

Recently, there have been arguments in the Egyptian press (*The Egyptian Gazette* 7 January 2010) that the MB may be moving in a new, more radical direction with younger, more radical members taking over from the moderate old guard. In the December 2009 elections to the MB Guidance Bureau, hardliners and conservatives won most of the seats at the expense of reformists and moderates.[24] Benraad and Abdelbaky (2009) have also argued that the crackdown by security forces on the MB since June 2009, in which thousands of MB members, including moderates,[25] have been arrested amid the uncertainty over Egypt's impending political succession (prior to the ousting of the Mubarak regime) and the attempt to curtail MB participation in political life, threatens the deradicalization process:

> After more than a decade of relative political moderation and successful de-radicalisation of the main Islamist groups, Cairo's policy of exclusion and persecution threatens to foment a return to radical Islamism in Egypt.
>
> *(Benraad and Abdelbaky 2009: 1)*

The failure of the former Mubarak regime to allow the MB to operate as a political party, and the 2007 constitutional amendments to Article 76 that made it much harder for MB members to run as independents in elections and for candidates to stand against Mubarak in the Presidential elections, run the risk of driving the MB and other groups, towards actions taken outside of the political system. In addition, the financial squeeze on the MB's resources has meant that the group is increasingly turning to external funding with the possibility that external funders may influence the group's ideology in a more radical direction.

It is unclear exactly what role the IG and al-Jihad want to take now that they have deradicalized. Karam Zohdy has stated that he would like the organization to provide welfare, education and social assistance within Egyptian society. Their attitude towards democracy remains ambiguous, although Abbud al-Zumur, a former al-Jihad leader has argued that members of the group should be given some political role in Egypt (Ashour 2009). His intentions to form a political party and run in the Presidential elections were thwarted by the previous Mubarak regime. In the late 1990s a number of individuals from former Jihadist groups, including the IG, attempted without success to petition the Political Parties Committee to establish political parties (Rashwan 1999). Likewise, the IG has stated that it wants a role in Egyptian society and reconciliation with the state and several former members participated in the 2005 parliamentary elections. The IG leader Karam Zohdy has stated that the official group attitude to the democratic process could change in favour of participation based on pragmatic considerations (Ashour 2009). An important way of furthering the deradicalization process towards political moderation is to ensure that groups like the MB, IG and al-Jihad are given a legitimate role to play in society and politics. The former Mubarak regime in its dying years did little in this respect and it remains to be seen, following the downfall of Mubarak in the Arab Spring of 2011, how the future political powers in Egypt accommodate religious-based political movements. The early signs as of November 2011 are that the MB is doing well in the early stages of the parliamentary elections. However, at present, former Jihadists released from prison are still prevented from speaking to the media without security clearance and are prevented from participating in conferences to share their experience of the deradicalization process. Conditions of release also include restrictions on travel, public speech and preaching in mosques. To quote el-Zayat:

> The government and the regime are thinking of their own interests in ending violence without changing any of their own policies. They are still controlling and restricting the role of Islamists in politics and social welfare provision.
>
> *(Personal interview, Cairo January 2010)*

There is some consensus that the current 'freedom deficit' in the Arab world, which has done much to provoke the uprisings of 2011, must be addressed by new regimes if radicalization is to be stemmed. To quote Carpenter *et al.* (2009: 305):

> A key part of an effective strategy will be rejuvenating efforts to encourage prosperity, reform and democracy in Arab countries … Prosperous democratic societies that respect the rights of their citizens are more resilient and less susceptible to political instability and radicalisation. If grievances can be peacefully expressed and mediated through democratic institutions, citizens are less apt to turn to more extreme options.

Likewise, tackling state corruption is an important element in any reform process in the region since this is often used as a pretext by extremists to challenge state legitimacy.

Economic reforms in Egypt, despite leading to healthy rates of economic growth over the past decade until the 2011 uprisings, have resulted in growing economic inequality (Harrigan and El-Said 2009a and b). This has resulted in unrest, and in response the government has come to rely increasingly on security forces, often acting beyond the law, and has shown a reluctance to allow various groups to participate in the political process.

According to al-Zayat (Personal interview, Cairo January 2010) there was a very clear list of things the Mubarak regime needed to do if it wanted a future with the Islamists. The same argument applies to the new regime that will hopefully be elected into power in free and fair democratic elections. Firstly, it needs to respect the rule of law and execute the decisions of the judiciary. This involves changing from a police-orientated government to a legally orientated one, respecting the emergency legislation, abiding by it and releasing prisoners that are wrongfully detained. Secondly, it needs to give Islamists freedom of expression and allow them to establish legal entities and political parties.

One foreign diplomat in Cairo supports the above argument. She asserts that the government has failed to address a number of grievances. These include: personal negative experiences with the police or security forces who are above the law, human rights abuses, corruption at all levels, a growing gap between the rich and poor, especially in Cairo and Upper Egypt, and a lack of faith in the political process as a peaceful means to obtain change, which at present can only be achieved by bribery, corruption or knowing the right person. Although Islamists were not at the forefront of the Arab Spring uprisings in Egypt, these uprisings clearly illustrate that a large cross section of the Egyptian population have finally had enough of the above type of political system. A study by RAND showed that 43 per cent of terrorist groups that are no longer involved in violence have begun the transition towards a legitimate political process (Bjørgo 2009). Such a fact indicates that political reform will be critical in Egypt if it is to encompass religious-based political groups and help prevent a return to more extremists and radical views.

Clearly, the fact that there has been a deradicalization process in Egypt does not mean that the underlying causes of radicalization have been addressed. Without socio-political reform and proper rehabilitation, deradicalization is likely to be only a short- to mid-term solution to religious-based violence.

Is deradicalization in Egypt durable?

The deradicalization of the IG and al-Jihad has, so far, been one of the most successful processes of its kind. Neither group has been responsible for any attacks since 1997 and it seems that they have genuinely laid down their arms. Although there have been several subsequent bombings in the Sinai Peninsula, it seems that neither the IG nor al-Jihad were responsible for these and there has been hardly any violence in the Nile Valley where over 90 per cent of the population lives, making Egypt one of the safer countries in the Arab world. The IG also condemned the October 2004 Sinai bombing at Taba and the terrorist attack near al-Azhar in Cairo on 7 April 2005 in which three tourists were killed. In addition Ashour claims that the process has removed more than 15,000 IG militants from the ranks of al-Qaeda (Ashour 2009: 2). In the case of al-Jihad, the al-Zawhiri camp abroad does not support the initiative and two factions inside Egyptian jails refuse to support the process. Al-Jihad has proved to be a harder organization to crack than the IG and was more dangerous than the latter both before and after deradicalization. This was partly due to its cell-like organizational structure and the covert nature of its operations. In addition, the deradicalization of al-Jihad is a much more recent process with many of the members still to be released from jail. Despite this, there have still not been any al-Jihad attacks in Egypt.

There remains, however, the danger that the younger generation in both the IG and al-Jihad, as well as in the MB, may revert to radicalism in the future. In the MB it is the older generation of leaders in their 60s and 70s who have been through a deradicalization process whilst there is some evidence that the younger members who have not gone through this process or experienced armed conflict with the regime may be becoming more radical and disillusioned with Egypt's repressive regime (Benraad and Abdelbaky 2009). It remains to be seen whether the post-Mubarak era can bring a halt to this via a more inclusive political system. In all groups, it is very unlikely that the older generation who have renounced violence will have yet another change of mind and revert to their old ways, but a lack of genuine political reform could drive younger people back towards radicalism. It will also prevent the IG and al-Jihad from moving the process of deradicalization forwards towards moderation by which they become fully integrated into the political process. This is an important point. The future role of both organizations in Egyptian society remains ambiguous, as does their stance towards democracy. Both groups continue to exist and although proscribed, they are tolerated by the state, with the IG for example having a website, focusing on outreach and engaging in public issues of political and religious debate.

In recent years, there has been a growth in the more fundamentalist Salafi Islam in Egypt. This has been partly due to the influence of migrant workers exposed to more radical Wahhabism, especially in Saudi Arabia. This more conservative and puritanical trend is evidenced by more women wearing the full veil and the preaching of more radical Imams in mosques and on radio and satellite television channels. So far, this Salafism has remained largely apolitical and non-violent and the former Mubarak government allowed the movement to develop as an alternative to the politically motivated MB. In addition, despite some evidence of slightly more radical preaching in mosques in recent years, the Egyptian authorities have been very successful in controlling religion and ensuring that there are no underground subversive mosques or Imams acting as centres for radicalization. This is in contrast to the 1980s and early 1990s.

As with any successful reduction in violence, it is difficult to ascribe causation. Has it been due to the deradicalization process or due to increased security and repression? Certainly, the released detainees are kept under close watch by an extensive network of security services which are largely able to operate beyond the law. A dependency relationship between the released detainees and the security forces has also been created. If resources to support this become stretched in the future, or if pressure to improve the country's human rights record mounts, this system of control could well be weakened. On the other hand it does seem, if many analysts and commentators are to be believed, that there has been a genuine deradicalization process amongst both the IG and al-Jihad members and it seems unlikely, with so many released from jail, that violence would have ceased completely had this not been the case. One aspect of repression was however, crucial and that was the imprisonment of leaders and members as it was largely within the prison system that the process of deradicalization took place.

In terms of the deradicalization process itself, there is another issue of causation concerning the role played by state actions. Was the process purely the result of an initiative undertaken by the leaders of the groups or did state action to facilitate the process also play an important role? Was state action a catalyst or just a product of an already changing situation? The analysis above suggests that although the process was initiated by the leadership of the Jihadist groups, once in progress the state played an important role in facilitating it, both by allowing interaction and providing selective inducements.

An issue raised by al-Anani (2009) is whether the deradicalization process in Egypt, especially that of al-Jihad that had close links to al-Qaeda, will impact at a global level and encourage more people to reappraise the beliefs and strategies of groups like al-Qaeda, and initiate a global process of deradicalization. On the one hand, it is possible that al-Sharif's document, coming as it does from one of the leading and most influential ideologues of the Jihadist movement, will influence others abroad. On the other hand, many have pointed out that al-Qaeda's leadership has become dispersed, making it harder to influence the organization and its beliefs. In addition, new ideologues have emerged to replace al-Sharif and represent a new influential generation of Jihadists. Whatever the global outcome, it would seem that for the time being the deradicalization process seems to have succeeded in Egypt. To ensure that it is durable, the unfinished agenda needs to be addressed by tackling grievances such as the lack of political participation in an authoritarian regime, corruption, human rights abuses and growing economic inequality. In this respect, the way in which the interim Ruling Council and any newly elected government behaves will be critical in helping to determine the durability of Egypt's impressive deradicalization.

Notes

1 The MB's influence in the region increased in the 1950s and 1960s as a result of Nasser's persecution of the movement, causing a large number of its members to flee to other countries, such as Saudi Arabia, Morocco and Algeria, where they started to spread their message and proselytize against Nasser's socialism and Arab secularism in general.

2 Instead of dismantling the SA al-Hudaybi succeeded in transforming it with a new leadership and a new name the 'Secret Organization' (SO).

3 Prior to this the MB was characterized by factional leadership with each faction pursuing its own agenda such that the leadership was unable to give a clear message on the group's attitude to the use of violence.

4 This book, *Ma'alim Fi al-Tariq*, which can be translated as *Milestones* or *Signposts* was published by Dar al-Shuruq in Cairo and is undated. It had a profound influence on many Jihadists, particularly with its concept of *al-Hakimiyya,* which denies humans the right to legislate, which is the exclusive province of God and hence declares as *Takfir* (an apostate or non Muslim) anyone or any regime that legislates. The ideological countering of this

work represents a concerted attempt by the MB to prevent the interpretations of Sayyid Qutb's works along Takfir lines as well as to prevent the development of a Takfiri organization by former MB members in Egypt. In addition to the ideological basis for the renunciation of violence there was also a degree of pragmatism involved. A now united leadership agreed that the previous violent stance by the MB had led to disastrous consequences in the form of severe state repression, imprisonment of many MB members and torture. Not only did state repression contribute to the decision to renounce violence for pragmatic reasons it had also produced a leadership in the form of al-Haudaybi and others who had gained credibility amongst followers for their endurance of harsh methods of repression by the state (Ashour 2009: 83).

5 These leaders included Umar al-Tilmisani, Muhammad Hamid Abu al-Nasr, Salah Shadi and Mustafa Mashhur.

6 Other much smaller and more radical clandestine Islamic groups also emerged in the 1970s including *Takfir wal Hijra* (Excommunication and Exile) and *Al-Nagoun min al-Nar* (Salvation from Hell).

7 Blaydes and Rubin (2008: 465–7) suggest that following the assassination of Sadat until the late 1980s the IG had 'entered some sort of agreement with the regime to limit violence' in return for being allowed to preach freely in Upper Egypt. They argue that this tacit agreement ended in the late 1980s when the IG started operating in Cairo and Lower Egypt so crossing a government red line by moving out of rural Egypt into working class areas of Cairo.

8 Prior to this time there were several small cells operating under the name of al-Jihad, including cells led by al-Zawhiri and Kamal Habib and some of these, although lacking a clear organizational structure, were involved along with the IG in the assassination of Sadat.

9 Al-Qaeda was established on 11 August 1988 following a meeting in Peshawar that included senior leaders of Al-Jihad (including Zawahiri and Sayyid Sharif), Abdullah Azzam, a Palestinian who oversaw the recruitment of Arab mujahedeen in Afghanistan, and Osama Bin Laden. Senior members of Al-Jihad saw in the establishment of al-Qaeda an opportunity to 'use their well-trained warriors to overthrow the Egyptian government'. Soon Al-Jihad started a terror campaign inside Egypt that targeted police officers, state symbols and the 'tourist industry, declaring that it corrupted Egyptian society by bringing alien customs and morals which offend Islam' (Wright 2008).

10 The previous year one of the IG leaders, Khaled Ibrahim, had called for a one-year ceasefire so that the group could prepare for and concentrate on the more important need for armed conflict with Israel. He argued that instead of spilling blood in Egypt the IG should concentrate on the true secular enemy which was Israel, the USA and the West (al-Hashimi and Goerzig 2007: 13).

11 The journalist Makram Mohammed Ahmed was asked by the authorities to provide journalistic coverage of the IG deradicalization process. He carried out a number of interviews with IG leadership in prison which were subsequently published in the prestigious magazine *al-Mussawar* in June 2002. These interviews were translated by Lisa Blaydes in 2004 and placed on the web.

12 Abdul Rahman was the key ideologue of the IG group and gave his approval from his prison cell in the USA, although he later withdrew this.

13 Al-Anani 2009 and Gunaratna and Bin Ali 2009 outline in more detail the content of each of these aspects of Jihadist revisionism.

14 According to Bjørgo (2009) this seems to be an example of Leon Festinger's (1957) theory of cognitive dissonance ' … if there is inconsistency between a person's beliefs and his or her behaviours or social reality it will cause an uncomfortable psychological tension. This will lead people to change their beliefs to fit their actual behaviour or the new realities, rather than the other way around, as suggested by popular wisdom … I think this is what happened with the leaders of Gama'a al-Islamiyya and al-Jihad in Egypt' (Bjørgo 2009: 2–3).

15 According to Ashour, (2010) a second wave of modern Islamist deradicalization is now underway with books such as Abbud al-Zumur's *The Third Alternative: Between Authoritarianism and Surrender* (2009), in which al-Zumur, a former member of both IG and al-Jihad, analyses the causes of violent radicalism and sets out ways of ending political violence in Muslim majority states.
16 Al-Azhar is a world renowned Islamic university and mosque based in Cairo regarded by Sunni Muslims as an important source of Islamic teaching.
17 Blaydes and Rubin (2008: 466) state that in the late 1980s ' … .there was some suggestion that IG members and the regime engaged in a bargaining dialogue to end the violence' but this dialogue involved IG issuing demands. Even so, although 'no agreement was reached, the two sides were in the process of continued negotiation'.
18 As mentioned earlier, former al-Jihad leaders are co-founders and leaders of al-Qaeda and part of al-Jihad merged with al-Qaeda in 1998. Commanders of al-Qaeda in Afghanistan and Iraq are former mid-ranking commanders in al-Jihad and al-Zawhiri, the former leader of al-Jihad between 1993 and 2000 became Bin Laden's second in command (Ashour 2009: 91).
19 Magdi Salim in al-Marj prison and Ahmad Mabruk in Abu Za'abal prison.
20 Anani (2009: 3–4) and Gunaratna and Bin Ali (2009: 283–4) outline the nature of this revisionism in terms of a changed attitude towards engaging in Jihad, rebellion against rulers, attacks on Western countries and killing innocent civilians, attacks on foreign tourists and Takfir and the treatment of Copts.
21 Harith was a former lawyer who defended many Islamic militants. He was appalled by the spiralling violence in his country and was determined to broker a ceasefire between the Egyptian state and militant Islamists.
22 The magazine is over one hundred years old and the second oldest after al-Ahram.
23 Although the state press covered the release of Karam Zohdy in the autumn of 2003 and two other leaders and this coincided with the publications of some of the IG's books. As a political gesture Mubarak timed the release to coincide with the 30th anniversary of Egypt's 1973 war with Israel.
24 These recent reports need to be viewed with some scepticism in the year running up to the parliamentary elections in that in such years the government often portrays the MB as a radical group to dissuade people from voting for the MB, which is the only credible opposition to the ruling NDP, and to justify the usual crack down on the MB in election year.
25 These arrests were made following the MB criticism of the regime's attitude to the Gaza war.

Bibliography

Abdul Rahman, H., Ibrahim, N. and al-Sharif, A. (2002) *Taslit al-Adwa' 'ala ma Waqa'a fi al-Jihad min Akhta* (Shedding light on what went wrong during the Jihad), Al-Turath al-Islami, Cairo.

Ahmad, M.M. (2002) *Ahmad Yuhawir Qiyadat al-Jama'a al-Islamiyya Kharji al-Sujun* (Ahmad Interviews the Leadership of the Islamic Group Outside Prisons), Al-Mussawar, 5 July 2002: 4–18.

Al-Anani, K. (2009) 'Jihadi Revisionism: Will it Save the World?', Brandeis University, Crown Center for Middle East Studies, *Middle East Brief*, April 2009, no. 35.

Al-Hashimi, H. and Goerzig, C. 'Change through debate – Egypt's counterterrorism strategy towards the Gama'a Islamia', paper prepared for the 2007 Annual Meeting of the American Political Science Association, 30 August–2 September 2007.

Al-Hudaybi, H. (1985) *Du'ah La Qudah* (Preachers not Judges), al-Faysal al-Islami, Kuwait.

Al-Sharif, S. (2007) *Wathiqat Tarshid al-Jihad fi Misr wa al-'Alam* (Document for Guiding Jihad in Egypt and the World), Al-Jarida.

——(2008), *Unveiling al-Zawhiri's Deceptions.* (unpublished)

Al-Urdun Al-Jadidi Research Centre (1996) *The Democratic Process in Jordan, Amman*: Sinbad Publishing House.
Al-Zawhiri, A. (undated) *Al-Tabri'ah* (The Vindication), (unpublished)
Al-Zumar, A. (2009) *The Third Alternative: Between Authoritarianism and Surrender*, al-Shuruq, Cairo.
Ashmawy, A. (2005) *Al-Tarikh al-Sirri li Jama'at al-Ikhwan al-Muslimyin* (The Secret History of the Muslim Brothers), Ibn Kkaldun, Cairo.
Ashour, O. (2009) *The De-Radicalisation of Jihadists*, London and New York: Routledge.
——(2010) *Post-Jihadism and the Inevitability of Democratisation*. Available HTTP: http://www.icsr.info/blog/post-jihadism-and-the-inevitabilityofdemocratisation
Benraad, M. and Abdelbaky, M. (2009) 'Transition in Egypt: Radicals on the Rise?' *Policy Watch* no. 1588.
Bjørgo, T. (2009) *What is 'De-Radicalisation' and 'Disengagement'? Some Conceptual Clarifications*, unpublished paper.
Blaydes, L. (2004a) Makram Mohammed Ahmed Interviews the Historic Leadership of al-Gama'a al-Islamiyya inside the 'Scorpion' Prison. Available HTTP: http://www.stanford.edu/blaydes/part1.pdf
——(2004b) *Makram Mohammed Ahmed writes from the Wadi al-Natroun Penitentiary: The Rank and File has a Discussion with their Leadership in the Courtyard of the Penitentiary*. Available HTTP: http://www.stanford.edu/blaydes/part2.pdf.
Blaydes, L. and Rubin, L. (2008) 'Ideological reorientation and counterterrorism: confronting militant Islam in Egypt', *Terrorism and Political Violence*, Vol. 20, No. 4: 461–79.
Carpenter, J. S., Levitt, M. and Jacobson, M. (2009) 'Confronting the ideology of radical extremism', *Journal of National Security Law and Policy*, Vol. 3: 303–29.
Festinger, L. (1957) *A Theory of Cognitive Dissonance*, Evanston, IL.
Guardian (2007) *Violence Won't Work: How Author of 'Jihadist's Bible' Stirred up a Storm*, 27 July.
Gunaratna, R. and Bin Ali, M. (2009) 'De-radicalisation initiatives in Egypt: a preliminary insight', *Studies in Conflict and Terrorism*, Vol. 32: 277–91.
Hafiz, U. and Majid, A.A. (2002) *Mubadarit Waqf Al-'unf: Ru'ya Waqi'iya wa Nazra Shar'iya* (Initiative for Ceasing Violence: A Realistic View and a Legitimate Perspective), Al-Turath al-Islami, Cairo.
Harrigan, J. and El-Said, H. (2009a) *Economic Liberalisation, Social Capital and Islamic Welfare Provision*, Palgrave Macmillan: Basingstoke.
——(2009b) *Aid and Power in the Arab World: IMF and World Bank Policy-Based Lending in the Middle East and North Africa*, Palgrave Macmillan: Basingstoke.
Khatab, S. (2009) *Towards a General Counterterrorism Strategy*. Available HTTP: <http://arts.monash.edu.au/politics/terror-research/proceedings/gtrec-proceedings-2009-02-sayed-khatab.pdf
Qutb, S. (1964), *Ma'alim Fi al-Tariq* (Milestones), Kazi Publications, Cairo.
Rashwan, D. (1999) 'Islamists Crash the Party', *Al-Ahram Weekly*, 16–22 September 1999, Issue no. 447.
Richards, A. and Waterbury J. (1996) *A Political Economy of the Middle East*, 2nd edn, London: Westview.
Stracke, N. (2007) 'Arab prisons: a place for dialogue and reform', *Perspectives on Terrorism*, Volume I, Issue 4.
The Economist (2010) *The Long Wait: A Special Report on Egypt*, 15 July.
The Egyptian Gazette (2010) *Brotherhood's Future Uncertain Under Radicals*, 7 January.
Weaver, A. (1995) The Novelist and the Sheikh, in *The New Yorker*, 30 January.
Wright, L. (2008) The Rebellion Within: An Al-Qaeda Mastermind Questions Terrorism, in *The New Yorker*, 2 June.
Zohdy, K. *et al.* (2002) *Istratijiyat wa Tafjirat al-Qaeda: al-Akhta' wa al-Akhtar* (The Strategy and Bombings of al-Qaeda: The Mistakes and Dangers), al-Turath al-Islami, Cairo.
Zohdy, K. *et al.* (2003a) *Tafjirat al-Riyadh:Al-Ahkam wa ak-Athar* (The Riyadh Bombings: The Rulings and the Effects), al-Turatf al-Islami, Cairo.
Zohdy, K. *et al.* (2003b) *Nahr al-Zikrayat* (River of Memories), al-Turath al-Islami, Cairo.

5

JORDAN'S RESPONSE TO JIHADI SALAFISM

Hamed El-Said

Introduction

Jordan's experience with violent extremism shows little correlation to cultural theories of violence. The country has a relatively peaceful past, having never experienced a suicide terrorist attack in her entire history (until 2005), a strong, but historically loyal Islamic movement, a secular and a Westernized regime that turned the desert into a modern, well-established and internationally recognized state. Even the colonial past of the country stands out in the region as uniquely bloodless, described by Adnan Abu Odeh (1999), the late King Hussein's political advisor, as a successful story of colonization, in reference to a rare, and in most parts non-violent, coexistence between colonial power and colonized subjects in what was then known as Transjordan.

Jordan's political stability, moreover, and her relative liberal political posture, have historically motivated and attracted many from neighbouring countries to settle in Jordan, including from Syria, Lebanon, Palestine, Iraq and Saudi Arabia (Rogan and Tell 1994). Stability notwithstanding the country's sensitive geopolitical location which is surrounded by inconsistently friendly, if not at times hostile regimes, have always been more powerful and resourceful than Jordan itself. It was this ability to carefully and skilfully juggle the country's otherwise surmountable internal and external threats that earned the late King Hussein the reputation of being a master of political balancing, 'macho … strongman [who] had few political prisoners.' (Dallas 1999: xviii).

This small, peaceful, stable and Westernized country, however, has recently produced some of the most notorious violent extremists on Earth, as well as ideologues, radical preachers and theorists that have had a momentous impact on the global Jihadi movement. Examples of such figures include: Ahamd Fadil Nazzal al-Khalayleh, aka Abu Musab al-Zarqawi, the former leader of Al-Qaeda in Iraq, who was responsible for some of the worst atrocities in Iraq post-2003 and who was responsible for Jordan's 2005 hotel bombings ('Jordan's 9/11'); Issam Bin Mohammed Taher al-Barqawi, alias Abu

Mohammad al Magdisi, who is considered one of the most prominent theorists in developing the ideology of the Jihadi Salafist movement on a global scale; and Abu Qatada al-Filistini, who is considered to be the spiritual leader of the Jihadi groups in the Arab Maghreb and al-Qaeda's man in Europe. Jordan has also produced hundreds of Jihadis who flocked to Afghanistan, Iraq, Chechnya, Bosnia and Iraq to participate in what they perceived as holy war (jihad) in these countries. 'These Jordanian stars … shone' in the world of violent extremism, illuminated al-Qaeda's global frontier and became its emblem, wrote Abu Ruman and Abu Hanieh (2009: 12 and 13).

Jordan's experience with violent extremism thus raises key questions: how is it that such a peaceful, Westernized and for the most part secular country, has come to produce some of the most notorious violent extremists, ideologues and theorists on earth? What factors turned a small number of Jordanians against their own and other states, inside and outside the region? Where can the root causes of violent extremism be found in the country? How did the state react and respond to this phenomenon? How successful has this response been? What lessons can be learned from the Jordanian experience with countering violent extremism? These are the key questions, which this chapter seeks to answer.

The chapter proceeds as follows. First it divides the period between 1946–2010 into three main phases, 1946–69, 1970–88, and 1989–2010. These divisions are based on the challenges faced by the regime and strategies and methods used by its oppositional forces. Each period is then analyzed separately. The next section provides a historical context to the main challenges faced by the regime during the first two decades after independence in 1946. The section also provides a background analysis to the birth and evolution of Jordan's most organized and enduring Islamic movement, The Muslim Brotherhood (MB), with special emphasis on its relationship with the Jordanian regime. The third section analyses the main developments and challenges during 1970–88. The fourth section then looks at the 1989–2010 period, with special emphasis on the process of political opening that started in 1989, the response of the MB to the democratization process and how that response changed the nature of the movement's relationship with the monarchy and other ideologically driven groups, which began to emerge in the early 1990s and thereafter. Section five pays special attention to the evolution of the Jihadist Salafist movement in Jordan, as well as to national, regional and global factors that influenced its emergence in the country. Section six analyses the state's response to this phenomenon. The final section provides a tentative analysis for Jordan's counter-terrorism strategies and concludes with some remarks.

1946–69: the rise of Arab nationalism and Muslim Brotherhood

Before political independence in 1946, Jordan was first part of the Ottoman Empire which collapsed after the First Wold War in 1914. In 1921, Transjordan was established as an Emirate, governed by the son of the then governor of Hejaz, Prince Abdullah, under British mandate. Under both the Ottomans and the British, Transjordan enjoyed relative stability and economic prosperity, a fact that encouraged a large number of merchants and families from Palestine and Syria, but also from Lebanon and Saudi Arabia, to settle in the country (Rogan and Tell 1994).

The British in Transjordan did not seek either to transform Jordan into a British land or Transjordanians into British subjects, as the French attempted in Algeria. On the contrary, both the Ottomans and the British colonial authorities ruled via local leaders and figures, and maintained and protected local tribal traditions, institutions and beliefs. Indeed, most British officials lived a Transjordanian way of life, rather than forcing their 'Britishness' on the local population (Gubser 1973). Although Muslims, the Ottomans avoided a political version of Islam and promoted instead an apolitical version of religion, one that is closer to the current Sufi version of Islam promoted in some countries, like Morocco, today.

Despite small pockets of resistance (mainly on economic grounds) by some tribes to the presence of British soldiers in Transjordan, the latter did not provoke religious sentiments. Nor did it lead to the emergence of either a nationalist or radical religious movement morally outraged by an attack against Islam, local tradition, institutions or beliefs, seeking to protect them from the invading modern and secular European culture. This led Adnan Abu Odeh (1999) to state that Britain's presence in Transjordan represented the most successful case of colonization in history.

Jordan's first real challenge came after independence, particularly following the 1948 war, which led to the birth of the Israeli State by force. The war brought hundreds of thousands of Palestinian refugees to Jordan and tipped the demographic balance against Jordanians. Having lost their property, livelihood, close family members and friends, and now having been driven out of their country, a large number of refugees, and the overwhelmingly local Muslim population of Jordan, were naturally radicalized by what they experienced, heard about and watched on TV screens. This coincided with the emergence of a powerful but secular brand of National Socialism, led and guided from Cairo by President Nasser himself.

'Nasserism' and Nasserites, therefore, presented the new Jordanian regime (the young King Hussein who ascended to the thrown in 1951) with its first real challenge after independence. The 1950s and 1960s were described extensively elsewhere to warrant repetition here (Oren 1990; Richards and Waterbury 1996). Suffice it to say that the nationalist, pro-Nasserites demonstrated, rioted and attacked state buildings and institutions. Some even implemented such tactics as targeting the assassination of some state officials and planting explosives in state institutions to express their opposition to the regime's policies (Satloff 1986). Oren (1990) even argues that the Jordanian regime, as a result of the strength of opposition, was on the verge of collapse in the 1950s.

For the nationalists, the most radicalizing factor was not simply the regime's refusal to align itself with Nasser, instead it was the monarchy's close relations with Britain. Most nationalists perceived Great Britain as being biased against the Arab cause and held it responsible for the creation of the Israeli state over Arab land. Indeed, then, and until 1956, even the Arab Legion was led by British officers who dictated Jordan's foreign, defence and budgetary policies (Rogan and Tell 1994). These facts were not missed by the opposition, who launched a substantial smear campaign against the monarchy.

Following an alleged military coup attempt in the mid-1950s, the regime reacted to these developments by, first, introducing emergency measures and marshal law, suspending the parliament and banning all political parties, as well as briefly arresting leaders of the opposition. Some measures to placate the masses and boost the popularity of the regime were also taken. For example, the young King also fired all British officials in his army and administration and replaced them with loyal elements of his constituencies. In a similar fashion to President Sadat of Egypt, King Hassan II of Morocco and King Faisal of Saudi Arabia, King Hussein also encouraged the rise of the Islamic current to counter the influence of Arab nationalists and socialists, particularly in schools, universities, professional associations and trade unions where repression alone can have the opposite effect.

The Muslim Brotherhood Movement (MBM), Jordan's oldest and most enduring Islamic movement undeniably owes its creation to Haj Abdullatif Abu Qourah, who was inspired by the work of Sheikh Hassan al-Bana, the founder of the mother Muslim Brotherhood Movement in Egypt in the late 1920s. Sheikh al-Bana's call for Muslims to stand up for the Zionist scheme in Palestine appealed to Haj Abu Qourah who contacted al-Bana, began subscribing and reading enthusiastically the writings of the mother movement, and pledged to spread its ideas, values and influence in Jordan, and the entire region.[1]

Haj Abu Qourah was known for his love of charity work and his nationalism. He even sold his house and other properties to support charity, as well as the work of Mujahedeen in Palestine. In 1936, he lost his nephew in the Palestinian revolution and later mobilized members of his movement to participate in the 1948 war against Israel (Kazem 1997; Gharaibeh 1997). From its inception, the MBM was consequently linked to the question of Palestine and this came to affect the organization's relationship with the regime later on, particularly after the restoration of parliamentary elections in 1989 and the regime's signing of a peace treaty with Israel in 1994. Although the MBM was created in, and its central headquarters were inaugurated on 19 November 1945 (under the patronage of King Abdullah I himself), the MBM was later used and supported by the regime in the 1950s and 1960s to counter the nationalist-pan Arab movement that dominated the political scene in the post-independence period. The MBM, therefore, enjoyed political support from the highest echelon of the state, as well as freedom to operate and preach their moderate version of Islam. In return, the MBM became a staunch defender of the regime. Anybody who wanted to attack the monarchy had to go through the MBM first. They were seen as part of the regime, a loyal and co-opted movement under the arm of the Hashemites. As a result, the MBM was the only movement to survive a political ban on all political parties and associations which was imposed in 1957 following a political episode of instability that involved an alleged coup attempt. Its legal status as a society, rather than as a party, allowed the MBM to continue to operate freely in the country, although the MBM was simultaneously licensed in 1953 as a 'general multifunction Islamic body', a fact which allowed it to engage in various political activities (Kazem 1997: 17).

Put differently, the MBM was born out of, rather than against, the wishes of the Jordanian regime. Jordan also managed to avoid the kind of bloody conflict that implicated and entangled some neighbouring Arab regimes with their Islamists, such as Egypt, Syria, Iraq and Algeria. This is partly because the Jordanian MBM, unlike Islamists in other countries in the region, was always moderate and its members were not radicalized by repression and other oppressive state policies. As Milton-Edwards (1996: 124 and 126) wrote: 'the notion of "fundamentalism" was never part and parcel of Jordan's Islamist movement ... the Muslim Brotherhood ... is a reformist rather than a fundamentalist anti-regime movement'.

Blind loyalty to the monarchy however, and royal and political privileges bestowed on the MBM by the Royal Palace, undermined the movement's popularity among the masses and was translated into poor political gains in parliament, trade and professional associations. MBM candidates for example, garnered no seats in the 1951[2] elections and only four seats in the 1956 elections. Their representation deteriorated to just two seats in the 1963 elections, an experience which was repeated in the 1967 poll (Gharaibeh 1997: 48). This unpopularity was evidenced not only in parliament, but also in the trade unions, professional associations and student movements which were all dominated instead by the nationalists, socialists and Ba'athists, who maintained a strong influence over the masses and over public opinion. The MBM's alliance with the regime was largely seen as a liability, undermining the movement's popular support base in favour of the suppressed, but more radical-secular-nationalist movements. Perceived elitism was another factor that undermined the popular base of MBM's support. The MBM was, and to a large extent continues to be, comprised of educated middle and upper-class elements, unlike trade unions or other nationalist movements that prevailed in the 1950s and 1960s. As Engineer Murad Adaileh, Chairman of Social Care Department at the Islamic Charity Society of the MBM put it: 'While Communist parties rely on labour and Ba'athists rely on army junta, we rely on the intellect and educated' (Personal interview, December 2008 Amman). This perception advanced the Islamist movement's isolation from the masses and starved it from significant political gains.

The MBM's influence was undermined even more in the mid-1960s by the emergence of another more radical group in Jordan: the Palestinian Liberation Organization (PLO). The PLO attempted to infiltrate society by recruiting new cadres of members and their sympathizers in Palestinian refugee camps. They also attracted a large number of nationalist, pro-Nasserite Transjordanians. Not only did the more radical PLO, whose publically stated objective was to liberate Arab land occupied by Israel through 'force', start to attract more recruits than the MBM itself, but some MBM's members disassociated themselves with the movement and joined the PLO instead. The PLO, however, soon turned its weapons against the Jordanian state and sought to bring down the Jordanian regime through a revolutionary change. Despite being secular, the PLO was made up of various cells, some of which implemented violent extremist tactics not dissimilar to the kind of terror tactics implemented by today's al-Qaeda. This included the launching of guerrilla warfare against the Jordanian state, the assassinations of key state officials, the hijacking and detonation of civilian planes and a massive public propaganda campaign aimed at besmirching the reputation of the monarchy, and winning the hearts and minds of the people. Their tactics also included planting explosions in state institutions and terrorizing Jordanians via regular check-up points and kidnappings (El-Said and Harrigan 2009; Dallas 1999).

The history of Jordan and indeed most Arab states, suggests that movements that resort to violence are defeated. The experience of the PLO in Jordan was no exception. Even large sections of the Palestinian population in Jordan shifted positions and turned against the PLO. To counter the threat of the guerrillas, the regime reorganized the armed forces and launched in September 1970 a substantial military operation that defeated the *Fedayeen* (Palestinian fighters) and ended their presence in Jordan. They were, following their military defeat in what is referred to in Jordan today as 'Black September', transferred to Lebanon.

Jordanization: planting the roots of radicalization: 1971–89

Designing and successfully implementing a carefully drawn up and tailor-made reconciliation process, particularly in multi-ethnic societies which experience communal strife, is necessary in order to heal the wounds of the past and restore peace, stability and prevent further communal or ethnic conflicts in the future (World Bank 2004). This should have occupied the top priority of the Jordanian regime after the 1970–1 conflict, in order to prevent 'Black September' from being seen as a conflict between Jordanians and Palestinians in general. A genuine reconciliation process would have prevented the scars of the conflict from lingering and thus affecting the relationship between the two communities in the medium- and long-run at the expense of the country's economic development and political stability. As Jane Harrigan has shown in her chapter on Malaysia, reconciliation there after the communal conflict erupted between the Chinese and Malays in 1969 took the form of a multi-prong strategy that included a re-settlement programme to move the Chinese population away from communist strongholds to safe, well-defended, well equipped and economically viable new villages. This part of the strategy sought to break the link between the Communist insurgency and their sympathizers among the Chinese community. The strategy also included the participation of the military in civic activities, for instance in rural development projects, in order to create an amiable relationship with soldiers who had fought the insurgents, create a new cordial environment between the state and Chinese ethnic communities and change the image of the army as simply a fighting and repressive machine. Both the army and civil authorities were also tasked to eradicate the insurgents' radical ideology among the population through socioeconomic projects and psychological operations and public campaigns.

A New Economic Policy (NEP) was implemented by the Malaysian authorities from 1971–91 and was designed to eliminate absolute poverty, reduce inequities and create jobs to overcome unemployment and improve the living standards of all citizens. This was to be done by reorienting national economic strategy from inward looking, import-substitution industrialization to the globally-oriented export-expansion strategy based on attracting foreign investment. The NEP was part of an overall counter-radicalization programme which was deliberately, consciously and successfully designed and implemented to restore 'trust' between Malays and other ethnic communities living in Malaysia, including in particular the Chinese community. More importantly, 'The bargain struck at independence granted Malays special privileges in the political realm and the Chinese minority freedom to compete as Malaysian citizens in the economic realm' (all quotations from Lubeck 1996: 311). Although the 'bargain' created a division of labour between a Malay public sector and a Chinese private sector, it was acceptable for both communities and became the foundation of a 'new deal' that laid the ground for political stability, sustainable economic development and prosperity for all citizens.

Jordan's policies in the post-1970–1 civil strife stand in stark contradiction to those of Malaysia. The public campaign programme which the Jordanian state initiated after 1971 aimed at idealizing the Arab Legion for inflicting a severe and memorable defeat against the *Fedayeen*, rather than restoring trust and achieving reconciliation between Palestinians and Transjordanians. Although most members of the Arab Legion, until at least the early 1970s, were of Palestinian origin that fought and defended the regime and state against the *Fedayeen*, the Jordanian authorities began generally viewing Palestinians with suspicion and disloyalty. A 'Jordanization' process was launched, with the intention of purging the public sector, the security forces and the army of Jordanians of Palestinian (JP) origin. As a result, a division of labour has developed between a Jordanian public sector and a Palestinian private sector. While Palestinians have mostly been confined to the private sector, Tranjordanians have been free to move between the two sectors as they wish. Rather than striking a bargain however (as the Malaysian government did), to guarantee Transjordanians special privileges in the public sector and JPs freedom to compete as Jordanian citizens in the economic realm, 'stories of civil servants … obstruct[ing] Palestinian official transactions' in the private sector were well documented by Abu-Odeh (1999: 197). The upshot has been a general environment of mistrust that has permeated every aspect of the Jordanian society. Lauri Brand (1994) described this relationship, particularly between the Jordanian public sector and the overwhelmingly Palestinian private sector as 'parasitic', with each sector not only distrustful of the other, but also predacious on one another. Most Palestinians remained, and continue to do so, in refugee camps that suffer from poor conditions, poor infrastructure and poor defences, and are politically isolated and under-equipped. Their living conditions and political treatment make them vulnerable and subject to regular propaganda campaigns launched by the state's rivals.

As in the case of Morocco, fixation with survival or 'Jordanization' has been at the expense of economic development. In many ways, the 'Jordanization' process undermined the economic capacity of the state to efficiently design and implement a successful economic and industrial programme capable of achieving structural transformation and sustainable development. Jordan's government, to be sure, did introduce economic planning in 1974, which brought massive state intervention into Jordan's economy and society, but this was not a NEP or industrial strategy aimed at transforming the economy into an economy equal to those of newly industrializing countries. Indeed, while countries like Malaysia were reorienting their country and economy towards the global arena and world market, Jordan began looking inward and intensified instead import-substitution strategy. With its usual arsenal of protective measures and tax exemptions, this strategy only benefited a few small, but powerful interest groups.

Amawi referred to those groups as the former 'merchant class' with historical, financial and political ties to the Palace.

Between 1972–82, Jordan still experienced an unprecedented high real GDP growth rate of 7.9 per cent. Not only did unemployment disappear, thanks to labour migration to oil-rich Arab states, but the Jordanian economy actually began suffering from severe labour shortages, which were filled by less skilled workers coming predominantly from Egypt. Unprecedented growth, prosperity, economic intervention and planning however, were made possible by a hitherto unparalleled level of official aid in the 1970s and early 1980s, mainly from oil-rich Arab states. It was not from an accumulation of capital arising from a disciplined structural transformation of economy, as had been the case in East Asia's giants, namely, Singapore, Hong Kong, Korea and Taiwan. Foreign assistance per capita rose from $26 in 1967 to $257 and $428 in 1976 and 1980–3, respectively. By the late 1970s, more than a third of Jordan's labour (mostly Palestinians) had been attracted to work in the Gulf, remitting approximately $1 million on an annual basis between 1976–85 (Ilissa 2007: 6). Jordan's bonanza was, and continues to be, as Lubeck (1996: 297) put in a different context, 'an unearned windfall, like manna from heaven' that has been badly mismanaged, as later analyses will demonstrate.

Economic growth, planning and foreign aid provided further opportunities to buy loyalty and political stability, by expanding the public sector and providing jobs and other largess, to loyal members of Jordanian tribes and other elites. These jobs and largess were provided on the basis of loyalty to the regime, rather than on the basis of skills and competences. Lacking strong institutions or political parties to monitor the system and prevent abuse of power (similar to Malaysia's United Malay National Organization – UMNO), the patronage system ran out of control: 'an agency head would fill positions with employees from his extended family of origin. For example, a cabinet minister would appoint many people from his town. Their qualifications and job performance would be questionable … ' (Cunningham and Sarayrah 1993: 10 and 46). By 1980, the state was employing more than 60 per cent of the labour force, at least a third of which were considered by some observers as 'excessive capacity' who could be dismissed without affecting productivity of the state sector. Their wages and salaries represented more than 60 per cent of total government expenditure (Alissa 2007: 13).

Instead of creating an efficient and flexible state sector to oversee and facilitate economic and industrial development, Jordan's public sector and bureaucracy became bloated and inflexible, and were seen as dumping grounds for patronage by successive governments. Widespread corruption, nepotism and rent-seeking sapped the capacity of the state and created feeble state institutions. 'Feeble institutions [are] incapable of pursuing a sustained development policy' and 'networks of patronage prevent[.] merit-based career advancement' (Lubeck 1996: 298).

Jordan's economic planning and intervention, therefore, did not usher in an epoch of sustained economic development. The global collapse of oil prices in the early 1980s diminished the inflow of foreign assistance and remittances to Jordan, exposing the country's poor economic management and feeble state institutions. Economic growth rate in the 1980s (5.7 per cent between 1982–6) was maintained by following an expansionary policy based on foreign borrowing in the midst of austerity. The only economic reorientation Jordan's economy underwent was towards the protected Iraqi economy, whose longer than expected war with Iran led to reliance on Jordan's economy, sea and land to provide Iraq's war needs in return for handsome financial rewards. Until 2003, Iraq remained Jordan's main trading partner.

The accumulation of foreign borrowing within a context of widespread corruption, economic mismanagement and unfavourable external environment meant that Jordan, by the late 1980s, was no longer able to service its foreign debt, with foreign creditors refusing to extend further credit facilities. The upshot was a severe debt crisis, escorted with a twin banking and currency crisis in 1989. The crisis not only forced the government to turn to the International Monetary Fund (IMF) and World Bank for financial and technical assistance, but it also provoked civil unrest for the first time in the country in almost three decades. Ironically, rioters were Jordanian, seen as the backbone of the regime, not Palestinian. These Jordanians turned out to be the ones who lost most from their government's economic policies[3] (Harrigan and El-Said 2009a: 45).

Indeed, the economic crisis led to a colossal increase in the number of Jordanians living under the poverty line and was associated with an unprecedented deterioration in the living standards of most Jordanians. Equities also worsened dramatically, with the middle-class shrinking overnight. All Jordanians came to blame their government for mismanaging the economy and for their economic plights. Coupled with the return of the 'Jordanian Afghanis' outbreak of 1990–1 Gulf war, and deteriorating relations between the Palestinians and Israelis, the stage was set for radicalization and extremism that lead to terrorism.

Feigned democracy, rise of political Islam and fundamentalism: 1989–2010

One of the main beneficiaries of the 1970s and 1980s environment was the MBM. Aware of its poor and deteriorating ratings and popular support in the 1950s and 1960s, the MBM intensified its *da'wa* (calling) campaign to teach and spread Islamic values and principles, and began simultaneously to focus on the social sector in order to broaden its interaction with people and garner public support. The MBM launched in 1963–5 the Islamic Centre Society to organize, manage and oversee social activities of the movement in various sectors, including in health, education, sport, accommodation and renovations of the housing units belonging to the poor. Robust economic conditions in the 1970s and early 1980s, political stability enjoyed by the country after ousting the PLO fighters to Lebanon in 1971 and huge financial support extended to the MBM, mostly in the form of donations from members and sympathizers, enabled it to expand its social services to the poor and needy in urban areas.[4]

Signs of an increased popular base for the MBM began to emerge in the mid-1980s. The most solid evidence of their increased popularity came in 1984 when MBM candidates won three out of eight vacant parliamentary seats in the complementary elections, which the late King Hussein decided to summon after 17 years of non-parliamentary life.[5] MBM candidates and other independent Islamists were also achieving rapid gains in trade unions, students' movements and professional associations, thus ending a traditional monopoly by nationalist and leftist candidates (Abdul Kazem 1997: 23–4; Al-Urdun Al-Jadid Research Centre 1997). A poll called for by King Hussein himself and implemented by the government in 1988 showed a very high level of public support for the MBM and that under free and fair elections they would dominate the parliament (Harrigan and El-Said 2009a).

Aware of the increased popularity of Islamists and facing the most serious economic and financial crisis in its history, the regime restored parliamentary elections in 1989. Islamists stood to immediately benefit from the elections: they won almost half of all seats (36 out of the 80) in the Lower House of Parliament, which came as no surprise to the monarchy.

The results of the 1989 elections should not be seen as a reflection on the organizational capacity and resources of a movement (MBM) that had benefited from a monopoly of association since the late 1950s. The results reflected a wider regional trend, typified by the rise of both moderate and radical Islam. In Jordan in particular, at least five Islamic currents rose simultaneously to the fore of political activism in the late 1980s and early 1990s. These were the traditional MBM, the Islamic Action Front (IAF), independent Islamists, the Muslim Centre Party and jihadi salafists.

The MBM remains loyal to the regime and constitution, although not always satisfied with its policies, particularly regarding the Palestinian question and US policies in the region. After 1992, the MBM opted to take a step back from direct involvement in politics and began focusing only on *da'wa* and social services. Its *da'wa* mission seeks to spread true Islamic principles and values that would prepare society, one day, for an Islamic state to be achieved through peaceful and gradual change, not revolution. The 1989 economic and financial crisis led to a massive and sudden jump in poverty and unemployment in Jordan, as mentioned earlier. As in Morocco and Egypt, the IMF and World Bank's stabilization and structural adjustment lending policies promoted in Jordan from 1989–2005 reduced the state's resources and resulted in further social dislocations. A social vacuum developed in the country, which has been filled by the MBM's expanded social networks and provisions. Through the Islamic Centre Society, the MBM extended its activities in almost every aspect of the social sector, including in health and education. By the end of the 1990s the MBM's large and far-reaching social network activities were described as a state within a state (Harrigan and El-Said 2009b). By 2005, the MBM owned two large hospitals, 15 clinics, one university, one female community college, 28 primary and male and female high schools, and 23 kindergartens. The MBM's health and education sectors alone provided jobs for more than 4,000 Jordanian families. Other activities included the adoption of almost 10,000 orphans, supporting more than 3,700 poor Jordanian families, providing school packs and student support to poor children at the beginning of each academic year, food parcels to the poor, winter support and house renovations and medicine to the needy. On average these services cost more than $10 million annually. Finally, more than 3,000 poor Jordanians and 300 poor students benefit annually from the

MBM's Poor Patient Fund and Poor Student Fund, respectively. These funds were created to provide free treatment and studentships to poor Jordanians at a cost of more than $557,000 annually (El-Said and Rauch 2011. Also see Harrigan and El-Said 2009b). A government committee estimated the MBM's assets in 2008 at more than $2 billion (Interview with state officials and members of MBM, Amman December 2008).

Such a vast network of social services, stimulated by social retirement of the state, has important political implications. It enhances the legitimacy and credibility of faith-based providers at the expense of the state. As noted earlier, widespread corruption, nepotism, the lack of democratic outlets and the weakened developmental capacity of the state had already undermined the credibility and legitimacy of the regime. This was reflected by the severity of the riots and the demands of the rioters in 1989, overwhelmingly Jordanian in origin. After 1989, Islamists[6] framed their demands in a language that captured the meaning and essence of the problems which all Jordanians faced. Their demands were framed in a manner that resonated well with the public at large and ended up mobilizing further sympathizers. For example, Islamists attacked corruption, corrupt officials and a lack of democratic institutions. While in Parliament from 1989–92, they demanded and insisted on the following: a new anti-corruption law; expansion of political freedoms and associational rights, as well as the protection of freedom of expression; cutting government expenditure, except on necessities, as a way to reduce government corruption by spending less on unnecessary projects that benefit only the 'elite' or a small number of individuals. Within months of the elections, Islamists got all of their demands, forced the state to make significant reforms[7] and nearly succeeded in indicting the former Prime Minister, Mr Zaid al-Rifa'i, King Hussein's long life friend, with corruption.

Having achieved all of the above, the MBM, following the introduction of a new political parties' law in 1992, created their own political party (the Islamic Action Front – IAF) to act as both a political wing for the Movement and as an umbrella organization for all Islamist groups in the country. The IAF has benefited tremendously from the MBM's vast social network in its political discourse, a fact that has paid, and continues to pay, dividends in terms of votes obtained in elections. The IAF is today the largest oppositional bloc in the parliament, but, like the MBM, is also not a revolutionary party. It is often described as a 'loyal opposition'. It calls for democratization and political reform, and accepts the state as the main framework for competition, political activity and dispute settlement. It also calls for eliminating corruption, judicial independence and strong social network to compact poverty and unemployment. The IFA:

> ... announced its complete commitment to the regime, the king, and the democratisation program ... There is a marked change in our attitude towards what appears not to be Islamist. We now believe we cannot judge by appearances and that the Jordanian society is basically Muslim at heart if not in appearance.
>
> *(Milton-Edwards 1996: 134)*

One of the key issues which has been a thorn in the relationship between the regime on the one hand, and the MBM and IAF on the other, since the 1989 parliamentary elections is related to the question of Palestine and US policies in the region. The MBM and IAF adamantly oppose a peace treaty with Israel because of what they perceive as unfair and bias US policy towards Israel. We will return to this issue later in what follows.

The so-called 'independent Islamists' reflect the third Islamic current in Jordan. Independent Islamists resigned from the ranks of the IAF almost immediately after its establishment in 1992, initially on representational, not policy grounds. They argued that, despite promises to the contrary, the IAF is dominated and controlled by MBM's members. For example, the IAF's Consultative Council (*Majlis al-Shura*), the most powerful entity in the party and its decision-making body, was dominated by MBM members. Out of 120 seats, independents controlled only 15 per cent (or 18 seats) of the 1992 *Shura* Council, a minority representation. The number of Independent Islamists who resigned from the IAF in 1992 reached 17, and they were (and continue to be) mainly led by Engineer Laith Shubailat and his colleague Sheikh Ya'qub Qarrash. Both were former MPs who were imprisoned and jailed for 'allegedly' undertaking hostile activities and joining and establishing illegal-terrorist groups, such as the Islamic Liberation Front and Vanguard of Islamic Youth.

The main difference between Independent Islamists, and MBM and IAF's members is that they (independent Islamists) had taken a far less compromising stand on such issues as corruption, promotion of democracy and freedom of expression, peace with Israel and other moral and ethical issues than either the MBM or IAF. Indeed, while the IAF backed down and sought to entrench and integrate itself further in the political system after the trial of Shubailat and Qarrash in 1992, the latter two underwent further radicalization. Most observers inside and outside Jordan agree that the trial and accusations of Shubailat and Qarrash were deliberately manipulated and fabricated by the state. As Sheihk Qarrash stated after their trial in 1992 in which he and Shubailat were first sentenced to death before King Hussein later pardoned them:

> The sentence was no surprise. After all those lies, this was the biggest lie of all. Since the pardon though, I feel stronger, although I am very angry at what happened to me. I'm angry at my brothers in parliament, at the government, and the *Mukhabarat*.
>
> *(Quoted in Milton-Edwards 1996: 133)*

The Independent Islamists neither called for nor condoned violence, nor have they attacked the regime directly or called for a revolutionary change. Indeed, immediately after his trial and pardon in 1992, Shubailat 'cited the King as the most democratic person in the country; and only criticised the "Islamic movement" for its stand on the promotion of "true" democracy' (Quoted in Milton-Edwards 1996: 133). Their opposition to the government had taken a democratic form and always used democratic platforms in their attempt to promote their anti-corruption and democratic agenda. In this regard, they were not much different from the Saudi *sahwists* who remained critical of the government after their deradicalization in the mid- to late-1990s while opposing and rejecting violence. They (the *sahwists*) later, with facilitation and tacit support of the Saudi state, played a key a role in countering radicalization in the Kingdom and deradicalizing a large number of Saudi youth who joined al-Qaeda.

But the Jordanian regime, particularly after 1992 while preparing for peace with Israel, was growing less tolerant of opposition to its policies, particularly regarding peace with Israel. Independent Islamists held the potential of deradicalizing a large number of Jordanians who were radicalized either by their experience in Afghanistan, widespread corruption and repression in Jordan, regional politics or all of the above. However, they were marginalized, repressed and undermined by the authorities. The latter therefore, and as later sections show, missed an opportunity to use the independent Islamists as a deradicalization tool (Al-Rantawi 2009).

The fourth Islamic trend in Jordan is expressed in the form of a relatively new political party, namely the Muslim Centre Party (MCP). The MCP was established in 2001 with the explicit support of the new regime (King Abdullah II who ascended to the throne after the death of his father in 1999) in an attempt to divide further and undermine the increased influence of both the MBM and its political wing, the IAF. The MCP is, therefore, more closely allied to the regime and attempts to target and recruit members of the Islamic movements. The MCP's declared programme calls for a strengthening of democracy in Jordan and the promotion of pluralism, economic, social and educational reform on the basis of Islamic law. The MCP promotes itself as more moderate than the IAF and calls for increasing the political role of women in Jordan. It has a small following in the country, with only two members in the Jordanian parliament between 2007–09. The MCP is also adamant about the creation of a Palestinian State in the West Bank and Gaza Strip, seeing this as the only way to counter the Israeli Likud's project, known as the 'Jordan option', which seeks to solve the Palestinian problem by creating a Palestinian state in Jordan instead (LLC Books 2010).

The final form of (political) Islam in Jordan is the Jihadi salafist. Due to the significance of this group to the subject of this chapter (and book), it is worth discussing its evolution and root causes in a separate section.

The emergence of Jordanian jihadi salafism

A traditional Salafi movement first emerged in Jordan in the 1960s and was led by young Jordanian men who had studied in Egypt, Syria and Lebanon. It was inspired by the teachings of the Syrian scholar, Nasr al-Din al-Albani (1909–99). This movement was apolitical and missionary (*Da'aweyah*) in nature, following a Sufi version of Islam. It operated within a framework of allegiance and loyalty to the ruler, even if the latter was not perceived to be ruling according to Islamic principles. The movement was strengthened and expanded in the 1980s by the relocation of al-Albani from Syria to Jordan following the Syrian Ba'thist regime's onslaught on its Muslim Brotherhood movement in the early 1980s. The authorities, fearing its growth and transformation into a more radical movement following the persecution of its members in Syria, cracked-down on al-Albani and his followers. This pushed the movement underground and into informal social networks where members met secretly in private houses and practised their Sufi-style religious form of Islam (ICG 2005: 5).

Although it did not go as far as the Saudi government did in issuing a fatwa that justified jihad in Afghanistan, still the Jordanian government not only encouraged Jordanian volunteers to travel, but also facilitated their participation in the 'holy war' in Afghanistan against Russian forces. Indeed, the late Abdullah Azzam, a Jordanian of Palestinian origin, could not have established and run the Services Office in Peshawar (which used to greet and orient incoming Arab mujahedeen on their way to Afghanistan) without the support of many Arab states, including that of Jordan. Economic, security-political and regional concerns shaped the Jordanian regime's policies, which all led in one direction: supporting the mujahedeen's war in Afghanistan.

Politically, and like elsewhere in the region, the 1979 Iranian revolution inspired a large number of Jordanians, particularly among the followers of al-Albani and some members of the MBM. Economically, Jordan, after 1983, was facing an economic slowdown with thousands of Jordanians, up to 25,000, returning home in the mid-1980s after losing their jobs in the then depressed economies of the Gulf States. With the Jordanian economy already struggling to provide jobs for its own graduates, unemployment began mounting (El-Said 1996). Fearing the security implications of mounting unemployment, as well as spread of radical Islam from Syria to Jordan through al-Albani's movement, sending Jordanian mujahedeen to Afghanistan looked appealing not only politically and economically, but also theologically. It placed the Jordanian regime, which derives legitimacy from its prophetical lineage, in a religious uniform. The Jordanian monarchy, moreover, was also seeking in the mid-1980s rapprochement with the Syrian Baathist regime, which just a few years earlier had persecuted its own Islamists. Encouraging al-Albani's followers and their sympathizers in Jordan to leave to Afghanistan was also appealing on regional grounds, given the fact that Saudi Arabia, then a key financial backer, went as far as issuing a fatwa that justified the war in Afghanistan as a 'holy' one.

The return of 'Jordanian Afghans' in the early 1990s also coincided with the first 1990–1 Gulf war. The invasion of Iraq by Western powers, with the participation of armies from several Arab states, was a turning point in the evolution of Jihadi Salafism in Jordan, and, indeed, in the entire Muslim world. Having supported the Mujahedeen in Afghanistan in the 1980s, Iraq, an overwhelmingly Muslim state, had now been attacked by the same forces that supported the mujahedeen in Afghanistan a decade earlier, including in particular the US, facilitated by Saudi Arabia. This caused confusion among Jordanian, as well as other 'Arab Afghans'. 'Who is now a friend and who is a foe?' they asked (Personal interview with Hassan Abu Hanieh, Amman August 2010).

For Jordanians in particular, nothing could have been more radicalizing than the inhuman international embargo which the US and its allies imposed on Iraq after 1991 and which led to the deaths of hundreds of thousands of Iraqi children. Iraq, after all, had for years provided Jordan and Jordanians, with cheap and largely subsidized fuel, imported most products that Jordanian factories manufactured and invested billions of dollars in the infrastructure and roads that transformed Jordan's economic development, despite the political motives behind these polices. Iraq not only kept Jordanians warm in their bitter winters, but also kept their economy growing and provided a large number of them with jobs and lucrative contracts. Although King Hussein, unlike many other Arab leaders, refused to send his soldiers to participate in the war against Iraq, the embargo on Iraq was mortifying and humiliating for all Jordanians, who were further angered by their regime's lack of ability to provide any basic indemnifying role for fellow Iraqis or even to influence events in the region (See ICG 2003a & b and 2005).

The return of the 'Jordanian Afghans' in the early 1990s should have received some attention from the government. Having spent years fighting in Afghanistan, most lacked any marketable skills, had no jobs or training and were no longer familiar with their now ever-changing Jordanian environment. In fact, one other major implication of the 1991 Gulf Crisis was the sudden return of more than 300,000 Jordanians from the Gulf. While some of the returnees were saturated with a radical salafi ideology already, such as al-Magdisi, the majority were more liberal in their attitudes, more exposed in their clothes and more Westernized in their consumption and spending habits. They brought with them more liberal values and principles, some of which were completely alien to Jordanians and certainly alien to all 'Jordanian Afghans'. For the latter, what they saw in Jordan after their return from Afghanistan contradicted their expectations of a true Muslim society that they had become accustomed to in Afghanistan (Abu Ruman and Abu Hanieh 2009; ICG 2005). 'Is that what we fought for?' many of them asked (Personal interview with Abu Ruman and Abu Hanieh, Amman August 2010).

Finally, the arrival of 'Jordanian Afghans' coincided with the country's worst-ever economic and financial crisis, caused largely by widespread official corruption and economic mismanagement – in themselves as radicalizing as the 1989 riots demonstrated. Not only were poverty and unemployment high (and continue to be so), ranging according to government sources anywhere between 15 and 30 per cent, but also inequalities deteriorated rapidly and were further exposed by the return of generally better-off returnees from the Gulf in 1991–2 (Harrigan, El-Said and Wang 2006; Harrigan and El-Said 2009a). Add to that, of course, the lack of a genuine democratic process in Jordan that could have absorbed and provided more peaceful outlets for many disappointed and disgruntled young Jordanians.

It was no coincidence therefore that Jordan witnessed the birth of several jihadi movements in the early 1990s, such as The Islamic Liberation Front, Islamic Jihad, al-Aqsa Battalions, The Armed Vanguard of Islamic Youth and Mohammad's Army (Milton-Edwards 1996). As reflected by their names, these groups and individuals, who did not exceed a few hundred, adopted:

> … a discourse founded on the principle of '*takfir*' (disavowal as blasphemous or excommunication). The movement finds all Arab governments guilty of blasphemy. It claimed that they shun the very principle of politics and reject the notion of public political life, as well as democracy, representative assemblies and elections. Their ideological cornerstone is based on the belief that subversive, armed struggle and action are the only means for changing today's political reality.
>
> *(Abu Ruman and Abu Hanieh 2009)*

Many of the 'Jordanian Afghans' met in Afghanistan and became pals and buddies in the battlefield. There, they built a network of social groups that led them to developing bonds for one another. Upon their return to Jordan, they re-contacted and reconnected with one another and began to spread the calling (*al-Da'wa*). Among the returnees from Afghanistan in 1993 was Abu Musa'b al-Zarqawi who had earlier met his mentor, al-Magdisi, in Peshawar. As al-Magdisi stated:

> I met with Abu Musab [al-Zarqawi] for the first time in Peshawar ... Then, when he returned from Afghanistan, he visited me at my home, eager for the triumph of the calling to God and for al-Tawhid (Unitarianism: Belief in the Oneness of God). [...] So we cooperated together in this capacity. I arranged lessons to be conducted in all parts of the country. We began to publish and distribute some of my literature amongst the people; young men began to flock towards the "calling" (*da'wa*), and began to exchange the literature and messages of this "calling" (*da'wa*).
>
> *(Quoted in Abu Ruman and Abu Hanieh 2009: 23)*

Initially, the cluster of radical movements that emerged in Jordan in the early 1990s had 'confused' choices, priorities and vague and unclear organizational structure. This was reflected in their first attack in January 1991, which included stores selling alcohol, members of the Christian community (such as the Greek-Orthodox priest Kamil Haddad who was a victim of a rocket attack), as well as targeting a Jordanian intelligence officer involved in investigating violent extremist organizations in Jordan (Milton-Edwards 1996: 128–9). It was not before Zarqawi returned to Jordan from Afghanistan and got together with al-Magdisi in 1993 that these groups were united more or less under one organization, *Bay'at al-Imam* (Pledging of Allegiance to the Imam) *Group*. This group was 'the fruit of the union between Zarqawi and al-Magdisi's joint activities in disseminating Jihadi salafism, and between the contemporary expertise of al-Magdisi's theories and intellect and Zarqawi's practical experience' (Abu Ruman and Abu Hanieh 2009: 24).

In the 1990s, Jordanian security forces successfully penetrated and neutralized most groups before carrying out their operations. By the end of 1993, almost all 'Jordanian Afghans' and several of their followers were imprisoned with serious allegations of torture, abuse and malfeasance (ICG 2003a, 2003b and 2005). As Abu Ruman and Abu Hanieh (2009: 17) noted, 'Jordanian courts were flooded with tens of cases, and jails were replete with hundreds of detainees and prisoners'. Arrested individuals included members of Mohammad's Army and The Armed Vanguard of Islamic Youth (detained between 1991–2), as well as Zarqawi and al-Magdisi along with around 20 of their followers in *Bay'at al-Imam* Group who were detained in 1993.

An important issue that prison reformers all over the world have begun to face is how to prevent prisons from becoming breeding grounds for violent extremism and terrorist recruitment centres. Increasingly, sophisticated extremists have managed to devise ways to turn prisons into training camps under their control (UN 2008; Bjørge and Horgan 2008). The issue here is not simply whether to isolate radical violent extremists from other inmates or from one another in order to prevent them from 'growing together' (Shelley 2008). Prisons can and have been used as an important rehabilitation tool to train and prepare violent extremists to rejoin their society, as the Saudi Case in this volume clearly demonstrates. Jordan, on the other hand, had to learn the hard way how prisons can be turned into recruitment centres for violent extremists and their ideologies.

The prison phase was vital for the evolution of Jordanian Jihadi Salafism. Al-Magdisi (2008) himself wrote on his website (www.tawhed.ws/r?u=dtwiam56.) describing the significance of this phase for the *Bay'at al-Imam Group*:

> The regime was feeling the threat of the proliferation of the calling (*da'wa*) to Jihadi Salafism amongst the general prison population; and feeling the risk of it spreading beyond the prison bars to the outside; and the dissemination of my books and publications while I was still bound my shackles. They tried to isolate us from the rest of the prisoners; they kept a tight rein on them and banned them from praying with us. They pushed anyone who tried to make contact with us, even greet us. Then they completely isolated us from them in dorms set-aside solely for us. No one else was allowed to come in; then they started to move us to different prisons also set-aside just for us; the last one was the al-Jaffar Prison, in the desert near the border, where they tried to isolate us from the rest of the world. But they did not succeed. Because everything they did brought us closer together. And they made it easier for us to contact a wider range of our brothers, which is what happened when they transferred us to the prison in Salt – they made it easier for our brothers from Salt to visit us after suffering the distance to the prison in Suwaqa; so that transfer made it easier for us to remain in contact with them. When they transferred us to the prison in al-Jaffar, we became close to the city of Ma'an and that made it easier for us to communicate with our brothers there, as well as provided us with another opportunity to get to know new people from there.
>
> *(Also cited in Abu Ruman and Abu Hanieh 2009: 31–2)*

Jihadi Salafism was not only growing inside Jordanian prisons, but also within outside incarceration centres too, and while al-Magdisi and Zarqawi were still in prison:

> During that period, other groups of Jihadi Salafists began to emerge, the most prominent of which was called the 'Reform and Challenge' (*al-Tahadi wal Islah*) movement, which appeared on the scene in 1997. Abu Qatada al-Falastini was accused of commanding this group from his headquarters in London … another group of Jihadi Salafists based in the *Baqa'a* were dismantled by the security services in September 1998 … and during this period, communication channels and contact between the Global Jihadi Salafist and Jordanian Jihadi Salafist movements were actually quite easy and effortless.
>
> *(Abu Ruman and Abu Hanieh 2009: 32)*

It is important to note here that the Monarchy's decision to restore parliamentary elections in 1989 was a tactical, rather than a strategic one. The regime had no intention of loosening its grip on power, receding control or changing the structure of power in the country. King Hussein's decision to restore parliamentary elections in 1989 was preceded and triggered by large-scale riots in several southern cities traditionally known for their blind loyalty to the Hashemites. Demonstrators and rioters demanded political liberalization, elimination of corruption and dismissal of the prime minister, Mr al-Rifa'I, who they viewed as an emblem of corruption in the country. As such, the restoration of parliamentary elections was no more than a temporary measure, a survival strategy. The regime also aimed at convincing the American administration of its 'irreplaceability'. The US, in the late 1980s, cut all financial support to Jordan over the question of peace with Israel. By restoring democracy and allowing the Islamists, who have always opposed negotiations with Israel and opposed US policies in the region, to win elections, the regime was sending a clear message to the US Administration.

'Budget constraints' (the need for financial assistance to maintain its patronage system that was so vital for regime survival) soon forced the Jordanian regime to shift gears and reverse its policies towards Iraq and democratization process (Brand 1994). It began collaborating with the American administration against Saddam Hussein's regime and soon thereafter entered into direct, secret negotiations with Israel, culminating in the 1994 Wadi Araba Peace Accord.

Meanwhile, following the trials of Independent Islamists and other violent extremists in the early 1990s, the IAF, realizing the shift in the political mood of the country, moderated further its views and decided to entrench themselves further in the political system. The IAF therefore 'announced that the goal of an Islamic state would be temporarily shelved and that they identified with the goal of the Hashemite Kingdom and its monarch ... even if these appeared to contradict "Islamic goals"' (Milton-Edwards 1996: 134–5). Further moderation by the IAF was met with further restriction of freedoms of expression and participation by Jordanian authorities. This undermined the credibility of the MBM and IAF, at least in the eyes of more radical Jihadi Salafists, who began to treat the MBM and its political wing as regime stooges.

Indeed, while the IAF started to prepare enthusiastically for the 1993 elections with expectations of a landslide victory, the regime moved quickly to undermine the IAF's power and influence inside the parliament. The most important mechanism through which the monarchy achieved its objective was through changing the election law into what came to be known as the 'one-person one-vote' system. The new electoral system was introduced a few months before the 1993 election despite the objections of the Islamists and 16 of the then 20 registered political parties. While the old system allowed voters to cast as many votes as the number of candidates in their area, the 'one-person one-vote' system compelled voters to vote only for one person. While the new system is not strictly illegal and does not prevent anybody from voting, voters in a country with a strong tribal and family structure like Jordan, were forced to choose between tribal and party loyalties. 'As expected, tribal ties won out over party affiliation, with the Islamists being hit the hardest. Islamist representation dropped from 32 to 22 seats, 16 of which were won by the IAF' (Robinson 1997: 376). The upshot has been a docile and pliant parliament that ratified the peace accord with Israel, although at the expense of democratic process.

Peace with Israel was one of the key issues which the MBM and Independent Islamists, as well as most Jordanians, adamantly opposed, certainly not before concrete guarantees were at least provided for a durable and lasting peaceful resolution to the Palestinian question and not at the expense of Jordan. Jordanians in general and Islamists in particular, who have deep-rooted historical links with the question of Palestine, were shocked at the pace of negotiations and the declaration of peace with the Jewish state. This brought to the surface long held suspicions of secret negotiations and relations between the Hashemites and Israeli officials. Jordanian opposition to the peace treaty grew stronger as the much lauded 'peace dividends' failed to materialize. As Fahid Al-Fanik, the most outspoken Transjordanian nationalist and columnist, wrote:

> Jordan volunteered in 1994 to sign a comprehensive peace treaty with Israel after hasty one-day negotiations at the top level, which took only a few hours, without American mediation and for free. For some unknown reason, Jordan opted to make the cheapest peace treaty in the history of the region, making no demands [in return] whatsoever.
>
> *(Al-Fanik 2000)*

By the time King Hussein died in 1999, the peace treaty looked and continues to be seen today, as a treaty between the Hashemites and the Israeli State. The emergence of marginal violent extremist groups in the early 1990s was used to silence any opposition against the Peace Accord and the regime's foreign policy. An 'open war on radical Islam' and anybody who opposes peace with Israel, was launched by a regime that traditionally derived a great deal of its legitimacy from its prophetical lineage. An open war on Islam was launched with explicit support and the full backing of the US administration. In his speech during the signing of the peace treaty ceremony between Jordan and Israel in Wadi-Araba in 1994, President Bill Clinton used a 'strongly worded message to the Islamists … that Islamic fundamentalism must not be allowed to succeed … that the United States would not allow the "extremists forces" of Islam to torpedo the peace process' (All quotations from Milton-Edwards 1996: 139–40).

The next 17 years, between 1993–2010, saw such a constant back-pedalling on the democratic process that all hard won gains made in the late 1980s and 1990s evaporated. New press and publication laws were introduced in 1995 and 1997, which imposed broad restrictions on media and press that criticized the government on a range of questions, including corruption and condemned normalization with Israel. The new restrictions also included a far-reaching censorship regime, enforcement of substantial fines on journalists and editors violating them, empowered the government to suspend and shut down newspapers for a variety of broadly defined offences and introduced prohibitive increases in start-up capital requirements of weekly newspapers. As the ICG (2003a: 5) noted, these measures drastically undermined the opposition and freedom of expression in Jordan, hitting hardest the weekly newspapers that served as a key source of criticism of the government.

In 1999, unknown Abdullah II ascended to the throne. To shore up his credibility, Abdullah II made a strong commitment to institute both economic and democratic reform, pledging to improve the living standards of all Jordanians and to turn Jordan into 'a society that empowers its people, and offers opportunity to all … an inclusive, democratic civil society, one that provides real hope'. He also promised to protect and accelerate Jordan's 'rigorous process of domestic reform [which] began some years ago … .'[8] As a good-will gesture, Abdullah II also issued a royal pardon in 1999 that released most prisoners, including al-Magdisi, Zarqawi and several of their colleagues.

Contrary to his declarations, Abdullah II's first move was to suspend the parliament for two years until July 2003, during which time he ruled the country by royal decree. Between 1999–2003 a 'massacre of legislations' occurred with more than 200 temporary laws enacted in the absence of the parliament (ICG 2003a & b: 7). Several of these pieces of legislations further harmed the credibility of the legislative process and accelerated a process of de-democratization. Incorporated in the new legislation were a new Panel Code, and Press and Publication Law that punishes all of those who express dissent, as well as tightening the government's grip on media and press. For instance, the new law introduced new licensing and censorship practices, imposed new restrictions on who may practice journalism, enforced prohibitively minimum-capital requirements for daily newspapers and imposed limitations for research centres (ICG 2003a & b: 3). Leading allegations of torture committed against opposition became widespread.

In 2001 a new election law was issued by royal decree, the 'single non-transferable vote'. The new law further disadvantaged the development of political parties by encouraging votes being cast for individual candidates or those representing specific groups in tribal districts supportive of the regime instead of those standing for political party platform. People's rights to gather or hold demonstrations were also undermined by new legislation, which demanded at least a three-day prior government approval for any form of political activity (European Forum 2010: 3).

Contrary to general perceptions, Islamists, particularly the MBM, IAF and Independent Islamists, did not advocate violence or become revolutionaries. Although they continued to oppose the peace treaty with Israel, the way it was implemented with the one-man one-vote system, and the new press and publication laws, they continued to do so through democratic channels and political participation. Robinson described the behaviour of the Islamic party in the 1990s in the following words:

> In contradiction to the usual arguments about Islamist movements being the greatest threat to democratic transitions in the Middle East … the Islamist movement in Jordan has been a force for democratic expansion since liberalization began there in 1989 … When Jordan and Israel signed their October 1994 peace treaty, the Islamists criticized the treaty, voted against it in parliament, and boycotted US president Bill Clinton's address to the Jordanian parliament on the occasion of its signing. In the aftermath of the signing, the Islamists (and others) continued their vocal criticism of the agreement, both on principle and on what they saw as an unseemly rush to sign it, but did so without violating the norms of acceptable democratic dissent.
>
> *Robinson (1997: 373–6)*

The same applies for the post-1999 period. Although Islamists criticized many of the new legislations that were introduced under King Abdullah II and further arrested political reform and democratization process in the country, they still did so within the democratic rules of the game. Although they boycotted the 1997 elections, they came back to take part in the 2003 elections under the 'single non-transferable vote' which disadvantaged them most (European Forum 2010: 3). The regime's refusal to reform the political system as it promised and its continual arrest of the democratic process, has led the IAF to boycott the 2010 parliamentary elections, the second boycott in just over a decade. They continued their participation in politics, however, mainly through professional associations, trade and student unions, and expressing their opinions openly in organized lectures, conferences, campaigns, radio and TV shows and interviews.

The regime's policy of 'controlled democracy' has succeeded in diminishing the influence of Islamists inside the parliament. As Table 5.1 clearly shows, the number of seats controlled by Islamists declined over time from 34 in 1989 to only six seats in 2007 and only one seat in the last election (November 2010). More alarmingly, the share of Independent Islamists which were likely to provide the only real alternative to counter-radicalization in the country and/or to convince those who have become radical to repent, has equally shrunk from 12 in 1989 to one (female) in 2010 (see the European Forum 2010; Al-Rantawi 2009).[9] These developments have had major implications for Jordan's relations with Jihadi Salafists.

First, the Jordanian regime by constantly manipulating the political and electoral system and ramming a peace treaty down the Jordanians' throats via undemocratic means, has constantly undermined the credibility of Jordan's Islamist movement, whose stand on democracy, and several other issues, has been severely criticized by both independent Islamists and Jihadi Salafists. These latter two came to view the MBM and IAF as weak and complacent, sacrificing Islamic principles for survival and

TABLE 5.1 House of deputies: general legislative elections 1989–2007

	1989	*1993*	*1997*	*2003**	*2007*	*2010*
MBM/IAF	34[a]	22[b]	Boycotted[c]	24[d]	6	1
Nationalists, Ba'athests & Socialists	13				5	
Independents (Royal Loyalists)	35				75	105
Turnout	60%			58%	54%	53%

Notes:

a. Out of 34 seats, 22 were IAF candidates and 12 were independent Islamists.

b. The IAF took 16 seats and six more went to independent Islamists.

c. Although the IAF boycotted the 1997 elections, six independent Islamists still won seats in the 1997 elections.

d. Out of 24 seats won in the 2003 elections by Islamists, 18 were IAF candidates and six were independents.

* In 2001 a royal decree increased the number of parliamentary seats from 80 to 110. It also reserved a quota of six seats for women.

Sources: European Forum 2009 and Curtis 2004.

incapable of effecting any change through democratic process. Secondly, the regime by arresting Islamists (moderates and radicals) and manipulating court system and trials, as well as the democratic process, has also undermined the only real alternative source capable of countering radicalization and deradicalizing Jihadi Salafists in the country, namely, Independent Islamists. The state's ulama were not in a position to do anything either, they were used to issuing fatwas justifying royalist policies and behaviour, and had little credibility or legitimacy to counter radical ideology. In other words, no credible body was left to deliver true Islam to the people and the only forums left to discuss politics openly were mosques. Even the state's appointed imams blatantly denounced peace with Israel and American policies in the region. A theological vacuum developed, which was filled by those with a distorted image about Jihad and its interpretation. It is within this context that 'Jordan's 9/11' hotel bombings in 2005 should be understood.

New regime, old approach: Jordan's response to terrorism

In February 1999, King Abdullah II ascended to the throne following the death of his father King Hussein. The arrival of a new regime (cf. Algeria and Morocco in 1999 and Bangladesh in 2005) provides an excellent opportunity to reconcile the state with society and initiate a new social contract to achieve peace and reconciliation, and prevent radicalization and extremism from developing into terrorism. Initially King Abdullah II seemed, as alluded to earlier, to be heading towards reconciliation when he promised far-reaching economic and political reforms. He also started his reign by decreeing a general amnesty to all prisoners, which included more than 30 Jihadi Salafists. Those with death sentences had their sentences commuted to life imprisonment. Among those released were Al-Zarqawi and Al-Magdisi (ICG 2005: 9).

It soon became clear, however, that King Abdullah II did not intend to initiate a reconciliation process. On the contrary, King Abdullah II has relied on security and military approaches more rigorously than his predecessor. According to Amnesty International, by the year 2000 more than 1,700 people had been arrested in connection with their religious beliefs. While most of these did go to trial, the trials were neither free nor fair. The state refused to establish a constitutional court, as recommended by the 1991 National Charter and the 2002 Jordan First initiative,[10] in order to resolve disputes over constitutionality of laws and hence enhance credibility of the court and judicial system. Allegations of torture, extracting confessions under duress, even fabrication of cases and witnesses have been well documented by Milton-Edwards (1996), Robinson (1997), Jordan National Centre for Human Rights (2008) and recognized by the ICG (2003a, 2003b and 2005).

Jordan, in other words, provided no exit strategy for its radical groups or Jihadi Salafists. Despite repeated calls by several state officials and Islamists alike to take the threat of violent extremism seriously and to introduce an integrated approach to counter violent extremism, the regime believed that security alone can deal with the problem at hand and overcome Jihadi ideology and scheme. The state thus persisted in its traditional approach based first and foremost on the ability of security forces to continue to penetrate Jihadi networks, followed by arrests and imprisonments. Indeed, only five months after his release, Al-Magdisi was re-arrested on charges of belonging to a terror group and remained in custody until March 2008, despite the fact that he was exonerated of all charges by the courts. His disciple, Zarqawi, chose to go back to Afghanistan and following the invasion of Iraq in 2003, he found his way through Iran and Kurdistan to Mesopotamia. There, Zarqawi established and assumed leadership of al-Qaeda in Mesopotamia, which soon became al-Qaeda's headquarters in the region. From Iraq, Zarqawi began attracting followers from Jordan and other Arab states, and started to plan his next operation in Jordan.

In the meantime, Jordan had been undergoing further processes of de-democratization, including further restraints being placed on the freedom of expression and association. Even professional associations, which had become the only place for political activity following the weakening of the parliament and political parties in the 1990s, were undermined. A new draft law in March 2005 banned professional associations from engaging in any political activity, changed voting procedures in order to weaken the MBM's influence inside municipalities and professional associations, and prevented them (associations) from using their funds for any political activity; restricting their use to internal purposes only. This was accompanied by further modifications for the parties' law, which also banned the use of mosques and other public spaces for political party activities (ICG 2005: 15). Jordan looked like a 'police state', a state unofficially under martial law and intolerant of any opposition regardless of its form, shape, ideology and approach (*The Jordan Times* 2005).

The outcome of such an environment has been a rapid increase in violent activism in the country. King Abdullah II publicly admitted that his security thwarted more than 150 attempts between 2001–05 (ICG 2005: 1). Some operations were more successful than others. Examples of successful operations include the assassination of the US diplomat Lawrence Foley in 2002 and missiles fired on US ships in the Gulf of Aqaba in March 2005. According to Abu Ruman and Abu Hanieh (2009), these operations were planned and supervised by Zarqawi personally.

From the point of view of the Jordanian state (and regime), violent extremism 'is not an issue of Jordanian policy ... [it is an] ideological struggle ... not an issue of politics', the King publicly stated. The attackers, he added, are 'misguided groups' that have a 'perverse view of Islam' which 'justifies the killing of everyone and seeks to do precisely that'. While still refusing to reconcile and carry out any dialogue with violent extremists inside or outside incarceration centres, King Abdullah launched an unprecedented ideological attack against what he calls 'misguided groups' and their '*takfiri* ideology'. This came in the form of the Amman Letter (Risalat Amman), which he personally launched in November 2004 and aimed at refuting the *takfiri* culture of Jihadi Salafists and 'to say that they have nothing to do with Islam' (All quotations from *The Jordan Times* 2005). The objective of the Amman Letter was to pull the rug from under the feet of the radicals and their ideologues by delegitimizing their ability to issue fatwas. The Amman Letter was issued by a convention of 180 Muslim scholars which the King organized from various schools of Islamic thought to spread a more tolerant but apolitical version of Islam, advocate coexistence between people based upon respect and mutual pacts and agreements, and refute the *takfiri* ideology of the Jihadi Salafists.

In addition to presenting a wide consensus against *takfiri* ideology and thought, and attempting to de-link it from the Islamic faith, the Amman Letter also sought to delegitimize extremist fatwas that justify terrorism and excommunicate the other. The regime therefore organized a conference in Amman in July 2005 of prominent Islamic scholars representing all schools of Islamic thought, including Shi'a and Sunni schools. The conference adopted the Amman Letter in full and approved fatwas advocating co-existence, moderation, the middle way (*al-Wasatiyya*) and rejected violence as un-Islamic and a distortion of the basic peaceful principles of Islam (Minzili 2007).

Almost one year after the Amman Letter was initiated and five months after the Amman conference was organized, Jihadi Salafists launched their most devastating attack in the history of Jordan, namely the Amman Hotel Bombing or 'Jordan's 9/11' in local idiom. The attack took place on 9 November 2005 and targeted three key hotels in the capital, killing 60 people and injuring more than 100. The operation was planned personally by al-Zarqawi, who used Iraqi citizens instead of Jordanians to carry out the terrorist attack, thus making it difficult for Jordanian security to infiltrate and pre-empt the operation before it took place. Commenting on the operation, the king highlighted how the terrorist group who carried out the deadly bombing in Amman 'has been transformed from a local organization whose attacks were once constantly thwarted into one that is slowly being fuelled by Iraqi insurgents' (*New York Times* 2005).

Immediately after the attacks, the regime increased confrontational rhetoric, announced measures to counter violent extremists and intensified ideological and cultural campaign against Jihadi Salafists. To mobilize the Islamic world and win its support for its policies, the regime organized and sponsored four major international conferences within the first five months of 2006, including a summit conference of the Islamic Council organization. Muslim scholars from all over the world were invited to endorse the Amman Letter (which they did), to delegitimize *takfiri* ideology and the role and qualifications of Jihadi Salafists as fatwa makers, promote a modern and tolerant version of Islam and advocate instead co-existence and respect for agreements and treaties signed with other nations, including the peace treaty with Israel (Minzili 2007).

In addition to making more rigorous use of the ulama to justify his policies and behaviours, the regime also began to rely more forcefully on its religious roots to gain religious legitimacy for its actions and undermine the religious authority of the Salafists. For example, he began publicly reiterating: 'the problems Jordan has had with Al Qaeda … because the Hashemite Kingdom of Jordan represents descendants of the Prophet Mohammad – the moderate Islam' (*The Jordan Times* 2005).

There is an agreement inside and outside Jordan that the regime's educational and cultural efforts (the Amman Letter and conferences) were no more than a camouflage to justify its deeply rooted security and military approach. Indeed, in 2006 a new Anti-Terror Law and a new Preaching and Guidance Law were introduced which further undermined political space and association, freedom of expression and gave security forces extra discretionary powers. Although the IAF and most other political parties opposed both laws (the Anti-Terror and Preaching and Guidance Law), they were still passed by a pliant parliament (Curtis 2010).

An important shift in security strategy also occurred. While the traditional approach of infiltrating and arresting Jihadi groups (reactive or containment approach) remains paramount, a new pre-emptive approach has simultaneously been adopted after 2005. The new approach relies on striking at Jihadists before they carry out their operations, even if they are based outside Jordan. To that effect, the government intensified operations and exchange of information with the US intelligence services. Jordan has now openly and explicitly joined the so-called 'global war on terror' and has linked its security and interests more than ever with those of the US. In a recent interview with CNN, Jordan's Foreign Minister, Nasser Judeh, described Jordan's struggle with Jihadists in the following words: 'this is a global war on terrorism' and 'we are in this together' (Judeh 2010). Judeh's use of the term 'war on terror' contradicts a growing global consensus against even the use of this terminology. As David Miliband, the UK's former Foreign Minister, eloquently put it: 'the use of the term "war on terror" was wrong [because] The phrase gives a false idea of a unified global enemy, and encourages a primarily military reply' and that 'The call for a "war on terror" was a call to arms, an attempt to build solidarity for a fight against a single shared enemy', which is misleading, inaccurate and which backfired (Miliband 2009).

As part of its new pre-emptive strategy, the JID (Jordan's Intelligence Department) formed what it called *Fursan al-Haq* (Righteous Knights) Unit, whose main task was to track Jihadists outside Jordan, including in Iraq and Afghanistan (Personal interviews with Jordanian officials, Amman December 2008). In his interview with CNN on 8 January 2010, following the Jordanian suicide bomber incident which killed seven CIA agents along with his Jordanian handler (who, embarrassingly enough, turned out to be a member of the royal family) in Afghanistan on 30 December 2009,[11] Nasser Judeh (2010), Jordan's Foreign Minister, summarized Jordan's new approach in countering violent extremism since 2005 in the following words:

> It's a religious order […] And we will do everything that we can to prevent these terrorists from carrying out their plans. […] And we don't wait for terrorists to implement their plans. We try to uproot them before they implement their plans … we've got to look at the track record and we've seen many success stories and we've seen many effective ways of dealing with terror and terrorism and pursuing terrorists. Let's look at how Zarqawi was pursued, for example. And there was another. Karbuli, who was arrested by Jordanian intelligence officers in Iraq itself because he was planning to attack in Jordan again … but let me just go back to Afghanistan and the war on terror. You know that Jordan is present in Afghanistan and has been present right from the beginning. We have humanitarian operations there, we have logistical operations, and of course we have operations that target terror and terrorism, because we have been a target of that, and we like to prevent that. And our presence in Afghanistan will not only continue, but it will be enhanced and increased. […] And that

commitment not only stays but it's going to be increased and in different ways and we'll see that.

(*Judeh 2010*)

Missed opportunities inside prisons

Fixation with traditional-military approach and foreign policy has deviated attention away from the important deradicalization process, even when the conditions inside prisons became ripe for such a process.

While the prison environment could be and in many cases has been, a fertile place for recruitment and spreading violent extremist ideology and thought, it can also be and in many cases it has also proved to be, a place where individuals and groups undergo a process of self-revision or *muraja'h* (Bjørgo and Horgan 2008). Prisons provide plenty of time for inmates to read the Koran, *Hadith* (Prophet's stories and speeches) and other religious material more carefully, sometimes leading to a better and deeper understanding of religion. This is more likely to happen when the prison environment provides opportunities for reading and interacting with other more secular, moderate and charismatic leaders (Ashour 2008).

In June 2008, a regional 'domino effect' reached Jordanian prisons. A small group of inmates (50 in total) in Jordan's prisons unilaterally declared repentance and denounced violence, either inside or outside prisons.[12] They called upon authorities to debate them and construct dialogues between them and prominent Jordanian scholars and scientists, 'exactly like Saudi authorities debate and dialogue their extremists' (Personal interview with Colonel Sharif Al-Omari, Director of the Rehabilitation and Correction Centres, Amman December 2008). As a result, the authorities, in collaboration with the JID (the latter micro manages literally everything to do with Jihadi Salafists' and counter-terrorism policies in Jordan), organized a two-month *ad hoc* programme, the aim of which was not so much to debate the inmates as much as to lecture them on key religious ideas that represented the gist of the Amman Letter, which espouses a moderate version of Islam and attempts to refute *takfiri* ideology. Lecturers and professors from various Jordanian universities were chosen by the government to deliver the programme.

The programme started with 50 inmates, 14 of which were released before the programme was completed, as they had served their sentences in full and therefore left in the middle of the programme or before it was completed. Only 36 inmates attended the whole programme from beginning to end. The 50 inmates came from different incarceration centres in Jordan and 'were mainly of a criminal background and not a security background' (Personal interview with Colonel Sharif Al-Omari, Amman December 2008). Colonel Al-Omari continues:

> The 50 were targeted because, as a result of monitoring, watching and surveillance, we noticed a change in their behaviour and thinking. They started to embrace salafists' ideas and thoughts inside prison. Therefore, we isolated them, gave them the course and then sent them back later to various incarceration

> centres where we brought them from. It is important to note here that these were only brought to the course as a result of our inclinations that they have become radicals. For example, some of them might have had tendencies to become radical salafists, others we might have gotten things wrong altogether with them and brought them by a mistake, and the third might have been carriers of *takfiri* ideology.
>
> *(Personal interview with Colonel Sharif Al-Omari, Amman December 2008)*

The main objective of the programme, according to Colonel Al-Omarai, was security and safety inside prison; to prevent proliferation of fundamentalism inside prisons; to promote harmony inside prison in general and among various groups there; and to prevent empowerment of one group over another.

The programme took the shape of weekly lectures and did not exceed two hours a week. According to Dr Bassam Al-Emoush (2005), one of the key professors chosen by the authorities to engage with inmates and lead the programme, the programme focused on four key points: relations between Muslims and non-Muslims, particularly the presence of foreign forces in Arab lands; sources and legitimate authorities of fatwa; the role and conditions of Jihad in Islam; and Islam and violence.[13]

At the end of the programme, the Jordanian authorities celebrated with much flair and publicity, the success of its deradicalization programme. Success was measured in the following way: '36 inmates of infidel thoughts who attended seven sessions of a religious dialogue [have declared] repentance from extremists' thoughts' (NCHR 2008: Endnote No. 9). Also, graduates at the end of the programme 'all swore oath to the King and shouted inside the prison "long live the King"'. A strong evidence, Colonel Omari stated, that these repentances were genuine and not feign was the fact that 'one of the inmates who shouted and declared repentance had a death penalty and had therefore no other reason to repent except genuine conviction' (Personal Interview, Amman December 2008).

Evaluating Jordan's counter-terrorism efforts

Observers of developments in Jordan and of the country's counter-terrorism policies are sceptical of the government's ability to reduce the threat of violent extremism. On the contrary, the nature of these policies and the response of the regime to the 2005 attacks seemed to have caused more, not less, radicalization in the country in general. The available empirical evidence supports the thesis that Jordan is actually creating and radicalizing more individuals than the ones it is arresting or deradicalizing. Abu Ruman and Abu Hanieh recently described the situation in Jordan as follows:

> Indeed, over the past 15 years, there has been no ebb in the number of official announcements declaring this armed group or that armed group of Jihadi Salafist has been exposed. […] Certainly, the courts in the capital Amman have been inundated with the names of hundreds charged in cases related to the country's national security.
>
> *(Abu Ruman and Abu Hanieh 2009: 13)*

Evidently, the Amman Letter and the ensuing cultural and ideological campaign, which the government launched afterwards, have had little impact either. The Amman Letter and the conferences and seminars it engendered and produced seemed more designed to the outside world than to Jordanian citizens or Jihadi Salafists. King Abdullah II himself acknowledged this fact in a speech delivered in Washington, DC at the Catholic University of America on 13 September 2005 when he stated that:

> The Amman Message is an all-Islamic initiative. It currently involves opinion-makers from across the Islamic world. God willing, it will expand to engage the popular preachers and grass-roots activists – what is called the "Muslim street".
>
> *(HKH 2005)*

The Amman Letter remains out of reach of the grass roots. Recently, many Jordanian officials and experts have raised questions about the effectiveness of authorities' anti-*takfiri* campaigns. As Ibrahim Gharbiya, a senior Jordanian expert on extremist Islamic organizations stated:

> … [the] denunciations of terrorism and the information campaign to inculcate moderate Islam have not reached deeply into the general public, except among those who were already moderates. Extremist ideas and violent groups … continue to serve as an instrument for recruiting activists … Our ideological and administrative campaign to forestall extremism has not succeeded because it has not yet reached the sources of violence and crime. The existing simplistic solutions have not helped in the war against violence and have even served it. The search for the correct approach cannot be postponed.
>
> *(Quoted in Minzili 2007: 67)*

As it is, the Amman Letter represents no more than a PR campaign 'for presenting Jordan as the role model and representative of "Moderate Islam"' (Abu Ruman Abu Hanieh 2009: 158). For most Jordanians, the Amman Letter is no more than a means to justify an end, and the end is maintaining hold on power, strangling and stifling political and democratic process in the country, and preserving the current structure of power, with the monarchy at its head with little competition. Worse, there is a feeling among most Jordanians of various political backgrounds, including among Jihadi Salafists, that the regime is doing the 'US's bidding and is trading on the global war on terror' (Personal interviews, Amman December 2008). This feeling is frequently reinforced by continuous assurances provided publicly by high Jordanian officials to the US administration; the last of these assurances was given as recently as January 2010 by Jordan's Foreign Minister, Nasser Judeh, who stated in an interview with CNN that:

> We are in this together … Suffice it to say, once again, that this is an ongoing war on – on terror … [and our] commitment not only stays but it's going to be increased and in different ways and we'll see that.
>
> *(Judeh 2010)*

It is no secret that the US is Jordan's main patron, providing the regime with around U$ 450 million in annual grants, which has become the mainstay of the country's polity. For most Jordanians, the Foreign Minister's above statement translates into the following: 'we will do whatever you want us to do, just keep the money flowing in'. To this effect, the regime not only tended to exaggerate the threat of terror, but also to 'trade on' the war on terror in return for financial and military support from the US government, a policy that proved fatal for both the former presidents of Egypt and Tunisia (Mubarak and Ben Ali).[14] As the ICG noted:

> Rather than vigilance the feeling was that the regime exaggerated threat of terror and over-zealousness by rounding suspects up. To the regime, the benefits of such actions, however overbroad, are clear. Defendants who are found guilty can be closely monitored; even if their links to militant groups are loose, this arguably provides added security. Moreover, by demonstrating not only the existence of radical elements but also the security services' success in fighting them, the authorities demonstrate their mettle in the war on terror to the local population as well as to the US, and can hope to gain increased assistance in exchange.
>
> *ICG (2005: 13)*

The ad hoc deradicalization programme, which started by default and was implemented by the authorities in late 2008, was disjointed, unstructured and is also extremely limited in its impact and reach. The Jordanian authorities admit that most of the participants in the programme were not hard-core radicals or Jihadi Salafists. Rather, they were former criminals whom the authorities believed were embracing radical ideas based on the 'inclinations' of prison guards. The most radical inmates[15] actually refused to take part in the programme because the individuals whom the state chose to deliver lectures and debate incarcerated radical individuals, had little credibility from the point of view of Jihadi salafists. As Dr Bassam Al-Emoush, one of key professors chosen by the authorities to participate in the delivery of lectures to the inmates, stated:

> ... the more radical elements not only did not take part in the program, but they also even refused to talk to me because they believed I was sent by the government which made me an infidel in their eyes. They even refused to pray behind me.
>
> *(Personal interview, Amman December 2008)*

Moreover, several individuals who were jailed for formerly allegedly joining violent extremist groups have already been released after spending their sentences in prison. But all of them remain under constant and strong monitoring by Jordanian security (Abu Ruman and Aby Hanieh 2009). Knowing very well that they are under constant surveillance and having experienced first-hand the inhuman treatment of security authorities, they have little incentive to re-offend or recede back to violent extremism. Lack of recidivism in this case does not reflect success. Rather, it reflects increased repressive measures. This makes it impossible to judge whether their repentance, assuming that they did repent, is genuine or feign.

Many high-ranking officials, including several former prime ministers like Taher Al-Masri (a former prime minister and the current head of the Upper House of Parliament), Ahmad Obeidat (a former head of Jordan Department of Intelligence and a former prime minister) and Adnan Abu Odeh (King Hussein's former and longest serving political adviser), openly warn that if political liberalization does not go far enough and the regime does not deliver on its promises of democratization and inclusivity, 'Jordanians may in time revert to undemocratic means to express their growing frustrations, effectively swelling the ranks of extremists' (ICG 2003a: 15. Also see ICG 2003b and 2005). Their fears were well placed. In 2006, the hardliners in the IFA have taken control of the *Shura* Council for the first time since 1994. In November 2010, the IAF boycotted the last elections and in December issued a fatwa declaring that supporting American military activities in either Iraq or Afghanistan or any other Muslim state is 'Un-Islamic' and violates the spirit and letter of Islam (IAF 2010). This is the first time they openly attacked the regime on theological grounds. The IAF's decision to boycott the elections has also been welcomed by both moderates and hardliners within the movement, as well as by Jihadi Salafists (Curtis 2010). Such developments are bound to have far-reaching consequences for Jordan and its relations with Jihadi Salafists.

The Jordanian authorities are not yet prepared to engage, deliberate or debate with their Jihadi Salafists because they perceive them as lunatics, or at best 'misguided individuals' whose major objective is to kill everyone because of their *takfiri* ideology. This view ignores volumes of theoretical and empirical research which clearly demonstrates that violent extremists are rationale, knowing exactly what they are doing and are primarily motivated by political, not ideological or religious factors (El-Said and Harrigan 2010; Sageman 2008). As long as this view pervades the minds of Jordanian authorities and shapes their actions in countering violent activism, moving away from a purely radicalizing military approach towards incorporating 'soft' but more effective measures, will not be possible. Ridding the country of violent extremist ideology will be even harder to overcome.

Notes

1 Although born in Salt, Haj Abdullatif Abu Qourah's ancestral roots are traced back to Syria and Palestine. For full information on the history of the MBM, see Al-Urdun Al-Jadid Research Centre, Islamic Movements in Jordan (Amman: Sindbad Publishing House 1997) and Harrigan Jane and El-Said, Hamed, *Economic Liberalisation, Social Capital, and Islamic Welfare* (London: Palgrave Macmillan 2009).

2 A new constitution was produced in 1951, accompanied by a political liberalization process initiated by the short reign of the late King Talal led to the introduction of a short-lived democratization process in Jordan.

3 This is mainly because Transjordanians became so dependent on the public sector for jobs, wages, subsidies, grants and other handouts. But with the onset of economic downturn in the early 1980s, the state was no longer able to provide its constituents with all of these benefits.

4 No figures or data exist for the exact size of social welfare provided by the MBM prior to 2002 when the MBM's Society began collecting and documenting all of its social activities.

5 While political parties were banned in 1957, parliamentary elections were suspended after the 1967 war and the resultant loss of the West Bank to Israel. The winning of three out of eight vacant seats by MBM candidates raised their share in the parliament to five.

6 By Islamists we refer to the MBM here.

7 Within months of winning the 1989 elections, the parliament, probed by Islamists, ratified six important bills: ratifying the agreement with the IMF and World Bank for market-oriented reforms and cuts in government spending; lifting martial law imposed since 1957; passing a new Press and Publication Law that provided freedom of expression; legalizing political parties; delegitimizing illegal gains and combating financial and administrative corruption; and endorsing the National Charter, which was designed to act as a blueprint for the democratization process in the country (Al Urdun Al-Jadid Research Centre 1996 and 1997: 50).

8 All quotations are taken from Remarks Prepared for Delivery to the Council on Foreign Relations, Washington, DC, 18 September 2003, posted on the King's website, at www.kingabdullah.jo/ main.php?main_page = 0&lang_hmka1 = 1.

9 It is important to note that Islamists boycotted both the 2007 and the 2010 elections to contest the regime's refusal to initiate a far-reaching political and electoral reform. One female independent Islamist (Wafa Bani Mustafa), however, defied the boycott and won a seat in her home district of Jerash.

10 The Jordan First campaign was initiated in the midst of regional turmoil and uncertainties, including increased US rhetoric against Iraq and the outbreak of the second intifada in 2000. It emphasized the need to change the status of women in society, or at least the way in which they are perceived. It also called for large investment in education, health and communications, fighting poverty and unemployment, and enhancing public freedom, accountability and transparency. According to the ICG (2003: 10), the goals of the Jordan First Initiative 'were to shift the public's attention from the crises on the borders to domestic issues and, in so doing, promote national unity'.

11 It was the *Fursan al-Haq* Unit which attempted to manipulate Dr Beblawi to help them uncover top al-Qaeda leaders in Afghanistan. On the other hand, the Unit played a key role in infiltrating Zarqawi's group and locating his place in Iraq when an American missile ended his life on 9 June 2006. See the next quotation from Jordan's Foreign Minister, Mr Judeh, below in the text.

12 Jordanian prisons have on more than one occasion engaged in violent actions with security forces. See National Centre for Human Rights (2007 and 2008).

13 All of these elements are now common themes in almost every deradicalization programme from Saudi Arabia, to Malaysia, Indonesia, Yemen and Egypt.

14 In fact, following the formation of Fursan Al-Haq in 2005, the US increased its financial assistance to Jordan by $100 million.

15 The exact total number of incarcerated Jihadi Salafists at the end of 2008 and who refused to participate in the programme is not known. While Colonel Omari stated that their number is 100, Dr Bassam Al-Emoush stated that they number around 200.

Bibliography

Abu-Odeh, A. (1999) *Jordanians, Palestinians, and the Hashemite Kingdom in the Middle East Peace Process*, United States Institute of Peace Press.

Abu Ruman, M. and Abu Hanieh, H. (2009) *The Jihadi Salafist Movement in Jordan After Zarqawi: Identity, Leadership Crisis and Obscured Vision*, Amman: Friedrich Ebert Stiftung.

Al-Emoush, B. (2005) *Refuting the Intellectual Fundamentals of Al-Qaeda, Al-Ra'I*, Amman, 14 November.

Al-Fanik, F. (2000) *We Made Peace with No Dividend*, in *The Jordan Times*, 14 August.

Alissa, S. (2007) *Rethinking economic reform in Jordan; confronting socio-economic realities*. Carnegie Endowment for International Peace, Carnegie Middle East Centre, Paper No. 4, July.

Al-Magdisi, Abu M. (2008) *Zarqawi: Advocacy and Advice*. Available HTTP: <www.tawhed.ws/r?u=dtwiam56.

Al-Rantawi, O. (2009) 'Breaking Apart: Hamas and Jordan's Muslim Bortherhood', in *The Daily Star*, 29 September. Available HTTP: http://www.dailystar.com.lb/article.asp?edition_id=10&categ_id=5&article_id=106940.

Al-Urdun Al-Jadid Research Centre (1997) *Islamic Movements in Jordon*, Amman: Sinbad Publishing House.

Amnesty International, *Annual Report* 2001. Available HTTP: <http://web.amnesty.org/web/ar2001.nsf/webmepcountries/JORDAN?OpenDocument

Ashour, O. (2008) 'De-Radicalization of Jihad? The impact of Egyptian Islamist revisionists on Al-Qaeda', *Perspectives on Terrorism*, Volume II, Issue 5: 11–14.

Bjørgo, T. and Horgan, J. (eds.) (2008) *Leaving Terrorism Behind: Individual and Collective Disengagement*, London: Routledge.

Boucek, C. (2008) *Saudi Arabia's Soft Counter-Terrorism Strategy, Prevention, Rehabilitation and Aftercare*, Carnegie Paper, No. 97, September.

Brand, L. (1994) *Jordan's Inter-Arab Relations: The Political Economy of Alliance Making*, Columbia: Columbia University Press.

Cunningham, R. and Sarayrah, Y. (1993) *Wasta: The Hidden Force in Middle Eastern Society*, London: Praeger.

Curtis, R.R. (2004) *Islamic Action Front, Encyclopaedia of the Modern Middle East and North Africa*, The Gale Group Inc, Encyclopedia.com. Available HTTP: http://www.encyclopedia.com.

——(2010) Déjà-vu All Over Again?: Jordan's 2010 Elections, in *Foreign Policy*, 15 November. Available HTTP: http://mideast.foreignpolicy.com/posts/2010/11/15/jordanians_go_to_the_polls

Dallas, R. (1999) King Hussein: A Life on the Edge, London: Profile Books.

El-Said, H. (1996) 'Jordan: the political economy of industrialisation in a rentier state', PhD Thesis, The University of Manchester, Department of Economics and Social Sciences.

——(2002) 'The political economy of reform in Jordan: breaking resistance to reform?' in G. Joffe (ed.), Jordan in Transition 1990–2000, London: Hurst 257–73.

El-Said, H., and Harrigan, J. (2009) 'You Reap What You Plant': Social Networks in the Arab World – The Hashemite Kingdom of Jordan, in *World Development*, 37(7), pp. 1235–1249.

——(2010) *Globalisation, Democratisation and Radicalisation in the Arab World*, London: Routledge.

El-Said, H. and Rauch, J. (2011) 'Education, political participation and Islamist parties: the case of Jordan's Islamic action front', *Middle East Journal*, forthcoming.

European Forum for Democracy and Solidarity (2010) *Jordan, Amsterdam, EUDS, November*. Available HTTP: http://www.europeanforum.net/country/jordan.

Gharaibeh, I. (1997) *The Muslim Brotherhood Political and Organisational Performance*, in Al-Urdun Al-Jadid Research Centre, Islamic Movements in Jordan, Amman: Sindbad Publishing House 47–77.

Gubser, P. (1973) *Politics in Al-Karak Jordan*, London: Oxford University Press.

Harrigan, J. and El-Said H. (2009a) Aid and Power: The IMF and World Bank Policy Lending in the Arab World, London: Palgrave Macmillan.

—— (2009b) Economic Reform, Social Capital and Islamic Welfare, London: Palgrave Macmillan.

Harrigan, J., El-Said, H. and Chengang, W. (2006) The IMF and World Bank in Jordan: Elusive Growth and Social Instability, *Review of International Organisations*, 1, September issue, 236–51.

His Majesty King Abdullah II (HKH) (2005) *Remarks by His Majesty King Abdullah II at the Catholic University of America*, Washington D.C. 13 September. Available HTTP: http://www.jordanembassyus.org/hmka09132005.htm

IAF (2010) *Fatwa* on Participation with American Forces in Islamic Countries, Amman, June.

International Crisis Group (ICG) (2003a). The Challenge of Political Reform: Jordanian Democratisation and Regional Instability Amman/Brussels, 8 October 2003: Jordan has weathered the Middle East's recent storms, but to maintain stability it must decide how much democracy it now needs and can afford.

—— (2003b) Red Alert in Jordan: Recurrent Unrest in Maan, *Middle East Briefing*, Amman and Brussels, 19 February.

——(2005). Jordan's 9/11: Dealing With Jihadi Islamism, *Middle East Report* N°47, Amman and Brussels, 23 November.

Jordan National Centre for Human Rights (2008) Human Rights Report 2008, Amman.

Jordan Times, The (2005) 'King Says Terror Won't Divide Jordan', Iraq, 13 November. Available HTTP: http://www.jordanembassyus.org/11132005002.htm

Judeh, N. (2010) *CNN Interview with Foreign Minister Nasser Judeh by Wolf Blitzer*, 8 January, Washington, DC. Available HTTP: http://www.jordanembassyus.org/new/jib/speeches/hefm/hefm_01082010cnn.htm

Kazem, A. A. (1997) 'The Muslim Brotherhood: the historic background and the ideological origin', in *Al-Urdun Al-Jadid Research Centre, Islamic Movements in Jordan*, Amman: Sindbad Publishing House, 13–43.

LLC Books (2010) *Political Parties in Jordan: Jordanian Communist Party*, Islamic Action Front, List of Political Parties in Jordan, Muslim Centre Party.

Lubeck, P. (1996) 'Islamic responses to globalization: cultural conflict in Egypt, Algeria and Malaysia' in B. Crawford and R. Lipschutz (eds) *The Causes of Cultural Conflict,* International and Area Studies. Retrieved HTTP: http//scholarship.org/uc/item/90v5s45r, 293–319.

Miliband, D. (2009) War on Terror Was Wrong, *Guardian*, 15 January. Available HTTP: http://www.guardian.co.uk/commentisfree/2009/jan/15/david-miliband-war-terror.

Milton-Edwards, B. (1996) 'Climate of change in Jordan's Islamist's movement', in S. Abdelsalam and E. Annoushiravan (eds) *Islamic Fundamentalism,* 123–42.

Minzili, Y. (2007) 'The Jordanian regime fights the war of ideas', *Current Trends in Islamic Ideology*, Vol. 5, The Hudson Institute, May 23, 55–69.

National Centre for Human Rights (NCHR) (2007 and 2008). *State of Human Rights in the Hashemite Kingdom of Jordan*, 4th and 5th Reports, Amman, NCHT.

New York Times (2005) 11 Top Jordanian Advisors Resign in Wake of Attacks, 16 November. Available HTTP: http://query.nytimes.com/gst/fullpage.html?res=9D03E4DF113EF935A25752C1A9639C8B63& sec=&spon=&pagewanted=print.

Oren, M. (1990) 'A winter of discontent: Britain's crisis in Jordan', *International Journal of Middle East*, Vol. 22. December 1955-March 1956.

Richards, A., and Waterbury, J. (1996) *A Political Economy of the Middle East,* Oxford: Westview.

Robinson, G. E. (1997) 'Can Islamists be democrats? The case of Jordan', *Middle East Journal*, Vol. 51, No. 3: 373–87.

Rogan, E. L. and Tell, T. (1994) *Village, Steppe and State: The Social Origins of Modern Jordan*, London: British Academic Press.

Sageman, M. (2008) *Leaderless Jihad: Terror Networks in the Twenty-First Century*, Philadelphia: University of Pennsylvania Press.

Satloff, R. (1986) *Trouble on the East Bank: Challenges to the Domestic Stability of Jordan*, London: Praeger.

Shelley, L. (2008) *Growing Together: Ideological and Operational Linkages Between Terrorist and Criminal Networks.* Terrorism, Transnational Crime and Corruption Center American University, Washington, DC Available HTTP: http://www.fundforpeace.org/web/images/pdf/shelley.pdf

UN (2008) *First Report of the Working Group on Radicalisation and Extremism that Lead to Terrorism: Inventory of State Programmes, Counter-Terrorism Implementation Task Force*, UN, New York.

World Bank (2004) *Jordan: An Evaluation of World Bank Assistance for Poverty Reduction, Health and Education.* Washington DC, World Bank.

6

MALAYSIA

A history of dealing with insurgency and extremism

Jane Harrigan

Introduction

Malaysia is a multi-racial, multi-religious Muslim majority society where approximately 60 per cent of the 28 million population is Muslim. It has a high level of religious and racial harmony as well as possessing a strong developmental state. The state retains control over Islam as practiced in the country and most Muslims are moderate and tolerant. These factors have helped the country avoid any major terrorist incidents in the past 20 years.[1] The country has, however, a long history of terrorist insurgency dating back to the 1940s and involving the communist insurrection, which ended in 1989. This history has shaped the way that the state deals with the current threat of extremism and violence. The use of preventative legislation, in the form of the Internal Security Act (ISA) inherited from the colonial period, along with a prison-based rehabilitation and deradicalization programme, is at the core of Malaysia's approach to violent extremism. This approach has been adapted from the approach to the communist insurrection.

The deradicalization programme in Malaysia is not one of collective deradicalization whereby entire extremist groups revise their ideology and renounce violence, as in Egypt, but an individual-based programme whereby imprisoned extremists undergo a relatively well-developed programme of re-education, including religious-based re-education as well as rehabilitation. The treatment of imprisoned extremists is essentially one of rehabilitation rather than punishment and preventative rather than punitive legislation, in the form of the ISA, is used to this effect. Malaysia's programme is small in size with only 154 extremists detained under the ISA between 2001 and 2009, and only 6 currently undergoing the rehabilitation programme at the time of this research in May 2010. This means that the programme can be a relatively resource intensive yet low cost holistic programme that involves the coordinated effort of several different agencies.

Although Malaysia has a clear and well thought out deradicalization programme, in terms of counter-radicalization aimed at preventing society as a whole becoming radicalized, its approach is more ad hoc. The state and civic society have a number of initiatives aimed at counter-radicalization but this does not really constitute a programme. The lack of a strong thrust towards counter-radicalization is probably because Malaysia is already a relatively tolerant, liberal and inclusive society such that many believe there is not a need for a comprehensive, counter-radicalization programme.

As with all deradicalization programmes, it is difficult to judge the success of the Malaysian programme. There has been no recidivism by those released so far, but this may be due to the fact that most are still under Restriction Orders under the ISA with close monitoring and reporting arrangements. In addition, the ISA, under which all religious extremists are imprisoned in Malaysia, involves indefinite detention without charge such that the detainees' only option for release is to visibly cooperate with the rehabilitation programme even if they do not actually change their thinking. The fact that there have been no major terrorist attacks in Malaysia over the past 20 years, however, suggests that the country's overall approach to counter-terrorism, including its deradicalization programme, has been a success. A large part of this has been a soft approach as opposed to a hard military approach and this is well summed up in a quote from the former Prime Minister, Mahathir Mohamad:

> We should seek to fight all terrorists everywhere and we should fight them not just by direct action but more by winning the hearts and minds of the people so as to reduce support for acts of terrorism and to reduce the attraction of acts of terror for those who see no means of redress for their own sufferings.
>
> *(Mahathir Mohamad 2003: 47)*

The next section of this chapter outlines the way in which Malaysia's dealing with the communist insurgency of 1948–89 has helped influence the current approach to the counter radicalization and deradicalization of religious based extremism. This is followed by an assessment of the current threat from violent extremism. The present day counter and deradicalization programmes in Malaysia are then described and critically appraised.

Lessons from the Communist Insurgency

Malaysia faced a communist insurgency in Peninsular Malaysia that spanned 41 years (1948–89) in which almost 20,000 lives were lost and which was waged largely by ethnic Chinese. In confronting this, the state realized that something more than a purely military approach was necessary and security measures were complemented by a viable socio-economic development programme, which eventually became known as the KESBAN[2] programme, as well as both deradicalization and counter-radicalization programmes. In the words of former Deputy Prime Minister, Dr Ismail bin Adbul Rahman in 1977:

> The fight against communist insurrection cannot and should not rest on the force of arms alone. The very important battle, one that can produce decisive victory and lasting peace, lies in the field of social and economic development.
>
> *(quoted in Sharom Bin Hashim* et al. *2001:169)*

The communist insurgency spanned two periods, the Emergency of 1948–60 and the second phase of 1968–89. Both phases consisted of guerrilla-style, armed rebellion by an ideologically driven group that wanted to topple the government and take control of the country. Terrorist tactics were widely employed by the communists, including attacks on rubber estate managers, tin mine operators, the security forces and members of the public as well as the sabotage of rural development projects. In this respect, the communists were not dissimilar to currently ideologically driven religious groups such as Jemaah Islamiah (JI). During the Emergency period, the Communist Party of Malaya (CPM)[3] sought to seize power from the British and then Malaya governments through guerrilla warfare. The second phase sought to take advantage of the withdrawal of British forces in 1967 following independence in 1957, and the armed wing of the CPM, the Malayan National Liberation Army (MNLA) engaged in 21 years of combat with the country's armed forces.

The Communist Party attempted to infiltrate society by recruiting new cadres of communist family members and their sympathizers in Peninsular Malaysia as well as in South Thailand. Through underground elements, they mobilized support in order to obtain food supplies, money, clothing and medicine in their stronghold areas. They also used communist propaganda through radio broadcasts and pamphlets such as the Vanguard and the Torch and tried to infiltrate trade unions, political organizations, and youth and student bodies. Realizing that armed struggle would need to be supported by the people, they attempted to win hearts and minds with their ideological propaganda.

To counter the communist threat the state strengthened the armed forces,[4] revised the Internal Security Act in 1960 and launched psychological activities and counter-insurgency warfare. This included resettlement programmes to move the population away from communist strongholds to safe areas as well as military civic activities such as involvement in rural development projects. Members of the Chinese population in particular were resettled into well-defended, well-equipped and economically viable new villages to help break the link between the Communist Party and the Chinese community. In addition to the army, the civil authorities were tasked to eradicate the CPM ideology among the population through socioeconomic projects and psychological operations. This was essentially a well-designed counter-radicalization programme. In 1979, this was formalized into the KESBAN programme, a unique socioeconomic security programme through which the operations of the security forces were merged with the government's national development strategy. Under KESBAN the security forces helped public authorities carry out development projects, both by providing security in the project areas and by directly helping with the projects. The aim was to improve the socioeconomic condition of the population so as to remove any source of discontent that the insurgents might exploit to gain support:

> The KESBAN concept has been defined as the sum of total measures undertaken by all agencies of the government to strengthen and defend society from subversion, lawlessness and insurrection. It involves economic, political, psychological and civic actions as well as security operations.
>
> (*Sharom Bin Hashim* et al. *2001: 169)*

KESBAN also involved psychological operations (Psyops) and psychological warfare (Psywar) in the form of a counter-radicalization programme run by the civil agencies, the police and the military and coordinated by the National Security Council (NSC). This was designed to gain the allegiance and loyalty of the population by undermining the insurgents' propaganda and to prevent their appeal to the strategically important Chinese squatters, tin miners and rubber tappers. The programme involved the dissemination of leaflets directed towards the insurgents and their supporters containing messages designed to lower their morale, create dissention and to persuade them to surrender, as well as the use of aircraft and loudspeakers to similar effect. Surrendered enemy personnel were also used in the campaign particularly as part of the anti-communist propaganda effort in Chinese villages. Using television, radio and other selected audiences the surrendered personnel would explain what had radicalized them and why they had subsequently abandoned the insurrection. In order to win hearts and minds the armed forces also engaged in civic actions to help meet the needs of the population, especially those living in remote, rural areas vulnerable to the insurgency. This involved quick impact projects with tangible benefits such as provision of medical and dental services, troop participation in community self-help projects and the construction of minor engineering projects. Civil–military relations were also strengthened by joint sporting activities, dialogue and local military displays to establish a rapport between the local population and the troops. KESBAN also involved a Populace and Resources Control Programme to resettle those in remote areas vulnerable to the insurgency and to improve their socioeconomic status.

In the implementation of KESBAN an area 15 miles south of the Malaysia–Thailand border covering 358 square miles was designated as the KESBAN belt. All socio-economic development projects in this belt fell under the responsibility of the National KESBAN Committee and between 1981 and 1990, 786 projects were implemented in this belt. These included infrastructure development, the upgrading of agricultural productivity, the construction of the East–West Highway, educational development, construction of houses for the very poor, and the construction of dams and hydroelectric plants.

In addition to the counter-radicalization programme contained within KESBAN, the government also had a deradicalization programme for the captured communist insurgents, which aimed to reshape their ideology and reintegrate them into society as well as providing support to their families. In the latter years of the struggle, the communist leaders were detained in the detention centre at Kamunting, which is still used to detain today's violent extremists undergoing the deradicalization programme. To facilitate the communist deradicalization the authorities used the Internal Security Act, initially enacted by the British colonial occupiers and then revised in 1960. Generally speaking, those communists released after undergoing the deradicalization and rehabilitation programme did not return to the insurgents' struggle.

The entire national programme aimed at defeating the communists involved many agencies and was coordinated by the National Security Council (NSC). The defeat of the communist insurgents and the signing of a peace treaty in December 1989 was not only due to the military approach adopted by the government, but was also due to the counter- and deradicalization programmes as well as to the developmental approach contained within KASBAN which helped isolate the Communist Party from the masses. This soft approach paid dividends by alienating the population from the insurgents and countering their ideological messages.[5] The peace process was bolstered by the fact that the Malaysian government took steps to address the grievances of the insurgents and the Chinese community in Malaysia by giving over one million of them citizenship and by providing them with land, business opportunities and a meaningful stake in the process of government. This rehabilitation of the former insurgents and their supporters was in accord with Article 4 of the *Agreement between the Government of Malaysia and the Communist Party of Malaya to Terminate Hostilities*, which stated that in addition to the citizenship clause contained in Article 3:

> The Malaysian authorities shall assist members of the Communist Party of Malaya and members of its disbanded armed units in order to help them start their peaceful life afresh.

To quote the former Prime Minster:

> They laid down arms because the Government of Malaysia did not just fight them with arms … We carried out a campaign to win the hearts and minds of the people so as to ensure that the terrorists lost their civilian support. We studied the causes of the disaffection of these terrorists and their supporters and we took remedial action.
>
> *(Mahathir Mohamad 2003: 34–5)*

In dealing with subsequent threats from violent religious extremists such as Jemaah Islamiah (JI), the Government of Malaysia has built upon the lessons learnt from the communist insurgency. It has clearly accepted that a hard military approach alone is unlikely to succeed and even in terms of the hard approach, it is the police rather than the military that deal with arrests and intelligence under the ISA. The propaganda war is also seen as important, a comprehensive deradicalization programme has been developed and in keeping with the KESBAN concept, a strong developmental state has ensured socioeconomic progress amongst all members of the population. Although Psyops and Psywar are not used in the same manner as under the communist insurgency, nevertheless various ad hoc approaches to counter-radicalization are employed to ensure Malaysia remains a tolerant and harmonious, multi-racial and multi-religious society. Although repentant extremists are not used in the mainstream deradicalization programme some are used in the special programme tailored to hard core extremists and run by the Royal Malaysian Police. This approach has built upon the experience of using surrendered enemy personnel during the communist insurgency. As with the communist insurgency, the struggle against today's violent extremists is a nationwide effort involving multiple agencies, coordinated by the National Security Council and chaired by the Prime Minister. In short, the experience of dealing with 41 years of ideologically-based communist insurgency and the existence of legislation in the form of the ISA have played a major role in shaping the government's approach to the more recent extremist threats:

> Malaysia can claim to know how to deal with terrorists be they Muslims or non-Muslims. We have been successful so far and we believe we can successfully handle future problems. In fact, we think that we can be of help in dealing with modern terrorism elsewhere.
>
> *(Mahathir Mohamad 2003: 46)*

The nature of the current violent extremist threat

In the past two decades, a number of religious-based extremist groups have emerged in Malaysia. These include Jemaah Islamiah (JI), al-Maunah, Kampulan Mujahiddin Malaysia (KMM), Daar al Islam (DI) and Abu Sayaf Group (ASG), which is Philippine related. DI, JI and ASG have trans-border operational capabilities and share a common ideology and militants often use Malaysia's Sabah on the island of Borneo as transit for travel between the southern Philippines and Indonesia. Of these groups, JI, which is a militant Islamic group active in several Southeast Asian countries, poses the greatest threat with its aim to set up a Pan-Islamic state in the Southeast Asian region incorporating Indonesia, Malaysia, the southern Philippines, Singapore and Brunei, which directly challenges the legitimacy and national integrity of nation states.

Jemaah Islamiah can be roughly translated to mean 'broader Muslim community' or 'Islamic congregation'. The name dates from the late 1970s but the group has its roots in Darul Islam, a violent radical movement that advocated the establishment of Islamic law in Indonesia during the Dutch rule of the 1940s. The formal group came into being as a result of the actions of a small number of Indonesian exiles based in Malaysia in the 1980s and it was formally founded on 1 January 1993 by JI leaders Abu Bakar Bashir and Abdullah Sungkar.[6] Initially JI rejected violence, but senior members who trained in the Saudi-financed Afghan Mujahidin camps returned with a more violent ideology and during the late 1990s JI became a violent organization as a result of links with al-Qaeda.

Following the launch of the USA's War on Terror, JI shifted its targets to US and Western interests in Indonesia, and the wider Southeast Asian region. JI was responsible for the 2002 Bali attack, after which it was designated as a foreign terrorist organization by the USA. JI also carried out the August 2003 attack on the Marriott Hotel in Indonesia, the 2004 Australian Embassy bombing in Jakarta and the 2005 Bali bombing. It has also been linked directly and indirectly to dozens of bombings in the southern Philippines. Whilst Malaysia was the country in which JI was created and incubated, between the mid-1980s and mid-1990s, the country did not experience any JI-related terrorist attack. JI was added to the United Nation's 1267 Committee's list of terrorist organizations linked to al-Qaeda or the Taliban on 25 October 2002 under UN Security Council Resolution 1267.[7] The US State Department estimates JI membership to vary from hundreds to one thousand. The group is held together not just by ideology but also by an intricate network of marriages which gives it a family-like structure[8] and it also depends on a small number of Muslim boarding schools in Indonesia to propagate its jihadist teachings (International Crisis Group 2003). According to Abuza:

> JI recruitment is based on four primary factors: kinship, mosque, madrasa and friendship; in short, recruitment is based on trust.
>
> *(Abuza 2009: 195)*

JI has been able to recruit from across the socioeconomic and educational spectrum, and consists of both the middle class, who are secularly and technically educated, as well as those with only a basic Qur'anic education (Abuza 2009: 196).

In response to the threat posed by JI the Malaysian state outlawed the group and, like Singapore, the state took a strong stance against terrorism, particularly after the Bali bombings of October 2002 when the Special Branch of the Royal Malaysian Police (RMP) intensified its counter-terrorism intelligence and security activities. With the help of regional counterparts, the JI threat has been neutralized to some extent with the capture of more than 240 of its members. The JI in Peninsular Malaysia and Saba was seriously disrupted in December 2002 when key leaders like Riduanb Isamuddin, Dr Azahari Husin, Noor Din Top and Zulkifli Marzuki were forced to flee the country. The shutting down of the JI-run Luqmanul Haki Islamic School in Johor forced the leadership to send recruits to Pakistan for ideological and military training, but this was further disrupted when Pakistani security forces unearthed the JI Al-Ghuraba cell in September 2003. Most of JI's top leaders, including Hambali, Abu Dujana, Azahari Husin and Noor Din Top have been captured or killed, mainly by Indonesia's anti-terrorist squad Detachment 88, whilst former Malaysian JI jihadist, Nasir Abbas, has renounced violence and now assists both the Malaysian and Indonesian governments in their fight against the extremists.

Security crackdowns and the arrest of key JI leaders has created a schism within the group between a radical branch that advocates violent jihad and a more mainstream one that favours peaceful means to achieve its aims. Some members were unhappy at the choice of targets by JI, such as the Jakarta Marriott in which mainly Indonesian workers were killed and there is disagreement about the appropriate focus for jihad and the practice of robbery of non-Muslims to support the organization (International Crisis Group 2003). Following the arrests of most of its founding leaders, JI has become a less cohesive organization and has become more horizontal with autonomous cells. In addition, its financial links to al-Qaeda have been disrupted. It remains active and dangerous in the region, however and Malaysia cannot afford to be complacent. To quote Sidney Jones:

> There is no longer any reason to think of Jemaah Islamiyah as the biggest threat in the region … it's no longer appropriate to think of JI as a regional organisation; structurally, it's a wholly Indonesian one. The Singapore and Malaysian members who are still active are more associated with splinter groups. That said, JI, despite rifts and fissures, remains dangerous as a recruiting pool for jihadi

> groups, and there is always the potential for a younger, militant movement emerging, particularly given the regeneration going on in JI schools.
>
> *(Jones 2008: 1)*

Malaysia's problem has largely been with external groups, such as the JI, using the country as a base due to its location in the centre of the Southeast Asian region. Malaysia has, however, periodically, faced threats from more home-grown religious-based extremist groups. In the early 2000s, a small group of Muslim Malays attempted to mount a violent struggle to take over the government of the country. They mostly consisted of young members of the opposition Pan Malaysia Islamic Party (PAS)[9] who had been religious students in Pakistan and were trained by the Taliban. They killed a Christian State Assemblyman, tried to steal arms from a police station, robbed banks and exploded a few ineffectual bombs but they were eventually tracked down and arrested.

Al-Arqm is another religious movement which initially concentrated on the provision of social welfare but then started to demand an Islamic state. Although it was disbanded in the 1980s, there was an attempt in the mid-2000s to revive its ideology but this was effectively suppressed by the government. Al-Maunah is yet another radical group that stole weapons from the military but it has again been disbanded with three of its leaders hanged and others detained under the ISA and put through the deradicalization programme. More alarmingly, in January 2010 an al-Qaeda cell of nine people was arrested in Gumba Malaysia. This was linked to the attempted Detroit airliner bombing and the cell was in the process of planning attacks in Malaysia. The cell consisted of one Malaysian national along with Jordanians, Yemenis and Iraqis. The tip off came from external agencies and the cell did not seem to be linked with JI.

In both Malaysia and Indonesia, where there are Islamist political parties, society has in the past decade shifted to the right and become religiously more conservative (Abuza 2009). PAS, however, did not gain much support in the March 2008 elections (gaining only 23 seats in the National Assembly) and likewise nor did Anwar Ibrahim's People's Justice Party.

According to the Malaysian authorities, the main radicalizing factors in the country have been ideological rather than socioeconomic. Causes of recent religious-based radicalism in Malaysia mainly relate to international politics such as the Palestinian issue and the wars in Iraq and Afghanistan with Muslims seen as being targeted by American foreign policy. Radicals experience secondary trauma via exposure to violent, associated images on the TV and internet, and recruiters use the internet extensively. Unlike the communist era, poverty and low education are not a primary radicalizing factor. This is partly due to the success of the developmental state in Malaysia and a degree of social engineering that has transformed the country into a middle-income country with a high degree of equality and with intentions of becoming an upper income country by 2020.

The fact that external factors are largely responsible for recent radicalization in Malaysia makes it difficult for the authorities to deal with root causes apart from their efforts in the international community to campaign against aspects of Western foreign policy in the Muslim world. This contrasts to the communist insurgency period when a lack of domestic socioeconomic development and a lack of citizenship were key radicalizing factors, which the government could effectively address. The fact that authorities have recognized the problem as being ideologically driven means that deradicalization and counter-radicalization programmes have become an important part of their battle against extremism alongside the more hard approach involving the security forces.

Malaysia's deradicalization programme

Malaysia's approach to today's violent extremists is based on its experience of defeating the communist insurgents and consists of preventative legislation, in the form of the ISA, combined with a prison-based deradicalization and rehabilitation programme. The ISA is an important pre-emptive sweeping law that gives the police extra-judicial powers to search, arrest, and detain without trial in order to prevent any acts 'prejudicial to the security of Malaysia'. Detainees under the ISA include those who threaten national security, those who threaten the national economy, and those who support a terrorist movement by: giving terrorists confidential information; providing financial aid to terrorists; involvement in military training; involvement with religious deviationists; supplying firearms or explosives to terrorists; communicating with a terrorist group; attempting to topple the government through force or providing shelter or accommodation to those involved in terrorist activities. According to Section 8 (1) of the ISA:

> If the Minster is satisfied that the detention of any person is necessary with a view to prevent him from acting in any manner prejudicial to the security of Malaysia, he may make an order directing that person to be detained for any period not exceeding two years.

The ISA, as well as providing powers for 'preventative detention' for the promotion of national security, also allows for the rehabilitation of detainees under Section 8 (4) and Section 8 (5) and the main purpose of the detention is that of rehabilitation.

In addition to this preventative legislation, there is harsh punitive legislation that includes the death penalty for unlicensed possession of firearms, explosives and ammunition. As a result of this existing legislation, which was originally intended to combat communist terrorism, Malaysia has not needed to pass any specific anti-terrorist legislation in the wake of 9/11, with the exception of the 2001 Anti-Money Laundering and Anti-Terrorist Financing Act (AMLTFA).

Under the ISA, suspected militants are arrested on the basis of intelligence that they are involved in militant activity. If the threat of violent action is imminent, the arrest is immediate, otherwise there may be a period of observation and intelligence gathering before the arrest is made. The threat level is assessed on the basis of intention and capabilities. The arrest takes place before any acts of violence are committed and there is no trial in court even if there is enough evidence for a court case to be brought. The lack of a court case is often justified by the need to protect information sources. Instead, the ISA allows for a 60-day interrogation period by the police. If the arrested individual is not released after the 60-day period, he either receives a Detention Order for a two-year period which can be renewed indefinitely, or is placed under a Restriction Order which also lasts two years and can be renewed indefinitely. Under Restriction Orders a person must report to the local police either daily or weekly and is not allowed to leave home between 8.00 p.m. and 6.00 a.m. Restrictions are also placed on their travel and they are not allowed to speak in public or hold public office.

Although human rights groups have frequently criticized the ISA, detainees are accorded certain rights under the legislation and under the constitution. An Advisory Board of three independent experts equivalent to Federal Court Judges is appointed by the King and during the 60-day interrogation period the Board meets the detainee and can make a recommendation to the King for release. The Board then interviews the detainee or his representative at least every six months and, at any time, can make a recommendation to the King for release. The Board sits like a court and listens to the detainee or his representative who can make a case for release. The Board's recommendation overrides any counter recommendation made by the normal monitoring committee, the Assessment, Placement and Welfare Committee (APWC), although in practice the Advisory Board and the APWC have always seen eye to eye. The detainee also has a right for application for writ of *habeas corpus* and can file a case in court at any time. In addition, the detainee has the right to file for representation to the Advisory Board at any time, the right to visits by a defence counsel, the rights to visits by family members and the right to medical check-ups. Nevertheless, if the detainee does not repent such that the APWC recommends release and if the Advisory Board does not intervene he can be held indefinitely without trial.

Militants arrested under the ISA are all held at the Kamunting detention centre[10] and are put through a deradicalization and rehabilitation programme, which is overseen by the Rehabilitation Unit based at the Security and Public Order Division of the Ministry of Home Affairs.

Between 2001 and early 2010, 154 religious-based militants were arrested under the ISA. Of these 117 were members of JI, 16 were members of DI, 14 of al-Qaeda and 7 ASG. They included 25 Indonesians, 9 Singaporeans and 12 Philippinos as well as several other nationalities. Not all of them were detained with some being placed under Restriction Orders rather than Detention Orders. Of those detained most have now been released (although many are still under Restriction Orders and most foreign nationals have been deported) and as of April 2010 only six JI militants remained in detention at Kamunting (four Malaysian and two foreigners), of which five were new cases. A further nine people were held under the ISA for human trafficking and false documentation. Not all of those detained agreed to participate in the rehabilitation programme although over 100 have undergone the Kamunting programme whilst nearly 30 hard-core detainees have been put through a special programme run separately by the Royal Malaysian Police (RMP). In the past, at any one time there were a maximum of 20–30 ISA detainees undergoing these programmes. Even amongst the non-hard core, very few are released after the initial two year detention period is over and according to Abuza (2009: 206) the average period of detention is roughly three years. In October 2006, the authorities released 17 members of JI and KMM, the largest single release to date.

Within the Kamunting detention centre, which also holds other low-level criminals convicted in court, ISA detainees are separated from other prisoners and held together in dormitories where they socialize amongst themselves. Cell confinement is used as a form of punishment of the ISA detainees and for hard-core detainees but in general, the approach is one of rehabilitation rather than punishment. In general, the conditions under which ISA detainees are held are better than those for ordinary criminals, and the objective is to provide safe custody in accordance with the UN Standard Minimum Rules for the Treatment of Prisoners, as well as to provide effective rehabilitation. According to one staff member of Kamunting, detainees are 'treated humanely, reasonably and lawfully so as to reduce the risk of re-offending'. There exists, however, a regime of strict discipline with wake up time, prayer time, study time, counselling time and exercise time. Whilst held in detention militants undergo continuous rehabilitation and monitoring with the objective of reintegrating them back into mainstream society and the core curriculum is designed to provide skills for reintegration.

According to staff at Kamunting the mission of the centre is to protect the public by providing safe detention and effective rehabilitation programmes and the role of the detention centre is to ensure:

- Detainees become good citizens and will not be involved in crimes or activities detrimental to national security.
- Detainees gain skills and are able to find decent jobs after release.
- Detainees have good physical and mental health.
- Society and the community accept and support detainees when they are released.

The objectives of the detention period are:

- To ensure detainees undergo the detention period until their release.
- To ensure the safety of detainees, staff and the public.
- To ensure detainees are treated based on humanitarian values.
- To ensure that the detainees' rehabilitation programmes are effectively implemented.

The deradicalization and rehabilitation programme for detainees can be divided into three phases – the 60-day interrogation period which is mainly intelligence-led and where the role of the investigating officer is to 'win over the detainee', the period of detention in Kamunting, and the post release phase of monitoring and rehabilitation. The core of the programme for detainees draws on elements from the Saudi and Yemeni programme. The objective of the programme is to ensure that detainees understand that their activities are a threat to the country and against the true teachings of Islam, and to instil an awareness of the responsibilities of citizenship regarding race, religion, loyalty to the nation and obeying the ruler. The programme involves religious instruction, counselling, welfare assessment and outreach work. The Kamunting phase of the programme is itself split into three distinct phases that detainees must pass through, which are designed and run by the Prisons Department with approval from the Ministry of Home Affairs and with monitoring by the Rehabilitation Unit of the Ministry.

Phase one lasts for three months, consisting of orientation, the design of an appropriate rehabilitation programme, security classification, spiritual and religious classes, civil, hygiene and moral education classes, an introduction to counselling and discipline development as well as recreation. The main emphasis in phase one is on discipline and ensuring that the detainee becomes familiar with his environment. Phase two is a 'personality enhancement phase' and is offered to those who show a positive response to rehabilitation. Detainees' recovery begins with religious counselling which is the core of the programme. At this point, each detainee's treatment route map is further defined and individualized. It is an intensive programme with help from The Department of Malaysian Islamic Development (Jakim) and is designed to provide a deepened understanding of moderate Islam with ongoing advanced, religious and spiritual classes, as well as a motivational programme combined with counselling. In Phase three detainees continue to learn through a structured rehabilitation programme that includes work, recreation, social and religious counselling and, depending on which category they fall into, educational or vocational training and a variety of specialized treatment programmes ranging from anger and emotional management to family relationships and parenting education. The vocational training programme includes training in agricultural production and in entrepreneurial skills. This phase also consists of an evaluation of the detainee by the APWC in the last three months of the initial two-year detention order with a view to possible release.

The overall programme is designed as a progressive stage system with good behaviour noted by officers and rewarded with a points system as well as counting towards the evaluation for release. Strict discipline is maintained with cell and restricted diet punishments and deprivation of privileges for those who transgress. Privileges include face-to-face family visits, buying extra food with money provided by the family, use of the library, writing and receiving letters, TV and newspapers, and attending family funerals and visiting family members in hospital. The prison authorities are anxious to point out that whilst detained there is equal treatment of all and that the programme is not intelligence-led with special rewards given for the provision of information. In addition, there is no discrimination between prisoners according to the nature of their pre-detention offences. In fact, the prison officers do not assess the initial level of offence and are given little information by the police as to the nature of the pre-detention activities with intelligence gathering and offence assessment largely left to the 60-day pre-detention interrogation phase carried out by the police.

Given that the authorities view ideology as a key radicalizing factor, much of the deradicalization programmes concentrate on ideological re-programming. Unlike Indonesia's deradicalization programme, Malaysia does not ask former militants to counsel detainees.

Religious scholars mainly drawn from Jakim, the state religious department, provide religious instruction sessions for the detainees and prison officers have worked closely with Jakim scholars to produce a tailored programme. Sessions with religious scholars involve lectures, debates and discussions. Religious classes are on a daily basis for one-and-a-half hours, but outside scholars only visit once per week with the rest of the daily classes being given by the prison staff. University professors who are knowledgeable and respected are also used, as they are not seen as government servants, unlike the religious officials.

Scholars try to convince the detainees to abandon the binary 'us-versus-them' dichotomized worldview in favour of religious pluralism. They also provide teaching on the correct interpretation of jihad i.e. an interpretation which stresses improvement of the individual and society. The focus is very much on trying to convince detainees to abandon the violent component of their ideology rather than to give up their ideology altogether. This draws on the theological dialogue developed by Islamic jurist Hamoud al-Hittar in Yemen in 2002. Militants are told that what they have done, and their rationale for violence is not approved by the Qu'ran and that they have an incorrect version of Islam and jihad and that only mufti can issue fatwa. The religious dialogue is designed to correct the misunderstandings of militants, including those relating to usulfiqh (Islamic jurisprudence), the concept of martyrdom, the concept of jihad, the interpretation of the Qu'ranic verses and the deviant teachings of Wahhabism and Salafism. In addition, it exposes them to different views of ulamas (religious scholars), teaches respect for other races and religions and diffuses the militant ideology by teaching that militant struggle is not the only means to obtain desired ends. Detainees are exposed to the views of other major religions including Buddhism, Christianity and Hinduism, with scholars from these religions giving classes. The authorities compile a religious profile of each detainee, including how deep his religious knowledge is. The religious education sessions are provided both on a group and where necessary, on a one-to-one basis. In addition to religious scholars, psychologists are involved in the rehabilitation programme with counselling sessions to discuss individual problems.

Although the authorities still regard ideology as a key radicalizing factor, in recent years the core of the deradicalization programme has been expanded to move beyond religious instruction alone, and now incorporates instruction on issues such as politics, international relations, relations with non-Muslims and non-Muslim states, living in multi-racial societies and other global issues. This contrasts to previous years when dialogue, debate and rehabilitation centred almost exclusively on religious issues. One of the reasons for this shift was a realization that detainees often had greater religious knowledge than their instructors and that there was a need to open up their minds more fully to other non-religious, contemporary issues linked to rehabilitation.

One particular facet of the Malaysian programme is that it does not denounce the JI goal of establishing an Islamic state. Instead, it stresses that the Malaysian government considers the country to be an Islamic state and the fact that sharia law is gradually becoming parallel to the secular legal system. JI members are not persuaded to give up this goal but rather to accept a slower rate of its implementation (Abuza 2009: 207).

Like the Saudi model, the Malaysian programme uses appeals by family members to try to convince detainees to renounce violence and to provide them with an incentive to reform by knowing they are still wanted by their families. This is less well institutionalized than in the Saudi programme, and is more reactive than proactive. In Saudi, family members are encouraged to visit at regular and frequent intervals and financial assistance and even accommodation is provided by the state for these visits. By contrast, in Malaysia, no help is provided for the family visits and it is up to family members to decide how frequently they visit. Although they are permitted to visit once per month in the initial two months of detention followed by once per week after this, some who live great distances from the Kamunting detention centre only visit once every six months.

A Special Re-Education Programme (SReP) is provided for the families of detainees by the Royal Malaysian Police so that they are able to help guide the detainee back into society. This programme instils awareness of deviant teachings of Islam and sometimes involves former detainees. It also explains why the family member has been arrested, and discusses and addresses all grievances and doubts with regard to legal procedures, ideology and welfare. Families are not forced to attend and no inducements or promises are offered. Although often initially hostile due to the arrest, the RMP report that a rapport soon develops with the family and family members can then be used to influence the detainee. So far, the RMP has run six such programmes for families in different regions of the country.

Whilst in detention a detainee or his family's case can be referred to the Social Welfare Department which is under the Ministry of Home Affairs. The Department will assess the needs of the detainee or his family and make recommendations for assistance. Financial aid is provided for detainees' families so that they are not forced to rely on the social networks of JI. Children in school are given books and uniforms if they need them, and jobs for the family as well as health care are also sometimes provided as well as help with any other family problems. This welfare assistance in some instances continues after the detainee has been released.

In the last few months of their initial two-year detention the Assessment, Placement and Welfare Committee (APWC), which is responsible for supervising and monitoring the detainee, reviews detainees' progress with the deradicalization and rehabilitation programme to see whether release can be recommended. The committee meets every month and consists of members of the Royal Malaysian Police, Ministry of Home Affairs, Social and Welfare Department, and Prison Department including rehabilitation officers and others involved in the rehabilitation process. The Committee, which is under the purview of the Ministry of Home Affairs and chaired by the Secretary General of the Ministry, reviews detainees' progress every four to six months and can recommend release at any time. There is, however, in practise, seldom any early release, with the average detention period being three years. Unlike the Advisory Board, the APWC does not actually meet with the detainee but reviews the documentation and reports on his progress with the report and recommendation of the prison officers being particularly influential. Recommendations are taken from the officer-in-charge, the rehabilitation officer, the counsellor, the welfare officer and the religious officer.

One strong point of the Malaysian programme is that it does not end at the prison gate but continues after the detainee has been released, with release normally being under a Supervision Order. The Police Department takes over from the Prison Department at this stage, and the released detainee is provided with continued counselling and religious education as well as with other assistance to help reintegrate into society. This includes training and the provision of a job if necessary. Some are provided with financial assistance to start up small businesses. As a result of the fact that the detainees are not recorded by the authorities as criminals and are not generally stigmatized by society as criminals, many are able to return to their former jobs – one former ISA detainee became Deputy Prime Minister. Periodic meetings take place between the ex-detainee and a member of the police force, to ensure the former's welfare is being taken care of and that they do not resort to their past militant activities.

A special deradicalization programme has been tailor-made for hard-core militants who prove resistant to the programme in Kamunting. This programme is run by the police rather than the prison authorities at separate locations. This special rehabilitation programme uses ex-detainees with religious experience who have repented and its aim is similar to the programme in Kamunting, namely, to dispel misconceptions relating to usulfiqh, the Qu'ran, martyrdom and jihad. In addition to dialogue with ex-detainees, there is dialogue with the police and religious scholars, although the authorities report that the use of the ex-detainees is especially effective in dealing with these hard core militants. The Royal Malaysian Police provides counselling in both group and one-to-one sessions and dialogue with the police is first used before the religious scholars are brought in. Some of those on the special programme have been detained for over six years and are particularly resistant to deradicalization and before they are released, they are subject to a polygraph test.

As with any deradicalization and rehabilitation programme, it is difficult to judge the success of the Malaysian programme. With a few exceptions, the government has not allowed independent researchers or journalists to meet with detainees. This makes it difficult to judge whether those going through the programme have genuinely renounced violence. The fact that most detainees, apart from six, have been deemed to have successfully completed the deradicalization programme and have hence been released without re-offending is one indicator of success. Many of those released, however, remain under Restriction Orders with tight supervision and monitoring which may explain the lack of recidivism. In addition, some have claimed that a coercive state also helps avoid recidivism:

> A number of former detainees speaking off the record have explicitly stated that government officials threatened them and their families with far harsher punishments if they engaged in militant and anti-state activities following their release.
>
> *(Abuza 2009: 208)*

The fact that the alternative to rehabilitation is indefinite renewal of the Detention Order under the ISA may also explain why so many detainees appear to be compliant with the deradicalization and rehabilitation programme, even though they may not have been genuinely rehabilitated.

Looking at the profile of those released it seems that most of them are junior members, sympathizers or logistical supporters rather than hard-core jihadist leaders (ibid.: 209). There is also a concern that the Malaysian government is releasing people without full rehabilitation as a rebuke to American foreign policy and the War on Terror, which Malaysia sees as anti-Muslim (ibid.: 208).

Regardless of the views on the success of the programme, there is a high level of state commitment to the programme, which is fairly resource intensive. This is possible due to the small size of the programme with only 154 radicals detained under the ISA since 2001 – this contrasts to the Saudi programme, which has involved thousands of participants and costs around US$ 12 million per year. The use of selective incentives in prison, as well as a clear understanding of the role of religion and faith in the radicalization process, and the use of clerics to counter this are also crucial to the success of the Malaysian programme.

Counter-radicalization in Malaysia

Malaysia does not have a specific counter-radicalization programme aimed at society as a whole. The general view is that Malaysia is a tolerant and harmonious multi-racial and multi-religious society,[11] which is not susceptible to religious-based radicalization. Muslims, Buddhists, Christians and Hindus live together in relative harmony. Nevertheless, a number of ad hoc measures have been taken to try to ensure that the country's religious views remain moderate. In the education field, the government tightly controls religious schools and their teachings, and uses the education system to build peace, foster tolerance and promote coexistence. To this effect government assistance to 500 Islamic religious schools, alleged to be misusing religion to promote anti-government sentiments and militant ideologies, was stopped and even private religious schools have to register with the state. The government is also monitoring students at religious schools in Pakistan. In contrast to countries like Pakistan and Indonesia, Malaysia does not have a problem with radical madrassas as a result of tight state control. All teachers are closely screened, especially teachers from abroad.

Islam is tightly controlled by the state. Clerics are state officials and are vetted before they are allowed to preach or teach and the religious authorities vet all sermons with the Friday sermon produced by the government. There is also a State Religious Department in each state, which manages the administration of Islamic affairs.

In terms of the electronic media, TV and radio are used occasionally by the government to help promote a moderate interpretation of Islam and other religions, and the state closely monitors radical websites, with the emphasis on monitoring rather than the closure of sites. The Malaysian authorities have good cooperation with cyber agencies such as the Malaysian Cooperation on Multimedia Commission (MCMC) and Cyber Security Malaysia to monitor and formulate counter mechanisms against the use of the internet for the dissemination of jihadist propaganda and other radicalization agendas.

Explanatory programmes on the danger of deviant teachings and militant ideology are often provided in schools, institutes of higher learning, government and non-governmental organizations. The danger of militant ideology is often stressed at meetings, seminars and workshops conducted by the government and institutes of higher learning. Officers from RMP who are specialized in terrorism and radicalization-related issues are often invited to give talks at such occasions.

The Southeast Asia Regional Centre for Counter-Terrorism (SEARCCT), based in Kuala Lumpur, also engages in capacity building and awareness building work in the fight against terror, with workshops, roundtables and lectures. SEARCCT also runs training programmes for enforcement officers on rehabilitation and on managing terrorists in the prison population.

One major counter to the spread of radicalism is the strength of the developmental state in Malaysia and the considerable socioeconomic development of the past few decades. As a result poverty and inequality are not driving radicalization forces in Malaysia. This is likely to continue in the future with Malaysia's Vision 2020 setting an economic target of fully developed industrial nation status and the eradication of poverty by 2020. The strong state in Malaysia and in Singapore, contrasts to the weaker states in Thailand and the Philippines, which have poor administrative coverage over their territories. To pre-empt radicals, former Prime Minister Mahathir Mohamad, who did much to promote the developmental state, also declared Malaysia an Islamic state that promotes a peaceful, moderate and democratic brand of Islam. Under the commitment to Islam, Prime Minster Mohamad formulated various Islamic policies in the field of education, economy and administration without alienating other religious groups:

> Malaysia is an Islamic state. At the same time, and without contradiction, it is democratic, diverse, tolerant, peaceful, economically and politically stable, progressive and forward looking. There is no inherent conflict between Islam and any of these achievements. In fact, we believe that the way we adhere to the essential or fundamental teachings and practice of Islam in Malaysia has contributed to our success as a nation.
>
> *(Mahathir Mohamad 2003: 78–9)*

Despite the tolerant nature of Malaysian society and the lack of any major terrorist incidents inside the country, the state cannot afford to be complacent. According to Abuza, there are signs of increased Islamic activity in Malaysia, although this does not necessarily imply any increase in radicalisation. Referring to both Malaysia and Indonesia, he states:

> … societies have become far more religiously conservative and pious in recent years, and which have a panoply of legal organisations and civil society committed to pursuing an Islamist agenda.
>
> *(Abuza 2009: 194)*

Conclusion – the strengths and weaknesses of Malaysia's approach

Malaysia has a unique advantage over many other countries when it comes to designing and implementing deradicalization and rehabilitation programmes for violent extremists. This advantage comes in the form of previous experience with the communist insurgency and the ISA legislation inherited from the colonial period. A 'soft approach' to 'win hearts and minds' has been used in Malaysia for decades. As a result, the current deradicalization and rehabilitation programme is a centre-piece of the country's counter-terrorism strategy. Detainees under the ISA are not stigmatized as criminals and the approach is one of rehabilitation, not punishment. Apart from the initial 60-day interrogation period under the ISA, the programme is also not intelligence-led and detainees are not forced to participate or rewarded for the provision of intelligence. The approach is also holistic with the overall welfare of the detainee and his family taken care of both during detention and after release, with family involvement in the deradicalization phase in prison. There is a strong post-detention phase, which not only involves close monitoring and supervision but also ensures that the detainee can find a job and reintegrate into society. Religious re-education programmes are provided for detainees' families as well as for those outside prisons on Supervision Orders, and there is a special deradicalization programme run by the Royal Malaysian Police for hard-core detainees resistant to the programme at Kamunting.

There are, however, a number of areas where the Malaysian programme could perhaps be improved. Apart from the special rehabilitation programme for hard-core detainees, which is run by the police, the prison-based rehabilitation programme does not use former repentant detainees to help convince militants to abandon violence. Instead, most of the religious counselling carried out by people from outside the prison is provided by clerics who work for the state in the form of Jakim. The use of state employees is possibly less effective than the use of ex-militants who are likely to have greater credibility amongst detainees, and the Malaysian authorities may do well to consider expanding the use of ex-detainees beyond the special hard core programme.

The prison-based deradicalization programme could also be improved by a more pro-active approach to family involvement, as in Saudi Arabia. In particular, the fact that families are not given financial help to ensure they visit detainees on a regular basis is a weakness of the programme which limits family involvement. The Saudi experience has shown that the family is a critical component in the rehabilitation process, especially as at the end of the day, it is back to the family that the detainee usually returns. Families should be integrated into the programme with regular visits, briefings on why their family member became radicalized and what the authorities are doing to rehabilitate them. Families need to be encouraged to talk to detainees and to point out what the authorities are doing to take care of the family in the community.

The programme of deradicalization and rehabilitation in Malaysia is a multi-agency one involving the Police Department, the Prison Department, social welfare agencies, religious authorities, psychologists, university professors, family members and other members from society. One possible weakness, however, is the division of responsibilities between the police and the Prison Department. The police are responsible for the first 60-day interrogation phase and the final post-release monitoring and rehabilitation stage whilst the Prison Department is responsible for the middle stage in detention. This means there is a lack of continuity which limits the detainees' ability to develop a close bond with one trusted individual. Prison officers for example stated that detainees seldom discuss their religious views or personal problems with them. In addition, there could be better communication between the police and the Prison Department with the latter complaining that they are often not briefed enough by the police on the nature of the detainees' actions that led to detention under the ISA, and that they are not involved in the initial and final stages of the process. It also seems, in contrast to Saudi Arabia, that the prison officers working with detainees function like traditional prison guards and do not build a close personal relationship with the detainee to encourage him to talk about his religious views and problems. The prison staff could perhaps learn from the Saudi experience, where guards eat and play sport with detainees, and build up close, one-to-one relationships, which are sustained throughout the entire rehabilitation process.

The library at Kamunting is very poor and there is not a tradition of encouraging detainees to undertake their own independent religious scholarship. Much can be learnt from the Egyptian experience in this respect where imprisoned militants are provided access to a rich supply of materials and are encouraged to use them to reformulate their own religious views. The Egyptian experience has also illustrated that allowing militant detainees to mix with other prisoners can have a moderating effect on their views. By contrast, the Malaysian militants held at Kamunting are isolated from other types of prisoners.

Human rights groups and a delegation from the Malaysian Bar Association have criticized the ISA and its indefinite detention without trial as well as harsh conditions under which detainees are held. According to Abuza:

> There are no doubts that fear and coercion play a central role in Malaysia's rehabilitation programme. Beatings, torture, long periods of solitary confinement and other punishments are routinely reported by human rights organisations looking at the conditions of ISA detainees.
>
> *(Abuza 2009: 207)*

The current government has released many held under the ISA and announced a review of the ISA in response to public pressure and is currently seeking the views of the RMP and other interested bodies. It remains to be seen whether the ISA will be abolished or revised. If so this could undermine Malaysia's current deradicalization process since the ISA forms the centre-piece of this programme. In recent years, the government has also become more open and transparent regarding the use of the ISA and the whole deradicalization process, and is anxious not to give the impression, as under previous regimes, that the ISA is used for political purposes to hold political detainees with too much power given to the Minister of Home Affairs. It is essential that the state ensures that there are no human rights abuses under the ISA. In addition, the state needs to make efforts to ensure that the outside world clearly understands the nature and functioning of the ISA whilst also being aware that detention without trial raises important human rights issues.

In terms of counter-radicalization for society as a whole, Malaysia does not have an integrated approach but rather an *ad hoc* series of policies. This includes close state control over religion and education. The lack of a strong programme in this area can be ascribed to the fact that Malaysia views itself as a tolerant and moderate multi-racial and multi-religious democracy not susceptible to radicalization. In this respect, a strong developmental state embodying the KESBAN concept has done much to promote such a society. This includes a vibrant democracy, with numerous political parties and free and fair elections every five years and good progress in stemming poverty and inequality under the developmental state. There is, however, room for civil society to play a greater role in both the deradicalization programme and the counter-radicalization initiatives. Indonesia, for example, makes greater use of civil society to counter radical ideology via the internet, TV and public debates and promotes important role models in their anti-terrorism propaganda.

Regardless of the above caveats, the lack of any terrorist attack in Malaysia despite the large number of releases possibly points to a successful programme. To quote Abuza's conclusion of his study on deradicalization in Singapore, Indonesia and Malaysia:

> Nonetheless, despite these many shortcomings and lack of transparency, the three governments have made disengagement and rehabilitation a corner-stone of their counter-terrorism efforts. As JI has been considerably weakened in the past few years, this strategy must be considered a component of that success.
>
> *(Abuza 2009: 211)*

Notes

1 The recent exception to this was the January 2010 firebombing of several Christian churches in an apparent response to the court ruling that allowed a local Catholic newspaper to use the word 'Allah' to refer to the Christian god.

2 KESBAN is the Malay language acronym for *Keselamatan* and *Pembangunan* which means security and development.

3 The CPM was founded in April 1930 and was recognized by the British at the end of the Second World War. It was banned on 20 July 1948 with the declaration of the Emergency in the Federation of Malaya following the launching of armed rebellion by the communists.

4 In 1970 another six brigades and two more divisions of the army were formed to help safeguard the country from the insurgency.

5 Another important reason for the defeat of the communists in Malaysia was that with the fall of communism in most parts of the world, the Chinese government took steps to foster closer relations with the vibrant economies of Malaysia and Thailand. The Communist Party of China subsequently stopped providing assistance and support to the communist insurgents in Malaysia.

6 Both leaders returned to Indonesia after the fall of the Suharto regime in 1998.

7 On 5 August 2006, al-Qaeda's al-Zawahiri appeared on a recorded video announcing that JI and al-Qaeda had joined forces and that the two groups will form 'one line, facing its enemies'.
8 Malaysian intelligence estimated that over 100 marriages had been conducted amongst the families of key JI leaders and that this comprised the core of the organization's membership (*The Star* 7 September 2004). As a result women are active in the organization, not in operations or leadership but in fund-raising, accounting, providing shelter to JI members and teaching and propaganda at JI schools (Abuza 2009).
9 Following the sacking of Deputy Prime Minister Anwar Ibrahim in September 1998, PAS became more radical and critical of the incumbent regime.
10 The Kamunting detention centre became operational in 1973 and was initially used to hold low level criminals and communist insurgents detained under the ISA. It currently holds 230 inmates and has 320 staff.
11 The exception to this was the so-called race riots of 1969, but the basic cause was economic rather than racial or religious.

Bibliography

Abuza, Z. (2009) 'The rehabilitation of Jemaah Islamiyah detainees in South East Asia', in T. Bjørgo and J. Horgan (eds), *Leaving Terrorism Behind: Individual and Collective Disengagement,* London and New York: Routledge.

Bin Hashim, S. *et al.* (2001) *The Malaysian Army's Battle Against Communist Insurgency in Peninsular Malaysia 1968–1989*, Army Headquarters, Kuala Lumpur.

International Crisis Group (2003) 'Jemaah Islamiyah in South East Asia: Damaged but still Dangerous', *Asia Report* no. 63, 26 August 2003.

Jones, S. (2008) 'Regional Trends in Southeast Asia Terrorism'. Available HTTP: http://www.Safeguardingaustraliasummit.org.au/uploads/sidney_jones.pdf

Mahathir, M. (2003) *Terrorism and the Real Issues*, Pelanduk Publications, Malaysia.

The Star, 7 September 2004, 'More than 100 marriages involve key JI members'.

7

COUNTER-RADICALIZATION WITHOUT DERADICALIZATION

The case of Morocco

Hamed El-Said

Introduction

The 16 May 2003 terrorist attacks in Casablanca,[1] and the follow up of attacks in 2007,[2] came as a surprise to most observers of Morocco's political situation. 'Morocco has always been viewed as a rare liberalising, modernising Islamic state, open to the West and a potential bridge to a calmer Middle East that can live in peace' not only with itself, but also with Israel (Erlanger and Mekhennet 2009). Morocco is also rare in the Arab World as a country with a political community that is more than 900 years old. The current ruling family, the Alawites, can be traced back to the eighteenth century, thus making it one of the longest and most enduring ruling families in the world. In addition to this historical, legitimizing role, the Alawite family's lineage and descent, directly from the Prophet Muhammad, confers upon the monarchy a unique source of religious legitimacy, shared only with the Hashemites in Jordan. More importantly, Morocco has been one of only two Arab States that have almost continuously maintained some form of political pluralism since political independence in 1956. The other is Lebanon. It was not surprising, therefore, that the attacks shook the regime to its foundations and were treated very seriously. The attacks themselves, however, remain largely unexplained, under-researched and little understood. The reaction of the regime to the attacks and the reforms they triggered, the most encompassing and wide-ranging in our eight-country case-study, has not only received little attention, but remains largely unknown.

Only a deep, historical analysis of Morocco's political, economic and Islamist evolution can provide a clear insight into the root causes of militant activism in the country today. Only through such an understanding can the opportunity to fashion effective counter-radicalization measures be realized. This chapter, therefore, is organized as follows. The following section traces the historical evolution of radical violent movements in Morocco in the pre-independence-protectorate period of 1912 and 1956. The chapter then divides the post-independence history of Morocco, based on opposition to the regime and strategies followed by opposition, into three main periods respectively: the 1956–65 consolidation of the regime and the rise of neo-left revolutionary; the 1966–74 rise of Islamist threat and the 1975–99 highly controlled democratic system and incorporation of Islamist and Neo-leftists into the political process. Section six sheds some light on the reconciliation process started by the late King Hassan II in the 1990s but gained momentum under the new king, Muhammad VI since 1999, while section seven documents counter-radicalization measures implemented since 2003 and triggered by the 2003 terrorist attacks. The final section concludes with some remarks.

Pacification *v.* assimilation: French protectorate and rise of militant activism

Unlike their assimilation approach in Algeria and to a lesser extent in Tunisia, the French authorities followed a completely different strategy in Morocco, one that is often referred to as 'association' or 'pacification'. While the old French cultural theory of assimilation hoped to turn Algerians into French and their economy and country into that of France, the 'association' or 'pacification' approach developed by the French colonial officer Marshal Lyautey, sought to rule, or at least be seen in theory as ruling according to native rather than European lines. 'Pacification' rested on a small number of select French officers who acquired deep knowledge of local Moroccan culture, religion (Islam), tradition, language and beliefs and sought to exploit strengths, weaknesses and divisions of the Moroccan society, the most important division of which was (and continues to be) that between Berber and Arabs. As Ayubi (1999: 90) wrote: the French formula in Morocco 'put a premium on the "subtle exploitation of the strengths and weaknesses of native society" and on respect for local religion, customs and law, rule through native institutions, and economic (though not necessary industrial) development'. Even the Sultan (the King before independence in 1956) was maintained in Morocco during the protectorate and his administrative apparatus expanded, although his powers were largely slimmed and reduced. While analysing the protectorate period, Waterbury (1970: 15) noted that, although Morocco experienced large transformations during 44 years of French protectorate, the country's continuity with the past was maintained, not least because the Alawites, who ruled before 1912, continued to rule during the French protectorate and even thereafter.

In other words, Islam did not face a direct threat under the French protectorate in Morocco as it was perceived to be under threat in Algeria. Attempts to turn Algerians into French antagonized the colony and revived strong religious sentiments that united all Algerians against the French. In Morocco, on the contrary, the French maintained traditional religious institutions and even protected them. It cannot be said, therefore, that a direct threat to Islam was responsible for the birth of radical organizations or movements acting violently in the name of defending national religion in Morocco. Several other intertwined factors, however, did – four of which are prominent.

First, was the fact that a Muslim country (Morocco) was occupied by a non-Muslim (Christian) country (France). Second, was the disposition and exile of the Moroccan Sultan (Muhammed V) in the early 1950s (Waterbury 1970; Ayubi 1999). These two factors, in particular the occupation of a Muslim country by a non-Muslim power and the absence of a Muslim leader to declare Jihad, traditionally form the most formidable case for Jihad in the Islamic religion.[3]

The third factor that radicalized a large section of Moroccans during the protectorate was the French's discriminatory economic, social and political policies. While the colonial authorities invested in ports, railways, infrastructure, dams, modern farming methods, public health and education services, most benefits accrued largely to the European community rather than to the average Moroccan. These projects aimed more at serving the needs of a European colony and sought to exploit Morocco's mineral and agricultural resources to its advantage. Politically and administratively, while the protectorate preferred to rule through native institutions and traditions, they still preferred a total subordination of native officials to the European civilian and military supervisors. In a similar vein, preserving the prestige of the Sultan at least until the early 1950s was accompanied by the trimming of its powers – a fact that represented an insult to all Moroccans.

Nor did the expansion of the administration bring many jobs to most Moroccans, as the administration was predominantly staffed by Europeans, while Moroccans were, at best, marginal participants in the running of their country. Similarly, only a handful of elite Moroccans were associated with, and benefited from, an expansion in administration and the development of a modern, advanced educational system that the protectorate authorities had built. Those beneficiaries were the sons of a few Moroccan notables, which the protectorate authorities relied upon as a façade for its pacification policy, to be *Morocco's Evolues*. That only a small number of Moroccans benefited from the protectorate's educational and cultural efforts was reflected in the fact that, when Morocco gained independence in 1956, more than 80 per cent of all Moroccans were still illiterate (Waterbury 1970: 33–43 and 82–4. Also see Ayubi 1999; Owen 1992; Richards and Waterbury 1996).

Discriminatory economic and political policies, occupation by a foreign, non-Muslim power, the undermining influence of the national leadership (the Sultan) and the desire to exploit and deepen national and local divisions, stimulated the emergence of a national movement in Morocco in the early 1920s. This national movement gained momentum in the early 1930s, following the public declaration of the Berber Dahir, which sought to divide Moroccans judicially between Arabs and Berbers.[4] The Dahir, which systematically excluded Berber areas from the influence of the *Makhzan* (government), was first introduced in 1914, but it was developed and defined more precisely in 1916 and 1921. That is, before the emergence of a committed nationalist movement capable of challenging it. It was not before 16 May 1930, however, that the Dahir was made public (Waterbury 1970: 41). Initially, the nationalist movement was secular and, at least until the birth of the nationalist Istiqlal Party in 1944, independence was not even one of its top priorities. The movement remained a clandestine movement for the most part and was thus unable to phrase its political demands or develop clear operational methods before 1944. Conversely, a Salafi movement was being born.[5] This Salafi movement had become concerned by the dilution of orthodox Islamic teaching and practice because of the European invasion of the country. In addition, the Salafi movement was concerned by the widespread application of unorthodox religious practice, including the worship of saints and a belief in *bid'a* (innovations that are usually linked to religion). The Salafis thus sought and 'called for a return to the tradition of the founders of the religion, the pious ancestors (*as-salaf as-salih*)' (Waterbury 1970: 44). This was, primarily at least, an apolitical, reformist movement not much concerned with nationalism. Its bearers were mainly influenced by the work of non-Moroccan ulama, particularly the work of Jamal al-Dine al-Afghani, Muhammad Abduh, Hassan al-Bana and later, Rashid Rida.

Traditionally however, and even still in contemporary Morocco, no movement, whether political or religious, succeeded without incorporating the traditional religious practices of Moroccans, including in particular the Sufi tradition (Ben al-Mustafa 2008; Dareef 1999). The marriage between the nationalists and the religious-salafi movement occurred immediately after the protectorate publicly declared the Berber Dahir in 1930. Since then, 'religion and nationalism [found] common ground within Morocco … From then on the twin objectives of the purification of the Muslim community and the expulsion of the foreign intruder became clearly linked'. (Waterbury 1970: 45. Also see Owen 1992; Ayubi 1999).

From 1930 on, the nationalists sought to revive religious sentiments in order to mobilize Moroccans for their cause. The mosques became the main theatres for protest and mass mobilization, drawing attention to the gravity and political implications of the Dahir and other policies of the protectorates. The marriage between nationalism and religious reform was strengthened by the spread of privately founded and funded schools in the 1930s and 1940s that sought to counter the French elitist educational system by emphasizing religious education and the Arabic language within a modern educational curriculum. These schools which were built in all major cities and towns were all under nationalist control and were later extended to rural areas to link the city-based nationalist movement with the rural population (Waterbury 1970: 46).

It was the exile of the Sultan in 1953 for supporting the agenda of the nationalists that eventually brought about the marriage between the nationalist and religious-reformist movement. The Sultan was challenged neither by the nationalists nor by the salafists. On the contrary, both viewed him as a symbol of religious and political unity. The marriage between religious movement and the nationalist Istiqlala Party enabled the latter to articulate, for the first time, national independence as a key objective and a top priority for all Moroccans. It further succeeded in mobilizing a large number of Moroccans from both rural and urban areas. Even before he supported its agenda, the religio-nationalist movement had already lent unconditional support to the Sultan, who by then was largely weakened and in many ways discredited. The Sultan had, after all, signed the protectorate document in 1912 and had thus proved unable to defend the religious, economic and social institutions of the country. The Sultan's value, at least in the 1920s, was being questioned. By openly reciprocating and supporting the demands of the nationalist movement, the Sultan guaranteed his stake in the future independent Moroccan state.

In addition to exiling the Sultan, the imprisonment and exile of other key leaders of the Istiqlal Party by the protectorates deprived the movement of its most moderating voices. The protectorates thus unintentionally succeeded in radicalizing many Moroccans and created a leadership vacuum that was filled by more radical elements – most of whom were not formal members of either the Salafi-reformist or nationalist movements. A militant extremist group, which Waterbury (1970: 47) referred to as 'a terrorist group', emerged as a result and they took matters into their own hands. This extremist group came from both an urban and a rural background, with the rural elements forming the majority, as well as being more radical and uncompromising with regard to the return of the Sultan. In 1955, even before Morocco had any regular armed forces, they created a rural Liberation Army and made the fight for independence and the restoration of the sultanate their primary objectives (Dareef 1999; Ben al-Mustafa 2008; Waterbury 1970: 47).

In 1956 the protectorate, after calculating its losses in Algeria, decided to cut its losses and depart. The Sultan returned to a hero's welcome and officially became the King of Morocco. After independence in 1956, the rural Liberation Army became the bedrock of support for the restored regime, reminiscent of an old pattern where rural and tribal support had always been a crucial factor behind the Sultan's survival and continuity.

To summarize the key point of this section, the phenomenon of militant extremism is not totally aligned to Morocco. In fact, Ben al-Mustafa (2008: 26) traces the first violent extremist movement in Morocco to 1117–20 CE by the Berber Ibn Tomort against the al-Murabitun regime which he accused of distorting and corrupting religious practices. Ibn Tomort called instead for *al-Amer Belma'roof and al-Nahe an al-Munkar* (implementing what God called for of good deeds and preventing what God forbade) and resorted to the Atlas tribes to destroy the strong Murabitun state in Spain and western Morocco. Violent extremism is not a new phenomenon in Morocco, but religion has often been used for that purpose. Religion is neither the essence nor the cause though.

Consolidation of the monarchy 1956–65

Like elsewhere in the region, political independence in 1956 brought high expectations of progress, prosperity, sustained development and democracy. When the Istiqlal Party lent its support publicly to the Sultan after its establishment in 1944, the party demanded in return the promise of a future democracy in Morocco. The Sultan subsequently refused to commit himself openly to democratization and to constitutionally introduce any notion of democracy in his public speeches, lest, allegedly, this affect the unity of the Moroccan people. It was thus agreed that:

> Istiqlal leaves to H.M the task of establishing a democratic regime similar to the form of government adopted in the Moslem countries of the Orient, safeguarding the rights of all elements and all classes of Moroccan society, and defining the obligations of each.
>
> *(Istiqlal Party 1946: 2–3)*

In 1956 the Sultan returned to the country as a hero. Realizing the popularity of the Istiqlal Party, King Muhammad V, the first king in post-independence Morocco, reverted to an old strategy to undermine the Istiqlal Party: divide and rule (Ayubi 1999; Richards and Waterbury 1996; Owen 1992). According to Waterbury (1970: 146) this strategy is referred to in the Moroccan context as 'divide and survive'. Internal divisions inside the Istiqlal Party were encouraged, as well as the formation of rival political parties, such as the Union National des Forces Populaires (UNFP),[6] Front pour le Defence des Institutions Constitutionelles (FDIC) and People's Movement (Mouvement Populaire-MP), which was established in 1959 following a split in the ranks of the Istiqlal.

Muhammad V and, after his death in 1961 his son King Hassan II, set themselves up as the leaders of the nationalist movement, modernizers and at the same time arbiters among the country's political and social forces. They created 'a system of government that centralised power in their own person' and set themselves up as the ultimate and only arbiters of social, economic and political conflicts, creating a veneer of credible neutrality (Owen 1992: 67).

Article 3 of the first 1962 constitution was consciously designed to create a political system that had been in permanent need of a nationally recognized arbiter (the King): 'While the political parties shall participate in the organisation and representation of the citizens, there shall be no single-party regime in Morocco'. When the regime was criticized for giving itself excessive powers, King Hassan II sought to justify those powers in a 1962 conference-speech with the following words: 'Imagine two football teams on a field, take away from the referee the power to whistle out and expulse a player, and then gentlemen, play. The problem is very simple, and thus is posited' (Ministry of Information 1965: 206. Also see Waterbury 1970).

According to Entelis (1980: 65) the Moroccan regime surrounded itself with a small number of elite politicians and notables whose number did not exceed 1,000. According to Waterbury (1970: 86) the total number of elite notables reached 1,080 including 100 army officers, 450 administrators of the ministry of interior, 300 high-ranked officials in the rest of the administration, 130 prominent politicians and union leaders, and 100 important members of economic organizations, independents and ulama.

> A key part of this system was his [the king's] ability to grant favoured courtiers and politicians access to the business opportunities that he could offer in his double role of manager of a large public sector and the country's leading private sector entrepreneur.
>
> *(Owen 1992: 67)*

Corruption, rent-seeking and patronage networks not only became widespread, but also came to characterize the new state as an important political instrument to maintain the elite's loyalty.

The King finally invoked his Sharifian roots (descent from the prophet), to enhance his legitimacy. Traditionally, the Moroccan regime relied on and exploited its prophetical lineage and religious sentiments to obtain and maintain legitimacy.

The post-independence regime continued to draw on its traditional and religious role, even choosing Koranic titles for itself (Commander of the Faithful). It is not surprising therefore, that the monarchy included a small number of handpicked ulama into its small circle of elite notables that executed the regime's policies. These nobles operated as the regime's eyes and ears throughout Morocco, and provided political and theological justifications for its policies and behaviour (Joffe 1992). As Ayubi (1999: 122) noted while analyzing the political evolution of Morocco in this period, the state, after political independence in 1956, was reformulated into a confusing mix of traditional and modern structures that permitted only a small margin of movement for political parties and actors. Although the first constitution (1962) declared Morocco to be a constitutional monarchy, the monarchy was also declared to be the Commander of the Faithful, the final arbiter and not subject to the laws of the country. Within this context, whatever political rights did exist in the system, were only seen as a 'gift' bestowed by the King himself on political actors.[7]

As in Algeria, therefore, the Islamic nature of the state was constitutionally and institutionally emphasized from the early days of independence. Simultaneously, religious practice was made a private affair. Article Six of the constitution thus states that 'Islam is the religion of the state and the state guarantees for each individual the right to practice his religious affairs'. The regime, in other words, makes a distinction between the religion of the state (Islam) and religiosity or practice, which is a personal matter. Religion, put differently, has been made to serve the state (monarchy). Whenever its policies and behaviours are consistent with the theological order, the nature of the regime with Islam is emphasized. That which is inconsistent is often explained by the forgiven nature of Islam (Dareef 1999: 192).

Pluralism got off to a relatively late start in Morocco and was, initially, short-lived. The first parliamentary elections were held in 1963, almost eight years after independence and two years after King Hassan II ascended to the throne. The objective was to provide ample time to Istiqlal's rival parties to consolidate their position. Before the elections were held, the monarchy established a Consultative Council to assist in the administration of the country. Its members were personally selected by the King himself. The council lasted from 1957 to 1959 before it was dissolved in preparation for the elections. When the election results turned out to be not to the King's liking,[8] he dissolved the parliament in 1965. Large and unexpected riots in the main city of Casablanca ensued that were ruthlessly suppressed. Leaders together with a large number of members of Istiqlal and UNFP, following an alleged plot against the King in 1965, were subject to severe harassment, arrests and other violations of human and political rights. It was not before the mid-1970s that parliamentary elections were to be restored.

The rise and fall of Arabism and revolutionary neo-leftist

The main aim of the previous section, which shed some light on the way the regime chose to consolidate its rule after independence, was to reflect on the internal factors that could have had radicalizing effects inside Morocco itself. The country emerged from independence underdeveloped, poor, unequal and largely illiterate, and most

Moroccans had little access to education, health and infrastructural services. Sustainable development, common sense would suggest, should have been the main priority of the new state. Economics, however, was neglected and relegated to a secondary stage, while regime stability and survival were elevated to the top. Not surprisingly, politics remained after independence as exclusive as it was during the protectorate. Little space for political action was given and the little that was given was short-lived. Rent-seeking, corruption and nepotism were, and continue to be, widespread. Those who managed to progress into higher education but lacked access to key patron networks in the country were systematically excluded from posts of real responsibility. Even today, Morocco's human indicators remain much lower than the average in comparator countries (World Bank 2005). The excluded and disgruntled became fodder for the nationalist movement.

Ironically, it was not the Islamists who first emerged as the main challengers of the regime, despite the contradictory nature inherent in monarchy's theological interpretations and behaviours. Rather, it was the pro-Nasserite nationalists and neo-revolutionary leftist-Marxists, popular in the Arab World in the 1950s and 1960s. Both internal and external factors coincided to create such a strong nationalist, revolutionary movement, some of whose elements believed strongly in revolutionary change (Ayubi 1999; Owen 1992).

Repression alone, despite its magnitude and unprecedented nature in the history of Morocco, proved ineffectual in undermining the Nasserites and neo-revolutionary leftists, particularly inside universities where their bedrock of support was based. Hence, the Moroccan regime began supporting the Islamic current as a strategy to counter Nasserites and neo-revolutionary leftists in the country. As Commander of the Faithful, the regime immediately incorporated the influential Ministry of Religious Affairs (MRA) under its direct control from the early days of its establishment on 2 July 1961. The MRA started to promote a traditional and even radical form of Islam to counter neo-leftists outreach in the country. In addition to the MRA, the regime also created in 1961 the Moroccan Scientist Foundation (*Mu'asasat al-Ulama al-Magharebah* – MSF) mainly to support the efforts of the MRA in countering neo-leftists influence.[9]

In fact, the Moroccan state followed a consciously open policy of attracting radical Egyptian (and Syrian) clerics and ulama, fleeing Nasser's repression. To that effect, the Moroccan state also established *Dar-Al-Hadith Al-Hassania* in 1964, a key religious institution specifically to fight neo-leftists, neo-Marxists and Arab nationalism in Morocco and the region. *Dar-Al-Hadith* began publishing books by radical Islamists, such as the work of Sayyid Qutb, including his most extreme book *Ma'lem al Tareeq* (Signposts on the Road), which he wrote when he was in prison and in which he calls openly for revolting against rulers who do not rule according to Islamic principles (Ben al-Mustafa 2008: 28 and 29).

Moreover, the regime began reviving the old Sufi tradition by 'consciously encouraging delegations to annual *Moussems* (anniversaries) of local saints,[10] and … insisting that all Moroccan students receive religious instruction and perform ritual prayers during school hours' (Waterbury 1970: 154). The MRA also started sending

Moroccans to Saudi Arabia as part of a student scholarship programme in order to study religion and the *Hadeeth* (the prophet's stories and speeches). Although this programme started in the early 1970s, it was candidly enlarged and augmented in the mid-1970s when Morocco was facing an economic crisis and was seeking financial support from Saudi Arabia. Many of these students returned from Saudi Arabia, which was itself hosting radical Egyptian and Syrian clerics that came to dominate the Saudi educational and religious institutions. Saturated with a radical ideology they began preaching in local mosques. Their reach and legitimacy were enhanced by serving on the Scientific Councils, which were suffering from shortages of personnel, as Imams and religious preachers (Ben al-Mustafa 2008: 63).

It was not surprising that these policies soon backfired, as they did in Egypt under Sadat and in Algeria under Bendjedid, and led to the emergence of a new, radical *salafi* movement that soon turned against the regime itself. The Youth Islamic Group (*Harakat al-Chabeba al-Islameya*), formally established in 1969, was the first radical-Islamic expression in post-independence Morocco. Since then, the country has experienced a growth in the number of Islamic expressions. We will shed some light on each of these movements in later sections.

Most observers agree that *al-Chabeba* started its operations a few years before its organizational emergence in 1969; benefiting from a 1958 law that permitted the establishment of civil society and charitable organizations. *Al-Chabeba* founder, Abdualkarim Mutee', was a member of the National Union for the Public Forces, before abandoning it for lack of vertical mobility. Mutee' established his Islamist movement (*al-Chabeba*) immediately after returning from Hajj (Saudi Arabia) in the late 1960s.

Mutee' had two faces: a public and a private face. Publicly he praised the regime and always stated that the movement was apolitical; focusing only on education and religious teaching through *da'wa* (calling or missionary) that follows a *belati heya ahssan* approach (peaceful means and conviction).

At street level, Mutee' mocked the primitive nature of the regime and exposed the contradictory nature of its religious behaviour. In his speeches the ideas and teachings of radical clerics such as Sayyid Qutb were openly promoted. Even as Mutee' always emphasized the religious and apolitical nature of his movement, he made 'fighting infidelism which the Left Marxism spreads' as well as 'teach[ing] the leftists a lesson and [their] infidel thinkers and supporters …' one of the key objectives of the movement (Ben al-Mustafa 2008: 63).

Al-Chabeba soon began attracting a large number of Moroccans as a result of the vacuum created by repeated attacks against leftists by the authorities and which reached their peak in 1973 when the National Union for Moroccan Students was banned.[11] Mutee' soon became known as 'Sayyid Qutb of Morocco' particularly after he established in 1970 a Jihadi wing to *Al-Chabeba*, to add to the original calling (*da'wa*) wing (Dareef 1999: 24). This was followed by the establishment of a legal entity (Jame'yat al Chabeba al Isamiya) for which *Al-Chabeba* received a license from the authorities in 1972. The objective of the *Jame'yat* was to provide a camouflage, a legal coverage for the underground work of the movement. With tacit support from the regime, members of the *al-Chabeba* and leftists began clashing regularly, particularly inside Moroccan universities and educational institutions. The situation culminated in the assassination of Omar Jaloon, a key leader in the Union Socialist Party and Abdulrahim al-Menawe of the Progress and Socialists Party in 1975. Members of the *al-Chabeba* were accused of carrying out the assassination. The regime, fearing an increase in the popularity of the al-*Chabeba*, seized the opportunity to undermine the movement. Members and key leaders of *al-Chabeba* were consequently arrested and exiled. Abdualkarim Mutee' became further radicalized when he was sentenced to death twice *in absentia* in the early and mid-1970s. He publicly attacked the regime and called for a revolutionary reform before fleeing to Libya where he established *Tantheem al-Jihad* (al-Jihad Organization) in 1983. Its members, however, were made destitute, jailed, exiled and pursued by the Libyan and Moroccan regimes alike. The *al-Chabeba* was banned in 1975 and has almost disappeared since then.[12]

Controlled democracy and rise of moderate Islam: 1975–99

The 1970s began with two failed military coups in 1971 and 1972. The repercussion of these coups was to alert the regime to the gravity of the situation and to the dangers inherent in the personal political system which the king created on a narrow base of support, one that is based more on a patron–client network format. In 1977 therefore, parliamentary elections were restored, but under very strict political conditions. Those included unconditional and unquestionable acquiescence in the *Alawite's* dynasty and particularly in the Commander of the Faithful institution, the state's ritual-religious custom of Sunni–Maliki–Sufi tradition, as well as endorsing the regime's highly nationalistic campaign to incorporate Western Sahara into Moroccan rule.[13] Since 1977, multiparty elections were held relatively regularly, though erratically, but only along the lines mentioned above. They were further subject to constant manipulation by the state, including what could and could not be discussed and were therefore, 'neither free nor fair' (Owen 1992: 299).

Under the veneer of democracy, 'divide and survive' continued to be a key strategy assiduously pursued by the state. New loyal parties were encouraged, fragmentation and weaknesses among existing parties, unions and associations exploited, along with other manipulative tactics that infiltrated, further divided and fragmented the political system. This was an important element of the political strategy pursued by the regime to maintain and reinforce its function as an ultimate arbiter in the country. Examples of new political parties that emerged, if not tacitly encouraged by the regime, in addition to the Mouvement Populaire (MP), include the short-lived Front pour la Défense des Institutions Constitutionelles (FDIC), the Rassemblement National des Indépendants (RNI – 1978), the Union Socialiste des Forces Populaires (USFP – 1975) and the Union Constitutionel (UC – 1983). By the time the fourth parliamentary elections took place in post-independence Morocco in 1984, with the third taking place only in 1977, the country had eight major political parties contesting elections.[14] None of these parties were, or allowed to become, strong enough to dominate the parliament and all of them were compelled to demonstrate their loyalty to the monarchy and its policies before being allowed to contest elections (Owen 1992: 233).[15]

'Islam', moreover, 'continued to be endorsed as a form of social control'. Religion underwent a form of nationalization, with no independent religious institution permitted to function autonomously from the state. Other measures included censorship and control of all religious publications, introducing stringent licensing requirements for new religious (and secular) movements, parties or activities, bringing mosques and Friday sermons more under the direction of the MRA and increasing 'funding of Islamic institutions of learning and the scholars who inhabit them', particularly those under state control (All quotations from Tripp 1996: 58).

The role of ulama received special and increasing attention, not only as moulders and shapers of the version of Islam which the state sought to promote among ordinary Moroccans, but also as providers of theological justifications for what many Moroccans perceived as the state's anti-Islamic behaviour. The need for bringing ulama more under the direction of the state became increasingly more urgent in the 1970s and early 1980s following the mounting of severe criticism by several ulama that openly began to challenge what they perceived as the anti-Islamic and contradictory behaviour of the regime.[16] The Moroccan Scientist Foundation was, therefore, reformed in a way to court the key ulama in the country and to prevent their drift in an opposite direction.[17]

Following the *al-Chabeba* saga, the regime became wary of creating religious political parties, although the establishment of loyal Islamic movements was condoned, actually encouraged, not least for social and economic reasons, as will be demonstrated later in this chapter. But out of Morocco's 33 officially acknowledged political parties today, only one, the Justice and Development Party, can be truly described as an Islamic party in the sense of openly campaigning on Islamic principles and values, and candidly lifting Islamic slogans.

Today it is possible to divide the Islamic expression in Morocco into four main currents, according to their strategy of operation and position *vis-à-vis* the state.[18] First, is a *salafi*-radical current (referred to by the Moroccan authorities as *al-Jihadiya al-Salafiya*). It calls for a complete severing of links with the regime, even with the entire society and calls for the use of violence to achieve its key objective, that is, the establishment of an Islamic State. This current, which some members of the former *al-Chabeba* represent, is very small and much marginalized in Morocco. It is perhaps more important outside than inside Morocco, as reflected by the 2004 Madrid attacks.

The second Islamic expression in Morocco is a political current, actively engaged with and incorporated in the Moroccan political system. It includes two main movements/groupings and one party: *Jamiat al-Adl wa al-Ihsan* (the Justice and Charity Group – JCG),[19] *Harakat al-Tawheed wal Islah* (Unity and Reform Movement – URM)[20] and *Hizab al-Adala wa al-Tanmeya* (Party of Justice and Development – PJD).[21] The JCG, URM and PJD are, by far, the largest Islamic groupings in Morocco today and are politically the most active, although the URM practices politics indirectly through PJD.

The fourth and final Islamic expression in Morocco is a calling (missionary) current, of which four are most prominent in Morocco today: *Tabligh wal-Da'wa* (TWD),[22] *al-Badeel al-Hadari* (Contemporary Alternative – CA),[23] *Al-Harakah Min Ajal al-Umah*

(The Movement for the Nation's Sake – MNS)[24] and *Rabitat al-Mustagbal al-Islami* (The Foundation of the Islamic Future – FIF).[25]

Apart from the marginalized *salafiya jihadiya,* all of the above-mentioned Islamic currents are either incorporated in the political system or accept pluralism, democracy and a tolerant version of Islam. They do not advocate violence and accept the state as the main framework of their political activity and as a final arbiter among all political activists. They also support a developmental role for women in society, including the right to work, vote and be active in societal issues. Most also accept the institution of the Commander of the Faithful, denounce violence and do not question the role of the monarchy. Although the JCG continues to boycott elections, they do not oppose democracy *per se*. Rather they oppose what they see as unfair and restricted democracy in Morocco (Willis 2004). While many, such as the PJD and URM, do not describe themselves as followers of Sufi tradition, they do not excommunicate Sufism or its followers, and support the country's Sunni-Maliki tradition. As Ben al-Mustafa recently wrote:

> In Morocco, it is not possible to talk of radical Islam, since the general direction is against violence. The violent Islamic movements which the country saw, the *al-Chabeba* al-Islameya, were banned in 1972, four years after it was established. Another oppositional movement emerged, Justice and Charity, but it does not adopt violence. And the Justice and Development party was incorporated with national democratic constitutional movement which adopts a *muhaden* [truce] position towards the regime.
>
> *(Ben al-Mustafa 2009: 34)*

It is safe to argue here that not only do the main and most Islamic groups in Morocco denounce violence and support pluralism, but they have also played an important role in forcing the regime to make important political concessions, including the opening up of the political environment in the 1990s. The result was a 'gradual political reforms in the 1990s' (EFDS 2009: 1), that 'Increas[ed] liberalisation of public life during the 1990s' (Mideast & N. Africa Encyclopaedia 2010). For example, Morocco ratified the UN Convention on torture, discrimination against women and children, followed by the appointment of the first ever Human Rights Minister in 1993 (EFDS 2009: 5). A constitutional reform in 1996 empowered the democratic process by making elections more direct, establishing a bicameral legislation in the parliament in 1997 and making the position of the speaker of the house subject to elections. More importantly, an 'alternate' government led by former opposition parties (Istiqlal, USFP and PPS) was appointed by the King in 1998, with Abderrahman Youssoufi, a long-time left-wing opposition leader, heading the new government (Pellicer 2008; Willis 2004: 54–5).

It is important not to exaggerate the extent of reform in Morocco. Political participation remains subject to strict conditions set by the regime. The parliament continues to lack real power as the King holds the constitutional and practical authority to dismiss it and also to appoint and dismiss the Prime Minister and the cabinet who are appointed directly by the King. The resurrection of leftists in the 1990s also aimed at curbing the rising popularity of Islamists, more than a true belief in the democratic rules of the game on behalf of the monarchy. As the Mideast and N. Africa Encyclopaedia recently wrote:

> … the fragmented nature of the Moroccan society … have rendered them [political parties] vulnerable to both manipulation and repression. Overall, Morocco's political parties have served a significant, albeit adjunct, function in what has been essentially a monarchy-dominated, traditional, patrimonial system of rule.
>
> *(Mideast and N. Africa Encyclopaedia 2010: 1)*

Developmental capacity of the state and rise of Islamic social capital

There is little question that, in addition to both internal and international political pressure, the socio-economic environment, particularly the rise of poverty, unemployment and inequities, was also an important factor behind King Hassan II's political liberalization drive of the 1990s. From the beginning, the Moroccan state, as shown in earlier analysis, afforded politics, the rhetoric of economic developmental notwithstanding, top priority at the expense of 'efforts to treat potentially critical problems of economic development and social change … ' (Waterbury 1970: 155). In this respect, the Moroccan State stands in vast contradiction to the Malaysian State, which made economic development a top priority after independence, as part of an overall strategy to terminate the then communist insurgency (Lubeck 1998).

Although Morocco never officially laid claims to socialism, unlike Iraq, Libya, Algeria, Egypt and Syria, it nevertheless behaved in a similar fashion. Morocco's stealth socialism, as elsewhere in the region, consisted of a large public sector, an extensive welfare programme and a battery of tariff and non-tariff barriers, the aim of which was to support a narrow base of patron–client network (Richards and Waterbury 1996: 31–2).

Morocco's interventionist, pro-industrial-urban strategy also undermined the rural economy through two key mechanisms: an overvalued exchange rate that undermined agricultural exports and a marketing board that monopolized the marketing of key crops, both domestic and international. By paying its farmers prices below world prices and pocketing the difference, the Board's policies, along with an overvalued exchange rate, acted as a tax against agriculture. This encouraged Moroccan farmers to shift their production to untaxed crops, thus further aggravating the country's food security (Richards and Waterbury 1996: 157; Owen 1992).

The outcome of anti-agricultural policies was to accelerate rural–urban migration, a phenomenon which had already started under the protectorate and gathered pace in post-independence as a result of anti-rural policies implemented by the state in this period. Unplanned for rural–urban migration has been responsible for the creation of large urban slums, the '*bidonvilles*' that were at the core of the riots that swept

Morocco in June 1981, January 1984 and December 1990 (Joffe 1992: 143). They have also provided the main fodder, human elements, for the 2003 Casablanca terrorist attacks, as well as a spate of attacks that struck the country in 2007. As Al-Jazeera news stated: 'Morocco slum bred suicide bomber' (Quoted Ashford University 2007).

The first economic crisis Morocco faced was not long after independence. It occurred in 1963 and triggered widespread demonstrations and riots that proved a good test of the regime's stability. The riots were largely motivated by economic as much as by political factors and led to the proclamation of a state of emergency in 1965 and the abrogation of parliamentary life for almost a decade (Owen 1992: 232). Macroeconomic mismanagement played an important role in weakening the developmental capacity of the Moroccan state. Corruption and nepotism sapped whatever capacity was left in the state.

For example, Morocco is one of the world's major producers and exporters of phosphates. A commodity price boom in the early- and mid-1970s led to brief economic growth. The government responded by expanding its subsidies, social and economic programmes. But even when price of phosphates collapsed in 1976, the state continued to expand through foreign borrowing. Subsidies, for instance, increased from 1 per cent of GDP in 1973 to 6.9 per cent in 1976. The state, fearing the social impact of reduced subsidy, continued to expand in the midst of austerity. In the late 1970s, the state granted a 10 per cent rise in the salaries of the civil servants, a 30–40 per cent increase in the minimum wage and expanded further food subsidy despite a large rise in the prices of imported farm products. Add to this the cost of the Sahara war since 1975 and Morocco found itself in 1980 with more than U$ 10 billion of foreign debt, with debt service consuming more than 33 per cent of exports. Yet the state continued to avoid reforms as it hoped it would grow out of the recession through expansionary fiscal policies, even if this meant more borrowing.[26] Between 1981–83, a third expansionary spike took place following the 1981 Casa 'Bread Riots' themselves caused by the state's attempt to reduce public expenditure. In 1983 foreign debt reached U$ 11.8 billion or 80 per cent of GDP. Bad weather (drought) did not help either, thus dampening the economic growth rate further, bringing more rural migrants to major urban centres and increasing the need for food imports. In mid-1983 Morocco's Central Bank announced exhaustion of its reserves, its inability to manage foreign debt and refusal of lenders to extend further credit. Emergency measures were announced following the resort by the Moroccan government to the IMF and World Bank for financial and technical assistance in 1983 (Owen 1992: 237; Richards and Waterbury 1996; Ayubi 1999).

The IMF and World Bank initiated a Structural Adjustment Lending Programme (SALP) that lasted for almost ten years from 1983–92. Typical of SALPs, they targeted, among other things, fiscal deficit in order to rein in inflation. This meant massive cuts in public spending, which included lowering real wages, freezing public employment and reducing public investment. A tax-modernizing and simplifying programme (meaning the imposition of new taxes) was also implemented. Reducing public investment in particular had a strong negative impact on the development of both economic infrastructure and social facilities, delaying the provision of basic infrastructure (transportation, telecommunications etc.) and social services (education, training, health, housing), with considerable impact on the poor (Hamdouch 1999: 19).

Although SALP had a positive macroeconomic impact,[27] its social impact was calamitous. It led to large social underdevelopment, or a 'lag in social and infrastructure development' (Hamdouch 1999: 18 and 19). 'The social retirement of the state' created a social-welfare vacuum, which faith-based organizations and other civil society institutions, moved quickly to fill (Dareef 1999: 261–4). The regime was happy to open up and encourage the role of civil society, including in particular faith-based organizations, in the social sector and allow such organizations to provide welfare services because the state was financially bankrupt and charitable organizations save a lot of public money (Harrigan and El-Said 2009). According to EFDS (2009: 6), Morocco, by 2004, counted some 20,000–30,000 associations working in the field of democratization, human rights and 'social work and economic development'. Most of these associations are faith-based and their social activism has a significant political impact: it increases their popularity and public support and simultaneously debilitates the credibility of state for failing to provide basic services to its citizens.

Social capital provided by civil society, including by faith-based organizations, nevertheless, is not a substitute for an effective state system. It is unsurprising therefore that 'Morocco's human development indicators … [remain today] much lower than those of countries with similar per capita incomes' (Hamdouch 1999: 18 and 19). This is in spite of the fact that the Moroccan state has been engaged in implementing a large social programme to fight poverty since the mid-1990s. Unemployment among the young and educated in 2005 reached 34 per cent and 26 per cent respectively. Adult literacy rates remained low at 50 per cent and more than 20 per cent of the population are presently considered to be poor, with the economy growing by an average annual rate of approximately 3 per cent since the beginning of the twenty-first century (Harrigan and El-Said 2009; World Bank 2005). For many observers of Morocco's development, 'Poverty, exclusion, and misery are viewed widely as fertile breeding grounds for extremists', with the World Bank recently warning that 'if growth rate and job creation over the coming decade do not accelerate significantly faster than the rates of past decade, poverty and exclusion could reach levels that incite unimaginable social tension' (World Bank 2005: 1 and 7).

Reconciliation: conditions conducive to success

As implied in earlier analysis, Morocco has experienced grave violations of human rights since independence in 1956. Moroccans describe the time of King Hassan II as *zaman al-rasas* (the time of bullets) and *al-sanawat al-sawda* (the black years) in Arabic (Slyomovics 2005). These included 'forcible disappearance, torture, and mass political trials … the repression has affected Moroccans of every political persuasion: Marxist, Islamist, nationalist, Sahrawi, feminist, and Amazigh/Berber' (Clouser 2009: 1). It was not surprising therefore that reconciling with the past by improving human rights conditions in the country has been an important element in the liberalization package which the Moroccan regime started in the early 1990s. Even before ratifying the UN

Convention on Torture in 1993, the regime created on 20 April 1990, the Advisory Council for Human Rights (ACHR). The ACHR's publicly declared objectives include, 'to assist His Majesty the King in all issues related to protection, defence and guarantee of human rights practices … [and] respecting dignity, freedom and rights of citizens, groups and individuals'. The establishment of the ACHR marked the beginning of a long, gradual and complicated reconciliation process. The key objective here is to avoid repeating the past dark days: to 'guarantee to never repeat the past' of human rights violations (all quotations from ACHR 2006: 11 and 14).

The ACHR is a semi-governmental organization, a mix of public officials and societal elements, such as political parties, professional associations and civil society. The ACHR was entrusted with 13 tasks, all of which relate to improving human rights record in Morocco, including providing recommendations to the King on human rights issues, as well as encountering any human rights violations in the country through investigating and reporting violations to proper authorities and institutions. The ACHR, however, remained, initially, dominated by conservative pro-regime elements. That is not surprising given the fact that the ACHR was the creation of the king. Its initial role therefore, remained advisory, although one of its recommendations was the release of several hundred prisoners, around 300–400, in the early 1990s which was sanctioned.

The efforts of the ACHR remained constrained and confined mainly to the release of prisoners. It was not able to extend its agenda to other areas that were deemed necessary for true reconciliation, such as victims of torture, their families, forceful disappearances and exiled individuals. A significant development in the role of the ACHR took place when Abderrahman al-Youssoufi headed the new government in 1998. Al-Youssoufi, who had previously been imprisoned and exiled by the regime, and his overwhelmingly socialist government, the first since the late 1950s took a personal interest in the issue of settling past human rights violations, which continued in the 1990s notwithstanding general freedoms and liberalizations introduced in the same decade. Al-Youssoufi's cabinet was influential behind a 1998 ACHR recommendation, which called for, and led in 1999, to the establishment of an Independent Committee (IC) to investigate and compensate victims of human rights between 1956 and 1999. Al-Youssoufi's position was strengthened by the regime's need to use leftists to undermine the rising influence of Islamists in the country.

The IC went beyond calling for the release of and amnesties for, political prisoners by introducing a new compensation scheme to include not only political prisoners, but also families of the victims, disappeared victims, as well as exiled individuals. The latter, along with political prisoners, were also offered full amnesties. The al-Youssoufi government also worked on returning released political prisoners and other victims of human rights violations between the years of 1956–99, to their former jobs. All losses incurred as a result of years in prison or exile, including pensions and promotions that would have been obtained had they stayed in their previous jobs, were calculated and included in the compensation scheme. Medical treatment and health insurances for the victims and their families were also part of the compensation scheme put forward by the IC in 1999.

The IC though remained bogged down with internal divisions, for example, the definition of who and who was not a victim, and the domination of pro-regime elements. These elements included, in particular, the then powerful Minister of the Interior. The minister insisted that the victims of human rights violations could only qualify for the programme if they signed a document agreeing not to pursue any legal case against the state or security officials that were involved in torturing them. This condition was rejected by the overwhelming majority of the victims and their families. According to some victims interviewed, no more than 1,000 individuals signed the document and benefited from the IC's initiative in 1999. Officials at the ACHR put the figure at 5,000. Whether 1,000 or 5,000, the 'IC did not go far enough' to meet the demands of the Moroccan victims and society at large (Personal interview with Abdulrazaq Rawan, Rabat December 2009).

The death of King Hassan II and the arrival of a new regime in 1999, severed links with many powerful domestic interest groups that opposed a comprehensive reconciliation programme. The new king, Muhammed VI, saw in the reconciliation process an important opportunity to enhance his legitimacy and credibility. His first move was to fire the powerful Interior Minister in 1999, followed by an important initiative in 2001 that reformed the ACHR and made it more transparent and credible by expanding the number of its members to 44 from all walks of Moroccan political life.[28] At the same time, the King on 9 October 2001, created *Diwan al-Mazalem* (Complaints Council), which receives, investigates and reports violations of human rights in the country. In 2002, the new King also accepted a recommendation from the ACHR to create Equity and Reconciliation Commission (ERC) to replace IC and move forward with the reconciliation programme.

The ERC (*Lajnat al-Insaaf wal Musalaha*) was established in 2004 and its role and operations were completed 22 months later, ending in November 2006. During its short life, the ERC abolished all bureaucratic red-tape attached to the reconciliation programme and investigated the fate of disappeared individuals. It also extended the compensation programme to deaths and disappearances which occurred during detention and to those who fled the country between 1965 and 1999 fearing for their lives, known in Morocco as forced migration. The ERC was also influential in the new legislation of 2005, which provided a legal definition for torture.[29] Before it completed its mission in late 2006, the ERC received requests for reparations concerning more than 16,000 Moroccans, more than 95 per cent of whom have already received their compensations. Only administrative difficulties, including a lack of proper documents submitted by beneficiaries, are delaying the rest of compensations (EFDS 2009: 6; Personal interview with officials at the ACHR, Rabat December, 2009).

The ACHR and the ERC have also been influential in bringing about other important changes in the judicial system that outlawed torture during investigation or extraction of information under duress, improved treatment of prisoners according to international standards, separated prisoners according to their crimes, provided for regular medical check-ups of detainees and prisoners, and gave prisoners the right to see and receive their families and friends regularly while in detention. The new legislative also prevented detention without trial for more than 96 hours renewable only once, demanded that families be informed about the fate of their sons within

24 hours of their arrest, provided and protected detainees' right for defence and legalized conjugal visits (ACHR 2006).

One of the most important inventions of the ERC was the *Jaber a Darar* Scheme, which extended compensation to areas where detention centres were located. This had previously suffered as a result from lack of development, including lack of public and private investment, infrastructure and other services. A developmental programme to improve these areas was put in place in 2005, in consultation with the inhabitants who 'developed a strong feeling that the marginalisation which they suffer is due to past human rights violations' and location of torture centres in their areas (ACHR 2006: 54). The inhabitants of these areas have also been made partners with state officials and civil society organizations involved in developmental projects and provision of welfare services.

Other important differences between the new and old regime have also contributed to what is widely seen as a successful reconciliation programme by almost all sections of Moroccan society, a fact that has contributed to the popularity of the new king (MCSCR 2008). The former regime refused, for political reasons, to provide amnesties for political prisoners and provided only pardons instead. The intention of this strategy was to remind all Moroccans, as Owen (1992: 122) noted, of the benevolent nature of the monarch, that the monarch is the final arbiter in the country and is therefore not subject to any law and that whatever political rights are given they simply reflect 'his gift'.

The reconciliation programme, which began in 1999 under King Muhammed VI, conversely, was based on a confession on behalf of the state for its past mistakes, including the violation of human rights. This process was based on consultation with the victims themselves, their families and civil society associations representing them. The authorities also invited the victims and their families not only to talk openly about abuses of their human rights publicly on national TV and radio stations, but also to talk to their former torturers face to face and to ask them candidly 'why did you do that to your brothers and sisters?' (ACHR 2006: 55; Personal interviews with former detainees and prisoners, Rabat December 2009).

There are also important differences between the reconciliation processes, which have been implemented in Morocco (since 1999) and Algeria (since 1997). While the latter deprived its former militants of political rights and participation, Morocco relied on its former neo-revolutionary members and officially entrusted them with the responsibility of managing the reconciliation process itself. Many former hardcore socialists were appointed as high-ranked state officials, including the former Prime Minister himself, al-Youssoufi. The post-1999 reconciliation programme's overriding objective 'closing the file on past human rights violations' however, has been undermined by the emergence of Salafi Jihadists in the early twentieth century. A series of terrorist attacks in the country in 2003 and 2007 have ensued and ushered in a new era of counter-radicalization policies.

Counter-radicalization without deradicalization

The 2003 terrorist attacks in Casablanca were taken very seriously by the regime, the final arbiter in Morocco and the Commander of the Faithful whose main religious credentials have been challenged by some factions within Moroccan society. In official Moroccan circles, those factions are referred to as *al-Jihadiyea al-Salafiya*. These factions include those who were tried following the 16 May 2003 attacks in Casablanca, those who were accused of carrying out and planning the attacks, and those who are being pursued by the authorities under the 2003 anti-terrorism law. Today, 'nearly 1,000 prisoners considered to be Islamic radicals remain in Moroccan jails' (Erlanger and Mekhennet 2009). According to the ICG (2008), the number of arrested is 'over 2,000 suspected militants or sympathizers', the majority of which refuse to be called Jihadi Salafists and consider this concept to be the making of media and Moroccan authorities.

There is no agreement in Morocco on the root causes of violent militancy in the country. Islamists and other nationalists cite external factors, particularly Palestine, Iraq and Afghanistan, in addition to corruption, exclusion and inequities inside Morocco, as the most radicalizing factors. For state officials, poverty, unemployment and slums are key factors. This latter argument has won the day, and King Muhammed VI initiated, in response, a massive social and economic programme to fight poverty and reduce unemployment in the country (Ben al-Mustafa 2008; EFDS 2009).

Ironically, for a country that has already implemented a massive reconciliation programme, Moroccan authorities adamantly refuse to carry out any dialogue with the detained radicals. As one cabinet minister publicly stated in 2008, 'I could not find any ulama who would carry out dialogue with the radicals' (Personal interview with Khadija Alimoussa, Rabat December 2009). Several ulama, however, including some from the Scientific Supreme Council and the Director of the *al-Muhamadiya* Foundation, Dr Ahmad Abadi, have publicly expressed their willingness to carry out a dialogue with the radicals if they were asked to do so (Personal interview with Dr Abadi, Rabat December 2009). Indeed, Dr Abadi has been conducting a weekly dialogue with radicals outside prisons through the *al-Muhamadiya*'s internet programmes since his appointment as the head of the Foundation in 2006 (see below).

There is a lack of consensus inside Morocco with regard to deradicalization, leading to contradictory statements and strings continuously being attached to dialogue. In summer 2007, for example, Morocco missed a golden opportunity to build on its reconciliation programme and fashion a unique deradicalization programme when some detainees initiated, in the main Sala Prison, internal intellectual revisions and debates among themselves through *halagat dirasiya* (intellectual circles) during breaks. The prison authorities initially permitted such discussions, which focused on studying al-Maliki faqih, prophet stories, the Arabic language and Qu'ran reading and interpretation. Shortly thereafter, the authorities ended these activities and insisted that the JSs must write a letter to the King first petitioning him for a Royal amnesty. Most of the detainees refused to do so because they considered themselves innocent[30] (MCSCR 2008: 417 and 418; Alimoussa 2008: 1).

In July 2008 Ahmad Hirzani, the Director of the ACHR, in an interview arranged to discuss the issue of JSs, suggested that before any dialogue commences 'the detainees must first issue a written confession absolving their responsibilities of terrorist acts, clarify their position with regard to the accusations which indicted them, as well as refuting radical ideology and clarifying their position from the Monarchy'. This though is precisely the aim of any deradicalization dialogue. The Saudi, Yemenis and Egyptian officials facilitated dialogue with their radicals in order to convince them to change their misled convictions that justified violent ideology and activism. Moroccan officials demand the opposite. In August 2008, however, at least a third of JSs detainees in Fiz prison accepted almost all key points in the Hirzani initiative and declared the monarchy as protector of Islamic faith in the country, preserver of stability and that they have no problem with monarchy. The authorities have failed to capitalize on the situation and no dialogue has been initiated (MCSCR 2008: 419).

Finally on 29 November 2008, Muhammed Yesif, the General Director of the Supreme Scientific Council (*al majlis al'ilmi al ala*) declared preparedness of the ulama of the Council to engage in dialogue with JSs,[31] but according to conditions:

> the detainees must uphold the basic Moroccan foundations first, including the *asha'riyah* precept, Maliki school, Sunni-Sufism, and the system of rule based on *al bay'a* (loyalty) to the regime. If they agreed to these principles then the *ulama* have no objection carrying out a dialogue with them. With regard to the other minor issues, these can be discussed later.
>
> *(MCSCR 2008: 418)*

Again, many of those conditions have already been accepted by a large number of JSs, but the lack of consensus and internal divisions among Moroccan officials continue to undermine the emergence of a comprehensive and effective deradicalization programme in the country.

In fact the Abdulwahab Irafiq, better known as Abi Hafis, who is considered by the authorities as one of the key leaders of JS in Morocco, recently wrote a book from inside his cell in which he refutes and denounces radical ideology, admits mistakes committed by him and his colleagues and declares loyalty to the King (Irafiq 2010). So far, every call and/or attempt to carry out a dialogue has failed. According to MCSCR (2008: 416 and 19) calls for dialogue from the radicals and their statements 'do not amount to revisions because these guys are not subject to revisions' because they 'are the new *khawaraj* (outlawed)' who are 'ignorant, radical and reckless'. A similar official attitude also prevented the emergence of well-articulated deradicalization in Jordan.

Paradoxically, at the same time Morocco has launched the most far-reaching and comprehensive counter-radicalization programme among our eight-country case study. The 2003 and 2007 terrorist attacks triggered one of the most far reaching and wide-ranging religious reforms found in any Arab state. These reforms included the restructuring and reorganization of the most important institutions of the Commander of the Faithful in the country, particularly the MRA, Supreme Scientist Councils and the *al-Muhamadiya* Foundation. The restructure included institutional, legislative and social aspects, with reforms expanding the responsibilities of each institution to reach almost every aspect of religion and religious life in the country. In short, religion has been completely nationalized in a way that Morocco has never seen before.[32]

To start with, the MRA was subject to the most extensive of these reforms. A 2003 Royal decree (Law No. 1-030-193) expanded the MRA to include under its umbrella the *Wagf* (charity) Department, the Department of Imams, the Department of Islamic Affairs, the Department of Studies and Public Affairs, the Mosques' Department and the Department of Old Houses Education. Its new tasks include correcting and exposing realities of Islamic religion, spreading its tolerant principles and values, and supervising charity work in the country. It is further responsible for spreading religious awareness and Islamic education in an atmosphere of tolerance, tranquillity and safety.

Before 2003, the MRA used to issue a few religious magazines every year, such as *da'wat al haq* (Calls for Truth) and *sabeel 'al Irshad* (Path to Guidance). In 2005, the MRA issued six religious publications, rising in 2006 to 17. They evolved around religious and Islamic issues, religion and society, religion and the state.

Places of worship were also brought more directly under the supervision and control of the MRA. In 2004 and 2007 respectively, new laws regarding places of religious worship were passed which, first, specified places where worship could take place and then regulated and brought under its control the processes of donations, construction and the renovation of mosques. The laws stipulated that any of these processes can only take place through licensed *jam'iyyat* (organizations). Charitable organizations donating to mosques or any religious activity were also forced to become members in one of these licensed *jam'yyat* themselves, before their donations and charity work would be accepted and provided to society members. New committees in the MRA have been created to supervise financial donations, oversee licensing process, and construction and renovations of mosques. Its extended powers led to a large reduction in the amount of charity work in the country, so much so that by 2008 Morocco was suffering from a shortage of mosques.

Friday sermons were also brought more directly under the control of the MRA. Fridays' *khutbas* (speeches) are now prepared in advance by the MRA and then delivered in the name of the King himself. They all preach a similar, moderate version of Islam, combined with lots of prayers for the monarchy. The role of the mosque itself has been expanded to include human development. Given the high illiteracy rate in Morocco and the vacuum in social services, the Five-Year Development Plan, 2006–2010, of the MRA incorporated illiteracy programmes to be delivered in and by mosques. Those programmes do not only teach how to read and write (overcome illiteracy), but also aim to overcome religious illiteracy and misled ideologies, and to promote a moderate, apolitical Sufi version of Islam. In 2007/08, the total number of beneficiaries from these programmes reached 108,000 in urban areas and 68,000 in rural areas, at least 35 per cent of which were females. Success rate (pass and completion) of these programmes reached 85 per cent. The programme is being implemented in 3,146 mosques, 1,404 in rural areas and the rest in urban areas.

Old Teaching Institutions, including Qu'ran Foundation Houses (QFSs), are traditionally important places to study the Qu'ran, its interpretations and religious studies in general. They are also viewed as important preservers of Moroccan religious specificities and religious traditions. They proliferated rapidly in the 1970s with the rise of

Islamic movements and their charity work. Their activities, after 2003, were brought under the direct control of the MRA by subjecting them to a licensing system that is renewable on an annual basis. Their curriculum has also been expanded in an attempt to merge them with the public educational system and steer them away from using religion to serve politics. Increased religiosity in Morocco in recent years increased the importance of QFHs as authentic institutions teaching Islamic studies. Today, there are 499 Old Educational Houses, funded jointly by charity and the state. In 2007 the total number of students registered in these Houses reached 306,000, rising to 311,000 in 2008, with 11,000 and 11,100 state teachers, respectively involved in delivering their curriculum. The total cost of running these houses reached MD 19,340 million and 28,852 million in 2007 and 2008 respectively.

Other institutions of the Commander of Faithful underwent similar reforms. At the level of scientists, the official *Mu'asata al owalama* (Scientist Foundation), has traditionally been organized at two levels: the Supreme Scientists Council (SSC) and Local Scientist Councils (mainly administrative, organizational and missionary institutions), and the *al Muhammadiyah Foundation*, which is more academic and intellectual in nature. Each of these institutions were also subject to a considerable degree of reform and following the 2007 terrorist attacks, were brought under direct Royal supervision and guidance.

Before 2003, the number of local Scientist Councils was limited to no more than 14 in total. Their number increased in 2004 and 2008 to 30 and 70 respectively. Supervised by the SSC, these local councils delivered 295,360 *wa'ath* (religious) lessons in their localities in 2007 alone. The same number of lessons was also delivered in 2008. This translates into 4,219 *wa'ath* lessons for each local council. On 19 May 2007, the SSC organized a huge international conference on the *Shar'a*'s Judgement for Calls to Terrorism. It was attended by more than 1,200 ulama from Morocco and other Muslim countries. The conference's focus was to refute violent thought and radical ideology. In addition to Islam's position *vis-à-vis* terrorism, the conference focused on culture and terrorism, *al-Amer bel Ma'roof wal Nahi an al- Munkar, al-Wala' wa al-Bara', al-jihad, al-Khawaraj, al-Takfir* ideology, the role of the rational caliphate and *al-Jaheliya* (ignorance).

Moreover, an *Ifta'* (religious ruling) Committee was created after 2003 under the umbrella of the SSC, a centralized official committee that has been put solely in charge of issuing fatwas in Morocco. The main aim of the Committee is to pull the rag from under the feet of the radicals who managed to undermine the official ulama and preach their brand of radical Islam. The Committee seeks to restore the credibility of official ulama by confining the right to fatwa to only qualified and credible ulama, that is, state recognised ulama. The position of the Committee in the society was reinforced in 2007–08 as a result of issuing several fatwas pertaining to Islam and societal issues, and also as a result of the King himself resorting to the Committee for fatwa on the role of ruler in managing public affairs.

The establishment of the *Ifta'* Committee was preceded by a large *takweeni* (preparation) programme, launched in 2003 to train new imams and *mursheedeen* (religious guides, both males and females) and to re-train already employed imams to better prepare them for their religious duties inside and outside the SSC, local councils and mosques. Since the start of its operations in 2005, the programme graduated 150 new male and 50 new female *imams* and religious guides, as well as re-training hundreds, if not thousands, of old *imams*. After 2007, imams and *mursheedeen* were also empowered to regularly organize *irshad* (guidance and awareness) lessons outside the mosques and in community centres. A direct public telephone phone line has been created and linked directly to the ulama in order to provide advice on religious matters directly to Moroccans inside and outside Morocco.

Material inducements were also provided not only to the victims of human rights violations between 1956–99, but also to the ulama in order to prevent the drift of the 67,000 ulama and religious workers registered as employees in the MRA against the tides of the state. In 2008 for example, the Muhammad VI Foundation was established to raise funds and take care of the social needs of the ulama in the country. Since its establishment, the Muhammed VI Foundation has been providing full medical treatment and health insurances to all of those working in the religious field in Morocco, a total of 166,000 individuals, if families and siblings are included.

The spread of telecommunication technology, including in particular the Internet, satellite TV and radio stations, have made it difficult for states to control the level and the source of religious information in the society. IT facilitated counter-fatwas issued by the radicals, often contradict and even challenge fatwas issued by regimes and state-recognized ulama. The fact that the Internet or TV religious channels broadcast free of charge and do not require subscription or a card system facilitated easy access and undermined states' ability to control these sources of information. Most also broadcast in Arabic in order to make a connection with the Arab population inside and outside of the Arab World. In countries with a high level of illiteracy, TV and mosques are the main sources of religious education and information. One recent study showed that mosques, TV and Satellite, and radio channels, respectively, have become the main sources of religious education for most Moroccans (MCSCR 2008).

To counter the influence of radio broadcasting, the Moroccan authorities licensed 28 new religious radio stations (both private and public) after 2003, including the popular government-owned and run the King Muhammad VI Radio Station. In 2008 alone, Morocco's religious radio stations broadcasted more than 200 *halaga dinyeah* (religious discussion) on issues related to *feqh*, modern Islam, *hadith*, family relations, state and society, Islamic practices, values and principles. The Moroccan authorities also established the King Muhammad VI TV Channel (*al-Sadisha*), which specializes in religion and religious education. It also regularly broadcasts a live question/answer programme as part of its daily 10–12-hour operations.

Moroccans are increasingly turning to the Internet for information on their religion. To counter the influence of radical websites, the Moroccan authorities encouraged the MRA, SSC, Moroccan faith-based movements, key Moroccan ulama and the Al-*Muhammadiyah* Foundation to establish their own counter websites. In this, the Al-*Muhammadiyah* Foundation is taking the lead.[33] It is leading the academic aspect of the institutions of the Commander of the Faithful. It thus publishes a quarterly magazine that discusses a wide range of issues relevant to Moroccan society. The Foundation also encourages debate and interaction with the public through regular lectures, conferences, workshops and seminars held in the Foundation's headquarters in Rabat. The focus of the *Al-Muhammadiya*'s work is on the context of religion.

> We treat religion in the same way we treat anthropology, economics and physics. We cannot understand these subjects without understanding their context. You cannot claim to understand religion very well without understanding its context too, and without going back to basics.
>
> *(Personal interview with Dr Ahmad Abadi, Rabat December 2009)*

Dr Abadi, the Director of the *Al-Muhammadiya*, also claims that the Foundation has the most effective anti-terrorism internet website in the entire region, judging from its daily 7,500 hits from inside and outside Morocco (**www.arrabita.ma**).

Al-Muhammadiya's internet activities include an Electronic Journal that discusses all aspects related to religion with articles written by some of the country's most eminent scholars. The Foundation also provides religious educational lessons and peer-club sessions on the internet. For example, Dr Abadi has a live dialogue programme on the internet once every two weeks, whereby:

> I simply answer questions on all religious aspects, including terrorism. It is an open encounter for two hours. We also have a weekly live dialogue on the Internet where we choose a subject and then we discuss it live openly. This week for example we are discussing Islamophobia. In addition, I also have a daily seven-minute program on Morocco's main TV channel. During those seven minutes, I provide a daily interpretation for the whole Qu'ran, verse by verse. My plan is to do the whole Qu'ran. Finally, I have a weekly interactive live program on Morocco's main radio channel that lasts for two hours from 9–11pm. This is also a kind of question and answer program. We frankly and openly promote Sufi version of Islam in our work, what we call "Islamic beauty".
>
> *(Personal interview with Dr Abadi, Rabat December 2009)*

Finally, the Moroccan state has even introduced measures to deradicalize and prevent radicalization among Moroccans in Europe, where more than 80 per cent of three million Moroccans or so living abroad reside. This came as a result of the strong Moroccan connection with 2004 Madrid bombings, which alerted the authorities to the dangers of radicalization of Moroccans abroad. In 2008 the Moroccan authorities created the Moroccan Scientific Council for Europe (law No. 5680, on November 6) to promote religious duties and Islamic *shaa'er* (tradition) in an atmosphere of tranquillity within the framework of Maliki school. The aims are to coordinate activities with the Moroccan Community Councils abroad; to provide assistance to the Moroccan immigrant community in Europe; to supervise work carried out by Moroccan charities abroad and to organize training workshops for the imams there. The Council also released in 2008 more than 200 hours of audio-visual religious programmes that especially targeted Moroccans in Europe (MCSCR 2008: 159–60).

Conclusion

Morocco provides supportive evidence to four theses that are vital to the findings of this book in general and to conditions conducive to successful deradicalization, reconciliation and counter-radicalization processes in particular. These are: 1) the role of a strong developmental state in reducing the risk of violent extremism, 2) The role of civil society in countering radicalization and deradicalization policies, 3) The role of a new, charismatic leader (at state-level) in injecting new life into the deradicalization, counter-radicalization or reconciliation processes that in most cases were initiated by the departing regime, 4) The importance of combining counter-radicalization with effective deradicalization programmes.

The arrival of King Muhammad VI to power in 1999 injected the reconciliation process, which was first introduced by his late father King Hassan II in the 1990s, with new rigour, dynamism and creative elements that produced conditions conducive to a genuine reconciliation process in the country. This process, however, has disappointingly failed to 'guarantee to never again repeat the past' of human rights violations. Since 2003, particularly following the adoption of a controversial anti-terrorism law that increased arbitrary power of security forces, the Moroccan state 'has slowed the pace of change, there has been a major and continuing crackdown on those suspected of being extremists here … [with] irregularities … [and] circumstantial evidence' characterizing many court cases against Islamists (Erlanger and Mekhennet 2009). Domestic and international human rights organizations, including Amnesty International and Human Rights Watch, have been very critical of recent human rights violations against many suspected Islamists, with King Muhammad VI himself publicly acknowledging some of these violations. Morocco, under King Muhammad VI, it is worth noting, was among the few Muslim states chosen by the former US president, Bush, for America's rendition policy, which included the torturing of former 'terrorism suspect[s] being held at Guantanamo Bay' (Bonner 2008).

Ironically, these violations have been taking place under a far reaching and one of the largest counter-radicalization programmes recorded among our eight-country case-study. Most Moroccan officials, academics and observers rightly argue that 'it is too early to evaluate the effectiveness' of the country's counter-radicalization measures, since although they were introduced in 2003, most elements of the programme did not come together before 2007 (MCSCR 2008). Yet, anecdotal evidence suggests that Morocco's counter-radicalization programme may suffer from several serious shortcomings.

Among those shortcomings is the fact that Morocco has so far chosen to focus on countering radicalization instead, with the latter being implemented in isolation of Morocco's dynamic and creative civil society organizations. Counter-radicalization measures are based on promoting an apolitical, Sufi version of Islam, itself not totally accepted by all mainstream Islamists in Morocco. For many, 'Sufism aims at undermining Islamist parties in Morocco' (Personal interview with Sa'ad al-Othmani, Rabat December 2009). This is already creating an intense relationship between Sunnism and Sufism in Morocco. Another equally serious tension is now taking place between the former socialist opposition of the regime, which has been entrusted with the responsibility of managing the reconciliation process since 1999 and the new victims of human rights violation, most of whom are Islamists-anti-leftists. The enmity between the two is historical and goes back to the 1950s and 1960s when the regime encouraged Islamist movements to counter the then powerful influence of the leftist and socialists. The equation has now been reversed, with socialists and leftists being used to undermine Islamists (Willis 2004; Pellicer 2008).

Second, although the new Ifta' Committee is made up of several prominent Moroccan ulama and has provided several religious fatwas since its creation, 'However, through looking at the site of the SSC what is clear is the small number of these fatwas despite the enormity of the challenges that are threatening the Moroccan society at all levels'. The Committee has issued no more than ten fatwas so far. These are on such trivial issues as interest rates in Islam, their religious position *vis-à-vis* the new withdrawal system which the MRA has recently adopted regarding Haj, the use of the word sexy on the internet, the use of Qur'anic verses as business titles and prayer while sitting down on a chair in mosques for disability purposes (MCSCR 2008: 150–1).

Third, the Moroccan Scientific Council for Europe, apart from releasing audio-visual religious programmes, has mainly confined its role to sending religious people to Europe during Ramadan and then attempting to open up to already existing and active charity organizations among Moroccans in Europe. The MCSCR (2008: 161) warned that 'the council will be subject to a challenging test to ensure its credibility as an authentic religious source capable of facing the challenges of the religious specificities of the Moroccans abroad ... '.

Socio-economically, the situation remains threatening in Morocco. Problems, including poverty, unemployment, inequities and widespread corruption remain a major challenge. Despite the al-Youssifi government's impressive performance in the reconciliation process, its economic performance and that of its successor governments, has been disappointing. The socio-economic situation remains politically destabilizing and conducive to radicalization. A recent report in *The Economist* suggested that the new government's performance does not give any reason for hope that it will be able to solve the country's socio-economic problems (quoted in At-Tajdid 2008).

Perhaps the most worrying aspect of Morocco's counter-radicalization programme is its lack of deradicalization measures. There is an increasing evidence of radicalization taking place inside various Moroccan prisons (At-Tajdid 2008). A father of one of the detainees, Ahmad Irfiqi, has recently warned Moroccan authorities 'to reconsider themselves regarding the file of the JSs before it is too late', adding that, 'the sons of the detainees who are living in this electrocuting environment are time bombs who will one day explode if the situation is not managed and treated properly' (Quoted in MCSCR 2008: 416).

While revisiting the country's counter-radicalization measures, Muhammad Dareef (2008), Morocco's leading academic expert on Islamists, concluded that 'we can say that Morocco unlike other countries, is still threatened' by terrorism, despite the dismantling of more than 16 terrorist cells in the country since 2003. The test of analysis did not have to wait for a long time. The recent terror attack in April 2011, which left 15 dead in a tourist café in Marrakech and which was carried out by a suicide operation, should be interpreted in light of Morocco's failure to deliver on its socio-economic promises, produce a comprehensive counter-radicalization programme involving its society and failure to combine counter radicalization with an effective deradicalization programme.

Notes

1 On 16 May 2003, five bombs exploded in different places in Casablanca, targeting mainly Western objectives. These included the Belgian Consulate, a Jewish Community Centre, a Spanish Restaurant and the Farrah Hotel. Forty-three people were killed during the attacks.

2 Two incidents occurred in 2007. The first was on 11 March, when a suicide bomber, while drawing attention to himself in an internet café in Casablanca, blew himself up and killed himself and injured four others, including his companion. The second incident took place on 13 August, when an armature man carrying a gas cylinder tried to blow himself up in what he wrongly believed to be a bus full of foreign tourists in Meknes. Nobody was killed or injured in the incident except the armature man who lost his arm only.

3 Indeed, these two factors are important components of both Saudi and Yemeni deradicalization and counter-radicalization programmes that seek to counter violent extremist narrative which calls rather hastily for jihad in Muslim countries and elsewhere.

4 The Berber Dahir stated: 'The tribes of Berber custom are and remain regulated and administered according to their own laws and customs under the control of the authorities' (Quoted in De Laubadere 1949: 59).

5 This was also consistent with the developments in the region where a religious movement emerged at the end of the nineteenth century and the beginning of the twentieth century. Initially, it was not anti-Western and sought reform and modernization by borrowing methods and approaches from the West. Later on, and mainly as a result of political developments that swept the region in the inter-war period, including the Sykes-Picot Agreement which divided the Arab World between France and Britain, and the Belfour Declaration which promised the Jews a homeland in Palestine, the reform movement became more anti-Western (for more details see ICG 2008).

6 The UNFP is an offshoot of the Istiqlal party, and both the Istiqlal and the UNFP led a vigorous challenge during the first decade of independence to the King's efforts to rule as well as reign. They were subjected to manipulation, arrests, imprisonment, repression and, allegedly, assassination, such as in the case of one of the UNFP's key leaders, Mehdi Ben Barka, who disappeared in the streets of Paris under suspicious circumstances in the 1960s.

7 In fact, Article 19 of the constitution stated that: 'The monarchy is the Commander of the Faithful and the supreme representative of the nation and symbol of its unity and the guarantor of state's continuity. He is the protector of the religion and seeker of the constitution's respect, and it is to him the maintenance of the rights and freedoms of citizens and groups and committees, and he is the guarantor of the country's independence and maintenance of the state in its just circle'.

8 While the Istiqlal could not dominate the parliament, it still acquired large enough shares to prevent other parties from dominating it. For example, the FDIC received 69 seats in

parliament, as opposed to 41 to Istiqlal and 28 to UNFP. The popularity of the Istiqlal still prevented the FDIC, the King's favoured party, from establishing a complete majority, therefore subjecting it, and the UNFP, to harassment and leading to the arrest of leaders of the UNFP in the same year after the discovery of an alleged plot against the King (Waterbury 1970: 232).

9 The objectives of the MSF were identified as 'calling (*da'wa*) for God with ration and good wisdom, carrying out the responsibilities of the *da'wa* in rural and urban areas, and teaching people their true religious principles from the book and the Sunna' (MCSCR 2008: 151).

10 This custom is linked to the old and historically most widespread form of religious expression in Morocco, namely, Sophism. Sophism entered the Islamic *Mashrq* (North Africa) in the eighth century, as a current opposing the then *fugaha*' forum of expression (Ulama). Some observers believe that Sophism was reinforced by the Turkish rule, which allegedly, took a Sophie form of Islam since it focused less on the political and more on the *Da'wa* (calling or missionary side). Sophism, however, first entered Morocco in the eleventh century through the *Hujaj* (pilgrims). But this was not yet a Moroccan form of sophism: it was an eastern form adopted by many Moroccans. The Moroccanization of Sophism took place in the thirteenth century at the hands of *Molay Abdualsalam ben Mshesh*, who is accredited today for developing Morocco's unique tradition of Sophism. Initially, Sophism was, and continues to be, seen as a ritual, apolitical form of practicing Islam. But in the fourteenth century it found itself enmeshed in politics when it started calling for the coming of the messiah as a saviour, an act which for many was seen as a pure political act aimed at rejecting incumbent leaders by waiting for the saviour. From the beginning of the fifteenth century, Sophism became an important, if not the most important source of legitimacy to incumbent regimes. It was also beginning to be seen as an important tradition not only necessary but also capable of applying the true *shari'ah*, the only protector of religious heritage, and may even aspire to replace incumbent regimes if it felt that they are no longer capable of protecting religion. The pre-independence nationalist movement also invoked Sophism in its attempt to mobilize Moroccans for *jihadi* against colonial authorities. This led some Moroccan observers, such as Dareef (1999: 81–5), to argue that no activist movement succeeded in Morocco's history by ignoring the form of religion traditionally followed by Moroccans. He also attributes the failure of the *al-Shebebay* movement (see the rest of the analyses in this section) and its demise by the late 1970s to the movement's opposition to and neglect of Sophie tradition of the country. For more details on Sophism in Morocco, (see Joffe 1992; Dareef 1999 and the Moroccan Centre for Studies and Contemporary Research 2008).

11 In 1968–9, both the Communist Party (Parti Communiste Maroccan) and the Party of Liberation and Socialism (Parti de la Liberation et du Socialisme) were also banned and their leaders arrested, harassed and exiled.

12 For more details on *al-Chabeba*, see Dareef 1997.

13 Morocco has formally occupied the former Spanish colony of Western Sahara since Spain left it in 1975. The Polisario Front, a national independence movement in control of a small part of the Sahara, took up arms against Morocco and is backed by neighbouring Algeria. The UN has been monitoring cease-fire between the two sides since 1991, but little movement towards peace occurred. A 'Baker Plan' was introduced in 2004 to solve the dispute peacefully, but its failure led both sides to propose alternative plans in 2007 with little progress. Currently, the UN has sponsored direct negotiations since June 2008. For more details, see ICG 2008; Reuters 2009; European Forum for Democracy and Consolidation 2009.

14 In the 2002 elections, 26 officially recognized political parties contested for seats in the parliament. This number increased to 33 parties in the 2007 elections. Even today, most of Morocco's political parties have a leftist leniency, with only one true religion (Islamic

Party, namely, the Justice and Development. For more details, see European Forum for Democracy and Solidarity 2009).

15 Even the Communist Party, banned in the late 1960s, was allowed to legally re-establish itself prior to the 1977 third parliamentary elections.

16 According to Dareef (1999: 135), the regime began to realize the threat of Islamists in the early 1970s, but this was reinforced in the late 1970s by the Iranian revolution, which transformed the Moroccan Islamist current from a reactionary to a proactive expression. A good indicator of this shift was seen in the al-Adel wa al-Ahsan Movement's decision to express itself as a movement. At the same time, several prominent Moroccan ulama, such as Abdullah ben al-Sedeeq and Abdulaziz ben Sedeeq, entered in direct confrontation with the regime when they openly called upon the ulama to sever their link with the monarchy, describing it as Jaheely (ignorant) because it is not ruling according to Islam. They went further and called upon the ulama to question the regime and not just to justify its policies. Both were arrested in late 1970s. It was these events which led the regime to establish the Supreme Scientist Council in the early 1980s.

17 The Scientists Foundation is organized at two levels: the Supreme Scientists Council and the Local Science Councils. Their role is mainly administrative, organizational and aims at da'wa (calling).

18 This classification is also followed by several Moroccan academics, such as Dareef 1999; Ben al-Mustafa 2008 and MCSCR 2008.

19 The first organizational expression of JCG appeared in September 1981, when its leader, Sheikh Abdul-Salam Yassin, announced the establishment of *Ausrat al-Jama'* (The Family of the Group). One year later in September 1982 he established *Jame'yat al-Jama'* (the Foundation of the Group). Licensing for the Group was rejected in both cases under the pretext of mixing politics with religion. This led Sheikh Yassin in March 1983 to establish *Jame'yat al_jama' al-kheriyah* as a charitable organization, thus benefiting from the 1958 charity and NGOs' law. In September 1987 the movement changed its name to Justice and Charity Group (JCG), which is taken directly from a verse in the Qu'ran. JCG remains unlicensed today, but is tolerated by the authorities. We classify JCG as a political movement not only because it is the largest religious movement in the country and has the largest number of followers, but also because it is generally interested in the daily politics of the country, constantly criticizes the regime's policies and democratic façade of Morocco, and therefore believes that political work should complement *da'wa* work. The JCG has therefore established a political unit in order to keep the JCG politically active. The movement's ideas and organization crystallizes around the person of Abdul-Salam Yassin himself, who spent most of the 1990s under house arrest. Unlike other Islamist movements in Morocco, the JCG has little ideological connections outside Morocco (Dareef 1999: 69–93; Ben al-Mustafa 2008; Slymovics 1999 and Willis 2004).

20 Most members of the URM originate from the *al-Chabeba*, who, since the early 1980s, sought to moderate their views and join the political process. Led by Benkeran, they established the *Jama' Islamiyyah* (JI) in 1983. JI latter applied formally for a license to establish a political party (*Hizb al-Islah al-Watani*) in the early 1980s but its request was rejected. This led the movement to change its name to Reform and Renewal Movement in 1985–6 (*Harakat al-Islah wal Tajdeed*), and to *Tawheed wal Islah* (Unity and Reform Movement) in 1996, when they were eventually permitted to enter politics by joining an already existing political party – the *Mouvement Populaire Democratique et Constitutionnel* (MPDC), led by the nationalist Abdul-Karim al-Khatib. This revived religious-nationalist sentiments and links that existed during the protectorate. One year later, after dominating the MPDC, the latter changed its name to PJD in 1997 (see endnote No. 21). The URM is a calling (missionary) movement, focuses on education, *da'wa* and social work, and leaves politics to PJD. The URM changed its name several times in order to indicate its severance with the past, particularly with the *al-Chabeba*. There is a great deal of overlapping in membership between the PJD and URM, and

members from the latter organization dominate the former, especially in the upper echelon of the administrative structure (Ben al-Mustafa 2008: 53; Willis 2004: 55–6).

21 Initially, the Party of Justice and Development (PJD) was created as the Constitutional and Democratic Popular Movement (MPDC). Its members come mostly from splinters of the Popular Movement (MP) and former *al-Chabeba* Movement. In October 1998 it became a political party under the name of PJD. Its creation followed the 1997 elections, which produced two main blocs with almost equal seats: the democratic bloc and *Ahzab al-wefag al-watani* (National Conciliation). It was not possible for any of the two blocs to rule without additional voices from independents. The regime wanted some Islamists in the political system but only those that have accepted his conditions and have been largely incorporated into his political strategy. This PJD met this condition and was thus licensed. It was also used as a pressure card against democratic bloc headed by socialist union to accept cabinet according to the conditions set by the regime (Dareef 1999: 276). The PJD is moderate Islamist and a growing force in the country. The electoral programme of the PJD had five key points: authenticity, sovereignty, democracy, equality and development – everything in accordance with Islam. In the run-off to the 2007 parliamentary elections, opinion-polls in the country showed a great victory for the PJD, with the possibility of winning up to 80 seats. However, the outcome of the elections was disappointing: although the PJD did increase its number of seats from 42 in 2002 to 46 in 2007, the increase was much less than expected (see European Forum for Democracy and Solidarity 2009: 11). The former PJD's Secretary General, Saad Eddine El-Othmani, explained this disappointing outcome as a result of 'state's deliberate rigging of the elections and manipulation of the electoral system'. (Personal interview, Rabat February 2010.) The party has an active and popular website in Arabic, and is developing a French website to reach Moroccans in Europe: http://www.pjd.ma/arabe/index.asp.

22 Tabligh wal-Da'wa (TWD) was established first in India in 1927 by Sheikh Muhamed Illias al-Helawi (1845–1944) within a context of tense relations between Muslims and Hindus and in response to what was perceived as Christian missionary movements. TWD has branches in several Muslim countries. The first Moroccan branch was established in 1964 by Sheikh Muhamed al-Hamdawi who was succeeded by al-Basheer Yousi in 1987. From the start, the TWD has been an apolitical movement concerned with calling (*da'wa*) mainly. It focuses on the spiritual, educational and tarbiya (bringing up) sides, including key Islamic principles of honesty, loyalty and imitating the prophet's ethics, manners and behaviours. Accessing authority is not one of the movement's priorities, which seeks to change society (Islamizing it) over the long run. In fact, other Islamic political movements criticize the TWD for ignoring politics and over-focusing on the individual (Ben al-Mustafa 2008: 47–8).

23 The al-Badeel al-Hadari (BH) Movement was established in *Fiz* on 22 October 1995. Most members also originally come from the Chabeba Group, with Kamal Ibrahim, the second man in the former Chabeba Group, being its spiritual father. It is the apolitical-da'wa movement that identifies its objectives as contributing to the social and civilized upbringing of the Moroccan society, support dialogue with the other and by extending bridges of communications with all other national activists to bridge gaps between them and find common grounds for action, and assist in solving problems of Morocco's society; support dialogue of civilizations. The movement has a small office, with only 11 elected members and publishes a weekly newspaper, *al-Jisser* (*The Bridge*) that expresses its opinions.

24 The MNS was established in November 1998 by Muhammed ben Mubarak al-Murwani. It is also an apolitical movement whose main objectives are to contribute to Islamic sahwa (awakening), protect political reforms and to be an active factor in new political openings which Morocco has been experiencing since the early 1990s. Like the PJD and BH, not only do most of the HMAU members also come from the former Chabeba Group, but it also has its own monthly newspaper, *al-Naba'* (*The News*). For details, see *al-Sahwa*, No. 38. December 1994: 13 and Dareef 1999: 100.

25 FIF was established in April 1994 as a result of merging of three small Islamic expressions and activists in Morocco: Jame'at al-Da'wa al-Islameya (The Group of Islamic Calling – GIC), first established in Fez in 1976 by Dr Abdulsalaam al-Haras: al-Jame'ya al-Islameya fi al-Qaser al-Kabeer (the Islamic Foundation in the Big Palace), established by Ahmad al-Reesoni in 1976, and Jame'yat al-Shorooq al-Islameya (The Islamic Enlightenment Foundation – IEF), established in 1986 by some older members of the former Chabeba Group who decided to freeze their activities with Chabeba after the latter became more radicalized in the early 1970s. All of the above-mentioned movements had one thing in common; they abandoned political Islam and joined educational, da'awee and Islam al-tarbawee only. FIF identified six key objectives for itself: strengthening historical links with Islam, spreading the spirit of cooperation, promoting dialogue and pluralism, creating conditions conducive for renaissance though deepening self-feeling, identity and belief in the divine message of the nation, working to counter negative social problems which lead to backwardness, such as illiteracy, ignorance, individualism, selfishness, laziness and atrophy; and spreading good ethics and principled values (Dareef 1999: 100–6).

26 Two spontaneous reform programmes were initiated in the late 1970s and early 1980s and both were abandoned shortly after their introduction because of a lack of political will and fear of social impact of reform. For more details, see Hamdouch 1999.

27 SALP was associated with a real average GDP growth rate of 3.8 per cent during the 1980s, a decline in inflation rate from 10.3 per cent in 1982 to 2.3 per cent in 1988, and rescheduling and stabilizing external debt at around $21 billion in 1993 (Hamdouch 1999: 14).

28 Many of the members were former opposition leaders who were themselves tortured and imprisoned for long periods by the former regime. Unlike Algeria, therefore, which prevented its former radicals from participating in any political activities, Morocco actually relied on them to bring about a true reconciliation process and thus appointed many of them in important positions and allowed them to establish and join political parties.

29 On 20 October 2005, the Moroccan Parliament ratified a new law which defined torture as 'Every act results in pain or severe physical and psychological pain deliberately committed, incited or not reported by an employer the aim of which is to create fear inside or force a person or another individual to provide information or documents or confessions in order to punish him for acts he committed or is suspected to have committed … ' (ACHR 2006: 44).

30 On November 2008 the Minister of Justice, Abdualwahid al-Radi, stated he did not know anything about this initiative and 'that all what we have is several amnesty calls from those detainees and that we are studying them but I am unaware of a dialogue with what is known as the ideologues salafi sheikhs' (MCSCR 2008: 417 and 418).

31 This followed a call from JSs detainees to the ulama to participate in a dialogue with them, similar to the one which the Saudi and Egyptians authorities implemented with their radicals, in order to avoid 'pessimistic analysis and wrong claims and the speeches of frustrations and failure, and to take into consideration sensitivity of the subject and the suffering of the families and siblings.' (MCSCR 2008: 416).

32 Unless otherwise stated, the rest of the section draws heavily on the Moroccan Centre for Studies and Contemporary Research 2008, Report on the Religious Case in Morocco, which was written by a group of Moroccan experts and considered the most comprehensive study on the subject.

33 Al-Muhammadiyah Foundation is an extension of the Moroccan Scientist Foundation, which was established in 1961 as a calling (*da'wa*) institution aiming at teaching people their true religious principles from the book and the Sunna. In 2006, a royal degree turned the Scientist Foundation into an independent institution, Al-Muhammadiyah, which carries the name of the King himself.

Bibliography

Advisory Council for Human Rights (2006) *The Foundation for Consolidating Reforms and Reconciliation*, National Committee for the Truth, Fairness and Reconciliation, Morocco. The Final Report.

Alimoussa, K. (2008) 'On the fifth anniversary of the terrorist attacks, Jihadi Salfist detainees call for arresting those behind May 16 attacks', in *Al-Tajdid*, Rabat, 16–18 May, pp.1.

Amnesty International (2007) *Amnesty International Report 2007 Morocco/Western Sahara.*

Ashford University (2007) *Terrorist Attacks in Morocco, the FAQ*, Ashford University. Available HTTP: http://www.militaryphotos.net/forums/showthread.php?109766-Terrorist-attack-in-morocco.

At-Tajdid (2008) *Special Report on the Fifth Anniversary of the 2003 Terrorist Attacks*, 16–18 May.

Ayubi, N. (1999) *Over-Stating the Arab State: Politics and Society in the Middle East*, London: I. B Tauris.

Ben al-Mustafa, O. (2008) *The Islamists in Morocco (Al-Islameyoona fi al-Magrib)*, Casablanca, Dar Toubkal Publications.

Bonner, R. (2008) 'Torture Claims Credible, Court Finds', *The New York Times*, 22 August.

Clouser, M. (2009) *The Performance of Human Rights in Morocco*, University of Texas, 3 March. Available HTTP: <http://www.cwrl.utexas.edu/.

Dareef, M. (1997) 'Political Islam in Morocco', Rabat, Al-Najah Publisher, *The Moroccan Magazine for Social Science.*

—— (1999). 'The Moroccan Islamist: The Political Calculations in the Islamic Work 1969–1999 (Al-Islamiyeen al-magharibah: Al-Hesabat al Siyasiyah fi al-amal al-Islami 1969–1999)', Rabat, Al-Najah Publisher, *The Moroccan Magazine for Political Social Science.*

—— (2008). 'Terrorism is the Outcome of External Contradictions and Morocco is Still Threatened', in *At-Tajdid*, 16–18 May, pp.4.

De Laubadere, A. (1949) *Les Reformes des Pouvoirs Publics au Maroc*, Paris.

Entelis, J. (1980) *Comparative Politics of North Africa: Algeria, Morocco and Tunisia*, New York: Syracuse University Press.

Erlanger, S. and Mekhennet, S. (2009) 'Islamic Radicalism Slows Moroccan Reforms', in *The New York Times*, 27 August.

European Forum for Democracy and Solidarity (EFDS) (2009) *Morocco*, London, Party of European Socialists, 15 July. Available HTTP: http://www.europeanforum.net/country/morocco.

Hamdouch, B. (1999) 'Adjustment, strategic planning and the Morocco economy', in N. Shafk (ed.), *Economic Challenges Facing MENA Countries: Alternative Futures,* 1999: 13–24.

Harrigan, J. and El-Said, H. (2009) *Economic Liberalisation, Social Capital and Islamic Welfare Provision*, London: Palgrave Macmillan.

ICG (2008) *Morocco Conflict History*, Brussels, an Update, September.

Irafiq, A. (2010) 'Be fair to us: for the sake of finding an exit for what is known as the Jihadi Salafist File', Local Prison, Fiz.

Istiqlal Party (1946) *Istiqlal Party Document*, Paris, September (Obtained from Istiqlal Party Headquarters in Rabat).

Joffe, G. (1992) 'The changing geography of North Africa: development, migration and the demographic time bomb', in G. Chapman and K. Baker (eds) *The Changing Geography of Africa and the Middle East*, London: Routledge, 139–64.

Lubeck, P. M. (1998) 'Islamist Responses to Globalization: Cultural Conflict in Egypt, Algeria, and Malaysia', in B. Crawford and R. Lipschutz (eds), *The Myth of 'Ethnic conflict': Politics, Economics and 'Cultural' Violence,* IIS/IAS-University of California Press: Berkeley, 293–319.

Mideast & N. Africa Encyclopaedia (2010) *Political Parties in Morocco*, August 8. Available HTTP: http://www.answers.com/topic/political-parties-in-morocco.

Ministry of Information (1965) *Le Maroc en Marche: discourse de Sa Majeste le Roi Hassan II depiuis Son Intronisation*, Rabat, Morocco.

Moroccan Centre for Studies and Contemporary Research (MCSCR) (2008). *Taqrir al-Hala al-Dineya* in Morocco (The Report of the Religious Status in Morocco), CEMERC, Morocco.

Owen, R. (1992) *State, Power and Politics in the Making of the Modern Middle East*, London: Routledge.

Pellicer, M. (2008) *Who Supports Islamist Parties? The Case of Morocco*, Macmillan Centre for International and Area Studies, Yale University.

Reuters (2009) Feature – 'Morocco Party Woos Western Saharan Hearts and Minds', 11 June. Available HTTP: http://www.reuters.com/article/idUSLB743581.

Richards, A. and Waterbury, J. (1996) *A Political Economy of the Middle East*, 2nd edn, Oxford: Westview.

Slymovics, S. (1999) *Stolen Lives: Twenty Years in a Desert Jail*, Paris, Grasset & Fasquelle.

—— (2005). *The Performance of Human Rights in Morocco*, Pennsylvania: University of Pennsylvania Press.

Tripp, C. (1996) 'Islam and the secular logic of the state in the Middle East', in A. S. Sidahmed and A. Ehteshami (eds) *Islamic Fundamentalism*, Westview Press: Oxford 1996: 51–69.

Waterbury, J. (1970) *The Commander of the Faithful: The Moroccan Political Elite*, London: Weidenfeld and Nicolson.

Willis, M. (2004) 'Morocco's Islamist and the legislative elections of 2002: the strange case of the party that did not want to win', in *Mediterranean Politics*, 9:1, pp. 53–81.

World Bank (2005) *Kingdom of Morocco: Country Assistance Strategy 2005–2009.*

8

SAUDI ARABIA

The master of deradicalization

Hamed El-Said and Richard Barrett

Introduction

Any study of counter-radicalization in general, and of deradicalization in particular, would be incomplete without an examination of the state-based programmes in Saudi Arabia. Saudi Arabia has long faced the problem of extremist violence and many of the leaders and operatives of Al-Qaeda have their origins there, including 15 of the 19 hijackers who ploughed airplanes into targets in the United States in September 2001. Saudi citizens continue to provide much of the Al-Qaeda leadership and have comprised the majority of foreign fighters in Iraq. More important still, many officials and commentators have pointed to the deliberate exportation by Saudi Arabia of Wahhabism, a rigid, puritanical brand of Islam, and a 'philosophy of *takfir*', that have led to the radicalization of Muslims in many parts of the world (Lake 2007. Also see Zakaria 2001). The ICG (2004a: 8) has gone so far as to claim that Saudi Arabia 'came to be portrayed as a breeding ground for terrorism, an anachronistic, backward country that professes official friendship to the US, while simultaneously teaching its children to hate the West and funding the religious extremists who attack Americans'.

Saudi Arabia has responded to its critics and to the rise of extremism and terrorism inside the Kingdom, by introducing 'one of the [.] best terrorist rehabilitation programs in the world' (Youssef 2009). Christopher Boucek (2008a: 64–5), a senior researcher at the Carnegie Institute, described the Saudi programme, which is known as PRAC (Prevention, Rehabilitation and Aftercare), as 'the best funded and longest continually run program' in the world and one that 'has become a *de facto* model for other countries seeking to implement a counter-radicalisation program'. Even 'the U.S. has praised Saudi Arabia's anti-terrorism efforts and its "unprecedented level of cooperation" [in the] war on terror' (BBC News Online, 30 April 2004).

Despite its global reputation, how PRAC 'is accomplished is not entirely clear', particularly given that the country does indeed promote Wahhabism, one of the most extreme versions of Islam, not only as the official religion of the State, but also 'as a basis of all of these [PRAC] efforts' (Seifert 2010: 3). This chapter aims to analyse Saudi Arabia's counter-radicalization and rehabilitation policies as they have evolved since the early 1990s, in particular in the context of the internal challenges the kingdom has faced since its establishment in the 1930s.

The chapter first looks at the roots of Wahhabism and the evolution of its relationship with the rulers of the country; it analyses the main challenges that the State faced internally and externally before 1990 and how it managed to overcome them. It goes on to describe the rise of the Islamic radical right in the 1990s and the State's response, examining a significant early process of deradicalization among a large number of radical Islamists (*sahwists*), a process which had considerable influence over the design of subsequent programmes. The chapter then looks at the current counter-radicalization, rehabilitation and aftercare programme and considers the difficulties of measuring its success. The final section provides some concluding remarks.

The chapter also argues that Wahhabism has been largely misunderstood, even deliberately misinterpreted, and that this focus on religious issues has diverted attention from political factors, which have had a far greater radicalizing effect.

The roots of Wahhabism: 1902–52

Saudi Arabia is unique in the region. It was never colonized by a foreign power and, compared to other states in the area, was not much subject to the influences of the Ottoman Empire. Its creation was mainly an internal affair, enabled by the religious, revivalist movement known as Wahhabism.

The origin of Wahhabism lies in early eighteenth century Nejd (central Arabia) as a puritan-hanabilte-revivalist movement initiated by Sheikh Muhammed Ibn Abdulwahhab of the Saudi Al-Shaikh tribe. Ibn Wahhab deplored what he perceived as the decay of Islamic society in the Arabian Peninsula and its degeneration into the state of ignorance (*jahiliya*) that had pertained before the Prophet Muhammad began his call to spread the Islamic religion. Ibn Abdulwahhab sought a return to the original and true Islamic path as existed during the time of the Prophet and his companions (*al-salaf al-salih*), rejecting all theological interpretations and intermediaries not derived from the Qu'ran, the *sunnoh* (speeches, stories and recommendations of the Prophet) or the consensus of the *salaf al-salih*. Religion was therefore politicized by 'eradicating all forms of popular Islam, including Sufism, saint worshipping and Shiism' and by 'imposing [a] ritual austerity on believers' (ICG 2004b: 1).

Ibn Abdulwahhab, while possessing the necessary spiritual influence, lacked sufficient military force to impose his views on a tribal, largely fragmented society that was naturally opposed to central authority. However, he found a powerful ally in Muhammad Ibn Saud, a tribal leader and head of a small town near modern day Riyadh (*Dir'iyya*) and their alliance, which began in 1744, survived over the years to provide the basis of the modern Saudi State. The key feature of the agreement was a division of labour between Al-Saud and Al-Wahhab, with the former in charge of politics, including running and managing the State, and the latter in control of religious affairs, including spreading Ibn Abdulwahhab's ideas and teachings (ICG 2004b: 1). It was this combination of the military power of Al-Saud and the spiritual influence of Al-Wahhab that led to the foundation of the modern Kingdom of Saudi Arabia (KSA).

The Saudi–Wahhabi state collapsed twice before being re-established for the third time in the early twentieth century through the same Saudi–Wahhabi alliance that had led to its creation in 1744; once in 1818 and again, after a 68-year revival, in 1891. The destruction of the first two Saudi–Wahhabi states came first at the hands of Muhammad Ali of Egypt (then the Ottoman Viceroy) and then by the British, helped by *Shiite* communities in the region who were all alarmed by the rise of this new power (Sharara 1981; Ayubi 1999: 283). Between 1902 and 1925 the Saudi–Wahhabi alliance reformed and re-established its power in all the territories it had controlled in the eighteenth century, this time with British support. It was a long, gradual, arduous process that began with the re-capture of Riyadh by Abd al-Aziz Al-Saud (Ibn Saud), in 1902 and ended with the conquest of Taif and Mecca in 1924[1] and the capture of Jidda in 1925.

> Instrumental in this process was the role played by the *Ikhwan* in their migratory camps (*hujar, sing.: hujra or hijra*). These were neo-Wahhabi agricultural/military colonies established outside normal Bedouin domicile for a process of training and organization as well as political acculturation. They were really the main force in defining the new Bedouin-state and in creating it in Arabia, in the name of Islam.
>
> *(Ayubi 1999: 127)*

The Ikhwan first became known around 1914 as a *salafi* movement seeking to revitalize and reinforce the eighteenth century puritanical doctrine of Ibn Abdulwahhab. Historians disagree as to its exact origin, some seeing it as an independent movement, while others argue that it was the creation of Ibn Saud who, up to 1915, showed little religious inclination but needed 'a religious rationale for his military expansion, understanding very well that nomads could not be subjugated for long by force or by money' (Ayubi 1999: 129). Either way, Ibn Saud co-opted the movement to achieve his political objectives.

The religious rationale for using the Ikhwan expired after 1925. The Ikhwan movement had become a liability, threatening both Ibn Saud's internal authority as supreme leader and his relations with the main imperialist power in the region, Great Britain, with whom he sought rapprochement in order to settle his tribal frontiers and his territorial disputes with neighbouring countries that were still under the British mandate.[2]

In September 1925, Ibn Saud signed two agreements with Britain: the *Hadda* Agreement on a Najd-Transjordan frontier and the *Bahra* Agreement which patched up some differences outstanding with Iraq concerning tribal rights. These agreements upset the Ikhwan; 'Both agreements outlawed giving refuge to groups involved in raiding or subverting tribal loyalties and confirmed the nomads' peaceful right to cross boundaries' (Wilkinson 2000: 53). This effectively put an end to the old tribal practice of raid and tribute (protection tax) being enforced on less powerful tribes. Instead, both an Islamic tax (zakat) and a non-Islamic commercial tax were imposed on Najdis (Helms 1981). Ibn Saud also destroyed the Ikhwan's agricultural–military settlements, the *hujar*, which, from the Ikhwan's point of view, simulated 'the Prophet Muhammad's flight from Mecca to Medina' (Habib 1978a: 14–15; Ayubi 1999: 83). This, in addition to dispossessing them of their weapons, infuriated the Ikhwan.

Also, the Ikhwan resented both Ibn Saud's modernization drive, which included the introduction of modern technology such as motor cars, the telegraph and a capitalist mode of production, and his increased dependence on the British, which they saw as a deviation from true Islamic principles:

> … this new state, supported by the English, was being established on foundations of a capitalist character, linked to foreign capital. Confrontation was inevitable between a mode of production moving towards capitalism, and the nomadic mode with its tribal system. The Saudi family was seeking to benefit from the oil funds in modern projects, whereas its nomadic masses, especially the Ikhwan, were brought up to values and traditions that are as far as can be from capitalist relations.
>
> *(Dahir 1986: 283–4; see also Ayubi 1999: 130)*

To be sure, the key issue for Ibn Saud was not the Ikhwan *per se*, but rather their ulama *(religious leadership)*, who in 1926 issued a fatwa (a religious order) that supported many of the Ikhwan's demands. The confrontation between Ibn Saud and the Ikhwan ended with their defeat in the Battle of *Sabala* in 1930, but Ibn Saud managed also to co-opt their ulama, leading them to issue a fatwa to say that the declaration of jihad (in the sense of a religiously sanctioned war) 'was the responsibility of the *imam* (leader) alone' (Ayubi 1999: 129). This fatwa has come to play a key role in the conduct of rehabilitation and deradicalization policies in modern Saudi Arabia.

Following the defeat of the Ikhwan, but still with the support of the Al Wahhab, Ibn Saud started to build his modern state and strengthen his new administration. He adopted a policy of pacification towards the tribes and in order to integrate them into a centralized state system, persuaded them to abandon their nomadic traditions and live in permanent settlements. In this context, jihad, which had been a key tool for mobilizing the tribes before 1930, was replaced by a new system of subsidy to assure their loyalty. A new National Guard was created in 1928, which played an important role in co-opting tribal warriors and the defeated remnants of the Ikhwan into a centralized state security system. The declaration of Saudi Arabia as a kingdom in 1932 without Ibn Saud having to revoke any of the policies which the Ikhwan had opposed before their defeat in 1930 enhanced his popularity, legitimacy and authority. The Wahhabi ulama were further incorporated into state institutions by making them state employees and putting them in charge of the country's educational, cultural and religious institutions and activities. Even today, 'the decedents of Al-Wahhab still dominate the religious official institutions of the state' (Okruhlik, 2004), thus providing religious legitimacy to state policies.

The death of a leader and consolidation of the Bedouin state: 1953–74

Although Ibn Saud was not able to complete his main projects before his death in 1953 (the settlement of nomads, fixing tribal frontiers and resolving territorial disputes with his neighbours), he succeeded in bringing the whole of Arabia under his rule. In doing so he resorted occasionally to force in order to counter internal threats and tribal insurrections, and until his death his rule remained based on a combination of religious manipulation, military coercion, and co-opting powerful tribes and social groups through a mixture of increased subsidies, particularly after the advent of oil wealth in the late 1940s, and marriage alliances with key tribes and social groups.

When Ibn Saud died in 1953, the country was still being ruled in very much the same way as it had been in the 1930s; it remained largely underdeveloped, under-modernized, nomadic and under Ibn Saud's personal control. ARAMCO, the main oil company, was the most important and modern institution in the country and it played an important role in helping the then small and inexperienced bureaucracy to manage the state. A modernization programme, which re-introduced the nomad settlement project in the early 1950s, had little success.[3]

Before his death, Ibn Saud did two important things that had significant impact on the political evolution of Saudi Arabia (Owen 1992: 70). The first was to regulate the succession and prepare for a future leader and he appointed his oldest son, Saud, as the Crown prince, supported closely by his more skilful and diplomatic brother, Faisal. The second was to create a council of ministers to run the daily affairs of the state and to oversee the country's economic development.

Faisal took a special interest in the council of ministers, which became the most important political institution in the country alongside the Royal family and partially compensated for the lack of a constitution. Faisal also focused on building state institutions and regulating the remuneration and roles of members of the Royal family. He encouraged their education and sought to develop the skills and experience of its younger, third-generation members. During this period, the United States had already replaced the United Kingdom as Saudi Arabia's key Western ally and Faisal bolstered relations with the USA when he sent his oldest son to attend school and then university there. Several other members of the Royal family followed suit.

During the 1950s, little attention was paid to the country's economic development; the focus was on consolidating the state itself. The creation of the council of ministers, and later of a higher committee of senior princes to advise the king on all major decisions, provided excellent opportunities to develop the administrative, political and diplomatic skills of the Royal family. Faisal also initiated a process of appointing family members to the most sensitive state positions, including in the cabinet, army and security sector (Owen 1992: 70; Ayubi 1999; Richards and Waterbury 1996).

The National Guard, which had been created in 1928, was expanded, trained and equipped with modern technology thus becoming the core of the country's modern armed forces. It played an important role in incorporating and co-opting tribal warriors, including remnants of the Ikhwan, into a loyal, dependable and salaried centralized state institution. Wahhabi clerics and ulama remained in charge of religious, educational and cultural activities. The Enforcement of Good and Prevention of Evil Unit, which was created in 1929, was also expanded in the 1950s and 1960s, and played an important role in integrating and co-opting radical elements into a religious police institution, the *mutawwa*, which monitored the behaviour of citizens to ensure compatibility with Wahhabi *Tawhidi*, doctrine. Wahhabism, therefore, continued to shape not only the religious practices of the country, but also its way of life. Through mechanisms of state control it kept the country firmly conservative and traditional. Following the death of the grand mufti in 1970, King Faisal took the opportunity to create a new Ministry of Justice, thus also bringing under state control an important sphere of Islamic jurisprudence (Owen 1992: 70–1).

Force was used only when needed and Saudi Arabia generally avoided the kind of violent confrontation with Islamic groups that other countries in the region (such as Egypt, Iraq and Syria) encountered, the 1929 rebellion by the Ikhwan being a striking exception. Saudi Arabia nonetheless experienced several instances of political unrest, including demonstrations and strikes by workers and the intelligentsia, as well as failed military coups leading to arrests and imprisonments in 1953, 1956, 1963, 1964 and 1969.[4] King Faisal himself was assassinated in the mid-1970s by a nephew. These instances of unrest occurred despite the fact that the 1950s and 1960s saw little extreme poverty in the country. Such events show, as Ayubi (1999: 232) has noted, that nothing about Saudi Arabia makes her more immune than any other place to coups, revolutions and rebellions; and if they could happen in the 1950s and 1960s, there is no reason why they could not also happen 15 or 25 years later.

The major threat to the state came from within. Faisal and Saud did not get on very well as the former opposed the latter's lifestyle and handling of the diplomatic and economic affairs of the country (which led to a series of financial crises that threatened both the bankruptcy of the economy and the credibility of the ruling family). Tensions between them intensified in the late 1950s and early 1960s, made worse by increasing political instability in neighbouring Yemen, where the pan-Arabist Nasser sent troops in 1962 and managed to overthrow the pro-Saudi regime of Imam Ahmad. This led to a protracted civil war in which Saudi-backed royalists faced an Egyptian expeditionary force of 70,000 men (Owen 1992: 210). Internal divisions in Saudi Arabia led to the replacement of Fahad as king by Faisal in 1964 (Owen 1992: 70; Richards and Waterbury 1996).

The Saudi authorities then launched and led a pan-Islamic counter movement, whose membership included Jordan, Morocco and other Gulf oil states. As a result:

> … the Saudi regime gave shelter to a large number of Syrian and Egyptian Muslim Brothers, who were persecuted in their home countries by Baathist and Nasserist regimes … Riyadh used the Muslim Brothers' politicised version of Islam as a weapon in its political–ideological dispute with Nasserist and Baathist neighbours … Muslim Brothers came to play a key role in the new and expanding administration, especially in education where they designed school and university curricula and were the bulk of the faculty. […] As one

> Saudi Islamist who was a student put it: "most of the books that could be found in bookshops in the 1970s were written by members of the Brotherhood".
>
> *(ICG 2004b: 2)*

The hosting of Egyptian and Syrian radical elements of the Muslim Brotherhood, in conjunction with other state policies (see below), helped, over the years, to radicalize certain sections of the Saudi population, particularly sheikhs, students and even professors and teachers who were educated at the hands of Egyptian and Syrian radicals. These in turn radicalized other Saudis, particularly friends and relatives. As Nasser Al-Bahri (better known as Abu Jandal), a former companion of Osama Bin Laden in Afghanistan, who grew up in Saudi Arabia at that time, stated, 'we were all radicalized at the hands of Egyptian and Syrian sheikhs, not Saudis' (Personal interview, Sana'a June 2010). These developments came back to haunt the Saudi state almost two decades later, particularly in the highly politicized and politically charged environment of the 1990s.

Thus the political system remained very narrowly based in Saudi Arabia and was overwhelmingly dominated by members of the Royal family. Although the Kingdom neither experienced violent confrontations with any internal Islamic groups, nor witnessed extreme poverty, it still experienced several instances of political unrest. More importantly, a new generation of students, academics and scholars became radicalized at the hands of Egyptian and Syrian clerics who flocked to the country in the 1950s and 1960s. The impact of these developments, however, was dampened by the sudden and massive inflow of oil revenues in the 1970s and was only truly felt in the 1990s.

Oil, wealth and retribalization 1975–90

The sudden large spike in oil prices in the early 1970s brought unprecedented wealth to the kingdom. This ushered in an era of substantial economic development and modernization, which included considerable investment in infrastructure, such as roads, power stations and electricity, water desalination plants, telecommunications, schools, hospitals, and large economic and developmental projects. Saudi Arabia was so awash with oil rents that it did not matter how much it spent, there were always large surpluses. Generous hand-outs, in terms of subsidized food, utilities, schools, hospitals, housing and land were extended to almost all citizens. While in the previous decades loyal tribes and social groups had been the main beneficiaries of state policies, in the post-1973 era almost everybody benefited, although some groups and individuals were more favoured than others (Owen 1992; Ayubi 1999). The state acquired what Hossein Mahdavy (1970) described in his work on Iran as a '*rentier*' character: a state that depends heavily on rent accrued to it from the rest of the world which it then *distributes* locally.

Oil rents also had important political implications:

> [In] allocation or distributive (or rentier) states … the state is independent of society … rentier states do not need to tax, or may tax more lightly, and their

> primary function is the distribution of resources accruing from abroad ... Spending therefore is the essential function of the rentier state, and generosity (as opposed to accountability) is the essential virtue of its ruler ... The rentier state paradigm has become most popular through the reversal of the well-known saying "no taxation without representation" into its mirror image: "no representation without taxation".
>
> *(Luciani 2005: 90–2)*

Mammoth oil wealth enabled the state to buy acquiescence and the expanded bureaucracy became a further political-distributive mechanism by providing jobs in the public sector. Not surprisingly, the 1970s and 1980s were decades of relative stability compared with the earlier two decades. The system, however, as predicated by the *rentier* state paradigm, became even narrower, based on a thin network of elite officials legitimized by a subservient Wahhabi doctrine.

One of the major social and political consequences of this system of state patronage was the 'retribalization' of society. As Crystal (1996: 269) noted, state policies led tribes to trade political support for 'housing, social services, scholarship, and jobs, especially as soldiers, police officers, guards and bodyguards. The result was strengthening of tribal identities, a process of political retribalization'. However, in undemocratic and particularly rentier states, 'no conflict arises over the ownership of the means of production. Instead, strictly moral and cultural considerations become the legitimising ideology of groups and opposing rentier states' (Shambayati 1994: 308). In undemocratic and tribal societies, opposition, particularly Islamic moderate and radical opposition, is often nurtured through strong informal institutions like the clan, the tribe, the family and other social networks. It is less reliant on formal organizations such as political parties, trade unions and students' associations, all of which are usually prohibited in undemocratic, Arab rentier states (Wiktorowics 2004).

Despite the relative stability of the decade, Saudi Arabia faced two significant challenges at the end of the 1970s. The first came in November 1979 from the Shiite community, which is concentrated mainly in the Eastern province where the oil fields are located. Saudi's Shiite population has always complained of economic, political and religious discrimination and it was emboldened by the 1979 Iranian revolution to celebrate openly *Ashura*, a Shiite religious festival long banned in Saudi Arabia. The second threat came almost two weeks after the Shiite uprising and was even more disturbing to the Saudi authorities: it came from a small group of Sunni-Wahhabists who took over the Great Mosque in Mecca in mid-November under the leadership of Juhaiman al-Utaibi, a grandson of one of the former Ikhwan warriors. Al-Utaibi and his colleagues hoped not only to attract attention but also to force the state to initiate reform in order to tackle what they perceived as widespread corruption, depravity among the Royal family, deviation from the true path of Islam, subservience to the United States, economic and social injustices, and the weakening of the Wahhabi religious establishment's role in guiding and monitoring societal behaviour. These demands for reform were similar to the historic demands of the Ikhwan who led the 1929 revolt, with one minor difference: while the Ikhwan had opposed Ibn

Saud's then close alliance with Great Britain, al-Utaibi and his colleagues opposed Saudi Arabia's close relations with the United States, which they saw as biased towards Israel and against Muslims (Okruhlik 2004).

The state's omnipotent coercive institutions overcame both challenges; but in addition to coercion, state authorities responded with more religion. As if Saudi Arabia was not religious enough, more funding was given to the creation of new and the expansion of existing religious institutions; more religious material was incorporated into the educational curricula leading to a large imbalance between religious and non-religious topics; more powers were given to the religious police and more restrictions were imposed on women and the freedom of speech. The reaction of the state seemed, at least on the surface, to validate the claim of the neo-Wahhabi movement of al-Utaibi that the state had deviated from the true path of Islam. These policies benefited most religious and cultural institutions, still overwhelmingly dominated by radical Egyptians, Syrians and, by now, their Saudi disciples and pupils (ICG 2004a and 2004b).

Even when oil prices plummeted in the early- and mid-1980s and cutbacks were forced on almost every sector of the economy, state religious expenditure remained intact and was even expanded. This led to more conservatism, a more inward-looking, narrower interpretation of sacred texts and the emergence of new forms of fundamentalism (ICG 2004a and 2004b). As a Saudi journalist put it: 'Different groups ended up competing with fundamentalists over who [could] appear more conservative in the public eye' (*Arab News* 20 May 2002. Also see Okruhlik 2004: 254).

The effects of new forms of fundamentalism, however, were temporarily dampened by the state's policy of encouraging up to 12,000 Saudi youths to go and fight a 'holy war' in Afghanistan in the 1980s.[5] The Saudi official religious establishment went as far as issuing a fatwa making Jihad in Afghanistan *fard kifayeh* (a collective duty). When the war in Afghanistan ended in 1989 with the defeat of the Soviet Union, the majority of Saudi mujahedeen, most of whom had either witnessed or participated in real battles and had developed a Jihadi culture and way of life, began returning home. This marked the beginning of the confrontation between the Saudi authorities and their Jihadists.

The rise and deradicalization of radical right: 1990–2003

Even before the 1990-91 Gulf War started, the Saudi environment was conducive to radicalization and politicization. Politically, the system remained narrow, with a small number of individuals controlling almost all important positions in the state. Formal forms of expression, such as political parties, labour and student unions remained banned, and associational life was further restricted after the 1979 twin Sunni–Shiite crises.

Economically, the price of oil plummeted in the early 1980s, thus reducing the capacity of the state to continue its generous hand-outs and its ability to fund development projects. Financing the Gulf War itself turned the once rich Saudi state into a net debtor, further undermining its ability to continue to buy loyalty through largess. Though unofficial, generally accepted unemployment rates rose to more than 30 per cent among university graduates. Per capita income in 1995 declined drastically to less than half its level in 1981. Saudi Arabia began experiencing new types of social problems, including drugs, crime, violence and poverty, as well as social inequalities (Okrunhlik 2004: 257; Ayubi 1999; Owen 1992). Within this context, little or no effort was made to rehabilitate, retrain and prepare returning Saudis who had fought in Afghanistan for reintegration into their society, families and the labour market.

Nothing, however, has been more radicalizing to Muslims in general and to Saudis in particular than the 1990–91 and the 2003 Gulf Wars, as well as the nature of bilateral relations between Saudi Arabia and the United States. ICG concurs:

> The 1990–1991 Gulf War was the most critical event in the history of Saudi Islamism and helps explain subsequent domestic politics. […] Indeed arguably no single factor contributed more to undermining the status of Saudi rulers and strengthened the appeal of the radical opponents than the nature of the bilateral relationship [with the USA] … Saudi militants regularly invoke the wrongs visited on the Palestinian and Iraqi people to justify their actions.[6]
>
> *(ICG 2004b: 5, 27, 28)*

Alarmed by Saddam Hussein's invasion of neighbouring Kuwait, Saudi Arabia responded by inviting/permitting a US-led multinational force to use Saudi territory to attack Iraq and simultaneously to base American troops in the kingdom. Saudi Arabia was one of a very few Muslim states in the region, along with Iran and Turkey, that had neither experienced colonization nor the presence of a large foreign army on its soil. Many Islamists, and even other progressive reformers, saw the presence of US soldiers in Saudi Arabia as tantamount to occupation. At the same time, Saudi authorities began to restrict the movement of the mujahedeen who had started to return from Afghanistan in the late 1980s and early 1990s. As Abu Jandal, Osama Bin Laden's former bodyguard in Afghanistan, explained:

> Yesterday we were told to go to Afghanistan for jihad against non-believers who occupied a Muslim country. Suddenly after returning from Afghanistan we were arrested and harassed to prevent us from fighting the Americans who now attacked another Muslim country, Iraq. We got very confused. We lost the ability to distinguish right from wrong. Who is a Muslim and who is not these days?
>
> *(Personal interview, Sana'a July 2010)*

Other state policies also seem to have had a role in radicalizing many Islamists in Saudi Arabia. Following the outbreak of the 1990–91 Gulf War the mujahedeen, now led by their undisputed leader Osama Bin Laden, offered to defend the Kingdom in case Saddam Hussein decided to attack after his invasion of Kuwait. The Saudi authorities naturally rejected Bin Laden's offer, but at the same time pushed its religious establishment to issue a fatwa that justified the presence of foreign (US) troops on Saudi soil. This was followed by another fatwa in 1993 justifying peace with Israel following the commencement of the Oslo Agreement between Palestinians and Israelis. These fatwas were read as American impositions on the Kingdom and led to the immediate loss of credibility of the Wahhabist religious establishment. This in turn led to the further radicalization of many Islamists, particularly jihadists, who started 'to move in directions more radical' than all other groups: these Islamists became more openly critical of the regime and its alliance with the United States, and in 1996 issued a 'Declaration of War on the USA' (ICG 2004a: 6 and 2004b). The 1990–91 Gulf War marked the emergence of a powerful and well-organized Islamist opposition movement[7] in Saudi Arabia.[8]

Whether *Sahwasts*, radical-right Islamists, rejectionists, liberals or Shiites – all opposition groups expressed similar demands. These were reflected in two important documents submitted to the King by Islamists in the early 1990s. The first, in March 1991, was a Letter of Demand (*Risalat Matalib*) signed by more than 400 religious intellectuals, mostly *sahwasts* but also including a number of official clerics and other Islamist groups. The second, in July 1992, was a Memorandum of Advice (*Muzakharat al Nasiha*), signed by 107 clerics and intellectuals. Islamists articulated their grievances in two forms: ideological and material. In the former the Islamists criticized the official Wahhabi establishment and called for a return to the true path of Islam through the 'strengthen[ing] of religious establishments over state and society'. In the latter, the Islamists called for political participation, an end to corruption, the introduction of justice and equity, and the end of the country's political alliance with the United States (ICG 2004b: 5).

Again, these demands were similar to those made by the Ikhwan in 1929 and by al-Utaibi's 1979 movement. The offer of *Nasiha* to the King fitted well with the religious and 'legitimate cultural repertoire' of the country and was 'compatible with the national organisational form of criticism and the status quo dogma in Saudi Arabia'. Islamists, nevertheless, ignored 'the norm for privacy in political discussion' by circulating their demands in schools and universities before reaching the King[9] (all quotations from Okruhlik 2004: 261, 262). This earned them the wrath of the official establishment, leading to their condemnation by the official religious leadership and when the Islamists decided to establish a Committee for the Defence of Legitimate Rights without official permission in 1993, a state crackdown followed. By the mid-1990s, most radical preachers and leaders had been arrested, exiled or even in some cases executed, particularly those who were involved in bombing attacks in 1995 and 1996.

Interestingly, this led to an important deradicalization process. After their release in the late 1990s, a large number of radical preachers and clerics 'openly discussed and criticised their old ideas, proposing more liberal interpretations of sacred texts in a process of *muraja'a* (revision). Despite significant differences, they formed the core of a "new Islamist" outlook' (ICG 2004b: 7). Their deradicalization process also provided a strong foundation upon which the Saudi State built its post-2003 counter-radicalization and deradicalization programme policies and programmes. These programmes, and the reasons for the *muraja'a* which took place in the second half of the 1990s, are the subject of the next section.

Muraja'a, prevention and deradicalization: 1995–2010

In many ways, 1995 was a turning point in the history of Saudi Arabia. On the one hand, it marked the pinnacle of radicalization and anti-Americanism in the country, witnessed most spectacularly by a car bomb which exploded in November at a National Guard facility, killing five Americans and two Indians, and injuring more than 60 bystanders. This attack was followed by another the following year (1996) on an American barracks in Khobar which killed 19 Americans and injured more than 400 others (ICG 2004b: 6). At the same time, in 1995, Saudi Arabia experienced a transfer of power. The then Crown Prince Abdullah became the *de facto* leader of the country after a heart attack incapacitated the late King Fahad. Known for his nationalist tendencies and religious credentials, Abdullah was seen by the majority of Saudis, including Islamists and reformists alike, as a far more credible and legitimate figure than his predecessor.

The shrewd Abdullah understood the cause, psychology and narrative of Islamists, and took a special interest in countering the rising tide of radicalization in the country. His first move was to take measures that reined in the pretentious behaviour of members of the Royal family. For example, he placed limits on the extent to which members of the Royal family could enjoy free access to utilities, telephone services, travel and airline tickets, and on their involvement in businesses, particularly in oil-related businesses (Okruhlik 2004: 259–67).

Secondly, Abdullah gradually distanced himself from the United States, another key demand of the Islamists, openly criticizing American policy in the region, especially towards Israel. He even delivered 'an extraordinary warning to Washington', following a perceived bias towards Israel, which the Saudi leadership held responsible for the escalation of hostilities in the region, 'threatening a reconsideration of bilateral relations' (ICG 2004a: 27). According to the *Washington Post* (10 February 2002), Abdullah warned Washington: 'from now on we will protect our national interests, regardless of where America's interests in the region lie'. In a country with a high level of anti-American sentiment, establishing distance from the United States can be an important element in a wider package of counter-radicalization policies.

The kingdom had also launched significant steps towards reform in the early 1990s and these gained momentum after 1995. In 1992, for example, the *Majlis al-Shura* (Consultative Council) was established to shore up popular support and to promote more participation in the politics of the country. The *Majlis* initially had 60 members, but this later increased to 90 and then to 120, all coming from outside the Royal family and all being highly respected and credible clerics and intellectuals.[10] Provincial councils were also created in the mid-1990s to provide advice to the leadership on the daily affairs of the state.

These developments were accompanied by another important reconciliatory step in the late 1990s when, having consolidated his internal position, Abdullah released a large number of radical prisoners as part of his general liberalization reform drive. As mentioned earlier, although they remained critical of the regime, a large number of these preachers, clerics and intellectuals had reviewed and moderated their opinions while in prison or did so upon their release. This seems to have been the result of a combination of factors not unique to Saudi Arabia, including repression, selective incentives, interaction with others and charismatic leadership.[11]

In the 1990s,[12] the influence of radical preachers and clerics was undermined 'by repression, exiles and internal wrangling' (ICG 2004b: 6), 'Islamists … were jailed, exiled, and tortured' (Okruhlik 2004: 264). Executions were also the fate of Al-Utaibi and key members of his movement, as well as perpetrators of the 1995 and 1996 terrorist attacks. The state proved itself strong, capable of taking drastic action to defend itself and society whenever faced with challenges, regardless of the price.

When in prison, liberals, Islamists, Shiites and other political inmates mixed, interacted and socialized with one another. In addition, the Saudi authorities encouraged respected religious figures to visit radicals incarcerated in different parts of the country to engage them in dialogue, encourage repentance and promote what the state saw as the true Islamic principles of tolerance. In doing so, the Saudi authorities drew on the social capital or tribal and familial networks of each region. Rather than sending clerics from the capital Riyadh with few regional links, 'The ministry [of the Interior] selected ten clerics from each province to visit prisons and interact with prisoners' in their own areas (Boucek 2008b: 6). After 2003, the Saudi authorities elicited the help of well-known Islamist movements (like Hamas) and individuals to condemn violence against fellow Muslims and other innocent citizens as un-Islamic. For example, the Saudi authorities invited Muntasir al-Zayyat, the chief lawyer of the Egyptian Muslim Brotherhood, to 'open channels of dialogue with the extremists' (www.arabicnews.com, 20 May 2004). Hamas, at Saudi request, also condemned terrorist attacks that took place in the Kingdom after 2003. As elsewhere, such as in Egypt (see Ashour 2009), such interactions, both internal and external, had a large moderating effect on incarcerated Saudi groups and individuals.

In addition to promoting repentance, regional clerics played another key function: they assured families that the detainees were in good health and allayed their fears regarding any possible abuse or torture. In tribal societies like Saudi Arabia, loyalty to one's family and tribe remains paramount. News of torture, real or perceived, can spread very quickly through patrimonial 'component units', including clan, tribe and even through regions with consequent radical reaction, such as terrorist attacks against the state and its perceived allies (Waterbury, 1970: 62). The clerics were able to reassure the families of incarcerated individuals that their sons were being treated satisfactorily and humanely. By encouraging regional clerics to visit prisons, the state drew on one of the country's rich cultural traditions. As Boucek (2008b: 7) noted:

> Asking a religious figure to intercede after the arrest of a loved one and to make inquiries after his welfare is not an uncommon practice. In rural Saudi Arabia if a son or nephew is arrested, it is acceptable to ask the village imam to visit the detainee and ask how he got into this situation. More generally, asking a cleric to speak to misguided youth transcends religions and culture.

Not surprisingly, improving the treatment of prisoners has been a key component of the reforms introduced by King Abdullah. Other incentives included the offer of amnesty[13] to repentant militants, assistance to families whose breadwinners were in prison, as well as for released prisoners to help their rehabilitation and reintegration into society and family. Here too, the state drew heavily on the rich traditions and culture of the country, namely, philanthropy. Boucek (2008a, 2008b: 6–7) has described a prisoner reintegration and rehabilitation network comprising a number of governmental, semi-governmental and private/voluntary specialized organizations and committees functioning according to Islamic jurisdiction.[14] These programmes provide various services ranging from one that facilitates marriage for both single men and women convicted of immorality offences; the delivery to released prisoners of social services, including the provision of food, clothes and even toys for Ramadan; granting loans that allow released prisoners to start a new business; to programmes that support women who have children and whose husbands are serving time in prison.

Charismatic leadership also played a role both within and outside prisons in moderating the views of radical groups and their followers. It was charismatic *sawha* leaders, such as Al-Hawali, Ayidh Al-Qarni and Al-Awda, among others, who mediated both between the state and society and between the state and Islamists, and played a key role in deradicalizing a large number of their followers inside and outside detention centres:

> Former *sahwa* leaders were determined to mediate between regime and radical Islamists … most former *sahwa* leaders tempered their views after release from prison in the late 1990s. Some even closed ranks with the regime; Ayidh al-Qarni, for example, took an official role, getting three extremist preachers (Nasir al-Fahd, Ali al-Khudayr and Ahmad al- Khalidi) to recant on national television their *fatwa* urging Saudis not to help the authorities seize wanted militants and to reverse their accusations of government apostasy. Others, such as al-Awda, while keeping a distance from the regime. both refused to call for jihad [during the 2003 war in Iraq] and urged Saudi youth to avoid any action that could disturb domestic peace. A third *sahwa* trend, personified by al-Hawali, has been more critical of the regime, albeit within bounds … and alternating understanding for the motivations of *jihadists* with condemnation of their acts …
>
> *(ICG 2004b: 7, 10)*

Charismatic leaders also emerged among the Shiite community to moderate their followers, a process which was also facilitated by the state. Shiites are known for their belief in the *wilayat al-Faqih* doctrine and are reluctant to follow Sunni clerics. Only charismatic Shiite clerics, like Al-Saffar, can moderate the views of their followers:[15]

> … many [Shiites] moderated their views by the late 1980s, distancing themselves from Khomeinism, and embracing principles of political pluralism and democracy … By most accounts, community leaders such as al-Saffar have persuaded the vast majority of the Shiite movement of the wisdom of this conciliatory approach. More radical factions have in effect been silenced.
>
> *(ICG 2004b: 4, 12)*

In order to enable charismatic leaders to perform their *wasta* (mediation) role (another important tool derived from the country's cultural repertoire), the Saudi authorities relaxed press censorship and provided the media with more freedom. In all societies, the media plays an important mediating role between the state and civil society by providing and facilitating access to information which 'ensures that citizens make responsible, informed choices rather than acting out of ignorance or misinformation' (USAID 1999: 3). The media has a powerful influence and can provide important advice from which sensible decisions can be made.

Saudi Arabia is no exception. There, the media has been used as an instrument to convey a message of tolerance and to promote reforms initiated by King Abdullah. Newspapers, for example, have opened their columns to unparalleled and extraordinary criticism of the status quo. This has included criticism of the quality of the kingdom's education and health services; its failure to provide solutions to poverty, rising unemployment, crime and drugs; and even the failure of the official Wahhabi establishment to promote a more tolerant message of Islam, thus holding it responsible for the wave of violent extremism that hit the country before and after 2003.

The internet has also been used in a similar fashion.[16] Religious figures and clerics were encouraged to have their own websites and e-mail addresses in order to answer questions from the public and to refute the radical ideology of the militants. The Ministry of Interior, which spearheads counter-radicalization and deradicalization efforts in the country, initiated a special website whose key function is to monitor and follow up what is being written in the virtual world by militants and prepare responses capable of refuting their arguments (www.murajaat.com). In 2004, a number of religious scholars were also encouraged to set up a web page to fight terrorism on ideological grounds. Named 'Sakeenah', or inner peace, the initiative offers open debates and answers questions. A similar website was established in October 2007 by Scientific Research and Religious Edicts (*Dar Al-Ift'a*), a Riyadh-based organization comprising prominent Islamic scholars that issues fatwas. 'The site (www.alifta.com) provides access to the fatwas issued by *Dar Al-Ift'a*, which is affiliated to the Council of Senior Islamic Scholars of Saudi Arabia headed by the Grand Mufti Sheikh Abdul Aziz Al-Sheikh' (Stracke 2007).

Other media outlets, such as television, newspapers and public campaigns, have also been used to defeat the militants and their violent narrative. The authorities, for example, regularly display repenting militants on television and frequently repudiate militant ideology on national TV channels. Hundreds of ulama have been mobilized by the state 'to preach against the militants and explain both in mosques and on television that their acts are breaches of Islam' (ICG 2004a: 2). According to Dr Abdulrahman al-Hadlaq of the Interior Ministry, in 2009–10 the Saudi authorities fired more than 1,300 radical preachers who were preaching violent ideology at schools and colleges (Personal interview, New York June 2010).

The media has also been used to highlight the suffering of victims of terrorism, particularly after Al-Qaeda in the Arabian Peninsula (AQAP) was established in 2003 and launched a string of attacks against the Saudi state. Explicit pictures of wounded, bloodstained and even murdered people were shown on TV. Newspaper articles focused attention on victims and their bereaved families.[17] The evil of terrorists, the dangerous consequences of their actions and their un-Islamic narrative were highlighted in signs and billboards put up by the authorities in public places.[18] The aim of such tactics was to elicit public support and cooperation against the militants by depicting terrorists as outsiders, who violated Islamic teachings and principles, and pursued their own personal agendas. The ICG (2004a: 2) believes that these tactics 'have had a powerful impact on public opinion'.

Finally, the Saudi authorities have organized, both inside and outside the Kingdom, tens of conferences a year to counter radical ideology and discredit the radical ideologues who have attempted to hijack the discussion of Saudi grievances, real or perceived, by relying 'on the power of ideas and cultural resources' (Okruhlik 2004: 252). In these conferences, Saudi authorities work closely with key religious figures from inside and outside the Kingdom to undermine the militant's narrative, expose their limited understanding of religion and highlight their deviant behaviour and practices. Most importantly, they aim to convey an important message: only credible and knowledgeable scholars can issue fatwas to justify jihad and this also requires permission from the head of the state himself.[19] This echoes the 1926 fatwa issued by Wahhabi clerics that confined the right to declare jihad to Ibn Saud, then the Head of State, and enabled him to defeat the Ikhwan in 1930.[20]

A case in point was a conference in Turkey in October 2010 attended by many key Islamic scholars from all over the world. The conference's final declaration stated that 'no Muslim individual or Muslim group has the right to declare war or join jihad on their own … to excommunicate other Muslims … or to divide the Muslims (or world) into *dar al kufur and dar al-Iman*' (the house of infidels and the house of religion) (Al-Arabiya 2010). This fatwa is aimed chiefly at undermining al-Qaeda's key source, Ibn Taymiyya, the fourteenth century Syrian theologian who is frequently cited in al-Qaeda's own pronouncements to justify their actions.

Prison deradicalization: the post-2003 Policies

While Saudi Arabia has been developing counter-radicalization and deradicalization policies since the early 1990s, since the turn of the century two factors have begun to pull reforms in opposite directions. These contrary forces led initially to the reforms gaining momentum, but then brought them to a halt before causing a shift in focus towards the prison environment.

Initially pressure for reform from Islamists in general, and *Shawists* in particular, continued beyond the start of the new millennium. Although they revised and moderated their views and tactics, *Shawists* remained generally autonomous and critical of the regime. They expressed their dissatisfaction through no fewer than six new petitions submitted to Crown Prince Abdullah, five in 2003 (including one from the Shiite community) and one in 2004. Some of these petitions (such as one in February 2004) carried the signatures of more than 900 reformers from a variety of backgrounds, but with the *Shawists* spearheading the campaign. The new petitions were generally the same, calling for religious and social reform, greater freedom of expression, more opportunity for participation in government, stronger institutions of state and the separation of legislative and executive powers. In order to galvanize popular support and pre-empt the authorities describing their demands as un-Islamic, all petitions were expressed in religious and Islamic terms (ICG 2004a and 2004b).

The 2003–4 petition campaigns brought further concessions. For example, following the first petition in January 2003, Abdullah met in June with its signatories and sponsored three National Dialogues (in June and December 2003, and June 2004) to discuss key issues, including education and political reform, religious differences and, more importantly, the causes of terrorism. In October 2003, the authorities announced that elections for half of all local council seats would take place within 12 months and that partial elections for the *Majlis al-Shura* would take place within three years. In November 2003 a royal decree empowered the *majlis* to act as a legislative as opposed to a purely advisory body by granting authority to its individual members to propose new legislation. Previously the sponsor of a new law had to receive support from at least nine colleagues before he could put forward a draft for consideration (ICG 2004a: 18–20 and 2004b; Boucek 2008a and 2008b).

A further significant reform that emerged from the National Dialogues concerned education. Religious material was dropped from the curriculum in favour of a higher proportion of professional and technical training, thus providing a better balance between religious and non-religious subjects. Textbooks were purged of lessons that tended to provoke hostility, particularly towards non-Muslims and especially towards Christians and Jews 'in order to guarantee a spirit of tolerance and moderation and the development of cognitive capacities' (ICG 2004a: 25 and 2004b: 10).

The Shiite community also attained modest but significant concessions. In March 2004, for example, the authorities granted them the right to celebrate *Ashura* (Reuters 3 March 2011). Also, more economic and financial resources were diverted to the Shiite region. Modest as they were, these developments strengthened the hands of moderate Shiite leaders, such as al-Saffar and allowed them to win over more sceptical members of their community, whilst at the same time undermining the radical extremists.

However, while the majority of Islamists moderated their views during the 1990s, a small group became more radicalized and joined Jihadists, particularly Al-Qaeda after Bin Laden returned to Afghanistan in the mid-1990s. Not only were these radicals responsible for the 1995 and 1996 terrorist bombings in Saudi Arabia, they also established in around 2003, Al Qaeda, in the Arabian Peninsula (AQAP) and launched a string of attacks against the authorities between 2003 and 2006.

These terrorist attacks not only undermined some of the earlier hard-won reforms (particularly with regard to the election of local councils and *majlis* members), but they also forced the state to initiate a large security operation based on either killing or capturing the militants. This anti-terrorist campaign led to a large number of detainees, which the Kingdom was ill prepared to deal with:

> The Kingdom was not really prepared for this situation. The number of prisoners in the 1980s and 1990s was relatively small and they used to spend a short

> period of time in jail. When this problem [violence in 2003] broke out the Ministry of Interior invited bids from certain companies and five big prisons were built in different parts of the country, including Jeddah, Riyadh, and Damam. These purpose-built prisons were equipped with state of the art technology and allowed the complete isolation of jihadists from other prisoners.
>
> *(Personal interview with Dr Abdlrahman Al.Hadlaq, Riyadh August 2009)*

Probably one of the most important outcomes of the violent campaign which started in 2003 was the establishment by the Ministry of the Interior in early 2004 of a coherent, centrally managed and well-funded deradicalization programme (known as the 'Advice and Counselling Program'), for which the Kingdom has now become particularly well known (Boucek 2008a: 60). What is interesting about the 2004 deradicalization programme is that it is based on an important Islamic historical precedent:

> We started with the *Munasaha* (advice) program back in 2004. The idea came from Ali Bin Abu Talib (the fourth Caliph) who sent Ibn Abbas to the radicals (*alkhawarji*). Ibn Abbas had many advantages: he was an intellectual, he was one of them and a well-respected member of their society, and he was the messenger of the Caliph. He managed to convince thousands to disengage from extremism and return to the true Islamic path. This is where our idea for the programme first came from.
>
> *(Personal interview with Sheikh Ahmed Jelan, Riyadh August 2009)*

Indeed, one of the most notable features of the Saudi deradicalization programme is the participation of distinguished scholars, scientists and clerics. They share similar advantages to Ibn Abbas: they originate from the same community that produced the militants: they are well respected because they have remained autonomous and critical of the regime and they became the messengers of the King because they understood the dangers of terrorism and its implications for the Islamic *umma*, and were determined to mediate between the state and society, including militants. They are proud of their job, committed to it because they believe it is their religious duty to protect society and they do not see themselves, nor are they seen by others, as working for the state,[21] a fact which they repeatedly stress to their pupils in the deradicalization programme. These same characteristics led scholars to look at detainees (called beneficiaries after 2004) in a sympathetic and paternalistic way, and as 'misled' requiring *nasiha* (advice) and help,[22] rather than as criminals needing punishment: 'Those boys are our misled sons, they need help. By helping them we provide a key to their lives'. The key is dialogue. 'Our aim is to change their culture of death for a culture of life' (Personal interview with a key scholar at the Prince Nayef Care Centre, Riyadh August 2009).

The key components of the deradicalization programme

The deradicalization programme consists of three main parts: the *Munasah* (advice) programme, the Care (rehabilitation) programme and the aftercare (reintegration) programme. Each part of the programme is 'contingent on the power of ideas and cultural resources' in order to counter the extremist narrative (Okruhlik 2004: 252).

The *munasah* programme is, in many ways, a development of the advice (*nasiha*) approach initiated by the Islamists in the early 1990s. While *nasiha* may imply less of a choice (for example, I advise you to do this or that), in *al-munasah* 'we do not force them to make a decision, but we help them to do so by offering them several options and let them choose from among them' (Personal interview with Sheikh Ahmed Jelani, Riyadh August 2009).

Dialogue and debate based on pragmatism and interaction with the beneficiaries are the key pillars of the Saudi deradicalization programme in general and the *al-Munasah* programme in particular. This approach is derived from the Qu'ran itself, which advises rulers to consult and debate with their people. According to the Ministry of the Interior, the aim of the counselling and the *al-Munasah* programme is:

> To deal with the wrong convictions of the detained person in order to change and substitute them with correct convictions that agree with the middle way of Islam and its tolerance. This is realized by using the method of dialogue, wisdom and gentle preaching by competent people, specialized in religious, psychological and social sciences, with a follow up by security experts …
>
> *(Ministry of the Interior 2009: 2)*

The *al-Munasah* programme is prison-based, taking place inside all security prisons affiliated with the General Directorate of Investigations[23] (five in total) and builds upon the approach that was implemented in the 1990s. Three committees undertake the process of *al-Munasah* and educate the detainees through two types of counselling or advice:[24] individual meetings and group educational courses. The individual meetings are short-term programmes that usually last for two weeks, but if need be can be extended for much longer. Here, a team made up of three professionals (a psychologist, a religious figure or cleric and a security individual) meet with each beneficiary on an individual basis. Individual dialogue is permitted only in very rare circumstances at this stage and this type of joint meeting is believed to be more beneficial as it leads to greater dynamism, provides more perspective and avoids boredom. Beneficiaries can attend up to six sessions (sometimes more) and each session lasts for between 90 minutes and three hours.

The second type, group educational courses, is more common. These can last up to six weeks, sometimes even longer, during which each beneficiary is subject to a minimum of ten sessions, sometimes many more. This programme takes the form of group sessions involving between six and ten beneficiaries.

The *al-Munasah* programme is voluntary, meaning that all security detainees can choose to attend, but nobody is forced to take part. Although a few may initially refuse to attend, they generally change their minds when they see the majority of their colleagues participating. Some repent very quickly, even after one session, others may require the completion of the entire *al-Munasah* programme before changing their views and some never repent at all.

During the short, individual two-week programme, beneficiaries are listened to and encouraged to speak about the extremist narrative and the reasons that they have ended up in prison. The scholars and scientists then debate with them, citing Qu'ranic verses and stories from the life of the prophet to correct their misguided ideas and convince them to repent. The six-week course is more structured in that debates and dialogues take place in the form of lectures and around certain subjects. These include: legal, religious and social duties and the responsibilities of the beneficiaries; *Huqooq welayat al amer,* conditions of jihad in Islam, treatment of non-Muslims in Muslim societies, the issue of heresy or *takfir,* the authority to issue fatwas and the rights of the ulama.

While in prison, detainees have access to books, fatwas, educational religious pamphlets and documentaries, television programmes and videos that support the objectives of the programme, and which detainees may view in their cells. These are equipped with VCRs, TVs and even intercoms in case beneficiaries need to debate or ask scholars any questions.

All security detainees qualify for the *al-Munasah* programme, regardless of their sentences or felonies. Until 2009, 4,300 detainees had passed through the *al-Munasah* programme, but only a small number had qualified for the second stage, the care or rehabilitation stage.

The care programme

The care phase of the programme lasts for six months and starts on completion of the beneficiary's sentence. It takes place outside the prison in a purpose-built halfway house (Muhammad Bin Nayef Care Centre) just outside Riyadh, which was built in late 2006. The programme consists of several activities, some of which are non-curricular while others are more structured and take place (in the form of lectures) in classrooms equipped with state-of-the-art technology. The programme is characterized by serious dialogue and debate developed through flexible methods of presentation.

Structured classroom activities consist of six main programmes.[25] First the religious programme, which attempts to correct deviant religious concepts embraced by the beneficiaries and promote repentance, the middle way, tolerance and moderation through the discussion of several topics. These are similar to those discussed in the *al-Munasah* programme but are examined in more depth and with a larger number of scholars participating. The religious programme reinforces the goals and objectives of the *al-Munasah* programme.

What scholars try to achieve is not to negate jihad or to even attempt to tell their pupils that jihad is un-Islamic, for jihad is rooted and enshrined in the Qu'ran itself and is therefore sacrosanct. What the scholars do is to focus on the conditions and circumstances that justify jihad in Islam, including first and foremost the need for permission from the ruler as the person with the sole right to declare jihad. Otherwise, beneficiaries are advised that individual jihad will bring calamity to the Islamic nation as evidenced by the occupation of Iraq and Afghanistan by foreign forces.

Second is the psychological programme. This involves not only a constant assessment of the psychological condition of the beneficiaries, but also their training in positive thinking, handling psychological pressure, discerning signs of psychological abnormality, building and boosting self-confidence and overcoming anxiety. The main premise of the psychological programme is that:

> Nobody is born a terrorist. Terrorism is a process. Our programme works according to this principle. We have not noticed any major psychological disorders among the beneficiaries. They may suffer from stress, even from depression or maladjustment but there has not even been one case of major psychological disorder. We try therefore to help them control their emotions by teaching them self-management.
>
> *(Personal interviews with staff at the Care Centre, Riyadh August 2009)*

Third is the social programme. Boucek (2008a: 60) rightly argues 'one of the keys to the [Saudi] programme's success is the extensive social support given to the detainee and his family'. The chief aim of the social programme is to develop the social skills of beneficiaries, enabling them to live in harmony with society and cope with the pressures of life after their release, especially significant for individuals who have spent a long time behind bars. The programme involves a series of social and educational lectures which discuss such topics as social behaviour, social problems and how to deal with them, social stigmatization and ways of coping with it, modernization and social development, as well as the roles and responsibilities of the family in society (Ministry of the Interior 2009: 5).

The social programme also studies the social and economic conditions of each beneficiary and his family. The authorities look after the families of prisoners while they are incarcerated (from health, to education, groceries, utilities and stipends). 'If we don't do this al-Qaeda will. Al-Qaeda usually sends the families of killed or incarcerated individuals an envelope full of money with the message: from your brothers the mujahedeen' (Personal interview with Dr Abdulrahman Al-Hadlaq, Riyadh August 2009). By easing the pain and hardship of the families of incarcerated breadwinners, the state hopes to promote a sense of gratitude and avoid turning spouses and children into radicals who might seek revenge against the state and its symbols.

While in earlier periods the authorities used regional clerics to communicate with the families of incarcerated individuals, today they encourage family members to witness the conditions of their sons for themselves. The Ministry of the Interior regularly invites families of the beneficiaries to visit their sons and relatives in the Care Centre and covers all costs involved, including transportation, accommodation and food. Families are also invited to participate in the care programme by talking to their sons and help to moderate their views. After the release of the beneficiaries, the families themselves become an important monitoring tool for the authorities, thus reducing the high costs associated with post-release probation:

> The family plays an extremely important role in our programs. We encourage families to visit the centre and we facilitate those visits. The aim is to let them see for themselves how we treat their sons. Some have not seen their sons for years, which means that their sons will have changed. Therefore, we introduce them to the new habits of their sons, their ideas and behaviour, and we teach them how to deal with them. We also provide for the social and economic needs of the family. What we try to do is to win their hearts and minds. Once their trust is won, the families start to provide information on their sons before, during and after they are released, whether positive or negative, especially when they know that such information will not be used against them.
>
> *(Personal interview with Sheikh Ahmed Jelani, Riyadh August 2009)*

While in the Care Centre, beneficiaries qualify for three to five days of 'family leave' once every two months, which they can use to visit their families and friends unescorted. They are also released for a day or two to participate in certain social events, such as marriages, funerals or visiting sick parents in hospital. The aim of all of this is to prepare them gradually for eventual reintegration into society. Key family and tribal figures are also asked to provide guarantees for the return of their sons from leave as a way to re-establish and reinforce these social networks.

> We usually like to have three of the beneficiary's family to guarantee his return. We usually call the father and two brothers. In theory, we know that nobody guarantees anybody and Prince Muhammad has now asked us to move towards self-guarantee instead. […] But involving families creates a moral obligation on behalf of the beneficiary to come back, become a moderate and repent.
>
> *(Interview with Sheik Ahmed Jelani and Dr Abdulrahman al-Hadlaq, Riyadh August 2009)*

When beneficiaries start their home leave from the Care Centre, each is given around 2,000 Saudi Riyals. This allows them to buy gifts so as not to go home empty-handed, which would be humiliating for the beneficiary and to help them to pay their way during their visit. All of this dovetails well with the tribal culture of the country, where gifts and *wasta* (mediation) go hand in hand.

Fourth is the art programme. Here, beneficiaries are encouraged to express their inner feelings and emotions through art:

> We use art to help beneficiaries express their feelings and inner emotions in a non-verbal way. Some beneficiaries are not able to express themselves easily, so we use art to allow them to do that. The beneficiaries are encouraged to make drawings and paintings, which are later discussed individually and in groups. This not only allows us to understand how their minds and psychology work, but also to correct any unsuitable behaviour they might have.[26]
>
> *(Personal interview with staff at the Care Centre, Riyadh August 2009)*

Fifth and sixth are training in culture and history. The latter focuses not simply on history lessons, but also on correcting misunderstandings and refuting al-Qaeda's argument that the Prophet spent most of his life in jihad. Beneficiaries are taught about the life of the Prophet and his emphasis on peace, not jihad. The cultural programme seeks to increase and clarify the understanding and cultural references of beneficiaries. In addition to lectures, the cultural programme includes the presentation of documentaries, films, newspaper articles and other media productions that support the objectives of the Centre. The aim of the cultural programme is to 'broaden the minds of the beneficiaries. to follow the coverage of the mass media [and] enrich cultural aspects' (Ministry of the Interior 2009: 7).

In addition to curricular programmes, the Care programme also includes non-curricular activities, such as teaching beneficiaries how to conduct scientific research; the coordination of open meetings with distinguished members of society and other prominent figures of various ranks and backgrounds; the preparation of various cultural contests to enhance the skills and competitive spirit of beneficiaries, and sporting activities. The last takes place among all members of the programme, including beneficiaries, scholars, scientists and security officials. The objective here is not only to create a cordial atmosphere and personal bonds,

> … but also it gives us the opportunity to study the attitudes of the beneficiaries. Some show aggression in the game, which may suggest that they need more counseling. We get the chance to know who is restless, reckless, or aggressive through the way they play.
>
> *(Interview with Dr Abdulrahman al-Hadlaq, Riyadh August 2009)*

The aftercare programme

The objective of the aftercare programme is 'to prevent recidivism and re-integrate people back into society' (Boucek 2008a: 60). When released, beneficiaries are supported in many ways to facilitate their reintegration into society and their families. For example, beneficiaries receive a stipend of SR 2,000–5,000 per month for a period of almost one year to help them stand on their own feet until the time comes when they can manage without state support. The state also facilitates the process of finding new jobs for beneficiaries, restoring them to their previous jobs and/or encourages them to return to education.

> We focus on education most because we believe that education is the most important facilitator of reintegration and self-management. Therefore, we encourage released beneficiaries to go back to education and we facilitate this process by supporting them financially and by intervening with educational institutions to secure them admission.
>
> *(Interview with Dr Abdulrahman al-Hadlaq, Riyadh August 2009)*

Single beneficiaries are encouraged to marry, a traditionally important step in all Muslim societies. 'Prince Muhammad has undertaken to cover all marriage costs, including accommodation, furniture, a car, and monthly stipend' (Interview with staff at the Care Centre, Riyadh August 2009). The idea here is that once a beneficiary is responsible for a family, an important traditional role in Muslim societies, he will have less time for terrorism.

According to staff at the Care Centre, the entire deradicalization programme costs the Saudi authorities SR1 million a month, or SR12 million a year. Nonetheless, the Interior Ministry plans to build a further five such facilities around the country to accommodate more beneficiaries and make it easier to engage families who live some distance from Riyadh.

While all categories of security prisoners qualify for the *al-Munasah* programme, only three categories qualify for the Care Centre and aftercare programmes: those at the end of their prison sentence, returnees from the American detention centre at Guantanamo Bay (although the programme was not designed for this particular category) and those recommended by the security authorities. The last category includes those who give themselves up voluntarily and reject violent extremism, those who have fought in or attempted to fight in Iraq, Afghanistan or Somalia and those,

> who have not been to prison but they, or their families, call us and tell us that they feel that they need help as they believe they might have been radicalised. But this group is very small. Those with blood on their hands, or who have committed a terrorist act that led to the death of another person do not qualify for the care or aftercare programs.
>
> *(Personal interview with staff at the Care Centre, Riyadh August 2009)*

Measuring the success of PRAC

Gauging the success of a country's effort to counter violent extremism is beset with statistical and empirical difficulties. Not only is there a lack of consensus on how best to gauge success, but obtaining precise data on such programmes is difficult and the available data is insufficient, contradictory and, in most cases, 'do not properly add up' (Boucek 2008b: 25).

Data on incidences of terrorism, for example, might be a good way to judge the success of policies designed to prevent further radicalization in society and these have declined drastically in Saudi Arabia since 2004. As Kurlantzick noted, not only:

> Major terrorist attacks in Saudi Arabia have plummeted compared with 2004. [But] The Saudi plan also appears to have a broader regional impact. General David Petraeus, commander of US forces in Iraq, has said that the Saudi initiative is maybe one reason for the sharp decline in the number of foreign fighters coming into Iraq.
>
> *(Kurlantzick 2008)*

However, a decline in the incidence of terrorism can also result from other factors, such as the intensification of security operations against militants, and the effective monitoring of released prisoners, both of which have accompanied the implementation of 'soft' policies in Saudi Arabia. Focusing on incidents of terrorism may also take too little account of failed attempts by militants to carry out terrorist acts. According to Prince Nayef, the Minister of the Interior whose ministry is spearheading efforts to counter terrorism in the country, Saudi Arabia has discovered and 'aborted more than 230 attempts over the past few years, but failed to prevent ten other operations from taking place' (Middle East Online 2010).

Boucek (2008a and 2008b: 21) has tended to measure the success of Saudi efforts by distinguishing between two types of data: the number of graduates from the counselling programme and the rate of recidivism. According to Boucek, between 2003 and November 2007, 3,000 Saudi prisoners participated in the counselling programme, about 1,400 of whom have been released, of which only 35, or '1 to 2 per cent … have been rearrested'. These figures are challenged by a more recent study by Cline (2009: 3), who argues that 'some 2,000 detainees have participated in the [counseling] program, with around 700 renouncing their jihadist beliefs and being subsequently released', although Cline agrees with Boucek on 'a two per cent recidivism rate'. Lake (2007) on the other hand speaks of 3,200 Saudi prisoners attending parts of the counselling programme, of whom only 1,500 have 'successfully' been reformed and 'released'. In the same year, *The Economist* (2007), stated that out of '3,000 terrorist suspects and sympathisers arrested since 2003, some two-thirds have agreed to re-education programmes. Of those, 700 have renounced former beliefs and been released'. Stracke (2007: 3) described the Saudi deradicalization programme as 'successful', as 'only 3 to 5 per cent of the hard-line prisoners from 2004 to 2007 relapsed into their old ways'. The Ministry of the Interior (2009: 3) itself has stated that 'The number of the detainees who have been advised is about 4,300', with up to a 20 per cent failure rate and 4 per cent recidivism rate (Interviews with staff at the Care Centre, Riyadh August 2009).

To complicate even more, an already complex matter, the Care Centre with its advanced and sophisticated social, psychological, historical, religious, art and other non-curricular programmes, was created in late 2006, almost 36 months after the *al-Munasah* programme was designed in early 2004. Only 221 former prisoners had actually graduated from the Care Centre as of 1 September 2009,[27] of whom 107 were former Guantanamo Bay prisoners and the rest were arrested for carrying out operations inside the Kingdom. In other words, the majority of the released Saudi prisoners were not subject to the same rigorous debates, dialogues, tests and selective incentives as their successors in the programme. Recidivism is likely therefore to have been higher among this group than for later graduates, especially among the ex-Guantanamo detainees who were early beneficiaries of the programme although it was never designed to accommodate them and there was little opportunity to gauge and deal with the trauma they may have suffered during their detention, nor the hard-line views that they held or had developed while in prison.

Recent estimates by Saudi officials suggest a 20 per cent recidivist rate among former Guantanamo Bay detainees and a 10 per cent rate among the rest. Most of the felonies committed by the latter group which led to their arrest did not amount to terrorist acts but rather were simple 'mistakes such as calling a relative or friend who is a terrorist, or being trapped by a terrorist group into renting a car or raising money' (Personal interview with Dr Abdulrahman al-Hadlaq, New York June 2010).

All figures, including those of failures and recidivism rates should be regarded cautiously because Saudi officials are 'somewhat self-selecting' in their approach (Cline 2009: 3). Neither those who have blood on their hands, nor those who refuse to denounce violent ideology or refuse to collaborate, qualify for the Care Centre or even for release. Even those who make it to the Care Centre are subject to regular, rigorous psychological, mental, sociological and physical testing 'and other evaluation methods [that] help reduce the number of opportunistic or insincere revisions' (Boucek 2008a: 61). Those whose repentance is found to be insincere or opportunistic will clearly not be released.

Put differently, the majority of Saudi prisoners who have been released were neither subjected to intensive teaching, debates and dialogues, nor were they 'hard-line jihadi[s]'. Instead they were less deeply indoctrinated and less versed in extremist ideology, being more in the way of sympathizers or aspirant jihadis whose deradicalization has been relatively easy (Seifert 2010: 3). This suggests that the Saudi authorities have been extremely cautious about whom they release and despite the general perception in the West, they have not put 'terrorists back onto the streets'. Not surprisingly, the recidivism rate among released individuals has been low. As Seifert (2010: 7) has argued, ultimately, any exercise will be unconvincing without comparing the behaviour and narrative of those who undergo such programmes with those who don't.

Even if there are recidivists among those who have completed the programme and been released, this is not necessarily a failure for the programme or an argument to change its focus. Prince Mohammed bin Nayef, Deputy Interior Minister and the patron of the programme, has pointed out that the Saudi public has no sympathy for recidivists. Beneficiaries of the care programme receive every benefit from the State and if they choose to go back to extremist violence, it is not for lack of effort on behalf of the authorities. The public reaction is therefore quite different than if prisoners on release had returned to opposition to the state claiming that they had been tortured or otherwise mistreated while in custody. Recidivism, as Prince Mohammed has pointed out, is regarded by the public as an expression of gross ingratitude, and has therefore undermined rather than promoted the radical cause (Private interview, Riyadh November 2010).

Concluding remarks

This chapter has looked at the evolution of violent extremist groups in Saudi Arabia, with special emphasis on the post-1990 environment. Islamists, moderate and radical, have risen in the Kingdom not because of inequities in the distribution of wealth, but rather they have challenged the State on cultural, ethical, theological and traditional grounds. The Saudi authorities have responded in a similar fashion, drawing mainly on the country's cultural, traditional and theological bases to counter radicalization and deradicalize those who have already crossed the line and committed violent extremist acts. This, in addition to the financial resources of the state, has been one of the key factors behind the success of Saudi counter-radicalization and deradicalization efforts.

The problem of gauging success notwithstanding, whatever available benchmarks *are* used to gauge the success of Saudi rehabilitation and preventive policies, their achievements are impressive. Terrorist incidents in the country have plummeted since they crested in 2003 and 2004, although they have not ceased altogether.[28] A success rate of at least 50 per cent in terms of beneficiaries being released after attending the counselling programme and an impressively low recidivism rate (around 5 per cent), have led many countries around the world, both Muslim-majority and Muslim-minority, to study Saudi efforts carefully and consider what aspects they could follow. The United Kingdom, the United States, Singapore, Indonesia, Canada, Malaysia and Bangladesh have all taken a close look. Such attention no doubt reflects a growing consensus on the part of the international community that violent extremism cannot be defeated solely by traditional security approaches. It also reflects the reputational gain the Saudi Kingdom achieved as a result of its deradicalisation and rehabilitation efforts. Saudi is no longer seen as a 'exporting' country terrorism. On the country, it is today seen as a country providing solutions to violent extremist ideology and action. This perhaps is one unintended consequence of deradicalisation programmes, but it is one among many spillovers that have hitherto been neglected in the literature as a result of obsession with analyzing 'recidivism' rate as the main indicator of success/failure.

It would be quite impossible to transplant or emulate the Saudi strategy anywhere else in the world, particularly in Western Muslim-minority states. For a start few countries possess the financial resources of Saudi Arabia or are willing to commit the amounts necessary to maintain such a programme, especially in the current global environment. Second, Saudi Arabia is probably the only country in the world that can call on hundreds, if not thousands, of competent, credible, trusted and largely independent scholars, clerics and scientists to help with such a programme – and it is worth noting here that all the professional staff who work at the Care Centre do so on a voluntary basis. While this rich resource results from several factors, including history, state investment in education, regional and national politics and coincidence, the presence of competent, credible and autonomous scholars and clerics able to deliver the right message through the right messengers is a prerequisite for success of counter-radicalization and deradicalization programmes.

Third, family relationships and networks, particularly in Muslim-minority states, are different and in most cases lack the solidarity and close structure enjoyed by Saudi society. This is why Boucek (2008a and 2008b) warned against establishing deradicalization programmes in countries where the families of incarcerated individuals do not live. Social and family networks have been an integral part of Saudi efforts to deal with radicalism and while similar family and social structures may be found in other Arab Muslim states, it is doubtful that they exist in the West, or to the same extent in other non-Arab Muslim states, such as Indonesia or Malaysia. These countries have been more exposed to globalization and global capitalism, which are known to weaken social and family relationships and replace them with individualistic ones.

Fourth, in many countries the public perception would be that the programme is too kind to extremists. They would resent the financial and other help that the beneficiaries get from the state as a direct consequence of their bad behaviour. They would argue that this was rewarding terrorists rather than punishing them, particularly as many young men with no involvement with extremism suffer from a similar lack of work, wife or money. In Saudi Arabia however, the protective support of the state for people who have gone astray is entirely within the country's tradition.

Finally, Saudi Arabia has developed effective counter-radicalization and deradicalization policies not only without Western financial and technical support, but also by distancing itself from Western leaders. Here lies an important lesson for countries engaged in, or planning to develop, similar policies to counter radicalization and deradicalize violent extremists of Muslim origin. While counter-radicalization and deradicalization cannot be isolated from the external-global environment, success at the end of the day must be achieved internally, derived from and dependent upon the cultural, financial, mores and traditional 'tool kit' of each country.

Notes

1 According to Wilkinson (2000: 53), not only did the Ikhwan forces move on the Hijaz region, but also 'attacked and slaughtered population of Ta'if'.

2 During this period, Ibn Saud began extensive negotiations with Great Britain to delineate the boundaries of his newly reformed state. While doing so, Ibn Saud expressed his rights purely in tribal and Islamic terms, arguing that he ruled by the laws of tribes and Islam (the Shari'a) and that his state's boundaries are based on the extent of submission to his rule, evidenced by the fact that his subjects (tribes) obeyed his call for holy war (Jihad) and paid zakat (Islamic tax), which was the main source of revenue of the new Saudi state. He thus used tribal and Islamic laws to call all tribal frontiers in his dispute with Britain, who did not want to see the new Saudi-Wahhabi state's boundaries extending to Northern Iraq, Yemen and modern-day Qatar, Bahrain and the United Arab Emirates. The Ikhwan's behaviour, including unauthorized cross-territory raids, thus threatened his relations and negotiations with Britain (Wilkinson 2000: 46).

3 The main objective of the sedentarization project was not to relocate tribes from one place to another but rather to let them settle in their own regions and areas of herding and grazing. But even when it was introduced for the second time in the 1950s, the sedentarization project still failed as most nomad tribes refused to take part in it because they felt that the benefits from the project were not equally distributed and that some tribes benefited much more than others. It was not before the spike in oil prices in the early 1970s that the sedentarization project began to take hold. For more details see Fabietti 2000 and Wilkinson 2000.

4 The most threatening of these was the 1969 nationalist-oriented coup organized by a number of military and civilian groups in the country's three main regions: Hijaz, Najd and eastern province. The coup was pre-empted by the authorities, leading to several hundred being arrested.

5 It is important to remember that Saudi Arabia was not alone in encouraging its Islamist youth to go to Afghanistan. Several Muslim states followed suit too, although less overtly and without issuing religious fatwas to justify jihad in Afghanistan. More importantly, the Saudis', and other countries' logistical and financial support to the mujahedeen pales in significance when compared to that provided by the US government. For more details, see Sageman 2008.

6 The ICG statement goes on to give a very good indication on how bilateral relations with the USA, which is seen by most Muslims around the world as a biased actor favouring Israel, has undermined the legitimacy of many Muslim regimes: 'The Saudi cell that beheaded an American engineer on 18 June 2004 pointedly called itself the *Al Falluja* Brigade. Likewise, the targeting of Americans in June 2004 was justified on the grounds that they were developing systems for the Apache helicopters that are used against Muslims by their enemies. 'This act is to heal the hearts of believers in Palestine, Afghanistan, Iraq and the Arabian Peninsula', said a statement by al-Qaeda that accompanied pictures of the severed head of American engineer Paul Johnson. Similar scenarios and statements by militants have also been observed in other countries studied in this book.

7 According to Ayubi (1999: 239), what emerged in SA in this period was not a pan-Arabist or socialist movement calling for democracy, rather, a radical Islamist branch of the Muslim Brotherhood calling for a more merit-based system, possibly a more flexible interpretation of some Islamic precepts (along lines set by Afghani and Abduh). They also believed that salafi-wahhabi Islam was being used in SA to mask deprivation and lack of freedom of expression and therefore set themselves to resist it. Ayubi also sees the group that took over the Grand Mosque in Mecca in 1979 as ultimately descending from the Ikhwan movement of Arabia and as a springboard for the emergence of radical Islamist movement later on in SA.

8 According to Okruhlik (2004: 253), it was the 1990–1 Gulf War that marked the 'emergence of Islamic social movements [particularly] with the stationing of US troops on Saudi Arabian soil during the first Gulf War (1990–1)'. Okruhlik adds however that Islamists used previous grievances existing in Saudi society to launch their campaign in a way consistent with the tradition, history, culture and religion of the country, or what he calls a 'cultural took kit' or reservoir. For the ICG (2004a and 2004b), various strands of Islamist movements were already present in Saudi society prior the Gulf War in 1990. The war, however, the argument continues, radicalized all of them without exception. These movements, according to the ICG, included the following: the reformist *al-Sahwa* al-Islamiyya (Islamic Awakening), referring to a strand of religious activism that gripped Saudi universities in the 1970s and 1980s, and who espoused a blend of the traditional Wahhabi outlook (mainly on social issues) and the more contemporary Muslim Brotherhood approach (especially on political issues); the Rejectionist group who, unlike *sahwa* reformers, focused more on questions of individual faith, morals and ritual practices, and were hostile to the concept of the nation-state, seeking not to modify it but to break with it either by withdrawal or revolt; Jihadists, who originated from Afghanistan and developed an international Jihadi culture while there and became critical of the regime and its Wahhabi establishment; and Shiite Islamists, mainly concentrated in the eastern province and expressing communal grievances. Towards the end of the 1990s, according to the ICG, these groups, none of which was monolithic, were decomposed into two main groups: a heterogeneous-centrist coalition of Islamists that included elements from former *Sahwa*, liberals, rejectionist, Shiites and deradicalized jihadi elements (this centrist coalition is today referred to in Saudi circles as the New Islamists); and the salafi jihadi trend that went further towards radicalization in the second half of the 1990s and seemed bent on destabilizing the country, bringing down the regime and establishing an Islamic caliphate. Okruhlik, on the other hand, does not make such clear distinctions in his analysis for Saudi Islamist movements and talks in general terms of two main groups: liberals and the right-wing radical Islamists. He describes the latter as more powerful, credible and legitimate and the ones responsible for breaking the tradition of public criticism and 'assumed the risk of political activity for Saudis who were hesitant to speak out themselves'. The former group, according to Okruhlik, were 'content to free ride on the back of the Islamist social movement' (2004: 262).

9 It is customary for senior members of the Saudi royal family to hold regular open gatherings during certain social occasions such as Ramadan or Eid 'where citizens can

[privately] air grievances, seek settlement of financial or other disputes or offer congratulations' (Al-Shihri 2009).

10 The idea of a CC first emerged in the early 1950s, but gained currency after the 1979 takeover of the Great Mosque in Mecca. But many feared that the country was not yet ready for such a drastic step leading to the idea being dropped quietly. For more details see Owen (1992: 72).

11 Omar Ashour (2009) has found these four elements to be key factors behind the deradicalization of the Egyptian Islamic Group and al-Jihad Organization in 1997 and 2007, respectively, as well as the Algerian Islamic Salvation Army (AIS) in the 1990s.

12 In SA, it is the Ministry of the Interior which played, and continues to play, the key role in countering radicalization and violent extremism in the country, both inside and outside prisons. For more details on the role of Ministry of the Interior, see Boucek (2008a and 2008b).

13 Amnesties continue to be an important element of Saudi deradicalizing policy up to today. For example, a speech delivered on behalf of the King in 2004, Crown Prince Abdullah announced: 'We offer a chance for whoever belongs to the misguided group and is still at large following involvement in terrorism operations to repent, plead guilty and voluntarily surrender within one month from the date of this address. Whoever does will be immune from prosecution and will be treated according to the Sharia law in relation to violated rights of third parties'. Saudi Press Agency, 23 June 2004.

14 These various organizations work hand in hand through joint committees to provide rehabilitation and reintegration services, as well as supporting convicts who are breadwinners. Examples of these organizations and committees include the following: the Committee for Supporting Prisoners and their Families; the National Committee for the Protection of Prisoners; the National Committee for the Care of Prisoners, Released Prisoners, and their Families; and the Family Reconciliation Committee, Best Mother Award and Centennial Fund grant loans. For more details see Boucek (2004b: 6, 7).

15 This approach stands in stark contradiction to Yemen, where official attempt to deradicalize the Shiite Huwthi community by using Sunni clerics failed miserably. For more details see the chapter on Yemen.

16 As IISS (2008: 2) noted, the Saudi authorities, or 'The Mabahith has devoted substantial resources to monitoring jihadist websites and has developed techniques, both overt and covert, for countering extremist ideologies'.

17 ICG (2004a: 2) has provided a couple of such sample headlines in newspapers: 'Lebanese Yassir Kanan: "I started helping the wounded but I became confused and started weeping when I saw my own daughter among the victims"' (in *Al-Sharq al-Awsat*, 23 April 2004); 'The mother of Wajdan, the victim of the al-Washm explosion in Riyadh: No one can imagine the amount of pain that Rami's family is going through right now' (in *Al-Sharq al-Awsat*, 1 June 2004.).

18 Boucek (2008b: 10) also provides few examples of these slogans used in public signs and billboards, some of which attempt to refute the militant narrative by stating that 'Our religion rejects terrorism' or 'We all say no to terrorism'. Others aim at depicting wreckage and carnage by asking 'Are these the actions of the sons of our nation'? Other slogans depict cooperation between security and public, thus showing images of security and emergency officers helping public, shootouts with terrorists.

19 At the end of 2007, the Grand Mufti, Sheikh Abdul Aziz bin Mohamed al-Sheikh, issued a fatwa declaring that participation in violent jihad is only permissible if it has the authority of the state (IISS Organization 2008).

20 This led Boucek (2008b: 4) to conclude that: 'These objectives dovetail with many of the traits of Wahhabi Islam practiced in the kingdom, which stresses such attributes as loyalty, recognition of authority, and obedience to leadership'.

21 As a former beneficiary stated: 'The *ma mashayeikh* (clerics) were excellent and very convincing. The teachers were honest and open. It was a dialogue from heart to the heart' (Personal interview, Riyadh August 2009).

22 This is supported by the findings of a study which was carried out by the Ministry of the Interior on detainees and which found that the majority of them actually lack a proper religious education and knowledge. For more details see Boucek (2008a and 2008b).
23 When individuals are first captured, the first step is to investigate them. Only after investigation can they join the programme, and no further investigation takes place after that. Hence, unlike the case situation in other countries studied in this book, such as Malaysia for example, the Saudi deradicalization programme is not an overwhelmingly intelligence-led programme.
24 These committees are: the Religious Committee whose main job is to rectify the deviated concepts and wrong ideas of the detainees about some religious issues using the method of dialogue and discussion; the Social Psychological Committee, whose main job is to test the psychological and mental state of detainees and to positively use those aspects in advice and counselling sessions – this also includes the provision of medical, psychological, cognitive and behavioural treatment to needy detainees; and the Security Committee whose main job is to provide advice and information to other committee members on the status, condition and case of the detainees inside the prison. The Security Committee is also concerned with drawing up a mechanism for releasing those who complete their terms in prison and preparing them to join the second stage, the Care Centre stage. For more information, see Ministry of the Interior (2009: 2–3).
25 For more details about these programmes, see Ministry of the Interior (2009: 4-9).
26 Staff at the Care Centre state that, at the beginning, many beneficiaries start by drawing aggressive and violent things, such as wars, weapons, bloodshed and fighter jets, but later on and as a result of the treatment provided they change and start drawing more peaceful things.
27 As of 1 September 2009, 57 beneficiaries were still present at the Care Centre waiting for their graduation and release, 10 of whom were former prisoners in Guantanamo Bay.
28 On 28 August 2009, the merged group carried out their first operation when a suicide bomber lightly wounded Prince Muhammad bin Nayef, a senior prince largely credited with Saudi Arabia's anti-terrorism campaign, blew himself up just before going into a gathering of well-wishers for the Muslim holy month of Ramadan. For more details see WTOP (2009).

Bibliography

Al-Arabiya (2010) 'La Yajooz Li Jama'a Islamiya an Tu'lin al-Harab Min Telqa'i Nafsaha' ('It is not Permissible for a Muslim Group to Declare war on their Own'), 7 October. Available HTTP: www.alarabiya.net/articles/2010/03/31/104561.html. Last seen on October 25, 2010.

Al-Shihri, A. (2009) 'Saudi Prince Vows to Fight Terrorism After Attack', Associated Press, 28 August. Available HTTP: http://news.yahoo.com/s/ap/20090828/ap_on_re_mi_ea/ml_saudi_assassination_attempt/print.

Ashour, O. (2009) *The De-Radicalisation of Jihadists: Transforming Armed Islamic Movements*, London: Routledge.

Ayubi, N. (1999) *Over-Stating the Arab State: Politics and Society in the Middle East*, London: I.B. Tauris.

Bjørgo, T. and Horgan, J. (2009) *Leaving Terrorism Behind: Individual and Collective Disengagement*, London: Routledge.

Boucek, C. (2008a) 'Counter-terrorism from within, assessing Saudi Arabia's religious rehabilitation and disengagement programme', *RUSI*, 153 (6): 60–5.

——(2008b) 'Saudi Arabia's "soft" counterterrorism strategy: prevention, rehabilitation, and aftercare', *Carnegie Paper Middle East Program*, Number 97, September.

BBC News (2010) '"Outrage" as deal ends BAE probes', 2 June. Available HTTP: http://newsvote.bbc.co.uk/mpapps/pagetools/print/news.bbc.co.uk/1/hi/business/8501689.stm?ad=1

Cline, L. (2009) 'Changing Jihadist Behaviour: The Saudi Model', in *Small Wars Journal*, 10 April.
Crystal, J. (1996) 'Civil society in the Arabian gulf', in A. Norton (ed.) *Civil Society in the Middle East*, Volume two, New York: E.J. Brill, pp. 259–86.
Dahir, M. (1986) 'Al-Mashriq al-'Arabi al mu'asir min al-badawa ila al-dawla al-haditha' ('The Contemporary Arab Levant from Nomadims to the Modern State'), Beirut, Ma'had al-Inma' al-'rabi.
Fabietti, U. (2000) 'State policies and bedouin adaptations in Saudi Arabia, 1900–1980', in M. Mundy and B. Musallam (eds.) *The Transformation of Nomadic Society in the Arab East*, Cambridge: Cambridge University Press, pp 82–9.
Habib, S.T. J. (1978a) *Ibn Sa'ud's Warriors of Islam*, London: Brill-Leiden.
Habib, S.T. J. (1978b) *Ibn Saud's Warriors of Islam: The Ikhwan of Najd and their Role in the Creation of the Saudi Kingdom, 1910- 1930*, London: Leiden.
Helms, C. M. (1981) *The Cohesion of Saudi Arabia*, London: Croom Helm.
ICG (2004a) 'Can Saudi Arabia Reform Itself?' *Middle East Report* No.28, Cairo/Brussels, 14 July.
——(2004b) 'Saudi Arabia Backgrounder: Who Are the Islamists?' *Middle East Report* No. 31, Brussels, 21 September.
——(2007) 'Deradicalisation and Indonesian Prisons', *Asia Report* No. 142, 19 November.
IISS Organization (2008) 'Rehabilitating the Jihadists: Saudi Arabia Tackles the Radical Threat from Within', 14 (5) June, pp.1–2.
Kurlantzick, J. (2008) 'Fighting Terrorism with Terrorism', *Los Angeles Times*, 6 January.
Lake, E. (2007) '1,500 Qaeda Members Freed After Counseling', *The New York Sun*, 27 November. Available HTTP: http://www.nysun.com/foreign/1500-qaeda-members-freed-after-counseling / 67016/.
Luciani, G. (2005) 'Oil and political economy in the international relations of the Middle East', in L. Fawcett (ed.) *International Relations of the Middle East*, Oxford: Oxford University Press.
Mahdavy, H. (1970) 'The patterns and problems of economic development in rentier states: the case of Iran', in M. Cook (ed.) *Studies in Economic History of the Middle East*, Oxford: Oxford University Press.
Middle East Online (2010) 'Al-Sau'diya Ahbatat 230 Amaliya Irhabiya' ('Saudi Arabia Aborted 230 Terrorist Operations'), 27 September.
Ministry of the Interior (2009) *Centre for Muhammad Bin Nayef for Advice, Counseling and Care*, Riyadh: Public Security Press.
Okruhlik, G. (2004) 'Making conversation permissible: Islamism and reform in Saudi Arabia', in Q. Wiktorowics (ed.) *Islamic Activism: A Social Movement Theory Approach*, Bloomington: Indiana University Press, pp. 250–70.
Owen, R. (1992) *State, Power and Politics in the Making of the Middle East*, London: Routledge.
Reuters (2011) 'Pro-reform Saudi activists launch political party', 10 February. Available HTTP: http://af.reuters.com/articlePrint?articleId=AFLDE71912K20110210
Richards, A., and Waterbury, J. (1996) *A Political Economy of the Middle East*, Oxford: Westview.
Ripley, A. (2008) 'Reverse Radicalism', in *The Times*, 13 March.
Sageman, M. (2008) *Leaderless Jihad: Terror Networks in the Twenty-first Century*, Philadelphia: University of Pennsylvania Press.
Seifert, K. (2010) 'Can Jihadis be Rehabilitated?' *Middle East Quarterly*, Spring, pp. 21–30, at: www.meforum.org/2660/can-jihadis-be-rehabilitated.
Shambayati, H. (1994). 'The rentier state, interest groups, and the paradox of autonomy: state and business in Turkey and Iran', in *Comparative Politics*, Vol. 26, No. 3: 307-31.
Sharara, W. (1981) 'Al-Ahl wa al-ghanima' ('Kin and Booty: the Foundation of Politics in the Kingdom of Saudi Arabia'), Beirut, Dar al-Tali'a.
Stracke, N. (2007) *Arab Prisons: A Place for Dialogue and Reform, Perspectives on Terrorism.*, I (4). Available HTTP: http://www.terrorismanalysts.com/pt/index.php?option=com_rokzine&view=article&id=14.

The Economist (2007) *Reforming Jihadists, Preachers to the Converted*, 13 December.
USAID (1999) *The Role of Media in Democracy: A Strategic Approach*, Technical Publication Series, Center for Democracy and Governance Bureau for Global Programs, Washington, DC. Available HTTP: http://www.usaid.gov/our_work/democracy_and_governance/publications/pdfs/pnace630.pdf.
Waterbury, J. (1970) *The Commander of the Faithful: the Moroccan Political Elite*, London: Weidenfeld & Nicolson.
Wiktorowicz, Q. (ed.) (2004) *Islamic Activism: A Social Movement Theory Approach*, Bloomington: Indiana University Press.
Wilkinson, J.C. (2000) 'Nomadic territory as a factor in defining Arabia's boundaries', in M. Mundy and B. Musallam (eds.) *The Transformation of Nomadic Society in the Arab East*, Cambridge: Cambridge University Press, pp 44–62.
WTOP (2009) 'Al-Qaida claims attack that injured Saudi prince', 30 August HTTP: http://www.wtop.com/?nid=500&sid=1749895.
Youssef, M. (2009) 'Al-Qaida claims attack that injured Saudi prince', Associated Press, 30 August. Available HTTP: http://www.wtop.com/?nid=500&sid=1749895.
Zakaria, F. (2001) 'The politics of rage: why do they hate us?', *Newsweek* (Reprinted on the following website on 22 August 2007). Available HTTP: http://fc.yarmouth.k12.me.us/~david_pearl/wikiresources/whydotheyhateus.pdf.

9

YEMEN'S PASSIVE APPROACH TO COUNTERING TERRORISM

Hamed El-Said

Introduction

Yemen was one of the first Muslim countries to officially develop a process of religious dialogue inside its prisons to convince its incarcerated detainees to repent and abandon violence. Yemen's programme not only 'inspired a number of copycats' in Muslim-majority states, including Saudi Arabia, Indonesia and Malaysia, but it also inspired counter-terrorism efforts in Western, Christian-majority states like the United Kingdom and the United States (Peraino 2009). Western officials and academics flocked to Sana'a to meet Judge Hattar, the highest Yemeni state official associated with the dialogue process, and invited him to their capitals, so that he might explain to them the components, intricacies and applicability of the Yemeni experience to Western environments.

Simultaneously, Yemen's counter-terrorism efforts are often described by Western officials and observers alike as 'passive … often schizophrenic in its pursuit of Islamic militants' (Johnsen 2006). If not already a 'failed' state, the argument continues, then 'Yemen is gradually becoming a failed state and safe haven for Al Qaeda operatives and as such should be considered an active theatre for U.S. counter-terrorism operations' (Sharp 2010: i).

Such operations, mostly military in nature, can, and have augmented Yemen's social, political and economic difficulties. They have also obscured the nature of the problems in Yemen and the root causes of violent extremism in the country. Indeed, Yemen has, for a long time, been largely ignored and 'overlooked' by the international community. It was only the recent attacks on Western targets, including the failed bomb attack against the Northwest flight on 25 December 2009 and the discovery of explosives almost a year later on a cargo plane that thrust Yemen into the spotlight international and heightened its relevance to the (Sharpe 2010: 3).

Internally stable, democratic and prosperous, Yemen is crucial to global security. This necessitates a holistic approach to understand the root causes of violent extremism in Yemen, not only in the prism of the 'war on terror'. It also necessitates a good understanding for the reasons that led to the failure, after 2005, of the Dialogue Committee, which was established by a presidential order in 2002 to convince Yemeni violent extremists to repent, abandon violence and peacefully rejoin their societies and families. This chapter does precisely that. It fills an important gap in the literature by analysing counter-violent extremism policy in a country which is 'not the easiest of countries to write about', namely, Yemen (Whitaker 2009). The chapter argues that Yemen's perceived 'passive' and 'schizophrenic' approach to violent extremism can only be understood by understanding the historical evolution of the country, its internal political, economic and social system, as well as the country's international and regional relations.

This chapter proceeds as follows. The next section provides a historical context to the evolution of the Arab Yemen Republic (AYR), including an account of the historical divisions that led to the birth of North and South Yemen in 1962 and 1968, respectively. Section three then analyses the developments that led to the 1990 unification of North and South Yemen. It further sheds light on the events that led to the 1994 civil war that re-united the two Yemens, albeit at the expense of a democratic process. Section four places the root causes of violent extremism in Yemen within their historical perspective, while sections five and six analyse and assess Yemen's counter-terrorism efforts, including the Dialogue Committee's policies and outcomes. The final section summarizes and concludes.

Historical background: evolution of North and South Yemen

Throughout its history, Yemen has always been subject to external influences, with important implications for its political system, demography and the boundaries of the state. The country also demonstrates the weakest developmental capacity among all of the eight countries studied in this book, with high levels of poverty, illiteracy, unemployment, malnutrition, ethnic conflicts and an unusually high level of tribalism that characterizes both state and society. Since the early 1990s, tribalism has become more intertwined not only with religion, but also with violent militancy.

As shown earlier in this volume and elsewhere (Ayubi 1999), tribalism and religiosity have become intertwined in the Arab world. Yemen is no exception. While state policies, particularly those providing tribes with state largess and positions in return for loyalty and support, as well as the manipulation of religious institutions by the state, have shaped conservative attitudes and re-tribalized states and societies such as Jordan and Saudi Arabia in recent years; religion penetrated Yemeni tribes more than a millennium ago. It did so through one of the most important tribal inventions, namely, *wasta* (mediation or arbitration). This interaction between tribalism and religious authority (Zaydi Shiites in the case of Yemen) has been eloquently expressed by Serjeant (1982), while describing the mediation system developed by Arabian tribes as:

> … concerned with protection, truces, the payment of blood monies, and damages, all of which involved the essential function of an arbiter … No

> potential arbiter is more acceptable than the member of a house upon which Allah has conferred some superior and supernatural quality – for who can quarrel with God's authority.
>
> *(Cited in Watkins 1996: 216)*

It was this tribal system that allowed Imam al-Hadi Yahya, a Hashemite descendent of the Prophet Mohammad, to establish the Imamate rule in Yemen after being dispatched to the Northern regions to settle a tribal dispute in the third Islamic century. Sheikh al-Hadi soon subjugated tribes to his rule and established a power base in Saada. This Zaydi-Imamic[1] rule lasted for more 1,000 years in Yemen, ruling more or less continuously until it was terminated by the 1962 revolution in North Yemen (Watkins 1996: 216; Serjeant 1982).

Trying to impose too much 'Islamic morality' on autonomous and largely non-religious tribes, as well as constantly weakening tribal authority through attempts to replace it by the authority of the Imam, were key factors behind the 1728 revolt by Lahej's Imam governor. This revolt led to the separation of the South from the North and in the process created the original division between North and South Yemen (Watkins 1996: 217). The 1728 revolt, moreover, paved the way almost 100 years later (in 1830) for the British reign over South Yemen, including the port city of Aden and hinterlands, which lasted for nearly 130 years until 1967.

While the British colonial power developed the port city of Aden and turned it into one of the major ports in the world (mainly in order to serve the colonial power's commercial and military links in the Red Sea and Asia), they paid little attention to the hinterland. The British brought the hinterland under their control to act as a buffer zone against the weak Ottoman influence in the North. Outside Aden, South Yemen remained largely tribal and underdeveloped (Ayubi 1999). When, on 14 October 1963, soldiers of the former British colonial authority in Aden shot dead seven Yemeni workers demonstrating against their poor conditions in the Radifan town of al-Habilayn, a nationalist movement, consisting mainly of workers, students, soldiers and women was born. It fought the British presence in the country, and achieved political independence four years later in November 1967 (Day 2008). When the British colonial authorities left Aden in 1968, the National Liberation Front (NLF), a very radical group with a strong Socialist-Marxist orientation took control in South Yemen. The NLF succeeded in creating a Socialist state in 1968, which became the only Arab state that is 'officially non-Muslim' (Richards and Waterbury 1996: 112) and 'the only Marxist state in the Arab world' (ICG 2003: 3). From the beginning, the newly born People's Democratic Republic of Yemen (PDRY) had strong financial and military backing from the former Soviet Union and China.

North Yemen, on the other hand, remained under the Imamate authority until 1962, when a revolution, led mainly by a group of Sunni officers who for a long time had opposed the Shiite-Imamate regime in the country, terminated the Imamate in Yemen. Since then, Yemen has been ruled by a coalition of military officers, tribal leaders and bureaucrats who were 'theoretically in the capitalist camp' but were republicans at heart (Whitaker 2009). The new state in the North became officially known as the Yemen Arab Republic (YAR).

It thus has become customary in the literature on Yemen, particularly before 1990, to discuss developments in the North and South separately. This is mainly a result of the fact that, from the time of rebellion by the Imam's governor of Lahj in the early eighteenth century and until 1990, there was no unified state on the land which today comprises the territory of Yemen. 'The terms North and South persist, however' and have recently gained renewed currency following the emergence of a southern separatist movement in 2007 (ICG 2003: 2; 2009). Due to the significance of the developments that took place in North and South Yemen in the pre-1990 period, on the one hand, and between North and South Yemen on the other, it is important to summarize briefly the dynamics of a regime's consolidation and evolution in this period in both states. It is imperative to avoid the common mistake of simply labelling a regime as 'Marxist', 'Capitalist', 'Socialist' or 'Republican' without looking at the important issue of the dynamics of the regime's evolution, consolidation, as well as the social and economic changes that usually accompany such developments (Richards and Waterbury 1996: 276).

North and South Yemen: between and within independence

South Yemen

As mentioned earlier, the NLF emerged as the main vehicle for resisting the British occupation, mobilizing students, workers, women, soldiers and peasants against colonial authorities. The NLF emerged after the departure of the colonial authorities in 1968 as the locus of decision-making in the country, eclipsing the Presidential Council, the Supreme People's Council and even the government. The NLF's constituency consisted mainly of intellectuals, soldiers and poor peasants who had grown bitter over the minority Shiites-Sayyid-Hashemite domination of the South. As Richards and Waterbury (1996: 293) state: 'Something of a Maoist scenario was enacted: revolutionary intellectuals allied with oppressed peasants surrounded and captured the city'. Both Nasser of Egypt and the Republicans who mounted a successful revolution in North Yemen in 1962 supported the Southern nationalist movement's quest for independence.

The new Marxist regime in the South inherited from the colonial era a largely conservative and stratified tribal society, not much different from the kind of society that emerged in North Yemen when the revolution occurred in 1962. One main difference though relates to the degree of religious homogeneity: the South was/is composed overwhelmingly of Shafi Sunnis, with few Christians, Jews and Hindus.

For the new rulers of the South, tribalism was seen as the main obstacle to economic development, social change and prosperity. A 'detribalization' process was thus launched and became the primary policy of the new Marxist regime, although 'detribalization efforts were not fully and thoroughly successful' (Ayubi 1999: 435). Detribalization policies included: the persecution and pursuit of tribes and individuals that had collaborated with the former colonial authorities, and the termination of all licenses to clubs, associations, societies and organizations that were linked to tribes, including the closure of their branches. Further policy included attempts for a semi-corporatist re-grouping that would mirror the Cuban model of progressive organizations, including the sitting of the People's Defence Committee, the General Union of Yemeni Workers and Peasants Union; and the launch of a popular militia that was able to mobilize more than 100,000 members overnight (Schwedler 2004: 207; Ayubi 1999: 435).

In 1970, the South was, as has been mentioned, renamed the People's Democratic Republic of Yemen and the country moved further to the Left by nationalizing, in the 1970s, most commercial concerns and carrying out a land reform in rural areas that uprooted most collaborators of the former colonial authorities (ICG 2003: 3). South Yemen became not only 'the only Marxist state in the Arab world', but also more Marxist than Leninist Russia.

Although the PDRY produced a stronger state, more liberal and more tolerant of its ethnic minorities (Christians, Jews and Hindus), with higher levels of education and health than the North, it remained poor, underdeveloped and highly dependent on the external assistance from the former Soviet Union. The country's political elite also remained largely divided. It is not surprising, therefore that the 1970s and 1980s were far from being stable, characterized not only by border skirmishes with the North,[2] but also continuous infighting and factional politics between the moderates and radicals in the NLF. During the 1970s and 1980s, the pendulum of power swung back and forth between the moderates and radicals. At first, the moderates were in favour in the mid-1970s under Salim Robaya Ali, then the chairman of the Presidential Council. Then the pendulum swung in favour of the radicals in the late 1970s, particularly in 1978 when Abd al-Fattah Ismail prevailed and changed the name of the NLF to Yemen Socialist Party – YSP. Finally the pendulum swung back to the moderates in 1980, when Ali Nasser Muhammad became the president and Secretary General of the YSP simultaneously. This resulted in the exile of his opponents, mainly to the former Soviet Union, North Yemen and Saudi Arabia. Factional politics reached its peak in 1986 when a bloody civil war broke out and there was fierce fighting in the streets of Aden and elsewhere between the supporters of moderate leaders of the YSP (Ali Nasser) and radicals, led by Ali Salim al-Baidh. The latter emerged victorious and persecuted and exiled his opponents, restoring to power former hard-core Marxist elements of the YSP (Richards and Waterbury 1996: 289).

The Socialist-Marxist policies of the PDRY, however, stifled private initiative and created a wasteful and inefficient public sector. Not only did detribalization have 'limited success', but the Marxist regime of the South also failed to impose Marxist secularism on all society (ICG 2003: 3). Instead, the PDRY's society and state remained stratified along tribal and regional lines, and became encumbered by factionalism and rivalry that further sapped the capacity of the state, bankrupted its institutions and evaporated the political capital of the government. Not only did the elite's rivalry and factionalism lead to the ousting of one president in 1971 and the assassination of a second in 1978, but it also culminated in the 1986 bloody power struggle that brought hard-core Marxists back into power. The abrupt end of developmental aid following the collapse of the former Soviet Union in the late 1980s not only exposed the country's economic inefficiencies and its stifling socialist policies, but also precipitated an economic and political crisis in the country, and necessitated fundamental reforms and action. Unification with the North appeared the only way for survival, regardless of the price that had to be paid (ICG 2003; Ayubi 1999; Richards and Waterbury 1996; Watkins 1996).

North Yemen

Like the South, North Yemen is also overwhelmingly Muslim, although the structure of its society is markedly different and theologically more heterogeneous. While almost all Yemenis in the South are Shafi-Sunnis, Yemenis in the North are divided between a sizeable minority of Zaydi-Shiite tribes from whom the former Imamates were drawn, and the majority of Shafi-Sunnis, urbanite merchants. As mentioned earlier, it was a series of Zaydi dynasties, however, that ruled parts of Yemen both directly and nominally from 1897 until 1962, which chafed the Sunni population of the North (Sharp 2010: 1). In 1962, Sunni officers seized power, terminated the Imamate and established a republican government in Sana'a officially known as YAR.

Although it left no country unaffected, Arab nationalism and socialism that swept through the Arab World in the 1950s and 1960s tore Yemen apart. The country found itself engulfed in a proxy cold war between Arab nationalism and anti-colonialism, on the one hand, and Arab conservatism on the other. While Shiites rejected the newly established republican in the North and looked to Saudi Arabia for support, the republicans in Sana'a reached out to Nasser of Egypt. A civil war lasting for most of the decade ensued, in which the republicans, notwithstanding large Egyptian expediency backing towards them, were incapable of extending their control over the entire North or to subdue tribes in the mountainous terrain of Yemen. Following the 1967 defeat at the hands of Israel, Egyptian troops were pulled out of Yemen, thus paving the way for a peace agreement in 1970, with royalists (and Saudi Arabia) eventually recognizing the YAR. In return, their (Zaydi-Shiites) leaders were given senior positions in the government as a form of reconciliation (Ayubi 1999: 281; ICG 2009).

Not unlike the South, North Yemen also suffered from internal elite rivalry and factionalism. For example, in addition to two border skirmishes with the South in 1972 and 1979, one president was exiled and his two successors were assassinated during the 1970s. Internal divisions, as well as an impoverished and weakened post-civil-war government, were responsible for a coup that in 1974 put the army in power. The army's hold on politics was consolidated further after 1978, when Ali Abdullah Saleh, then a little-known and relatively junior officer, was appointed President (ICG 2003: 3). Ali Saleh, a Zaydi-shiite himself, proved far more resilient than his predecessors. He remains in office today, although not without controversy and major challenges.

From a policy perspective, the North followed a completely different trajectory from that of the South. First, rather than attempting to eradicate tribes, the regime incorporated them from the very beginning. While the Southern, avowedly Marxist regime saw tribal structure as the main obstacle to development and prosperity, the Northern, 'theoretically capitalist' republican regime sought to incorporate tribes instead as a vehicle for balancing society's various influences. In a fashion contrary to the Southern eradicative trend, tribalism was encouraged, particularly in the rural areas, formalized and institutionalized:

> In … Yemen, tribal corps are regarded as a state institution whose position in the political system is virtually stipulated by law. The incorporation of sheikhly leaders took place soon after the revolution in 1962 to counter Saudi incorporation of tribal leaders into the Royal camp. In 1963, it was institutionalised with the establishment of the Higher Council for Tribes Affairs, which included leaders of major tribes and headed by the president of the Republic himself. Sheikhly Councils were also organised within each tribe and every province, and were provided with specific legal jurisdiction and allowed to hold regular proportional elections. Tribal corps were thus adapted to modern conditions and institutionalised as part of the state apparatus.
>
> *(Ayubi 1999: 243)*

Tribal support was not unconditional: it was premised on generous hand-outs from the state. Tribal leaders and influential groups and individuals were offered positions in state institutions, the army, security and economic organizations in return for their loyalty. The state also attempted to penetrate rural areas through the provision of services such as schools, hospitals and infrastructure. The price of these services was covered mainly from development aid and oil money, generated from the 500,000 barrels or so per day that Yemen produced until the late 1980s. The state's control over rural areas, however, remains almost non-existent up to today, and the state's services in rural areas continues to be weak, insufficient and incomprehensive (ICG 2003 and 2009). The state's control is confined to major cities where a new national identity, 'a melting pot', has been encouraged, while tribal identity was allowed to grow in rural areas (Ayubi 1999: 432).

Not surprisingly, tribalism not only remained strong in the North, but also came to inform almost all of the decision-making processes, including state contracts, employment, projects and other state benefits. Similar to the *rentier*-mentality prevalent in oil-rich states, a tribal mentality, or 'tribal ideology' permeated all practices, institutions and activities in Yemen (Ayubi 1999: 243). A state official or a cabinet member would use his position to serve his tribe or region and fill his ministry or institution with people from his own tribe or region. Halliday eloquently described this system:

> The 18th Brumaire of 'Ali Abdullah Saleh has created a Yemeni Bonapartism … Their calculation on government consolidation and a prudent Yemeni nationalism has led many Yemenis to support this hybrid regime … a fusion of tribal factions, military apparatus, and civil recruitment.
>
> *(Halliday 1985: 4-5; also quoted in Ayubi 1999: 432)*

Yemeni Bonapartism is antithetical to the developmental approach that was responsible for transforming countries like South Korea and Taiwan, by the late 1980s, into 'Asian tigers' or Newly Industrializing Countries (NICs). Yemeni 'Bonapartism' led instead to widespread 'corruption', rent-seeking, inefficiencies and waste that further weakened and inhibited the capacity of the state (Schwedler 2004: 219). The unfavourable and debilitating consequences of these factors, however, were temporarily concealed by foreign aid (mainly from Arab oil-rich states), a spike in international oil prices in the 1970s and early 1980s, and most importantly, a traditionally dynamic, vibrant and 'viable civil society' (Carapico 1996: 287).

Remittances from Yemenis working in the Gulf, particularly in Saudi Arabia, were one key factor behind Yemen's vibrant civil society. Unlike oil-income, which is accrued directly to the state, remittances are accrued to the private sector, a large chunk of which is sent via friends and relatives and therefore bypasses state and financial institutions (Chaudhry 1989: 117). Lacking jobs at home and bordering a rich oil state, Yemenis flocked to Saudi Arabia and other Arab oil-rich states for higher paid jobs and better living conditions.[3] Between 1971–83, remittances and financial assistance grew dramatically as a result of the 1.5 million Yemenis working in the Gulf. For example, aid, coming overwhelmingly from the Gulf States, represented 43 per cent of the budget in the early 1980s and covered all current expenditure. Remittances also grew in the same period, reaching an estimated $3.8-4 billion, or 126 per cent of GNP, with 1981 being the peak year (Ayubi 1999: 433). Migration and remittances not only improved food, nutrition and provided for better housing conditions in Yemen, but also benefited the poorer generally and state income via customs duties at the expense of previous agricultural tax (Richards and Waterbury 1996: 386). Migration and remittances, therefore, helped maintain political stability by preventing a higher number of Yemenis from falling into poverty and unemployment. As Carapico (1996: 291) wrote: 'stability was maintained by remittances and a façade of stability under semi-literate military officer [Ali Abdullah Saleh] after 1978'.

Simultaneously, the Yemeni state, lacking institutional and extractive capacity, as well as financial means to create a comprehensive and efficient social safety net or a system of distribution under wide-based prosperity, encouraged civil-society organizations (CSO) to provide social services. As a result, CSO proliferated in almost all fields, including education, health, orphanage, youth, women and philanthropic activities (Clark 2004; Schwedler 2004). While states like Morocco, Egypt and Jordan the state 'socially retired' from the provision of social services to their citizens under the conditions of austerity measures promoted in the 1980s and 1990s by the IMF and World Bank (Harrigan and El-Said 2009a), the state's social retirement in Yemen occurred under normal conditions. It was a natural path followed by a state that was more concerned with 'balancing the various influences present in Yemeni arena' (Al-Saqqaf 1989: 137-8. Also cited in Ayubi 1999: 432).

It has been shown elsewhere (Harrigan and El-Said 2009b), how CSOs can fill an important vacuum left by the state's withdrawal from social welfare provision during a period of austerity. Nevertheless, even under state prosperity, CSOs can only complement the state, not substitute it. No other institution in a country, no matter how large it is, can have the same resources and outreach as the state. The Bonapartist system of Saleh's regime, which used the state's meagre resources to balance various groups within Yemeni society and buy the loyalty of powerful tribes, as well as relying on CSOs to provide social welfare, could not be relied upon to maintain stability. It began to crackdown after 1983, a period which was characterized by a collapse in international oil prices. This not only reduced official financial assistance to Yemen, but it also reduced private remittances received by Yemeni society and its CSOs. The result was the weakening of SCOs' ability to continue to provide social services. The reduction in remittances also indirectly affected state's revenues, as it led to a drop in income from indirect taxes (customs revenues), thus reducing the state's ability to maintain its meagre social welfare services in rural areas (Richards and Waterbury 1996).

The fiscal crisis, precipitated by the decline in both financial assistance and remittances in the early 1980s, led to a large decline in the market value of the riyal, accompanied by a surge in inflationary pressure in the mid-1980s. The state responded by introducing a series of reform measures, including the curtailing of money changers to curb market speculation, the regulation of commercial banks and retail prices, and the state's importation of basic commodities to undermine monopolies and potential hikes in the price of basic commodities. Other reforms introduced included reforming the taxation system and land registry in order to raise revenues of the state. The Zakat Department was also merged with Local Councils in order to extend administration into the countryside through the use of local development cooperatives (Ayubi 1999: 145 and 434).

As Chaudhry (1989: 137–41) noted, however, the above-mentioned 'measures [were] astonishing in their simplicity' and did not go far enough to remedy the Yemeni economy's internal and external imbalances. In 1987 for example, total current revenues represented only 16.1 per cent of GNP. Taxes on international trade, a good proxy for the changes in the flow of remittances (which declined to $303 million in 1987 down from more than $1 billion in 1981), plummeted to $29.4 million in 1987, down from $56.5 million in 1972. The average rate of inflation rose to 11.4 per cent in 1980–7. The total official development assistance declined to $349 in 1987, down from $411 and $412 in 1981 and 1982 respectively (World Bank 1989). As the state struggled to replace aid revenues with local taxes, it relied further on CSOs to fill the widening social welfare gap in the country, which CSOs were unable to completely fulfil due to the decline in their own main source of income: remittances. It is against this economic background and dire financial situation that the 1990 unity agreement between North and South Yemen should be understood.

Unity destroys democracy

As demonstrated in the previous section, both South and North Yemen were fragile, neither politically nor economically viable states: 'Neither of which had a strong history of democratic or electoral policies' (Schwedler 2004: 207). Indeed, the 1970 constitution in North Yemen forbade all political parties. Although the trauma of the

1986 civil war in the South led to self-revisions, including some discussion about opening up the system, the pace and extent of the fiscal and political crises dominated events and pre-empted attempts to introduce wide-ranging reforms. Ali Saleh, however, attempted to compensate for the lack of genuine democracy by relying on civil society. Saleh brought together political and primordial forces in committees formed on a semi-corporatist fashion[4] as well as resorting to what Ayubi (1999: 432) called, 'direct democracy'. This programme relied on political figures meeting with citizens weekly, with President Ali Saleh spending most evenings during the months of Ramadan receiving various categories of society.

After 1989, however, the system began to crackdown in both South and North Yemen. While the economic crisis was precipitated in the South by stifling socialist policies and the collapse of developmental aid from the former Soviet Union, the economic crisis in North Yemen was precipitated by the decline in remittances, financial assistance, corruption and a debilitating patron-client system which had been developed under Saleh's 'Bonapartism' regime. 'But by 1989, tribes and regions', in both South and North Yemen, 'were again becoming restive, standards of living declining, and popular frustrations seemed barely contained' (Carapico 1996: 291).

Under these circumstances, unity between North and South not only seemed to be the only way out, but also 'appeared the only option to survive' regardless of the price and concessions involved in such a project (Richards and Waterbury 1996: 282). Unification, for both Ali Saleh and al-Badi, became a matter of 'regime survival' (Sharp 2010: 3).

In 1990, a unity agreement between Saleh and al-Badi's governments was publically proclaimed. The agreement, which proved popular among the people of both South and North Yemen, had been under negotiations since at least 1970.

Following the proclamation of the unity agreement in 1990, a new constitution stipulating an independent legislature, guaranteeing basic rights including rights of political expression and association, was promulgated (in May 1991). Despite the fact that the South represented only a fifth of the total population, the government was held jointly by the General People's Congress (GPC – President Saleh's party) and Yemen Socialist Party (YSP) of the South. After a one-year postponement, the first parliamentary elections were held in April 1993. Given the history of South and North Yemen, their tenuous and at times violent relationship and the lack of a strong history of democracy or electoral policies, not only did the unification surprise most observers, but also the adoption of democratic forms of governance. Schwedler eloquently captured the main developments in Yemen between unification in 1990 and the civil war that ensued in 1994:

> In 1989, the North's President Saleh and the South's President Ali Salim al-Badi negotiated the unification of the two Yemen in virtual secrecy … the idea of unification proved popular in both countries, and formal negotiations led to an agreement that the new state would have a representative democratic government … Liberalisation brought significant shift in political opportunity structures, creating new path for formal mobilization and political contestation.

> As Carapico (1998: 136) argues: "The relaxation of security, political, financial, and legal controls, the issuance of legal-constitutional guarantees to personal, press, and political freedom, and the unleashing of pent-up desires to travel within the country, publish, organize, and hold public debates were all unprecedented".
>
> *(Schwedler 2004: 208-9)*

Neither Ali Saleh nor Ali Salim were genuinely interested in the democratization process *per se*. As explained earlier, it was the mounting political and economic crises in both South and North Yemen that motivated the leadership of both countries to seek unification. In a similar fashion, Saleh and Salim used democratization to 'secure significant support among the population of the other' and NOT because they were genuine democrats. In fact, before unification in 1990, 'political parties were banned in both countries and their public spheres were highly restricted' (Schwedler 2004: 208).

In addition, external and regional factors initially strengthened the democratic process and national unity in Yemen, but later undermined them. On the one hand, unification and democratization allowed Yemen to collectively veto the war in Iraq and oppose the sending of Yemeni troops to participate in the 1991 Gulf War against Iraq. Although this led to a distinct feeling of pride and unity among all Yemenis, in a way never seen before, the price of opposing the war proved to be detrimental. The Arabian Gulf states which opposed a united and democratic Yemeni model on their doorsteps, cut off all financial assistance to Yemen and fired and sent home more than 800,000 Yemeni workers, most of whom had previously been working in Saudi Arabia. With the unemployment and poverty rates climbing tremendously overnight, with state aid completely exhausted and with tourism collapsed, state and tribal rivalry between and within the former two Yemeni states intensified over the meagre resources available. This revitalized old rivalries and suspicions, leading Ali Saleh and Ali Salam to use unity and democracy to mobilize their supporters and incite their followers in both countries against one another (Richards and Waterbury 1996; Ayubi 1999; Schwedler 2004: 208).

As in Algeria, democracy in Yemen proved equally destabilizing. Although 40 political parties contested the first parliamentary elections in Yemen in April 1993, no party won an overwhelming majority. The three main parties that between them won the majority of votes, and which continue to dominate the Yemeni political scene today, formed a coalition government. The first winner was President Ali Saleh's GPC, which won 123 seats in the parliament, followed by the newly established Islamically-oriented, Islah Party (62 seats). The YSP, which had previously ruled South Yemen, came third with 56 seats. Five other parties won a combined 12 seats, while there were an additional 48 seats won by independents (ICG 2003: 4; Schwedler 2004: 218).

Following the results of the elections, the main winners, GPC and Islah, fiercely opposed unity with the 'atheist-Marxists' forces of the South. At the same time, the results of the elections made al-Badi feel that the North would always dominate and the South would always be a subordinate. These feelings were consolidated following the formation of the first post-elections government, which gave six key portfolios to the Islah party. With support from Saudi Arabia, the South ceded from the union a few months after the elections, an act which was rejected by the Northern leader, Ali Saleh. One year after the elections, the former South and North Yemen went to war, which lasted from April to July 1994. A unified Yemen was restored, the old Socialist forces of the South were crushed and the experiment with democracy was, for the time being, shelved. Ali Saleh did become the head of the unified state, but at the expense of democracy (Ayubi 1999: 282; Schwedler 2004; ICG 2003).

The evolution of violent extremism in Yemen

Although Islamic activism 'has been present in Yemen since the beginning of the twentieth century', it has always taken a 'moderate' form (Clark 2004: 173). Violent militancy, however, has traditionally taken a tribal rather than a religious form in Yemen. As Serjeant (1982) noted, traditional Arabia, including Yemen, has been more dominated both politically and socially, by the arms-bearing tribal class and its chiefs, rather than by religious extremist groups. The phenomenon of radical religious militancy, the type of al-Qaeda, is a relatively new phenomenon in Yemen. Radical, al-Qaeda-type militant strands began to emerge in Yemen only in the late 1980s and throughout the 1990s, particularly after the unification of the former South and North in 1990. As one high-ranked Yemeni official stated: 'It was the ruthlessness of the South and lack of order in the North that led to, and facilitated, the proliferation of terrorism in Yemen after the unification' (Personal interview with Judge Hattar, Riyadh Saudi Arabia January 2011).

The root causes of violent extremism in Yemen can be traced back to the Imamate era, particularly to the early 1700s in the North and to the British colonial period in the South. Not only were most parts of the colonial South neglected under the British protectorate, but also the economic and financial benefits from the colonial authorities were not distributed evenly. Only two tribal Sultanates benefited from and were the virtual recipients of almost all British largess. These were the Sultanate of Fadhli of Abyan and the Sultanate of Lahej, the closest Sultanate to the port city of Aden. These two sultanates received the entire British subsidy in return for their assistance in maintaining order in Aden and Abyan regions. The new socialist-Marxist regime that took over in South Yemen following the departure of the British forces in 1968 persecuted all former collaborators with the British colonial authorities, and confiscated their lands and property without compensation. While some former collaborators were tried and executed, others were sentenced to death *in absentia* as they fled the country either to North Yemen or Saudi Arabia (Halliday 1975: 176-7). One prominent member of the former Fadhli Sultanate who took refuge in Saudi Arabia, Shaykh Tariq al-Fadhli, returned to Yemen to establish a violent extremist movement in the country in the 1990s, the Islamic Jihad Organization (IJO). The main objective of al-Fadhli was the restoration of his family's land and property, thereby avenging their treatment at the hands of the former Marxist regime in the South:

> Among federal leaders, the Fadhli family also took refuge in Saudi Arabia, where Shaykh Tariq al-Fadhli is said to have taken up Islamist causes. Indeed, reportedly funded by the Saudi Businessman Osama bin Laden, Shaykh Fadhli eventually "divided his time between Iran, the northern borders of Pakistan, and Afghanistan". ... Shaykh Fadhli fought with the Afghan mujahedeen against the Soviet Union. After leaving Afghanistan, he returned to Saudi Arabia and, with the continued patronage of bin Laden, quietly filtered into Yemen as head of its Islamic Jihad Organisation.
>
> *(Watkins 1996: 219)*

In the North, on the other hand, the Hashid confederation tribe was one of the main tribes that suffered at the hands of the Imamates, and it thus became a staunch supporter of the 1962 republican revolution. Though not the largest, the Hashid confederation tribe, thanks to its unified and charismatic leadership, is traditionally and presently the most powerful tribe in Yemen. Following a violent dispute with members of the Hashid tribe in the 1700s, Imam Husayn ordered the assassination of the prominent Hashid tribal leader, Ali bin Qassim al-Humar and had his head impaled on a spear for public display in Sana'a. Animosity between the Hashid and Imamate continued until the end of the Imamate in 1962. Imam Yehya, for instance, another in a series of Imam families that ruled parts of Yemen until 1962, seized Hajja in the twentieth century, the capital of the Hashid tribal confederation, and continued to destroy the power base of its ruling family, al-Ahmar. Further atrocities were committed in the 1950s, when Imam Ahmed – in a similar fashion to his forebears – ordered the execution and beheading of the prominent tribal leader Sheikh Husayn al-Ahmar and his son Hamid (Serjeant 1982: 29-30. Also cited in Watkins 1996: 217).

The above-mentioned historical events had important consequences for developments in Yemen since the 1960s and up to the present day. First, they explain the emergence of what Halliday (1975: 126) described as the state of 'republican tribalism' in North Yemen after the 1962 revolution, which was based on a strong alliance between military officers and tribes, particularly the Hashid tribal confederation, which had stood firmly behind and fully supported the revolution. This is why the tribes were incorporated into the newly established republican state from the very beginning, as was mentioned earlier (Also see Watkins 1996: 217).

Second, historical events also shed important light on the Huthi rebellion in the Saada region, which broke out in 2004.[5] Saada, during the civil war that ensued after the 1962 revolution, became the main opposition stronghold. After peace was achieved in 1970, the Saada region had been largely ignored and marginalized by the state, hence leading today to what is general prescribed in the media as the 'Huthi rebellion':[6]

> the Saada war can be seen as an extension of a process that began with the 1962 revolution and saw the decline of a social group of which the Huthi family were members. Zaydis also complain of state neglect of their

> strongholds, peripheral regions where … "people know the republic solely through the missiles and tanks". Saada remained on the margins, largely ignored by the government and developing solely thanks to commerce with neighboring Saudi Arabia on the one hand and the fertility of its land on the other. In early 1990s, a Zaydi intellectual recalled that the only hospital in Saada at that time had been built with Saudi money and that the city had waited more than twenty years after the revolution to be visited by a North Yemeni president. Alienated from the state that deprived them of their former status and failed to attend to their region's security or economic development, some Zaydi revivalist – notably Huthis – emerged as a key regime opponent.
>
> *(ICG 2009: 8)*

Put differently, neither in South nor North Yemen was there a comprehensive reconciliation programme initiated or put in place to restore lasting peace, stability and achieve national accord. Such a programme was neither initiated in the North, either following the 1962 revolution or civil war that ensued, nor in the South after persecuting collaborators with former colonial authorities. Such a programme should have also included policies to alleviate poverty, reduce illiteracy, create jobs, and provide prosperity and harmony. This stands in stark contradiction to the Malaysian state's efforts, which developed a comprehensive economic and stability programme to counter the rising influence of the Chinese insurgency after independence (see the chapter on Malaysia in this volume). Such a programme would have been necessary in Yemen to enable a reconciliation with the past, particularly since the emergence of the new regimes in the North (1962) and South (1968) brought abrupt changes to the long standing social, economic and political orders.

Peace in North Yemen in 1970, although most Royalists by then recognized the YAR, was certainly accompanied by the restoration of 'a few' Royalists to 'senior positions' in the republican state (ICG 2003: 3). That alone does not constitute a programme. It was rather a part of the Northern regime's 'Bonapartism' system of 'balancing' various influences in a society weakly ruled by a corrupt political system.

No attempt at a reconciliation occurred in the South after 1968 either. On the contrary, the new Marxist regime ruthlessly uprooted collaborators with the former British colonial authorities and confiscated their land and other properties. Many tribes who fled the persecution of the Marxist regime returned later to haunt the South, particularly after the 1990 unification, 'primarily to advance their own cause'[7] (Watkins 1996: 217).

Not only was there no reconciliation process within the South and North, which would have included a deradicalization programme to deradicalize and compensate the main losers from the abrupt changes brought about by the emergence of new regimes in the North and South in 1962 and 1968, respectively. There was also no real attempt at reconciliation between the North and South themselves after the short-lived 1990 unification bloodily ended in 1994. As a result, the unification itself proved destabilizing, self-destructive and radicalizing for many tribes and individuals. As a result, a cold war erupted between the South and North after 1970 supported by regional powers, which provided both finance and weaponry to competing tribes and states. The upshot has been not only the strengthening of tribalism, but also the production in Yemen of one of the 'most densely armed societies in the Arab World' (Ayubi 1999: 431). Meddling with Yemeni internal and tribal affairs, which is the cause and at the same time the effect of tribal national and regional 'overlapping' loyalties,[8] continues to the present day (ICG 2003 and 2009), with weapons remaining widespread. As Stracke noted:

> Weapons are widely available and regularly sold throughout the country ... Until today, Yemen remains one of the most heavily armed societies in the world, with, on average, around 40 guns per 100 people.
>
> *(Stracke 2006: 9)*

Immediately following the eruption of the cold war in 1970 between North and South Yemen, the Northern regime, in a fashion similar to that of Egypt under Sadat, Jordan under Hussein, Morocco under Hassan II and Saudi Arabia under Faisal deliberately encouraged the proliferation of Islamist movements to counter the influence of the more liberal, socialist regime of the YSP. Several Islamic conservative groups therefore emerged and joined 'in supporting Northern regime against socialist-leaning South' (Schwedler 2004: 211), including the Yemeni Muslim Brotherhood (YMB).[9] As the ICG (2003: 11) noted:

> Yemen's Islamist movements began to emerge in the 1970s. The *ma'ahid*, besides providing conventional training in Islamic orthodoxy, served somewhat as recruiting grounds not only for *mujahidin* who fought in Afghanistan but also for those who fought against Yemen's own "infidels". The pattern of government support for Islamist groups continued throughout the 1980s, as President Saleh sought to strengthen his position by improving ties to them.

The influence of Islamic activism in Yemen, both radical and moderate, increased rapidly after the 1990 unification, which also coincided with the return of thousands of Yemeni and Arab-Afghans. Although Yemeni authorities did not openly support Jihad in Afghanistan, or issue a fatwa declaring jihad in Afghanistan as '*fard ain*' (religious duty), thousands of Yemenis still flocked to Afghanistan to participate in what they perceived as a holy war against the Russian forces there. When the war ended in the late 1990s, however, Yemen welcomed mujahedeen and deliberately encouraged them to return to Yemen to counter the influence of YSP. It is now common knowledge that the Saleh regime cultivated Arab-Afghans in his cold and hard-military war against the former YSP (Sharp 2010: 16; ICG 2009: 15 and 16; Peraino 2009).

By the time the civil war erupted in 1994, there were more than 29,000 'Afghan-Arabs' in Yemen, including both Yemenis and other nationalities (ICG 2003: 9). Some chose Yemen because of a relaxation in security and legal controls, and the unprecedented freedoms provided to association, travel, organization, press and expression after the 1990 unification. Even Osama bin Laden expressed, in the mid-1990s, a desire 'to live in Yemen because it was one of the few places in the Arab world where one could still breathe the air of freedom', he stated (quoted in Johnsen 2006). Others chose Yemen in order to fight the socialist-Marxist regime[10] of the South.[11] Some simply chose Yemen in order to take advantage of the country's unprecedented freedoms and to leave Jihadism behind, settle there and start a new life. The Egyptian ideologue, Dr Fadl, born Sayyid Imam al-Sharif, was among them.[12]

One observes a similar pattern of regime-consolidation, a 'balancing' act and a lack of a comprehensive reconciliation programme after the 1994 civil war. In fact, the first act of the post-civil war state was to acknowledge the role of Islamists in the fight against the former socialist regime. After the war in 1994, 'the Yemeni constitution was changed according to their [Islamists] long-standing demand, to read that *shari'a* law would be the sole source of legislation in the country' (Watkins 1996: 221). Members of the newly-established Islah Party were given six portfolios in the first government after elections, rising to nine after the end of the civil war.[13] The leader of the al-Islah Party, al-Hamar, was elected as the speaker of the parliament in 1993 and 1997, thus opening more direct channels for Islamists to influence public opinion (Schwedler 2004: 217 and 218).

Rather than rebuilding the ravaged South and introducing an effectual reconciliation programme, the South continued to be neglected developmentally and politically. Although a general amnesty, excluding 16 of the top southern leaders, was declared and the PSY was not liquidated but was asked, instead, to reconsider its position with regard to unity (Ayubi 1999: 438), most southern 'officers and soldiers were forced to retire after the 1994 civil war, despite their young age and qualifications' (Day 2008). It was this negligence, which eventually triggered the separatist movement in the South in the second half of 2007, when tens of thousands of protesters gathered daily in several southern Yemeni cities and peacefully called 'for an end to corruption and regional discrimination inside the country'. Initially, most demonstrators were former soldiers who were forced to retire after the 1994 civil war, demanding work and a pension payment. Demonstrations were later extended to most Southern Yemeni districts. Since then, it has grown to be a separatist movement, demanding the restoration of a state in the former South[14] (all quotations from Day 2008).

Finally, corruption, nepotism, patronage and tribalism continued to inhibit the capacity of the state.[15] The 1990-1 Gulf Crisis, which cut off all developmental aid, sent more than 800,000 Yemenis home and diminished their remittances, and put tremendous pressure on the country's infrastructure and financial resources. It also exposed the corrupt, inefficient and incompetent nature of the ruling party and regime. Ayubi (1999) and Richards and Waterbury (1996) calculate the 1991 Gulf War cost on Yemen at more than two billion dollars in lost tourism revenue, remittances and developmental aid.

The severity of the situation forced Yemeni authorities in 1995 to turn to the IMF and World Bank for technical and financial assistance. As structural adjustment programmes promoted by the IMF and World Bank further reduced the state's resources, as they often do, Saleh's ability to continue to provide largess to all of his loyalists declined. This in turn forced the Yemeni authorities to rely more than ever on its civil society organizations to provide welfare services. As a result, 'Yemen witnessed a rapid proliferation of civil society organizations ... although the North in particular was characterized by a vibrant public sphere even before unification' (Schwedler 2004: 214).

One of the main social sectors that has been dominated by CSOs, some of which were, and still are, radical (preaching violent ideology) is education. While proselytization and incitement was common against the former Southern socialist regime, proselytization was extended after 1992 to include incitement against Shiite Huthis,[16] US foreign policy in the region[17] and even against Ali Saleh's regime itself (ICG 2003 and 2009). This came to be more the case after the 1994 civil war, which, by crushing former socialist forces and weakening the PSY, reduced the strategic importance of all Islamists in the country and triggered a gradual change in President Saleh's position towards Islamists in general.

Indeed, the Islamically-oriented Islah Party, after the end of the civil war in 1994, 'recognized that GPC members no longer looked at them as ready allies' (Schwedler 2004: 219). The GPC started a public campaign to smear Islah's reputation and undermine its electoral opportunities before the 1997 elections.[18] The response of Islah members, on the other hand, was rather surprising. Instead of relying on violence as expected by many observers, Islah members resorted to tools and instruments that were more traditionally and culturally acceptable and consistent with the mores of the country; instruments that the regime found difficult to constrain. They included the intensification of *da'wa* (calling) through conferences, seminars, charity work, education, lectures, *qat* sessions and private meetings in individual member's houses. These tools and instruments relied more on informal networks and aimed at 'islamiz [ing] society' and 'promote(ing) an environment through which Islam and Muslims flourish' (Clark 2004: 169).

The 'invention' or re-invention 'of tradition' by Islamists, as Dale Eickelman and James Piscaltori described it, opened the floodgates for criticism to be levelled against President Saleh, and further discredited his regime by focusing not only on political, but also on moral and cultural decay of his personal style of ruling the country. For example, they attacked Saleh's corrupt system of governance, his obsession with power, and criticized him for undermining multi-party democracy after 1996.[19] Even before the 11 September attacks, Saleh's domestic credibility had been largely undermined by criticism of corruption, the inability of his state to provide even the most basic of services to Yemeni citizens, his economic mismanagement that put the national economy firmly in the hands of foreign institutions (the IMF and World Bank) and the fragmentation of Yemeni political and social systems. By December 1997, all of Islah's cabinet members resigned from their positions, because 'they were prevented from taking steps to reduce corruption' in the public sector and in their own ministries (Clark 2004: 219-20).

Feeling the increased influence of Islamists, Ali Saleh's government moved to take measures in order to reduce the influence of all Islamists in the country. The first Islamists to be influenced by these measures were the 'Arab Afghans', who began to be viewed after 1995 with suspicions, prone to violent extremism and therefore problematic. Boucek *et al.* (2009: 181) described a UN-sponsored 'Sheikhs against terror' initiative, where the Yemeni government began paying 'millions of dollars to Yemeni tribes in order to purchase their loyalty and to deny refuge to extremists and militants'. In 1997, almost 7,000 'Arab Afghanis'[20] were deported from Yemen' (Personal interview with Judge Hattar, Riyadh January 2011). A large number of the deportees went back to Afghanistan, but since the number of the returnees was much higher than the number of deportees, thousands remained in Yemen. While the majority were incorporated in Saleh's security apparatus or abandoned jihad altogether for a more peaceful life, others were responsible for establishing several radical, militant movements in the country, such as the Islamic Army of Aden-Abyan (IAAA) and Yemeni Jihad Organization (YJO).

Yemen today enjoys, in addition to the al-Huthi rebellion movement in the North (and its radical Believing Youth arm) and a separatist movement in the South, at least three forms of Islamic activism: mobilizational, political and radical-violent militancy. The first two (represented by the Islah Party[21] and Islah Charitable Society,[22] respectively), tend to overwhelmingly dominate the Yemeni political scene. The movements played an important role in mobilizing Islamist grass-roots against the former socialist regime in the South, and strongly allied themselves with the Saleh's regime until at least the second parliamentary elections in 1997. Since then, they started to carve a more politically autonomous place for themselves. Still, they are today incorporated in the political system and the rules of the political game. They also accept democratic forms of governance and the state as the main frame for political competition and arbitration.

At least three main radical movements exist in Yemen today, however: the Islamic Army of Aden-Abyan (IAAA) Yemeni Jihad Organization (YJO)[23] and al-Qaeda's Yemen branch. The latter was announced in 2007, but became even more radicalized in 2009 when it merged, in January, with the Saudi branch of al-Qaeda to form al-Qaeda in the Arabian Peninsula (AQAP). Out of the three, AQAP is the most radical and violent organization in the country. Several of its members participated in the war against Southern secessionists, seeing the war as an opportunity to establish an Islamic state. When this failed after 1994, they turned against the Saleh's regime itself, which initially incorporated them and welcomed them back from Afghanistan. They represent a minority in Yemeni society and have a very small number of followers. According to Stracke (2009), the size of AQAP's membership remains modest. She estimates their size at between 100-150 active members in total. Sharp (2010: 9) estimates the number of AQAP's membership to be between 100 and 400 active members.

Yemen's passive deradicalization programme

As stated at the beginning of this chapter, Yemen is not 'the easiest of countries to write about'. This is not only because of paucity of data on Yemen, but also because 'Yemenis themselves often give conflicting accounts, as well as having differences of opinion about their interpretation' for the same phenomenon (Whitaker 2009).

In 2002, Yemen established the Committee for Dialogue (CD), the aim of which was to convince detained violent extremists to repent and abandon violence. Internal and international factors shed important light not only on the timing, but also on the motivations and the rationale behind the establishment of the CD.

Internal and international context: rationale for CD

Internally, violent extremism has been on the rise since the early 1990s. In addition to the bombing of two hotels in Aden in December 1992, which targeted American soldiers *en route* to Somalia and resulted in the deaths of several bystanders, a group of militants were captured in the same month at Yemen airport. They, allegedly, were preparing to launch rockets at an American aircraft. In 1998, a group of militants associated with the IAAA were detained on charges of planning to attack not only the British Embassy in Sana'a, but also churches and American interests in the country. Militants' operations soon assumed more sophistication and international consequences. For example, the IAAA, in early 1999, kidnapped 16 Western tourists in an attempt to force the government to release their comrades captured in the 1998 failed operation against the British Embassy. The hostage-taking operation was led by Zain al-Abidin abu Baker al Midhar, one of the key founders of the IAAA. He was tried, found guilty and executed in October 1999. In 2000, the American destroyer, the USS *Cole*, was attacked in Aden harbour as it re-fuelled, killing 17 sailors and wounding a further 39. Two years later, the French tanker, MV *Limburg*, was bombed off the cost of Yemen in the Gulf of Aden. The killing of three American missionaries in the same year at a southern Baptist missionary hospital in the town of Jibla followed these other attacks (Boucek *et al.* 2009: 182–3; Birk 2009: 7).

The 2000 and 2002 operations dealt a severe blow to the Yemeni economy. First, they led to the collapse of a plan to build a new free-zone area in Aden to alleviate unemployment and poverty by creating jobs and incomes. Second, the *Limburg* operation, which resulted in more than 90,000 tons of crude oil being spilled, led to massive increases in insurance rates with several international companies withdrawing their operations from Aden (Boucek *et al.* 2009: 182–3; Birk 2009: 15).

Yemen was thus quickly acquiring the reputation of a 'failing state' (Sharp, 2010), and 'a breeding ground for al-Qaeda members', which became a very dangerous label to acquire, particularly in the post-September 11 international environment characterised by 'war on terror' (Birk 2009: 1). As a result:

> many Yemenis, including prominent government officials, felt their country was next on a "hit list" after the U.S. finished in Afghanistan. That fear has been expressed more recently by President Ali Abdullah Saleh, during a speech in Aden in December 2005, when he claimed that he dissuaded the U.S. from occupying the country following the attack on the USS *Cole* in October 2000.
> *(Johnsen 2006)*

Internally, limited state resources, corruption and economic mismanagement continued to further undermine the legitimacy of the Ali Saleh's regime through the state's inability to provide basic services and welfare benefits to Yemeni citizens. The consequence of this was a tremendous increase in the kidnapping of state officials by tribes to force the government to provide infrastructure, jobs or other benefits to their members or areas, encountered by state's kidnapping of tribal members to force tribes to release kidnapped state officials[24] (ICG 2003 and 2009).

At the same time, mainstream Islamists were becoming more credible and legitimate, partly as a result of Ali Saleh government's continued mismanagement of the economy, widespread corruption, and partly as a result of their ability to provide social welfare services to a large segment of poor Yemenis through their *da'wa* and charity work. Ironically, as the relationship between state and mainstream Islamists in general began to deteriorate, the relationship between Islamists in general and tribes improved, including with al-Qaeda. Many tribes even started to protect and hide wanted militants by the state (Birk 2009; Sharp 2010; Peraino 2009).

On the other hand, fears of an American attack, or massive operation in Yemen after Afghanistan, which could topple the Yemeni regime, called for an immediate action to alleviate American fears and assure the US administration of Yemeni cooperation. It is against this background that the decision to establish the DC by President Ali Saleh in 2002 should be understood. It was part of Ali Saleh's Bonapartism system of balancing acts, including superpowers. It did not stem from the commitment to, or a belief in, the value of debating and dialoguing violent extremists: ' … the dialogue project was designed as a way to balance the need to appear tough in "the war on terror" with a need to appease and accommodate the wishes of a tribal population with some Islamist sympathies' (Birk 2009: 16).

The dialogue committee

By 2002, Yemen, as a result of the above-mentioned developments, had detained around 420 individuals under suspicion of involvement in violent extremist acts or who were linked to al-Qaeda. More than 100 of these people were arrested in relation to attack on the USS *Cole* in 2000 alone (Personal interview with Judge Hattar and Sheikh Hassan Abdullah al-Sheihk, Sana'a June 2010). The decision to debate and create a dialogue with detained individuals came from the head of the state, President Ali Saleh himself, who publically declared in the sixth annual party conference on 24 August 2002 that:

> … we have a group of young people who have dangerous beliefs. Those people have not committed any crime, but if we leave them on their own, they could cause great harm to themselves and to the country. We need to talk to them.
>
> *(Quoted in Boucek* et al. *2009: 184)*

Three important points can be derived from President's Saleh's public statement. First, ideology, or 'dangerous beliefs', were officially seen as the root cause of violent extremism in the country. Second, if this was the case, then the solution simply lay in unravelling ideology by 'talking to them' (detainees) and inject some rationale in their thinking. Brigadier Muhammad al-Daghwees, head of Yemeni Anti-Terrorist Unit at National Security Centre, concurs:

> We decided to carry out dialogue with detainees because their minds were washed by radical ideologies in order to correct their ideas and bring them back to society. They were attracted to radical thought in mosques and religious institutions.
>
> *(Personal interview, Sana'a 2010)*

Finally and more importantly, most of the detainees, as President Saleh himself admitted, 'have not committed any crime'. They were neither tried nor charged, and were, from a legal point of view, arrested unfairly and unjustly. Amnesty International (2003) referred to this phenomenon in Yemen as 'law sideline[ing] in the name of security'.

On 30 August 2002, President Saleh, four days after his sixth annual party's speech, invited his key state officials and the country's most influential 15 senior Yemeni ulama for a meeting. The aim of the meeting was 'to find a solution for the problem of terrorist detainees'. It was this meeting that led to the birth of the CD.[25] Among those who attended the meeting was Judge Hattar, a proud self-made former judge in the supreme court justice, who is known for his religious knowledge and personal integrity. Judge Hattar was to head the DC from the beginning. The DC's chief objective was identified as convincing the detainees to simply abandon violence and to accept a more moderate interpretation of Islam: 'to convert them from radical, militant understanding of Islam to a moderate peaceful understanding' (Birk 2009: 3).

Reflecting the fractured political nature of the Yemeni society, there was no consensus among the ulama regarding what approach the CD should follow:

> The *ulama* wanted to send all clerics to all prisons and then release all prisoners. They also wanted to bring all prisoners for dialogue at the same time. I refused and stated that we should establish a team or a dialogue committee of few clerics, which should be responsible for carrying out dialogue with the prisoners. Only four clerics accepted my idea of a dialogue committee, including myself and Judge Hattar, Sheikh Fadal al-Kerhi, and Sheikh Mushrif Abdul Karim. President Ali Saleh was informed about what happened and we were surprised to be informed that he supported our proposal and accepted it.[26]
>
> *(Personal interview with Sheikh Hassan Abdullah al-Sheihk and Judge Hattar, Sana'a June 2010)*

Judge Hattar and his colleagues developed two main components for the DC: theoretical and practical. The former focused on establishing a dialogue with incarcerated individuals. Rather than talking to all detained individuals simultaneously or collectively, the CD opted for debating the five or six most radical incarcerated individuals first:

> After taking the green light from the president, I asked the head of the Political Security Organisation (PSO) to arrange a meeting with the five or six most

> radical detained individuals. The rational was that if we could convince the most radical individuals to repent, then it would be easier to convince the rest of the prisoners. Better still, if we could convince the most radical elements to repent, then we could ask them to talk to their colleagues and deradicalise them, since the detainees are more likely to listen to their leaders than to us. It was like a trial, a pilot project.
>
> *(Personal interview with Judge Hattar, Sana'a June 2010)*

A meeting was arranged with the five most radical detained individuals on 15 September 2002. It was led by Judge Hattar and attended by the other three ulama who accepted to be part of the DC, the minister of the interior and the head of the PSO. Lacking the necessary logistics and tailor-made incarceration centres that Saudi Arabia enjoyed, the first meeting took place in the guest room of the main security prison in Sana'a at the PSO. To establish some sort of a level playing field and mutual trust and respect with the detainees, Judge Hattar and his colleagues followed the same approach used by Imam Al-Hadi when he first arrived in Yemen almost 1,000 years ago to solve a tribal dispute. 'Al-Hadi then ordered a Qu'ran to be brought and made them swear to one another to leave off dissension and hostility – which they did' (Watkins 1996: 216). Judge Hattar also brought in a copy of the Qu'ran with him and made ulama and detainees swear to one another to listen to each other, leave dissention and hostility aside, and to make the Qu'ran the ultimate source of arbitration between them. As Judge Hattar stated, in a now widely quoted statement, 'I told the detainees that if you are right we will follow you and if we are right you must follow us. But first let's agree to make the Qu'ran as our only and ultimate source of arbitration' (Personal interview, Sana'a June 2010. Also see Birk 2009: 18; Boucek *et al.* 2009: 186).

How the debate then proceeded has been discussed extensively elsewhere to warrant repetition here[27] (Boucek *et al.* 2009; Birk 2009). Suffice it to say the debate proceeded on a 'direct' basis, with the detainees raising their point of views first with the ulama then responding to them. At least four subjects, not dissimilar to those found in deradicalization programmes implemented in other Muslim-majority states discussed in this volume, were raised in the first meeting between the CD and the five detainees. These were the following: the Islamic status of the state and legitimacy of the president: the ethics of jihad; relations between Muslims and non-Muslims; and relations between Yemen and other non-Muslim states and international treaties.

Based on evidence derived from the Qu'ran and Sunni, Judge Hattar and his colleagues were able to convince the detainees during their first meeting that they got things wrong. For example, Judge Hattar presented a copy of the constitution, which proved to the detainees that '*shari'a* law is the sole source of legislation in the country', that the president is legitimate because he is elected democratically, and that democracy does not violate Islamic religion and is consistent with it. On the issue of relation with non-Muslims, Judge Hattar also cited verses from the Qu'ran, which shows beyond doubt that Allah forbad the killing of innocent souls regardless of their religion and under any circumstances. He also reminded them that the Qu'ran called for peace with anybody who seeks to establish peace with Muslims, and of how Muslim armies and leaders were always advised by the Qu'ran and the Prophet not to kill innocent human beings.

On the issue of international relations, Judge Hattar taught his interlocutors how the Prophet not only signed treaties and agreements with non-Muslims, but that he also always respected them and advised Muslim leaders after him to follow his footsteps. Judge Hattar collaborated with the detainees to make them understand that it is the duty of Muslims to protect non-Muslims who come to their country from overseas to work and serve Muslim states and their economies, and that the visa acquired by guest workers or visitors represents a form of agreement or oath made by a Muslim state to confer peace and tranquillity on its non-Muslim guests, which should be respected under all circumstances. Judge Hattar also explained to detainees the disastrous economic consequences of attacks on the USS *Cole* and French tanker, *Limburg*, which undermined Yemeni economy, led to more poverty and misery among Yemenis. Finally, the ulama reminded the detainees of the ethics of Jihad in Islam, that Jihad cannot be waged individually, that it requires permission from *wali al-Amer* (ruler), and that killing can only be justified in and as self-defence.

Assessment and outcomes

Attempts to evaluate and assess the effectiveness of the Yemeni DC have been fraught with difficulties pertaining to data availability, the lack of information on the socio-economic characteristics, as well as the identity of both incarcerated and released individuals. These difficulties have hampered a comprehensive assessment of the performance of the DC. Such an exercise, though, remains a necessity if we are to derive useful lessons from the Yemeni experience of religious dialogue.

Out of the 420 Yemeni arrested between 2002 and 2005, 364 (87 per cent) went through the DC and were later released. The rest were sentenced because they were believed to have committed crimes. Those who committed crimes do not go through the dialogue process.

How best to gauge the Yemeni DC has generated a great deal of controversy and many contradictions. Most Western observers and policy-makers have judged the DC to have 'failed', without fully understanding the goals, objectives and circumstances through which the DC had to operate (Birk 2009; Gannon 2007; Johnsen 2006; Shane 2009; Stracke 2006; Peraino 2009). While the performance of the DC has often 'annoy[ed] Western governments' (*The Economist* 2009), Yemeni officials are adamant that, at least until early 2006, the DC was 'successful, with the success rate among released individuals exceeding 90 percent' (Personal interview with Judge Hattar and other senior officials at PSO, Sana'a June 2010). The available empirical evidence also shows that from October 2002, the date that the dialogue commenced, and 2006, 'Yemen enjoyed a respite from terror attacks and it was during this period that the Dialogue Committee was established and worked to engage with militants detained in Yemen' (Boucek *et al.* 2009: 183).

Violent extremism, however, returned to Yemen after 2006, with a wave of attacks that targeted both state symbols and personal, as well as foreign objectives.

The attacks resulted in the killing of seven Spanish tourists by a suicide bomber while they were visiting a temple site linked to the biblical Queen of Sheba. Other attacks targeted the US Embassy in Sana'a, an attempt to assassinate Prince Mohammed bin Nayef[28] in August 2009, a failed attempt to blow up the Northwest flight on 25 December 2009 and the discovery of explosives almost one year later on a cargo plane (Sharp 2010; Gannon 2007). These attacks happened in absence of DC, which was terminated unilaterally by President Saleh in 2005.

From the Western point of view, 'al-Hittar's programme had failed' because:

> ... at least eight men from al-Hittar's program have found their way to Iraq to fight U.S. forces there ... [with] two former detainees, which al-Hittar had recommended for release, carried out a suicide bombing on U.S. forces in Baghdad ...
>
> *(Johnsen 2006)*

This evaluation raises important questions about the meaning of success, success to whom, and ways and means of gauging success. First, this kind of evaluation suggests that deradicalization, and religious dialogue programmes in general, cannot be evaluated in isolation from external (international and regional) environments. There is little doubt that the illegal invasion of Iraq in 2003, taking place in the middle of al-Hittar's dialogue, undermined the potential of the latter. Not only Yemenis, but also Saudis, Jordanians, Egyptians, Moroccans, Tunisians and Algerians, to mention but a few examples, were morally outraged by the 2003 invasion of Iraq. Like many Yemenis, they also found their way to Iraq to fight American forces there, despite their countries having very special and close relations with the US government. Images emanating from Iraq, with coalition forces bombing and attacking Muslims, led to what Speckhard and Ahkmedova (2006, 486) described as 'secondary traumatization', which develops through viewing downloaded footages of traumatic images, and which can lead to the radicalization of the young individuals in countries far away from the theatre of operation.

Second, not only is the external environment in which the religious dialogue programmes are being implemented significant, but also the internal environment. As the ICG (2007: i), while evaluating the Indonesian deradicalization programme wrote: such programmes 'cannot be evaluated in isolation and they are likely to founder unless incorporated into a broader program of prison [and non-prison] reform'. Not only did Yemen witness little prison and non-prison reforms, but 'corruption', nepotism and economic mismanagement remained widespread, leading to 'regional discrimination inside the country' (Day 2008). Along with improved collaboration with the US administration in the 'war on terror', this undermined several key messages of the DC. While Judge al-Hittar was at pains to teach his detainees that the president is legitimate, and the government of Yemen is truly Islamic, corruption and discrimination, as well as Saleh's endeavour to prove to the Americans that he is a reliable partner in the 'war on terror',[29] undermined both the credibility of the messages of the DC and of Saleh's regime itself.

There were also problems related to the dialogue process itself. Judge Hittar started the dialogue with the detainees by saying that:

> we are here on a mission: the president has asked us to come and talk to you. This was the first and most fatal mistake made by Judge Hittar. As soon as he said that, we all immediately recognised that the *ulama* are here to serve the interests of the state, not ours.[30]
>
> *(Personal interview with Abu Jandal and Judge Hittar, Sana'a June 2010)*

Divisions within the ulama, moreover, and a lack of consensus also undermined the DC's efforts. While Saudi Arabia mobilized and put thousands of clerics and scholars at the disposal of its deradicalization programme, Yemen was not able to mobilize more than three or four clerics. There were not a sufficient number of credible clerics able to talk to a large number of detainees (more than 400). The agenda of the dialogue itself was left, almost entirely, for one man, Judge Hittar, to determine. A powerful agency, such as the authoritative Saudi Ministry of Interior, was lacking to determine the goals of the dialogue, create consensus around its objectives, and to run and manage it centrally in collaboration with other stakeholders. The result was the emergence of contradictions and disagreements over the goals and objectives of the dialogue. The fact that 'Yemen's security forces were convinced that al-Hittar's programme had failed, and that it should be stopped' (Johnsen 2006) because several Yemenis appeared in Iraq, confirms a lack of internal agreement on the goals and objectives of the dialogue among Yemeni officials themselves. The fact that Judge Hattar's dialogue programme was terminated unilaterally, while the man was in Washington talking to American officials and practitioners about his unique experience with religious dialogue, also suggests that the Yemeni leadership itself had an entirely different set of goals and objectives. As Judge Hittar explained, 'It was not my problem to achieve peace and stability in Iraq. My concern was to achieve peace and stability in Yemen: Iraq was not part of the DC' (Personal interview, Sana'a June 2010).

The small number of clerics and scholars involved in the dialogue process also suggests that it is difficult to speak of a genuine and comprehensive dialogue process. Judge Hittar and his colleagues of ulama did not, in fact, meet more than two or three times with most detainees, who were divided into five or six groups and then talked to during individual sessions (Interviews with five former detainees who went through the DC, Sana'a June 2010). The aim of the sessions was more to inject 'ration' and pragmatism in the minds of the detainees, than leading to a cognitive and psychological change among them. This generated the wrong signals to the detainees, who understood this to be, essentially, a deal with the authorities: 'you simply repent and we will release you', the detainees thought. As a former detainee who attended the sessions with Judge Hittar stated, 'We all understood that it was just extortion to take money from the Americans'. The implications are obvious: 'If Satan himself told me to sign', stated Abu Jandal, 'I would have' (all quotations from Peraino 2009).

Boucek *et al.* (2009: 192) and Birk (2009) suggest several other reasons for the return of terrorism to Yemen after 2006. First were the conditions under which the detainees themselves were detained in the first place. As mentioned earlier, many of the detainees were detained without trial and were not charged with any offence as a result. Many felt that they were detained and kept in prison, some for well over three or four years, unjustly:

> While for some prison was a place for *muraja'ah* (revision), for others it was the opposite. They were asking themselves all the time why did they do that to us? Why are we here for? The prison hardened and embittered them against the state.
>
> *(Personal interview with a former detainee, Sana'a June 2010)*

When they were released from prison, they became an easy target for ideologues preaching violent militancy.

In 2006, 23 radical ideologues escaped from prison (Shane 2009). 'Before 2006, there was no terrorism in Yemen until 23 radical al-Qaeda members escaped from prison in 2006 and began spreading violent ideology again in the country', stated Judge Hattar (Personal interview, Sana'a June 2010). By that time, a new, younger group of radical extremists had emerged in Yemen. They were less compromising than the old group, and began seeing and treating Ali Saleh's regime as un-Islamic; a legitimate target of their attacks (Johnsen 2006; Boucek *et al.* 2009).

The eruption of the Huthi rebellion in 2004 further destabilized the DC's efforts. It may even have been the *real* catalyst for its termination in 2005. The rebellion put tremendous financial and military pressure on the limited resources of the state. The Yemen authorities were forced to shift resources to Saada, where they believed the real threat to the state lay (Stracke 2006). This meant terminating resources originally planned for the DC, particularly for released detainees. Under these circumstances:

> Marriage became a liability; we were no longer able to support our own family. Worse, we became a burden on our own parents and family members. Instead of supporting them, we began relying on them, but they are poor and had little to give. We started to feel that we lost our dignity as men. Al-Qaeda became an attractive option because it continues to give $300 for each member, much more than the state could give. Hence, several detainees rejoined al-Qaeda after their release.
>
> *(Interview with a former detainee, Sana'a June 2010)*

Three years after the DC was suspended, the Yemeni 'program … has restarted as of May 2008' (Boucek *et al.* 2009: 192). This time, significantly, without the DC and its ulama. The authorities instead started to rely more on released detainees, loyal officials, as well as 'family members' to talk to violent extremists, and convince them to repent and surrender (al-Mosawa 2010). To a large extent this approach worked: several high profile al-Qaeda members did surrender to the authorities in return for selective incentives. This includes several of al-Qaeda's local leaders, like Hizam Mujally in the Arhab district, Jumaan Sufian and Ghalib al-Zayidi, 'the most wanted Yemeni member in al-Qaeda in Marib who surrendered following protracted negotiation with the local authorities in Marib and also after being assured by Marib Governor, Naji Ali al-Zayidi that he will not be killed or harmed' (al-Mosawa 2010. Also see Xinhua 2010).

These efforts have, however, been largely undermined by US dawn attacks in Yemen, which killed several innocent Yemeni bystanders, including women and children, as well as some of state negotiators and family members mediating and intervening with their relatives to surrender to the Yemeni authorities. Following a US dawn attack in December 2010, in which 55 people including 42 civilians in Southern Yemen died, Oudeh and al-Mamari (2010) wrote:

> Just as high civilian causality in US attack on militants have fed extremism in Iraq and Afghanistan, the same phenomenon is now playing out in Yemen ... It is incredibly dangerous what the US is trying to do in Yemen at the moment because it really fits into AQAP's broader strategy, in which it says Yemen is not different from Iraq and Afghanistan ...

An earlier dawn attack by US forces on 25 May 2010, killed the Marib's province deputy governor, a respected local leader who had been trying to talk to al-Qaeda's members into giving up their weapons and fight against the Yemeni state. The attack 'had a devastating impact'. Not only did the mishaps embarrass the government of Yemen, but they also 'gave ammunition to Al Qaeda and the Salafists' in the Arabian Peninsula. Worse, US dawn attacks have undermined relations between the Yemeni state and many of its former loyal tribes. For example, the 25 May attack 'provoked a revenge attack on an oil pipeline by local tribesmen'. Another cruise missile attack by US forces in Yemen on 24 December 2010 led tribes to retaliate 'with a lethal attack on a government security compound in Aden that left 11 [state officials] dead' (all quotations from Shane *et al.* 2010).

Conclusion

The Yemeni experience with religious dialogue and deradicalization is consistent with at least three key empirical evidences that are crucial to the findings of this book. First, Yemeni authorities' failure to spread wealth, and reduce poverty and inequities, and manage relations with its various ethnic communities and tribes is a reflection of the country's weak developmental capacity. Developmentally weak states are at a higher risk of violent extremism than developmentally strong states. This is mainly because the environment in developmentally weak states, which are characterized by failure to manage economic growth, poverty, unemployment, inequities, as well as relations with their ethnic minorities, becomes more conducive to radicalization that in turn leads to violent extremism. Indeed, Yemen's social and economic indicators remain disturbing, as the analysis in this chapter has shown.

Second, not just developmentally but also politically Yemen is also a weak state. Not only does the state have little control outside the main cities, but also the state's control over its porous borders is equally weak, leading to the constant smuggling of weapons that are often used against the state itself, its subjects and foreign targets in the country. Indeed, it was the Yemeni state's inability to protect and control its porous borders that led many Yemenis to end up fighting in Iraq, a fact which not only undermined the process of religious dialogue that was created by a presidential request in 2002 but also led to the termination of the entire dialogue process in 2005.

Developmentally and politically weak states are almost invariably forced into politics of 'balancing' various forces in society to guarantee their survival. They have no credibility, either nationally or internationally, and they are in no position to fashion a credible and effective deradicalization or religious dialogue process. In fact, while Saudi Arabia has mobilized thousands of clerics and scholars that have become responsible for the success of the country's internationally touted deradicalization programme, Yemen has not been able to mobilize more than three or four clerics.

Unlike Saudi Arabia, Yemen lacks a consensus underpinning the dialogue process. Nor was the Yemeni religious dialogue ever backed by, run and micro-managed by a powerful state institution, such as the influential Saudi Ministry of Interior. The upshot has been the absence of generally agreed upon clear goals and objectives, factors that are equally necessary for an effective, and successful, religious dialogue process.

Finally, while the Saudi monarchy took measures to improve the credibility and legitimacy of its regime, including the placing of limits on the budget of members of the royal family and distancing itself from the US administration, in Yemen the opposite is true. The regime of Ali Saleh continued to lose credibility over time, as corruption, nepotism and inefficiencies became widespread and linked to him personally. The key message of the religious dialogue, that the president is legitimate and the regime is Islamic, was weakened not only by the political and developmental weakness of the state, but also by the corruptibility of the regime, state institutions and officials. Such a regime is only capable of radicalizing, not deradicalizing its citizens.

It is not surprising that the credibility of Ali Saleh's regime at the time of writing (March 2011), both nationally and internationally, is at its nadir. He is less likely to survive the Arab Spring, the first civil, mass, anti-violent movement in the region which has hitherto deposed two and killed a third of the region's most tyrant rulers: Hosni Mubarak of Egypt, Ben Ali of Tunisia and Gadaffi of Libya. Ali Saleh is highly unlikely to last until the next presidential elections in 2013. His departure could provide an excellent opportunity to fashion a new, effective and comprehensive religious dialogue programme that would bring about both a cognitive and behavioural changes. It could also incorporate a more global and regional agenda.

Notes

1 Imamate refers to Imam Al-Hadi Yahya who arrived in Yemen in the third Islamic century to mediate a large dispute between major Yemeni tribes, while Zaydim refers to tribes mostly in the North that recognized and submitted to his rule. Imamate is a form of Shiite Islam that believes in the Shiites' main Twelver principle which states that only a Hashemite (a decedent from the Prophet) can rule. Zaydis take their name from their fifth Imam, Zayd ibn Ali. Although they differ politically and theologically, Zaydis are more in line doctrinally with Sunni Islam and are distinct from the Twelvers, the

dominant branch of Shiite Islam in Iran, Iraq and Lebanon. For more details see ICG 2003 and 2009.

2 Both the YAR and the PDRY laid claim to Yemen in its entirety. This rivalry resulted in several, inconclusive border skirmishes in 1972 and 1979. Although no victor emerged, the skirmishes ended with commitments to unify the country. This, however, did not take place until May 1990, following the end of the Cold War and after decades of tense relations and unfulfilled promises between the PDRY and the YAR (ICG 2003: 3).

3 Labour migration is historically common in Yemen. Indeed, workers' migration from South Yemen goes back centuries as the British colonial authorities neglected development outside Aden Port, a coaling station on the way to India.

Wadi Hadramawt, the most heavily populated area in Eastern Aden protectorates, experienced most neglect. The region was also hindered by famine and constant tribal infighting. For centuries, therefore, the area had been highly dependent on remittances from expatriate *Hadramis* residing in East Africa, India, and especially Indonesia. The Yemeni Imamate itself was responsible for spreading Islam in several Asian countries, including Indonesia and Malaysia (ICG 2003: 2 and 2009).

4 Examples of such committees include a Council that was created in 1982 and aggregated all intellectual, tribal leaders, higher officers and businessmen. This Council was engaged in a two-year discussion, followed by a referendum and formation of General People's Congress, with 3,000 members including some women. In addition, 400 syndicates, cooperatives and societies as well as various tribal and rural councils were organized and some affiliated to the GPC (Ayubi 1999: 432).

5 According to ICG (2009: 2–3) the al-Huthi rebel movement was triggered by the death of its leader, Hussein al-Huthi at the hands of security forces on 10 September 2004. This incident was preceded in January 2003 by Believing Youth militants publically shouting 'God is great! Death to America! Death to Israel! Curse upon the Jews! Victory to Islam!' in a Saada mosque in President Ali Saleh's presence. The Believing Youth is a movement that was created in the 1990s by several Huthi leaders allegedly to 'revive Zaydi activism through education and proselytizing' (ICG 2003: 8). This incident was followed by continuous demonstrations by the al-Huthis in Saada region and Capital Sana'a, contesting their political and economic marginalization. After several reconciliation attempts between Saleh and Hussein al-Huthi failed, the government in June 2004 sought to arrest al-Huthi in his stronghold in Saada's Hayden district, leading to his death. His kin has taken over the leadership of the movement. Although the conflict has taken a more religious form in recent years and re-surfaced religious tension in the country, 'the [Saada] war expanded because it became a microcosm of a series of latent religious, social, political and economic tensions' (ibid.: i). For more details on the al-Huthi rebel movement and root causes of the problem (see Sharp 2010; Zelin 2010).

6 The Huthis are one of the core survivals of the old Zaydi regime in Yemen. They follow a Shiite form of Islam, like most Zaydists, although Zaydism and Sunni Shafeism are seen as relatively close within the doctrinal spectrum. Over the past four decades, Yemen enjoyed a cross-sectarian harmony, partly due to state's and CSOs' educational systems, which further narrowed the gulf between Zaydism and Shafeism. However, in recent years and mainly due to economic deprivation and political marginalization, as well as the spread of Salafi influence in Yemen (seen by the Huthi Shiites as a threat), a revivalist core of Zaydi-Huthis emerged. They are empowered by a sense of 'Zaydism' being under siege and undermined, despite the fact that the president himself is a Zaydi and most positions in security and army are filled by members of his tribe. Still, today 'Zaydi revivalists view the republic as fundamentally anti-Hashemite and anti-Zaydi' (ICG 2009: i). For a full account of the Huthi problem, also see ICG 2003; Sharp 2010; Zelin 2010; MEMRI 2009 and RULAC 2009.

7 In addition to Shaykh Tariq al-Fadhli, another example of an Afghan-Yemeni veteran who originally fled the rise of socialist regime in the South is Shaykh Abdul Majeed Zindani. See endnote No. 9.

8 As Ayubi 1999: 243 wrote: ' … tribal overlappings with kin-communities in both Saudi Arabia and South Yemen enabled some of their leaders to gain arms or donations from these two countries, which they used as a bargaining device with their own government for more generous support. In return, they have mobilized their folks for political or military support of the government against potential opposition and rebellion, as occurred, for example, during the war of December 1967 to February 1968, when the role played by tribal forces was more decisive than that played by the regular forces'.

9 Influenced by Hassan al-Banna of Egypt, Yemeni students and scholars initiated the YMB in the late 1930s and early 1940s to challenge the Shiites Imamate. YMB members played a key role in the Free Yemeni Movement, which challenged the Imamate in the 1930s and 1940s. It then sort of disappeared and played little role in Yemeni political scene until 1970 when it was reactivated by the post-revolutionary regime in North Yemen and was then headed by a radical cleric, Shaykh Abdul Majeed Zindani, after his return from Saudi Arabia in that year. Shaykh Zindani was born in 1936 in the central Yemeni province of Ibb and received early education in Aden. He then went to Ain Shams University in Cairo originally to study chemistry and biology, but later, influenced by Sayyid Qutb, switched to Islamic studies. In 1966 he returned to Aden but fled to Saudi Arabia after the rise of NLF in 1968. In 1970 Shaykh Zindani returned to North Yemen where he was appointed as an advisor to the ministry of education, and was encouraged by the post-revolutionary regime to re-activate the YMB. He shortly became its leader (Watkins 1996: 223–4). The YMB then joined other conservative groups in supporting the Northern regime against the Marxist Southern regime. But Zindani's popularity among members soon declined as he was seen as more motivated by personal, than religious factors. In what was tantamount to a coup, Zindani was ousted from the leadership of the YMB in the late 1970s and returned to Saudi Arabia where he established strong links with Wahhabis and participated with Bin Laden in the fight against the Soviet Union. After the departure of Zindani, the YMB experienced further moderation when several prominent leaders from the Yemeni Zaydi movement joined the movement to expand moderate Islamist influence in the country. The new elements in the YMB had confrontational relations with Wahhabis and their like-minded thinkers like Zindani. In 1991, the YMB merged with Islah Party (Schwedler 2004: 210-24).

10 Influence of radical Islam increased not only in North but also in South Yemen during this period. For example, radical salafists from the North began proselytizing in the South, attacking shafi'i mosques and shrines, as well as assassinating Southern leaders, allegedly in accord with Northern leadership. Attacks were also extended to foreign, particularly American targets in the country. In 1992, for instance, two hotels, one of which accommodated US troops on their way to Somalia, were bombed in Aden (ICG 2003: 11 and 24).

11 According to Wright (2008), a meeting took place in Peshawar in 1988 after the Soviets announced their intention to withdraw from Afghanistan between Abdullah Azzam, Dr Fadl, Bin Laden and other top al-Qaeda ranks. Each had a different vision, but Bin Laden wanted to establish a legion of Arab warriors, an all Arab-Foreign-Legion to chase the Russians into central Asia and also fight against the Marxist government that was then in control of South Yemen. That meeting, however, led to the birth of the al-Qaeda Organization.

12 Fadl worked in Afghanistan during the war against the Russian forces as a surgeon for the injured fighters and became a spiritual guide to the jihad. In 1994, Fadl moved to Yemen, where he resumed his medical practice and tried to put the work of jihad behind him. After 9/11 he was arrested by the Yemeni authorities and later handed over to the Egyptian government. He remains in prison today, spending a life sentence (Wright 2008).

13 These were: legal affairs, local governance, health, religious affairs and endowments, supply and trade. After 1994, electricity and water, justice and education were added to the Islah portfolio.

14 As Day (2008), noted, demonstrations soon turned into 'mass protests', particularly after security forces shot and killed four men on the eve of the country's 14 October holiday, which marked the 44th anniversary of events in late 1963 when soldiers of the former British colonial authority in Aden shot and killed seven men in the same Radfan town, al-Habilayn, protesting poor work and pay conditions under the protectorate. That incident triggered the nationalist movement which four years later forced the British colonial authorities to depart from Aden.

15 As Schwedler (2004: 225), wrote: 'Within Yemen's government bureaucracy, corruption is facilitated not only by ministers who wish to gain their share but also by the vast number of positions that, though unnecessary, cannot be eliminated for patronage reasons. Ministers from all political trends complain about their inability to fire employees, despite the fact that many never show up to work'.

16 According to RULAC (2009), it was the rise of the influence of Sunni-radical Islam which led the prominent Huthi leader, Hussien al-Huthi, to form in the 1990s the Believing Youth Movement, aimed at reviving Zaidi Islam and to counter growing influence of fundamentalist Sunni trends in the northern Yemeni governorates where Zaids dominate.

17 Especially after the 1991 Gulf War against Iraq, which seemed to have radicalized a large number of Yemenis, as it did elsewhere in the region including among 'Arab Afghans'. See endnote No. 10.

18 Indeed, the April 1997 elections brought a landslide victory for the GPC, which won 187, while Islah won only 53, down from 64 in the 1993 elections. Despite this decline, Islah remained the second most influential party in the parliament though.

19 Ali Saleh has taken several measures that undermined the democratization process in Yemen. The 1997 and 2010 elections for example, were marred by irregularities in voter registration and other major violations of the electoral law. Prior to the 1999 presidential elections, presidential elections law changed, requiring a nominee to win the support of at least 31 members of parliament to qualify for the ballot. Also, a potential candidate had to have the support of at least 10 per cent of the 301 members of parliament in order to be eligible for participation in the presidential election. 2001 saw another constitutional referendum which extended the terms of office of both the parliament and president, with further amendments that enhanced the power of the president *vis-à-vis* the parliament (ICG 2003: 6). In the second presidential elections in 2006, Ali Saleh received 77 per cent of votes, down from 96 per cent in the 1999 elections, in what would have been his last term in office, which theoretically expires in 2013. Saleh, however, sought to change the constitution to allow him a third term in office. This was the main reason behind the postponement of the last parliamentary elections in 2010. (Sharp 2010: 2). Following the collapse of ben Ali's and Hosni Mubarak's regimes in early 2011, as well as the eruption of widespread demonstrations against him in February, Ali Saleh publically announced that he would neither seek another term in office in 2013, nor would he nominate his son for that post.

20 According to ICG (2003: 9), '14,000' Arab-Afghans were deported at the time by the Yemeni government.

21 The IP was established in early 1991 in anticipation of the 1992 political party's law as a political arm of the ICS and in order to participate in post-unity parliamentary elections, the first of which took place in 1993. Although technically and financially independent, membership of IP and ICS overlaps greatly. The Islah Party brings together several conservative, not always religious, groups, including businessmen, tribal leaders, former members of YMB, a pro-Saudi Wahaabi group, and several ideologues with their own followings, some of which might be more radical than others. The IP is mostly Northern-based, with most members sharing, until recently, a common pro-northern regime and conservative social objective, including the eventual proclamation of *shari'a* as the sole basis of law (Clark 2004: 172).

22 The Islah Charitable Society (ICS), and Hizb al-Islah (Islah Party – IP), benefited from political liberalization that accompanied unification in 1990, including a new

political parties law in 1992. The ICS was established first in May 1990 as a mobilization-charity movement, concerned mainly with *da'wa* (calling) and welfare provision. Today not only the ICS' welfare provisions exceed, by far, those of the state, but it is also 'the most successful humanitarian, nonprofit, nongovernmental organization helping the poor in Yemen' (Clark 2004: 172).

23 The IAAA and YJO are home-grown organizations that were established in the 1990s by 'Arab-Afghans' to tap into returnees from the Afghan war. They consist of Yemenis and non-Yemenis and their members had already been converted to a radical form of Islam before returning to Yemen from Afghanistan. They shared a general Southern Yemeni dissatisfaction with the North's policies as well as socialists' domination of the South. They were involved in several large militant operations, including the kidnapping of a group of 16 tourists in 2008, the October 2000 bombing of the British Council in Sana'a and the suicide attack on the USS *Cole* in Aden in October 2000. In the late 1990s, the government arrested and tried a large number of IAAA and YJO members, including the British Council attackers, executed the leader of the IAAA and claimed to have destroyed the organizations. But the attack on USS *Cole* and *Limburg* in 2000 and 2002, respectively, and the return of violent extremism to Yemen after 2005 undermine this claim. The relationship between the IAAA and YJO, on the one hand, and al-Qaeda, on the other, however 'remain murky, although it is known that there have been personal links between Osama bin Laden and members of the YJO in the past' (ICG 2003: 1, 10, 11 and 17).

24 As the ICG (2003 and 2009) corroborates, kidnapping in Yemen is not new. Historically both the state under the Imamate and the tribes relied on kidnapping in order to force one another to make concessions. But since the mid-1990s, kidnapping became more frequent and began targeting foreigners as well as Yemeni officials to force the state to concede to tribal demands.

25 A detailed description of the meeting that led the establishment of the CD, components of CD, and a tentative assessment for its performance can also be found in Boucek *et al.* 2009.

26 According to Judge Hattar, most ulama refused to participate in dialogue because they 'feared being assassinated by the terrorists just like an Egyptian minister who tried to debate Egyptian terrorists in prison in the 1970s and ended up being assassinated by his interlocutors' (Personal interview, Sana'a June 2010). This story is inaccurate. The Egyptian minister referred to as Sheikh Muhammad al-Dahabi, former minister of Religious Affairs. He was first kidnapped by the *Takfir wal Hijra* group in 1977 and then assassinated (Boucek *et al.* 2009: 285).

27 The rest of the section is based on interviews with Judge Hattar and Sheikh Hassan Abdullah al-Sheihk, Sana'a June 2010.

28 Deputy Interior Minister and largely credited for Saudi's counter-radicalization programme.

29 The Saudi regime, for example, was careful to distance itself from the US administration's influence while implementing its much internationally touted deradicalization programme. See chapter on Saudi Arabia in this volume.

30 This approach is also in stark contradiction to the one followed by the Saudi ulama in the Prince Naif Care Centre where the Saudi clerics are careful to distance themselves from the state and to ensure their autonomy from the regime before carrying out a dialogue with the beneficiaries of the programme. For more details, see the chapter on Saudi Arabia in this volume.

Bibliography

Al-Mamari, I. (2010) Al-Qaeda Claims Responsibility for Killing al-Shabwani, *Yemen Observer*, 9 June, Vol. XII, Issue 42: 3.

Al-Mosawa, S. M. (2010) Wanted Yemeni Al-Qaeda Surrenders, *Yemen Observer*, 7 June 2010: pp.1.

Al-Saqqaf, A.A. (1989) 'Sigha yamaniyya jadida li al-adimuqratiyya [A New Yemini Formula for Democracy]', in S. Ibrahim (ed.) *Al-Ta' addidiyya al-siyasiyy [political pluralism and democracy in the Arab Fatherland]*, Amman: Arab Thought Forum.

Amnesty International (2003) *Yemen – The Rule of Law Sidelined in the Name of Security*, Amnesty International.

Ayubi, N. (1999) *Over Stating the Arab State: Politics and Society in the Middle East*, London: I.B. Tauris.

Birk, A. (2009). *Incredible Dialogues: Religious Dialogue as a Means of Counter-Terrorism in Yemen*, London: ICSR.

Boucek, C., Beg, S. and Horgan, J. (2009) 'Opening up the Jihadi debate: Yemen's committee for dialogue', in T. Bjorgo and J. Horgan (eds) *Leaving Terrorism Behind: Individual and Collective Disengagement*, London: Routledge pp. 181–211.

Carapico, S. (1996) 'Yemen between civil society and civil war', in *Civil Society in the Middle East*, Norton, Volume Two, Augustus, New York, E.J. Brill, pp. 287-316.

Chaudhry, K. A. (1989) *The Price of Wealth: Business and State in Labour Remittance and Oil Economies*, International Organisation, Vol. 43, No I, Winter.

Clark, J. (2004) *Islamist Women in Yemen: Informal Nodes of Activism, in Quintan Wiktorowicz, Islamic Activism: A Social Movement Theory Approach*, Indiana University Press: Bloomington & Indianapolis, pp. 164–84.

Day, S. (2008) 'Updating Yemeni national unity: could lingering regional divisions bring down the regime?' *The Middle East Journal*, Summer. Available HTTP: http://findarticles.com/p/articles/mi_7664/is_200807/ai_n32289537/?tag=content;col1

Gannon, K. (2007) 'Yemen Employs New Terror Approach', *The Associated Press*, 4 July. Available HTTP: http://www.washingtonpost.com/wpdyn/content/article/2007/07/04/AR2007070400992_pf.html.

Halliday, F. (1975) *Arabia Without Sultans: A Survey of Political Leadership in the Arab World*. London: Vintage Press.

——(1985) 'North Yemen Today', *MERIP Reports*, No. 130, Vol. 15, no. 2, February.

Harrigan, J. and El-Said, H. (2009a) *Aid and Power: The IMF and the World Bank Policy Lending in the Middle East and North Africa*, London: Palgrave Macmillan.

——(2009b) *Economic Liberalisation, Social Capital and Social Welfare*, London: Palgrave Macmillan.

International Crisis group (2003). *Middle East Report* No. 8, Brussels.

—— (2007). *Deradicalisation and Indonesian Prison: Asia Report* No. 142, 19 November.

——(2009). *Yemen: defusing the Saada Time Bomb, Middle East Report* No. 87, Brussels.

Johnsen, G. (2006). *Yemen's Passive Role in the War on Terrorism*, Terrorism Monitor Volume: 4 Issue: 4, 23 February. Jamestone Foundation. Available HTTP: http://www.jamestown.org/single/?no_cache=1&tx_ttnews%5Bswords%5D=8fd5893941d69d0be3f378576261ae3e&tx_ttnews%5Bany_of_the_words%5D=Gregory%20Johnsen&tx_ttnews%5Bpointer%5D=1&tx_ttnews%5Btt_news%5D=686&tx_ttnews%5BbackPid%5D=7&cHash=8a9e656962

MEMRI (The Middle East Media Research Institute) (2009) *Yemeni Houthis are Close to Iran and Khamenei*, Special Dispatch No. 2627, November 2. Available HTTP: http://www.shiachat.com/forum/index.php?/topic/234970804-yemeni-houthis-are-close-to-iran-and-khamenei/

Oudeh, A.A. and al-Mamari, I. (2010) *Amnesty Condemns Presence of US Cluster Bomb in Yemen, Yemen Observer*, 9 June, Vol. XII, Issue 42, pp. 1 & 4.

Peraino, K. (2009) 'The re-education of Abu Jandal: can jihadists really be reformed? Closing Guantanamo may depend on it', *Newsweek*, 29 May.

Richards, A. and Waterbury, J. (1996) *A Political Economy of the Middle East*, 2nd edn, London: Westview Press.

RULAC (Rule of Law in Armed Conflicts Project) (2009) *Yemen Current Conflicts: armed Conflict in Sa'ada Region*, November 1. Available HTTP: http://www.adh-geneva.ch/RULAC/.

Schwedler, J. (2004) 'The Islah party in Yemen: political opportunities and coalition building in a transitional polity', in *Islamic activism: a social movement theory approach*, Q. Wiktorowicz (ed.), Indiana University Press: Bloomington & Indianapolis, pp. 205-28.

Serjeant, R.B. (1982) 'The interplay between tribal affinities and religious (Zaydi) authority in the Yemen', in *Al-Abhath: Journal of the Centre for Arab and Middle East Studies, Faculty of Arts and Sciences, American University*, Beirut 30, 1982, pp. 11–50.

Shane, S. (2009) 'Detainee's Case Illustrates Bind of Prison's Fate', in *The New York Times*, 4 October. Available HTTP: http://www.nytimes.com/2009/10/04/world/middleeast/04gitmo.html?_r=1&pagewanted=print.

Shane, S., Mazzetti, M. and Worth, R. (2010) 'Secret Assault on Terrorism Widens on Two Continents', *The New York Times*, 14 August. Available HTTP: http://www.nytimes.com/2010/08/15/world/15shadowwar.html

Sharp, J. (2010) *Yemen; Background and US Relations*. CRS Report for Congress. Prepared for Members and Committees of Congress. Congressional Research Service. Available HTTP: http://www.fas.org/sgp/crs/.

Speckhard, A. and Ahkmedova, K. (2006) 'The making of a martyr: Chechen suicide terrorism', *Studies in Conflict and Terrorism*, 29: 429–92.

Stracke, N. (2006) *Counter Terrorism and Weapon Smuggling: Success and Failure of Yemeni-Saudi Collaboration*, Gulf Research Centre, November. Available HTTP: http://www.researchsea.com/html/article.php/aid/1188/cid/6?PHPSESSID=8gng8u1ofbhuc36beig98fn047.

——(2007) 'Arab Prisons: A Place for Dialogue and Reform', *Perspectives on Terrorism*, Vol 1(4).

The Economist (2009) *Yemen: Juggling Nerves*. 2 October.

Watkins, E. (1996) 'Islamism and tribalism in Yemen', A. S. Sidahamed and A. Ehteshami (eds) *Islamic Fundamentalism*, Colorado: Westview pp. 215–28.

Whitaker, B. (2009) *The Birth of Modern Yemen*, an e-book. Available HTTP: http://www.al-bab.com/yemen/birthofmodernyemen/default.htm.

World Bank (1989) *World Bank Report 1989*, Washington: World Bank.

Wright, L. (2008) 'The Rebellion Within', *The New Yorker*, 2 June. Available HTTP: http://www.newyorker.com/reporting/2008/06/02/080602fa_fact_wright?printable=true#ixzz14M1PCk4C.

Xinhua (2010). *Yemeni al-Qaida commander surrenders to security authority, Sana'a*, August. Available HTTP: http://news.xinhuanet.com/english2010/world/2010-08/20/c_13453140.htm.

Zelin, A. (2010) *Profile: al Houthi Movement*, in criticalthreats.org. Available HTTP: http://www.criticalthreats.org/print/1241.

10

CONCLUSION

Hamed El-Said

This book provided a systematic analysis for the counter-radicalization and deradicalization efforts in eight Muslim-majority states: Algeria, Bangladesh, Egypt, Jordan, Malaysia, Morocco, Saudi Arabia and Yemen. Various factors motivated the choice of these eight particular countries. Most important among these is the fact that all of them, except Jordan, have been engaged in implementing globally-touted counter-radicalization, deradicalization or both programmes at the same time. Their geographical distribution (from the Middle East, North Africa and Asia) also adds regional significance, as well as their ethnicity (while all are Muslim-majority, not all are Arabs). Their experience in countering the appeal of radical violent ideology and rehabilitating and reintegrating former radical groups and individuals provides important lessons to other countries, both Muslim-majority and Muslim-minority, facing threat of radical violent ideology, otherwise known as terrorism. We dare to hope that the book, its analysis and findings provide important new insights into the conditions conducive to successful counter-radicalization and deradicalization programmes. If this is the case, then practitioners, policy makers, international development agencies and other donors intent on assisting poor countries encountering the threat of terrorism will find the analysis in this book of special interest.

The point of departure here is a new realization that recognizes the utility of 'soft' measures that aim at winning hearts and minds in countering radicalization and convincing radical groups and individuals to repent and disengage from militant activities. As the International Peace Institute (2010: 1) noted, measures that aim at winning hearts and minds are 'more successful than military approaches and less likely to foment a new generation of violent extremists'. The former British Foreign Minister, David Miliband eloquently summed up the change in thinking with regard to the approach in countering terrorism in general and countering radicalization in particular:

> … the notion [of war on terror] is misleading and mistaken. The issue is not whether we need to attack the use of terror at its roots, with all the tools

> available. We must. The question is how … The "war on terror" also implied that the correct response was primarily military. But as General Petraeus said to me and others in Iraq, the coalition there could not kill its way out of the problems of insurgency and civil strife … We must respond to terrorism by championing the rule of law, not subordinating it, for it is the cornerstone of the democratic society. We must uphold our commitments to human rights and civil liberties at home and abroad. That is surely the lesson of Guantánamo and it is why we welcome President-elect Obama's commitment to close it.
>
> *(Miliband 2009)*

Not surprisingly, several countries have resorted to such 'soft' measures in countering radical violent ideology and in rehabilitating and reintegrating former radical elements. The eight Muslim-majority states studied in this first volume are a good example of such countries. Untangling the paradox of counter-radicalization and deradicalization sheds important light on how the appeal to violent ideology can best be countered. What happens in the global environment, and inside terror organizations (resources, unity of membership, charismatic leadership, interaction etc.), matters and is important. But the success of counter-radicalization and deradicalization programmes, in 'certain circumstances', suggests that the immediate environment is equally as important. Also, the implications and effects of such programmes go beyond national boundaries: they are also felt across national borders. The internationally-touted Saudi deradicalization programme, for example, seems to have reduced terrorism not only in the Kingdom itself, but also in the region too:

> Major terrorist attacks in Saudi Arabia have plummeted compared with 2004. [But] The Saudi plan also appears to have a broader regional impact. General David Petraeus, commander of US forces in Iraq, has said that the Saudi initiative is maybe one reason for the sharp decline in the number of foreign fighters coming into Iraq.
>
> *(Kurlantzick 2008)*

A study on countering radicalization and reintegration and rehabilitation of violent extremists has implications that stretch far beyond the eight Muslim-majority states studied in this volume. Numerous other countries are confronted with similar issues, including threats of terrorism and collapse of their state. Somalia, Afghanistan and Pakistan are just a few examples. How our eight country case studies respond, successfully or otherwise, to countering radicalization and convincing their radical violent elements to repent, have far-reaching implications and lessons for other countries facing a similar threat of terrorism and prospect of state failure.

Understanding counter-radicalization and rehabilitation efforts in Muslim-majority states is therefore important for several reasons. The success of some of these programmes, such as the Saudi rehabilitation programme, for example, has turned them into a *de facto* model for other countries facing and seeking to counter-radicalization in their societies. This includes Western states such as the United Kingdom, Australia, Canada and the Netherlands who have sent their officials to Riyadh, Cairo and Yemen, for example, seeking 'transferable applications' (Boucek 2008: 65). The growth, both in interest in and number of counter-radicalization and deradicalization programmes around the world, is consistent with the increasing realization on behalf of the international community of the failure of traditional hard, security approaches to defeat radical violent extremism in all shapes and forms.

What then are the main conditions conducive to successful counter-radicalization and deradicalization (counter-deradicalization) efforts? What lessons does the experience of eight Muslim-majority states studied in this volume provide to the rest of the world with regard to counter-deradicalization programmes? What are the chief factors that contribute to the success or failure of counter-radicalization, deradicalization or both measures in Muslim-majority states and beyond? These are some of the key questions which this book attempts to seek answers for. At least eight key factors seem to determine the success or failure of counter-deradicalization programmes in Muslim-majority states.

First, developmentally weak states (states which fail to manage sustainable economic growth, reduce poverty, create employment opportunities and manage relations with their ethnic communities) are more susceptible to radicalization. They are also less effective in fashioning successful counter-radicalization and deradicalization programmes. Indeed, not all Muslim-majority states face the problem of radicalization and violent extremism to the same extent. Some Muslim-majority states, like Malaysia, for example, have hitherto faced no major Islamic radicalization problems at societal level and there has been no support for radical ideology in the country. Also, Malaysia only experienced two small (*Islamist*) terrorist incidents since the beginning of the century, neither of which caused any fatalities or injuries whatsoever. This is not the case in the other seven Muslim-majority states studied in this volume. Countries like Algeria and Egypt in the 1990s and Saudi Arabia between 2002–05, experienced high-intensity warfare with their militants. One major feature distinguishes Malaysia from the other countries in our book and that is the country's possession of a state with strong developmental capacity. Malaysia's developmental focus had an important security element. It was seen as an important strategy in facing the threat of violent extremism posed by communist insurgents before and immediately after political independence in 1965. The communist insurgency lasted for well over two decades, ending in 1989. It was around that year, ironically, that Malaysia was classified by international development agencies as one of the 'Newly Industrializing Countries' or NICs. The classification of Malaysia as one of the NICs reflected the country's fast economic development and high and sustainable growth rate. The latter has been associated with the implementation of an export-oriented strategy, which turned the country into a major exporter of manufactured goods, allowed the government to provide its citizens with high-paid jobs, reduced unemployment and created one of the most egalitarian societies in the world.

Out of the eight Muslim-majority states studied in this book, only Malaysia possessed a strong developmental capacity. Such a state is lacking in all other countries presented in this volume. Even Saudi Arabia, despite its wealth, lacked Malaysia's developmental capacity. Although wealthy, Saudi Arabia's wealth is not derived from accumulation of capital arising from a disciplined structural transformation of the economy like the NIC's management of export-oriented industrialization. Rather, Saudi wealth is derived from external rents, oil revenues: 'an unearned windfall, like manna from heaven' (Lubeck 1999: 297). In this respect, the Kingdom's wealth has been seen by its citizens as a 'gift from God', not the result of wise economic policies implemented by state officials. By the mid-1980s, most Saudi citizens became disappointed with their government's failure to diversify the economy and continued reliance on external sources of rent, which undermined the country's economic and political independence. Not surprisingly, while Malaysia earned its status as a NIC, Saudi Arabia has been described as 'richer than it is developed' (UN 2002: 26).

It is true that the literature does not find a direct link between poverty and terrorism. However, the link is 'indirect' (Krueger and Maleckova 2003: 119). As Whitaker (2009) noted, 'a more highly-developed state can certainly provide better conditions' conducive for stability, democracy and counter-radicalization. Oil, and international assistance, do not alone create sustainable development or lead to the creation of developmental states. Nor do they create a sufficient number of jobs, sustainable growth or egalitarian societies. Not only are such sources subject to the vagaries of the market and political mood, but the number of people involved in either oil production (Saudi Arabia or Yemen) or international aid generation (Egypt, Jordan and Yemen) is very small. Oil and aid-dependent states rely more on distribution of largess than on extraction of taxes to buy political stability. The slogan of the American Revolution, 'No Taxation Without Representation', is reversed in the Arab World into 'No Taxation and No Representation'. Also, such sources of capital accumulation are neither unlimited nor large enough to buy political stability in the long run. Repression, corruption and other forms of rent-seeking, which have been associated with oil and aid-dependencies in the Arab World, lead to inequalities, political resentments, as well as the creation of an environment that is conducive to radicalization and extremism that lead to terrorism (UN 2002 and 2009).

Second, politically weak states, like developmentally weak states, also create conditions conducive to radicalization and violent extremism. The lure of 'failed states' to terrorist organizations is now well recognized. A recent (2008) report by the London-based think tank (International Institute for Strategic Studies – IISS) warned that a state, which 'lacks authority in much of the country', stands the risk of becoming a 'ready target of insurgents'. The Brussels-based think tank, International Crisis Group (2003: i), also warned that 'weak and lawless state[s] with porous borders' or countries 'with tenuous government control over vast parts of [their] territory' create conditions conducive to violent extremism and encourage terrorist organizations to create 'sanctuary for' their operatives over their soil. Such states also encourage even the more moderate elements of their opposition to take up arms in anticipation of benefits that could be obtained from the potential collapse of the state. As a former Amir in the Algerian Islamic Salvation Army (ISA) stated:

> Many members did not believe in violence but when the state weakened in the early 1990s and seemed on the verge of collapsing, many feared, in case the

> radicals take over the state, being seen as anti-radicals and pro-the departing regime. We felt that we could lose everything and therefore decided to carry arms with radicals rather than being seen against them and risk losing everything, including state perks, jobs and benefits.
>
> *(Personal interview, Algeria December 2009)*

It is not surprising therefore that al-Qaeda has found Yemen a fertile ground for its operations and operatives. Al-Qaeda in Yemen represents a major threat not only to Yemen itself, but also to the region and Western interests alike. In December 2009, a Nigerian trained and equipped in Yemen apparently attempted to bring down an airline as it approached Detroit. In October 2010, al-Qaeda operatives in Yemen attempted to send bombs concealed in printers to addresses in Chicago. Other Western interests have also been targeted by al-Qaeda in Yemen, including a French oil tanker and German, Korean, Spanish and United Kingdom nationals. A more immediate target is Saudi Arabia, where attacks and attempted attacks have targeted oil installations, security officials and members of the ruling family. Terrorist groups or organizations operating in politically weak states can also use such states to support terrorist organizations in other countries, such as Al-Qaeda operatives in Yemen which supports the al Shabaab movement in Somalia.

Third, national consensus is a prerequisite for successful counter-radicalization programmes. Building a national consensus is a collective exercise, one shared by the state and its various societal elements. However, the presence of a strong state institution to initiate, oversee, coordinate and administer the counter-radicalization efforts is necessary for effective implementation and optimal results. A key feature of the Saudi deradicalization programme is the presence of an omnipotent state institution (the Ministry of Foreign Affairs – MFA), which has taken ownership of the country's counter-terrorism strategy in general and promotion of 'soft' counter-deradicalization programmes in particular. The Saudi MFA also sought to build a consensus behind its efforts, including through such measures as using the internet, TV and radio to counter the appeal of violent extremism and to expose its detrimental effects to citizens; putting up billboards in public places that also show the traumatizing effects of terrorism on people's lives, the economy and the entire country; publically encouraging repented former violent extremists to talk about both their lives as terrorists and repentants; investing in religious education, which produced a large number of qualified and competent ulama that proved vital in promoting a moderate version of Islam and in convincing hundreds, if not thousands of former violent extremists to repent; and in inviting various societal organizations and personalities, including family and tribal members, to participate in and promote counter-deradicalization efforts in the country.

Compare the role of the Saudi MFA with that of the Yemeni Dialogue Committee (YDC). Although it was created in 2002 as a result of a direct instruction from President Ali Saleh himself, no state agency took ownership of the Committee or dialogue process. This was left entirely to one man: Judge Hamoud Hattar, the former Minister of Religious Affairs. Although the country has more than 600 officially registered ulama,

Judge Hattar, despite his best intentions, failed to galvanize the support of more than two other ulama for his programme, let alone to build a national consensus around his dialogue committee. The rest of the ulama, for various reasons, refused to participate in the YDC. Not only was the number of ulama who agreed to participate in the YDC (three including Judge Hattar) too small to allow a proper dialogue process, but the failure to galvanize the support of all or even the majority of the country's ulama undermined any opportunity of building a national consensus around the DC. In traditional, religious and tribal societies, like those in Yemen, the ulama are the most important source of national consensus building.

It is difficult, therefore, to talk of the YDC as representing a coherent programme of deradicalization, rehabilitation or dialogue. State officials, former graduates and even Judge Hattar himself admitted that the prisoners met with members of the DC no more than twice before they were released between 2002 and 2005, and even those meetings took a collective, rather than individual form. This stands in stark contrast to the Saudi deradicalization programme, which, among other things, consists of hundreds, if not thousands of ulama, who conduct tens, if not hundreds of meetings with graduates, on both a collective and an individual basis, before they are released. It is more accurate therefore to describe the Yemeni efforts in convincing their radicals to repent between 2002 and 2005 as a process, rather than a programme.[1]

It is also important to draw attention here to the quality and quantity of ulama involved in the dialogue process. The dialogue is a way to communicate with the other. It is an old, long-established practice in Islamic tradition. It was regularly resorted to by the Prophet Muhammad to offer advice to his relatives and close friends, even to convince his enemies to repent and follow the 'right path'. In addition, advice is rooted in the Qu'ran, which calls upon the prophet to debate and dialogue with his people. Not surprisingly, the Saudi authorities have skilfully invoked this tradition in their deradicalization programme, which they call the *al-Munasah* (the Advice) Programme. Yet, proper and effective advice requires competent and qualified advisors and messengers. Out of all the countries studied in this volume, only Saudi Arabia managed to prepare and come up with a sufficient number of competent, qualified and yet autonomous advisors, messengers, ulama and scholars. The apparently close relationship between religious scholars and authorities in other countries destroyed their credibility and autonomy. Preparing and providing competent, qualified and autonomous scholars is one of the key challenges that counter-deradicalization programmes face around the world.

Fourth, civil society is an important source of 'soft' power. It is an important mediator between state and society. Civil society organizations also have the ability to create far-reaching social networks, to multiply those networks and to reach the most recalcitrant members of society in ways that the state and its institutions cannot. States, therefore, with dynamic civil societies have greater capacity to craft effective counter-deradicalization programmes.

It is doubtful whether President Bouteflika, for example, would have been able to implement his deradicalization programme after 1999 had he not gained the full support of key societal organizations. The latter played a significant role in promoting the president's policies of national reconciliation, which included a large deradicalization programme. Bangladeshi authorities relied completely on their civil society to implement the country's counter-radicalization programme after 2005. Yemen, Morocco and Jordan have had little input from their civil societies. Their counter-deradicalization efforts remain incomplete and in many ways less successful.

In societies with weak or less dynamic civil societies but which have strong tribal structure, the gap is often filled by tribal and family members. Saudi Arabia is a case in point. The state invited and facilitated the participation of tribal and family members in its much touted rehabilitation programme. This, Boucek (2008) concurs, has been a key factor behind the success of the Kingdom's deradicalization policies.

Fifth, the timing of counter-deradicalization measures matters. In Algeria, for example, at least three attempts at deradicalization were tried before 1997, all of which led to nothing. In Egypt, also before the 1997 unilateral annunciation of ceasefire, there were at least 14 failed attempts to halt the violence between the IG and the state. A pertinent question here is why these earlier attempts failed, while the post-1997 processes both in Algeria and Egypt were a success. Answering this question will help identify further key conditions that are necessary for the successful deradicalization of violent extremist groups and may well have some important policy implications for international institutions, governments and donors seeking to promote such programmes in poor countries.

One time-relatable factor is the preparedness of violent extremist groups themselves to unilaterally denounce violence and disengage from militant discourse. It is safe to argue here that deradicalization is more effective and durable when ceasefire is called for by violent extremist groups themselves, not the state. In both Algeria and Egypt, ceasefire endured and gained credibility over time partly because it was initiated by the leaders of Algeria's Islamic Salvation Army (in 1997) and Egypt's IG and JI in 1997 and 2007, respectively. In his seminal work on Egypt and Algeria, Ashour (2009) has identified five key factors upon which 'The success of any deradicalisation process … depends heavily on: military defeat or repression; selective motivations and rewards provided by the state; internal dynamics between spiritual and organizational leadership within a group, on the one hand, and interaction between groups and more moderate members of society on the other; and presence of a charismatic leadership at group level' (also see Ashour and Boucek 2009).

Sixth, unilateral ceasefire and denunciation of violence by violent extremist groups alone, while necessary, is not sufficient for counter-deradicalization efforts either to take off or to be sustained over time. Despite a call for deradicalization by several incarcerated groups and individuals, Jordan has not introduced a genuine deradicalization process. The supply side of counter-deradicalization, the state, must also be taken into account: the state (or leadership at state level) must also be willing, capable and able of implementing them. It is not surprising therefore that the timing of most successful counter-deradicalization programmes studied also coincided with the arrival of new leadership at state level. Although Algeria's ISA unilaterally denounced violence and announced a ceasefire in 1997, it was not before a new leadership assumed power in 1999 that deradicalization actually took off. Bangladesh's large counter-radicalization programme was only implemented after a new caretaker government assumed responsibility in 2005, despite years of official promises to initiate such reforms earlier on. Similarly, Morocco's wide-ranging and most far-reaching counter-radicalization programme was also associated with the arrival of a new monarchy after 1999, King Mohammed VI.

The arrival of new leadership provides an exceptionally specific period of time during which counter-deradicalization and other reforms can be fully implemented. New leadership is usually less constrained by the relationship with powerful domestic interest groups that might oppose reform, such as the army or security forces. In fact, new leaders might see reform as an important way to shore up their credibility and popularity, as President Bouteflika did after winning presidential elections in 1999. Yet, as the experience of some other countries studied in this volume demonstrates, even a new charismatic leadership is not a sufficient factor for counter-deradicalization to succeed. Political commitment to such reforms trumps almost everything else.

Indeed, seventh, counter-deradicalization reform, particularly in Muslim-majority states, is an internal affair. It is not the business of Western states to promote counter-deradicalization in such states, although they could support reform in more indirect ways, such as through developmental projects, schools and education, health, human development and aid. The Saudi authorities were careful to present its much touted deradicalization programme as 'purely Saudi'. It was also funded completely by Saudi money. More importantly, the Saudi authorities sought to distance their country's policies from those of the US in the region during reforms. The point here is that unless national leadership is committed to counter-deradicalization measures, the chance of such reforms succeeding is minimal. Pouring aid on uncommitted regimes will not suffice. One of the key reasons behind the failure of YDC after 2005 is President Saleh's insistence on receiving financial support from the West first in order to continue and expand the country's DC's tasks. In fact, the entire YDC was motivated from the very beginning by political and financial incentives, rather than conviction and belief in the utility of dialogue, at least on behalf of the president Ali Saleh.

Eighth, prison policy that relies on separating violent extremists from one another and from other incarcerated inmates is not a deradicalization policy. On the contrary, it is a radicalization policy. While there is a case for isolating hard-core, unrepentable elements from the rest of the group, the available empirical evidence shows that internal and external interaction with more moderate and political elements can help the disengagement process and moderate the majority of radical elements. To succeed, moreover, deradicalization must also be accompanied by improvement of all aspects of human rights in order to prevent the formation of a new generation of violent extremists. Such fomentation could take place inside incarceration centres, whose harsh environment could further harden some prisoners and fill them with anger and hatred against the state and its officials. It could also take place outside the prison environment, as many siblings, progenies, family members or even friends could be radicalized by the mistreatment of their incarcerated members. Improving human rights environment should also be extended to society at large, as the available empirical evidence points to a strikingly strong relationship between repression and lack of democratic outlets, on the one hand and extremism and terrorism on the other. As David Miliband noted in the quotation cited at the beginning of this chapter, responding to terrorism does not mean subordinating the rule of law, or commitment to human rights. On the contrary, countering radicalization requires upholding both the rule of law and commitment to human rights, both at home and abroad.

Finally, reform in most cases is not a choice between counter-radicalization and deradicalization. It is not either/or. If a country is arresting a large number of violent extremist individuals and groups, then there must be radicalizing factors in the society itself that are producing radical elements and therefore require intervention. In this case, both counter-radicalization and deradicalization measures are needed. Nor are counter-deradicalization programmes immoral exhortations preached in prisons, schools, universities or on TV screens and other official ceremonies where such policies are being promoted. Promotion of moral principles inside prisons and on TV screens must also be accompanied by genuine immoral exhortation on behalf of the state, its officials and members of Royal and ruling families to end any contradiction between what is being preached and what is being practiced.

Before we end this volume, two points are in order. First, it is self-hypnotizing to believe, as some do, that terrorism is a 'Muslim problem' whose solutions lay in Muslim countries alone. Not all root causes of terrorism in the world are caused by, or stem from, Muslim countries. A great deal originates from external environment and is caused by policies of Western powers. These include the occupation of Muslim countries such as in Iraq and Afghanistan, dawn attacks in Muslim countries like Pakistan, Afghanistan and Yemen that invariably kill innocent bystanders, payment of lip service to genuine democracy in Muslim World by Western powers, as well as the latter's continued support for undemocratic and authoritarian regimes in the Arab World and elsewhere. The persistent Israeli transience and daily humiliation of Palestinians, Israeli refusal of any peaceful settlement with the Arabs based on international legitimacy and law, and prolonged and unceasing Israeli occupation of Arab lands, both in Palestine and the region also remain a significant radicalizing factor. Unless the external environment, which most Muslim-majority states have little control over, undergoes a similar reform process and ceases to be radicalizing, hoping to terminate terrorism through reform in Muslim-majority states alone is misleading and misplaced.

In fact, the Arab World, in early 2011 experienced the birth of the first Arab modern mass movement of nonviolent civil disorder, publically known as 'Arab Awakening' or 'Arab Spring'. The movement, which continues unabated, has succeeded so far in deposing two long-standing, authoritarian Arab leaders, Mubarak of Egypt and Zain al-Abiddin of Tunisia. It continues to threaten many other leaders in the region. The sudden and unexpected dawn of the Arab Spring through peaceful means not only reflects a conviction in the region that violence leads to violence and is thus less effective in bringing about desired change. It also suggests that reforms, which have hitherto been undertaken in the Arab World, including those pertinent to counter-radicalization and appeal of violent ideology, have not gone far enough. With perhaps the exception of Malaysia, reforms remain incomplete in almost all the Muslim-majority states studied in this volume, either in terms of breadth or extent of reform. Violent extremism therefore remains a major problem in the region and the world at large. For counter-deradicalization policies to be effective, they need to be part of an even larger package of reform, one that would include economic, political and social aspects too. Unless counter-deradicalization policies become part of a new social contract between state and society, a contract that will hold immoral exhortations at all levels and bring peace, stability and prosperity to all, not just to a powerful few, it is unlikely that we will see an imminent end to the phenomenon of violent extremism or terrorism.

Last but by no means least one size does not fit all. There is neither a silver bullet nor easily transferable practices. What works in Saudi Arabia might not work in another Muslim-majority state like Bangladesh, let alone in a Muslim-minority state like the United Kingdom. Conditions conducive to radicalization and extremism that lead to terrorism in one country might differ from those that exist in another, although there might be some common factors. Each country needs to develop its own counter-deradicalization programmes based on its own conditions, resources, mores, cultures, history and traditions. While there are general lessons and practices derived from studying the experience of counter-deradicalization of Muslim-majority states, such measures should only be seen as guidelines for conditions conducive to successful counter-deradicalization in all environments. What is certain, however, is that such measures and policies have proved more effective and successful when based, first, on a good understanding of the root causes of violent extremism in the national/local environment and second, linked to and/or based on the history and cultural 'tool-kit' of countries wishing to devise such policies.

Note

1 Even in other countries where counter- or deradicalization efforts have been more successful than in Yemen, one depicts at least one powerful state institution overseeing the entire process. In Malaysia, for example, deradicalization has been the prerogative of the Ministry of the Interior. In Algeria, the powerful security units, including the department of intelligence and some army units, took responsibility for the country's massive deradicalization programme. In Morocco, the Ministry of Religious Affairs, as well as the Ministry of Education, were the key state institutions in charge of the country's counter-radicalization programme initiated around the year 2003.

Bibliography

Ashour, O. (2009) *The De-radicalisation of Jihadist: Transforming Armed Islamic Movements*, London: Routledge.

Ashour, O. and Boucek, C. (2009) *De-Radicalization in Egypt, Algeria, and Libya*, Washington, DC, Carnegie Endowment, 16 April. http://www.carnegieendowment.org/events/?fa=eventDetail&id=1325

Boucek, C. (2008) 'Counter-terrorism from within assessing Saudi Arabia's religious rehabilitation and disengagement programme', in Rusi, 153-6 text.qxp 19 December: pp. 60-5.

International Crisis Group (2003) *Yemen: Coping with Terrorism and Violence in a Fragile State, Executive Summary and Recommendations*, Brussels, Jan 8. Available HTTP: http://www.crisisgroup.org/en/regions/middle-east-north-africa/iran-gulf/yemen/008-yemen-coping-with-terrorism-and-violence-in-a fragile-state.aspx.

International Institute for Strategic Studies (IISS) (2008) *The Military Balance*, London: IISS.
International Peace Institute (IPI) (2010) *A New Approach? Deradicalization Programs and Counterterrorism*, New York, June 2010.
Krueger, A. and Maleckova, J. (2003) 'Education, poverty and terrorism: is there a causal connection?' *Journal of Economic Perspectives*, Volume 17, No. 4: 119-44.
Kurlantzick, J. (2008) 'Fighting Terrorism with Terrorist', in *The Los Angeles Times*, 6 January.
Lubeck, P. (1999) 'Islamist responses to globalization: cultural conflict in Egypt, Algeria and Malaysia' in B. Crawford and R. Lipschutz (eds) *The Causes of Cultural Conflict*, Berkeley: International and Area Studies, 239-319. Retrieved HTTP: http://escholarship.org/uc/item/90v5s45r.
Miliband, D. (2009). 'War on Terror' was wrong, in *the Guardian*, 15 January. Available HTTP: http://www.guardian.co.uk/commentisfree/2009/jan/15/david-miliband-war-terror.
UN Arab Human Development Report (2002) *United Nations Development Programme*, Regional Bureau for Arab States (RBAS), New York, UN.
—— Arab Human Development Report (2009) *United Nations Development Programme*, Regional Bureau for Arab States (RBAS), New York, UN.
Whitaker, B. (2009) *The Birth of Modern Yemen*, An e-book. http://www.al-bab.com/yemen/birthofmodernyemen/default.htm.

INDEX